COLLECTED VERSE OF ROBERT SERVICE

VOLUME ONE

Uniform with this Volume

COLLECTED VERSE OF ROBERT SERVICE

VOLUME TWO

COLLECTED VERSE OF
ROBERT SERVICE

VOLUME ONE

ERNEST BENN LIMITED
LONDON & TONBRIDGE

Published by Ernest Benn Limited
Sovereign Way, Tonbridge, Kent and
25 New Street Square, London, EC4A 3JA

This Collected Edition first published 1930
Eighth impression 1943
Reset edition 1948
Second impression 1951
Third impression 1953
Fourth impression 1960
Fifth impression 1973

Printed in Great Britain

ISBN 0 510-32401-0

CONTENTS

SONGS OF A SOURDOUGH

v

CONTENTS

BALLADS OF A CHEECHAKO

CONTENTS

RHYMES OF A ROLLING STONE

CONTENTS

THE RHYMES OF A RED-CROSS MAN

CONTENTS

CONTENTS

BALLADS OF A BOHEMIAN

PART ONE

SPRING

I

II

CONTENTS

PART TWO

EARLY SUMMER

CONTENTS

xii

CONTENTS

PART FOUR

WINTER

I

II

III

CONTENTS

SONGS OF A SOURDOUGH

To
C. M.

The lonely sunsets flare forlorn
  Down valleys dreadly desolate;
The lordly mountains soar in scorn,
  As still as death, as stern as fate.

    The lonely sunsets flame and die;
      The giant valleys gulp the night;
    The monster mountains scrape the sky,
      Where eager stars are diamond-bright.

So gaunt against the gibbous moon,
  Piercing the silence velvet-piled,
A lone wolf howls his ancient rune,
  The fell arch-spirit of the Wild.

    O outcast land! O leper land!
      Let the lone wolf-cry all express—
    The hate insensate of thy hand,
      Thy heart's abysmal loneliness.

SONGS OF A SOURDOUGH

THE LAW OF THE YUKON

This is the law of the Yukon, and ever she makes it plain:
"Send not your foolish and feeble; send me your strong and
    your sane.
Strong for the red rage of battle; sane, for I harry them
    sore;
Send me men girt for the combat, men who are grit to the
    core;
Swift as the panther in triumph, fierce as the bear in defeat,
Sired of a bulldog parent, steeled in the furnace heat.
Send me the best of your breeding, lend me your chosen ones;
Them will I take to my bosom, them will I call my sons;
Them will I gild with my treasure, them will I glut with my
    meat;
But the others—the misfits, the failures—I trample under my
    feet.
Dissolute, damned, and despairful, crippled and palsied and
    slain,
Ye would send me the spawn of your gutters—Go! take back
    your spawn again.

"Wild and wide are my borders, stern as death is my sway;

From my ruthless throne I have ruled alone for a million years and a day;

Hugging my mighty treasure, waiting for man to come:

Till he swept like a turbid torrent, and after him swept—the scum.

The pallid pimp of the dead-line, the enervate of the pen.

One by one I weeded them out, for all that I sought was—Men.

One by one I dismayed them, frighting them sore with my glooms;

One by one I betrayed them unto my manifold dooms.

Drowned them like rats in my rivers, starved them like curs on my plains,

Rotted the flesh that was left them, poisoned the blood in their veins;

Burst with my winter upon them, searing forever their sight,

Lashed them with fungus-white faces, whimpering wild in the night;

Staggering blind through the storm-whirl, stumbling mad through the snow,

Frozen stiff in the ice pack, brittle and bent like a bow;

Featureless, formless, forsaken, scented by wolves in their flight,

Left for the wind to make music through ribs that are glittering white;

Gnawing the black crust of failure, searching the pit of despair,

Crooking the toe in the trigger, trying to patter a prayer;

Going outside with an escort, raving with lips all afoam;

Writing a cheque for a million, drivelling feebly of home;
Lost like a louse in the burning . . . or else in tented town
Seeking a drunkard's solace, sinking and sinking down;
Steeped in the slime at the bottom, dead to a decent world,
Lost 'mid the human flotsam, far on the frontier hurled;
In the camp at the bend of the river, with its dozen saloons
aglare,
Its gambling dens a-riot, its gramophones all a-blare;
Crimped with the crimes of a city, sin-ridden and bridled with
lies,
In the hush of my mountained vastness, in the flush of my
midnight skies.
Plague-spots, yet tools of my purpose, so natheless I suffer them
thrive,
Crushing my Weak in their clutches, that only my Strong may
survive.

"But the others, the men of my mettle, the men who would
'stablish my fame,
Unto its ultimate issue, winning me honour, not shame;
Searching my uttermost valleys, fighting each step as they go,
Shooting the wrath of my rapids, scaling my ramparts of
snow;
Ripping the guts of my mountains, looting the beds of my
creeks,
Them will I take to my bosom, and speak as a mother speaks.
I am the land that listens, I am the land that broods;
Steeped in eternal beauty, crystalline waters and woods.

Long have I waited lonely, shunned as a thing accurst,
Monstrous, moody, pathetic, the last of the lands and the first;
Visioning camp-fires at twilight, sad with a longing forlorn,
Feeling my womb o'er-pregnant with the seed of cities unborn.
Wild and wide are my borders, stern as death is my sway,
And I wait for the men who will win me—and I will not be
    won in a day;
And I will not be won by weaklings, subtile, suave, and mild,
But by men with the hearts of vikings, and the simple faith
    of a child;
Desperate, strong, and resistless, unthrottled by fear or defeat,
Them will I gild with my treasure, them will I glut with my
    meat.
"Lofty I stand from each sister land, patient and wearily wise,
With the weight of a world of sadness in my quiet, passionless
    eyes;
Dreaming alone of a people, dreaming alone of a day,
When men shall not rape my riches, and curse me and go
    away;
Making a bawd of my bounty, fouling the hand that gave—
Till I rise in my wrath and I sweep on their path and I stamp
    them into a grave.
Dreaming of men who will bless me, of women esteeming me
    good,
Of children born in my borders, of radiant motherhood;
Of cities leaping to stature, of fame like a flag unfurled,
As I pour the tide of my riches in the eager lap of the world."
This is the Law of the Yukon, that only the Strong shall thrive;
That surely the Weak shall perish, and only the Fit survive.

Dissolute, damned, and despairful, crippled and palsied and slain,

This is the Will of the Yukon,—Lo! how she makes it plain!

THE PARSON'S SON

This is the song of the parson's son, as he squats in his shack alone,
On the wild, weird nights when the Northern Lights shoot up from the frozen zone,
And it's sixty below, and couched in the snow the hungry huskies moan.

"I'm one of the Arctic brotherhood, I'm an old-time pioneer.
I came with the first—O God! how I've cursed this Yukon—but still I'm here.
I've sweated athirst in its summer heat, I've frozen and starved in its cold;
I've followed my dreams by its thousand streams, I've toiled and moiled for its gold.

"Look at my eyes—been snow-blind twice; look where my foot's half gone;
And that gruesome scar on my left cheek where the frost-fiend bit to the bone.

12

Each one a brand of this devil's land, where I've played and
    I've lost the game,
A broken wreck with a craze for 'hooch,' and never a cent to
    my name.

"This mining is only a gamble, the worst is as good as the best;
I was in with the bunch and I might have come out right on
    top with the rest;
With Cormack, Ladue and Macdonald—O God! but it's hell
    to think
Of the thousands and thousands I've squandered on cards and
    women and drink.

"In the early days we were just a few, and we hunted and
    fished around,
Nor dreamt by our lonely camp-fires of the wealth that lay
    under the ground.
We traded in skins and whiskey, and I've often slept under
    the shade.
Of that lone birch tree on Bonanza, where the first big find was
    made.

"We were just like a great big family, and every man had his
    squaw,
And we lived such a wild, free, fearless life beyond the pale of
    the law;

Till sudden there came a whisper, and it maddened us every
   man,
And I got in on Bonanza before the big rush began.

"Oh, those Dawson days, and the sin and the blaze, and the
   town all open wide!
(If God made me in His likeness, sure He let the devil inside.)
But we all were mad, both the good and the bad, and as for
   the women, well—
No spot on the map in so short a space has hustled more souls
   to hell.

"Money was just like dirt there, easy to get and to spend.
I was all caked in on a dance-hall jade, but she shook me in the
   end.
It put me queer, and for near a year I never drew sober breath,
Till I found myself in the bughouse ward with a claim staked
   out on death.

"Twenty years in the Yukon, struggling along its creeks;
Roaming its giant valleys, scaling its god-like peaks;
Bathed in its fiery sunsets, fighting its fiendish cold,
Twenty years in the Yukon . . . twenty years—and I'm old.

"Old and weak, but no matter, there's 'hooch' in the bottle still.
I'll hitch up the dogs to-morrow, and mush down the trail to
   Bill.

It's so long dark, and I'm lonesome—I'll just lay down on the
bed,
To-morrow I'll go . . . to-morrow . . . I guess I'll play on the
red.

". . . Come, Kit, your pony is saddled. I'm waiting, dear, in
the court . . .
. . . Minnie, you devil, I'll kill you if you skip with that flossy
sport . . .
. . . How much does it go to the pan, Bill? . . . play up, School,
and play the game . . .
. . . Our Father, which art in heaven, hallowed be Thy
name . . ."

*This was the song of the parson's son, as he lay in his bunk
alone,*
*Ere the fire went out and the cold crept in, and his blue lips
ceased to moan,*
*And the hunger-maddened malamutes had torn him flesh from
bone.*

THE SPELL OF THE YUKON

I wanted the gold, and I sought it;
 I scrabbled and mucked like a slave.
Was it famine or scurvy—I fought it,
 I hurled my youth into the grave.
I wanted the gold and I got it—
 Came out with a fortune last fall,—
Yet somehow life's not what I thought it,
 And somehow the gold isn't all.

No! There's the land. (Have you seen it?)
 It's the cussedest land that I know,
From the big, dizzy mountains that screen it,
 To the deep, deathlike valleys below.
Some say God was tired when He made it;
 Some say it's a fine land to shun;
Maybe: but there's some as would trade it
 For no land on earth—and I'm one.

You come to get rich (damned good reason),
 You feel like an exile at first;

16

You hate it like hell for a season,
  And then you are worse than the worst.
It grips you like some kinds of sinning;
  It twists you from foe to a friend;
It seems it's been since the beginning;
  It seems it will be to the end.

I've stood in some mighty-mouthed hollow
  That's plumb-full of hush to the brim;
I've watched the big, husky sun wallow
  In crimson and gold, and grow dim,
Till the moon set the pearly peaks gleaming,
  And the stars tumbled out, neck and crop;
And I've thought that I surely was dreaming,
  With the peace o' the world piled on top.

The summer—no sweeter was ever;
  The sunshiny woods all athrill;
The greyling aleap in the river,
  The bighorn asleep on the hill.
The strong life that never knows harness;
  The wilds where the caribou call;
The freshness, the freedom, the farness—
  O God! how I'm stuck on it all.

The winter! the brightness that blinds you,
  The white land locked tight as a drum,

The cold fear that follows and finds you,
  The silence that bludgeons you dumb.
The snows that are older than history,
  The woods where the weird shadows slant;
The stillness, the moonlight, the mystery,
  I've bade 'em good-bye—but I can't.

There's a land where the mountains are nameless,
  And the rivers all run God knows where;
There are lives that are erring and aimless,
  And deaths that just hang by a hair;
There are hardships that nobody reckons;
  There are valleys unpeopled and still;
There's a land—oh, it beckons and beckons,
  And I want to go back—and I will.

They're making my money diminish;
  I'm sick of the taste of champagne.
Thank God! when I'm skinned to a finish
  I'll pike to the Yukon again.
I'll fight—and you bet it's no sham-fight:
  It's hell!—but I've been there before;
And it's better than this by a damsite—
  So me for the Yukon once more.

There's gold, and it's haunting and haunting.
  It's luring me on as of old;

Yet it isn't the gold that I'm wanting
  So much as just finding the gold.
It's the great, big, broad land 'way up yonder,
  It's the forests where silence has lease;
It's the beauty that thrills me with wonder,
  It's the stillness that fills me with peace.

THE CALL OF THE WILD

HAVE you gazed on naked grandeur where there's nothing else
    to gaze on,
  Set pieces and drop-curtain scenes galore,
Big mountains heaved to heaven, which the blinding sunsets
    blazon,
  Black canyons where the rapids rip and roar?
Have you swept the visioned valley with the green stream
    streaking through it,
  Searched the Vastness for a something you have lost?
Have you strung your soul to silence? Then for God's sake
    go and do it;
  Hear the challenge, learn the lesson, pay the cost.

Have you wandered in the wilderness, the sage-brush desola-
    tion,
  The bunch-grass levels where the cattle graze?
Have you whistled bits of rag-time at the end of all creation,
  And learned to know the desert's little ways?
Have you camped upon the foothills, have you galloped o'er
    the ranges,
  Have you roamed the arid sun-lands through and through?

Have you chummed up with the mesa? Do you know its
    moods and changes?
  Then listen to the wild—it's calling you.

Have you known the Great White Silence, not a snow-gemmed
    twig a-quiver?
  (Eternal truths that shame our soothing lies.)
Have you broken trail on snowshoes? mushed your huskies up
    the river,
  Dared the unknown, led the way, and clutched the prize?
Have you marked the map's void spaces, mingled with the
    mongrel races,
  Felt the savage strength of brute in every thew?
And though grim as hell the worst is, can you round it off with
    curses?
  Then hearken to the wild—it's wanting you.

Have you suffered, starved, and triumphed, grovelled down,
    yet grasped at glory,
  Grown bigger in the bigness of the whole?
"Done things" just for the doing, letting babblers tell the story.
  Seeing through the nice veneer the naked soul?
Have you seen God in His splendours, heard the text that
    nature renders?
  (You'll never hear it in the family pew.)
The simple things, the true things, the silent men who do
    things—
  Then listen to the wild—it's calling you.

They have cradled you in custom, they have primed you with
      their preaching,
  They have soaked you in convention through and through;
They have put you in a showcase; you're a credit to their
      teaching—
  But can't you hear the wild?—it's calling you.
Let us probe the silent places, let us seek what luck betide us;
  Let us journey to a lonely land I know.
There's a whisper on the night-wind, there's a star agleam to
      guide us,
  And the wild is calling, calling . . . let us go.

THE LONE TRAIL

Ye who know the Lone Trail fain would follow it,
Though it lead to glory or the darkness of the pit.
Ye who take the Lone Trail, bid your love good-bye;
The Lone Trail, the Lone Trail follow till you die.

The trails of the world be countless, and most of the trails be
> tried;
You tread on the heels of the many, till you come where the
> ways divide;
And one lies safe in the sunlight, and the other is dreary and
> wan,
Yet you look aslant at the Lone Trail, and the Lone Trail
> lures you on.
And somehow you're sick of the highway, with its noise and
> its easy needs,
And you seek the risk of the by-way, and you reck not where
> it leads.
And sometimes it leads to the desert, and the tongue swells out
> of the mouth,
And you stagger blind to the mirage, to die in the mocking
> drouth.
And sometimes it leads to the mountain, to the light of the
> lone camp-fire,

And you gnaw your belt in the anguish of hunger-goaded
    desire.

And sometimes it leads to the Southland, to the swamp where
    the orchid glows,

And you rave to your grave with the fever, and they rob the
    corpse for its clothes.

And sometimes it leads to the Northland, and the scurvy softens
    your bones,

And your flesh dints in like putty, and you spit out your teeth
    like stones.

And sometimes it leads to a coral reef in the wash of a weedy
    sea,

And you sit and stare at the empty glare where the gulls wait
    greedily.

And sometimes it leads to an Arctic trail, and the snows where
    your torn feet freeze,

And you whittle away the useless clay, and crawl on your
    hands and knees.

Often it leads to the dead-pit; always it leads to pain;

By the bones of your brothers ye know it, but oh, to follow
    you're fain.

By your bones they will follow behind you, till the ways of
    the world are made plain.

Bid good-bye to sweetheart, bid good-bye to friend;
The Lone Trail, the Lone Trail follow to the end.
Tarry not, and fear not, chosen of the true;
Lover of the Lone Trail, the Lone Trail waits for you.

THE HEART OF THE SOURDOUGH

There where the mighty mountains bare their fangs unto the
    moon;
There where the sullen sun-dogs glare in the snow-bright,
    bitter noon,
And the glacier-gutted streams sweep down at the clarion call
    of June:

There where the livid tundras keep their tryst with the
    tranquil snows;
There where the Silences are spawned, and the light of hell-
    fire flows
Into the bowl of the midnight sky, violet, amber, and rose:

There where the rapids churn and roar, and the ice-floes bel-
    lowing run;
Where the tortured, twisted rivers of blood rush to the setting
    sun—
I've packed my kit and I'm going, boys, ere another day is gone.

I knew it would call, or soon or late, as it calls the whirring
    wings;
It's the olden lure, it's the golden lure, it's the lure of the
    timeless things;
And to-night, O God of the trails untrod, how it whines in my
    heart-strings!

I'm sick to death of your well-groomed gods, your make-believe
    and your show;
I long for a whiff of bacon and beans, a snug shake-down in
    the snow,
A trail to break, and a life at stake, and another bout with the
    foe;

With the raw-ribbed Wild that abhors all life, the Wild that
    would crush and rend;
I have clinched and closed with the naked North, I have
    learned to defy and defend;
Shoulder to shoulder we've fought it out—yet the Wild must
    win in the end.

I have flouted the Wild. I have followed its lure, fearless,
    familiar, alone;
By all that the battle means and makes I claim that land for
    mine own;
Yet the Wild must win, and a day will come when I shall be
    overthrown.

Then when as wolf-dogs fight we've fought, the lean wolf-land
    and I;
Fought and bled till the snows are red under the reeling sky;
Even as lean wolf-dog goes down will I go down and die.

THE THREE VOICES

THE waves have a story to tell me,
  As I lie on the lonely beach;
Chanting aloft in the pine-tops,
  The wind has a lesson to teach;
But the stars sing an anthem of glory
  I cannot put into speech.

The waves tell of ocean spaces,
  Of hearts that are wild and brave,
Of populous city places,
  Of desolate shores they lave;
Of men who sally in quest of gold
  To sink in an ocean grave.

The wind is a mighty roamer;
  He bids me keep me free,
Clean from the taint of the gold-lust,
  Hardy and pure as he;
Cling with my love to nature
  As a child to the mother-knee.

But the stars throng out in their glory,
   And they sing of the God in man;
They sing of the mighty Master,
   Of the loom His fingers span;
Where a star or a soul is a part of the whole,
   And weft in the wondrous plan.

Here by the camp-fire's flicker,
   Deep in my blanket curled,
I long for the peace of the pine-gloom
   When the scroll of the Lord is unfurled,
And the wind and the wave are silent,
   And world is singing to world.

THE PINES

WE sleep in the sleep of ages, the bleak, barbarian pines;
The grey moss drapes us like sages, and closer we lock our lines,
And deeper we clutch through the gelid gloom where never
   a sunbeam shines.

On the flanks of the storm-gored ridges are our black battalions
   massed;
We surge in a host to the sullen coast, and we sing in the
   ocean blast;
From empire of sea to empire of snow we grip our empire fast.

To the niggard lands were we driven; 'twixt desert and foe
   are we penned.
To us was the Northland given, ours to stronghold and defend;
Ours till the world be riven in the crash of the utter end.
Ours from the bleak beginning, through the æons of death-like
   sleep;
Ours from the shock when the naked rock was hurled from the
   hissing deep;
Ours through the twilight ages of weary glacier-creep.

Wind of the East, wind of the West, wandering to and fro,
Chant your songs in our topmost boughs, that the sons of
    men may know
The peerless pine was the first to come, and the pine will be
    last to go!

We pillar the halls of perfumed gloom; we plume where the
    eagles soar;
The North-wind swoops from the brooding Pole, and our
    ancients crash and roar;
But where one falls from the crumbling walls shoots up a
    hardy score.

We spring from the gloom of the canyon's womb; in the valley's
    lap we lie;
From the white foam-fringe where the breakers cringe to the
    peaks that tusk the sky
We climb, and we peer in the crag-locked mere that gleams
    like a golden eye,—

Gain to the verge of the hog-back ridge where the vision ranges
    free:
Pines and pines and the shadow of pines as far as the eye can
    see;
A steadfast legion of stalwart knights in dominant empery.

Sun, moon and stars, give answer; shall we not staunchly stand
Even as now, forever, wards of the wilder strand,
Sentinels of the stillness, lords of the last lone land!

THE HARPY

There was a woman, and she was wise; woefully wise was she;
She was old, so old, yet her years all told were but a score and
three;
And she knew by heart, from finish to start, the Book of
Iniquity.

There is no hope for such as I, on earth nor yet in Heaven;
Unloved I live, unloved I die, unpitied, unforgiven;
A loathèd jade I ply my trade, unhallowed and unshriven.

I paint my cheeks, for they are white, and cheeks of chalk
men hate;
Mine eyes with wine I make to shine, that men may seek and
sate;
With overhead a lamp of red I sit me down and wait.

Until they come, the nightly scum, with drunken eyes aflame;
Your sweethearts, sons, ye scornful ones—'tis I who know their
shame;
The gods ye see are brutes to me--and so I play my game.

For life is not the thing we thought, and not the thing we plan;
And woman in a bitter world must do the best she can;
Must yield the stroke, and bear the yoke, and serve the will of
      man;

Must serve his need and ever feed the flame of his desire;
Though be she loved for love alone, or be she loved for hire;
For every man since life began is tainted with the mire.

And though you know he love you so, and set you on love's
      throne,
Yet let your eyes but mock his sighs, and let your heart be
      stone,
Lest you be left (as I was left) attainted and alone.

From love's close kiss to hell's abyss is one sheer flight, I trow;
And wedding-ring and bridal bell are will-o'-wisps of woe;
And 'tis not wise to love too well, and this all women know.

Wherefore, the wolf-pack having gorged upon the lamb, their
      prey,
With siren smile and serpent guile I make the wolf-pack pay;
With velvet paws and flensing claws, a tigress roused to slay.

One who in youth sought truest truth, and found a devil's lies;
A symbol of the sin of man, a human sacrifice:
Yet shall I blame on man the shame? Could it be otherwise?

Was I not born to walk in scorn where others walk in pride?
The Maker marred, and evil-starred I drift upon His tide;
And He alone shall judge His own, so I His judgment bide.

Fate has written a tragedy; its name is "The Human Heart."
The theatre is the House of Life, Woman the mummer's part:
The Devil enters the prompter's box and the play is ready to
  start.

THE LURE OF LITTLE VOICES

THERE's a cry from out the Loneliness—Oh, listen, Honey,
    listen!
  Do you hear it, do you fear it, you're a-holding of me so?
You're a-sobbing in your sleep, dear, and your lashes, how they
    glisten—
  Do you hear the Little Voices all a-begging me to go?

All a-begging me to leave you. Day and night they're plead-
    ing, praying,
  On the North-wind, on the West-wind, from the peak and
    from the plain;
Night and day they never leave me—do you know what they
    are saying?
  "He was ours before you got him, and we want him once
    again."

Yes, they're wanting me, they're haunting me, the awful lonely
    places;
  They're whining and they're whimpering as if each had a
    soul;

They're calling from the wilderness, the vast and god-like
  spaces,
The stark and sullen solitudes that sentinel the Pole.

They miss my little camp-fires, ever brightly, bravely gleaming
  In the womb of desolation where was never man before;
As comradeless I sought them, lion-hearted, loving, dreaming;
  And they hailed me as a comrade, and they loved me ever-
  more.

And now they're all a-crying, and it's no use me denying:
  The spell of them is on me and I'm helpless as a child;
My heart is aching, aching, but I hear them sleeping, waking;
  It's the Lure of Little Voices, it's the mandate of the Wild.

I'm afraid to tell you, Honey, I can take no bitter leaving;
  But softly in the sleep-time from your love I'll steal away.
Oh, it's cruel, dearie, cruel, and it's God knows how I'm
  grieving;
  But His Loneliness is calling and He knows I must obey.

THE SONG OF THE WAGE-SLAVE

WHEN the long, long day is over, and the Big Boss gives me
   my pay,
I hope that it won't be hell-fire, as some of the parsons say.
And I hope that it won't be heaven, with some of the parsons
   I've met—
All I want is just quiet, just to rest and forget.
Look at my face, toil-furrowed; look at my calloused hands;
Master, I've done Thy bidding, wrought in Thy many lands—
Wrought for the little masters, big-bellied they be, and rich;
I've done their desire for a daily hire, and I die like a dog in a
   ditch.
I have used the strength Thou hast given, Thou knowest I did
   not shirk;
Threescore years of labour—Thine be the long day's work.
And now, Big Master, I'm broken and bent and twisted and
   scarred,
But I've held my job, and Thou knowest, and Thou wilt not
   judge me hard.
Thou knowest my sins are many, and often I've played the
   fool—
Whiskey and cards and women, they made me the devil's tool.
I was just like a child with money: I flung it away with a curse,

Feasting a fawning parasite, or glutting a harlot's purse,
Then back to the woods repentant, back to the mill or the
    mine,
I, the worker of workers, everything in my line.
Everything hard but headwork (I'd no more brains than a kid),
A brute with brute strength to labour, doing as I was bid;
Living in camps with men-folk, a lonely and loveless life;
Never knew kiss of sweetheart, never caress of wife.
A brute with brute strength to labour, and they were so far
    above—
Yet I'd gladly have gone to the gallows for one little look of
    Love.
I with the strength of two men, savage and shy and wild—
Yet how I'd ha' treasured a woman, and the sweet, warm kiss
    of a child.
Well, 'tis Thy world, and Thou knowest. I blaspheme and
    my ways be rude;
But I've lived my life as I found it, and I've done my best to
    be good;
I, the primitive toiler, half naked, and grimed to the eyes,
Sweating it deep in their ditches, swining it stark in their
    styes.
Hurling down forests before me, spanning tumultuous streams;
Down in the ditch building o'er me palaces fairer than dreams;
Boring the rock to the ore-bed, driving the road through the
    fen,
Resolute, dumb, uncomplaining, a man in a world of men.
Master, I've filled my contract, wrought in Thy many lands;

Not by my sins wilt Thou judge me, but by the work of my
    hands.
Master, I've done Thy bidding, and the light is low in the west,
And the long, long shift is over . . . Master, I've earned it—
    Rest.

GRIN

IF you're up against a bruiser and you're getting knocked
    about—
                        Grin.
If you're feeling pretty groggy, and you're licked beyond a
    doubt—
                        Grin.
Don't let him see you're funking, let him know with every
    clout,
Though your face is battered to a pulp, your blooming heart
    is stout:
Just stand upon your pins until the beggar knocks you out—
                And grin.

This life's a bally battle, and the same advice holds true,
                  Of grin.
If you're up against it badly, then it's only one on you,
                  So grin.
If the future's black as thunder, don't let people see you're
    blue;
Just cultivate a cast-iron smile of joy the whole day through;

If they call you "Little Sunshine," wish that *they'd* no troubles,
  too—

You may—grin.

Rise up in the morning with the will that, smooth or rough,
  You'll grin.
Sink to sleep at midnight, and although you're feeling tough,
  Yet grin.
There's nothing gained by whining, and you're not that kind
  of stuff;
You're a fighter from away back, and you *won't* take a rebuff:
Your trouble is that you don't know when you have had
  enough—

Don't give in.
If Fate should down you, just get up and take another cuff;
You may bank on it that there is no philosophy like bluff
  And grin.

THE SHOOTING OF DAN McGREW

A BUNCH of the boys were whooping it up in the Malamute
     saloon;
The kid that handles the music-box was hitting a rag-time
     tune;
Back of the bar, in a solo game, sat Dangerous Dan McGrew,
And watching his luck was his light-o'-love, the lady that's
     known as Lou.

When out of the night, which was fifty below, and into the
     din and the glare,
There stumbled a miner fresh from the creeks, dog-dirty and
     loaded for bear.
He looked like a man with a foot in the grave, and scarcely the
     strength of a louse,
Yet he tilted a poke of dust on the bar, and he called for
     drinks for the house.
There was none could place the stranger's face, though we
     searched ourselves for a clue;
But we drank his health, and the last to drink was Dangerous
     Dan McGrew.

There's men that somehow just grip your eyes, and hold them
    hard like a spell;
And such was he, and he looked to me like a man who had
    lived in hell;
With a face most hair, and the dreary stare of a dog whose
    day is done,
As he watered the green stuff in his glass, and the drops fell
    one by one.
Then I got to figgering who he was, and wondering what he'd
    do,
And I turned my head—and there watching him was the lady
    that's known as Lou.

His eyes went rubbering round the room, and he seemed in a
    kind of daze,
Till at last that old piano fell in the way of his wandering
    gaze.
The rag-time kid was having a drink; there was no one else
    on the stool,
So the stranger stumbles across the room, and flops down there
    like a fool.
In a buckskin shirt that was glazed with dirt he sat, and I saw
    him sway;
Then he clutched the keys with his talon hands—my God! but
    that man could play!

Were you ever out in the Great Alone, when the moon was
    awful clear,

And the icy mountains hemmed you in with a silence you
most could *hear*;
With only the howl of a timber wolf, and you camped there in
the cold,
A half-dead thing in a stark, dead-world, clean mad for the
muck called gold;
While high overhead, green, yellow, and red, the North Light
swept in bars—
Then you've a haunch what the music meant . . . hunger and
night and the stars.

And hunger not of the belly kind, that's banished with bacon
and beans;
But the gnawing hunger of lonely men for a home and all
that it means;
For a fireside far from the cares that are, four walls and a roof
above;
But oh! so cramful of cosy joy, and crowned with a woman's
love:
A woman dearer than all the world, and true as Heaven is
true—
(God! how ghastly she looks through her rouge,—the lady
that's known as Lou.)

Then on a sudden the music changed, so soft that you scarce
could hear;
But you felt that your life had been looted clean of all that it
once held dear;

That someone had stolen the woman you loved; that her love
was a devil's lie;
That your guts were gone, and the best for you was to crawl
away and die.
'Twas the crowning cry of a heart's despair, and it thrilled you
through and through—
"I guess I'll make it a spread misere," said Dangerous Dan
McGrew.

The music almost died away . . . then it burst like a pent-up
flood;
And it seemed to say, "Repay, repay," and my eyes were blind
with blood.
The thought came back of an ancient wrong, and it stung like
a frozen lash,
And the lust awoke to kill, to kill . . . then the music stopped
with a crash.

And the stranger turned, and his eyes they burned in a most
peculiar way;
In a buckskin shirt that was glazed with dirt he sat, and I saw
him sway;
Then his lips went in in a kind of grin, and he spoke, and
his voice was calm;
And, "Boys," says he, "you don't know me, and none of you
care a damn;
But I want to state, and my words are straight, and I'll bet my
poke they're true,

That one of you is a hound of hell . . . and that one is Dan
  McGrew."

Then I ducked my head, and the lights went out, and two
  guns blazed in the dark;
And a woman screamed, and the lights went up, and two men
  lay stiff and stark.
Pitched on his head, and pumped full of lead, was Dangerous
  Dan McGrew,
While the man from the creeks lay clutched to the breast of
  the lady that's known as Lou.

These are the simple facts of the case, and I guess I ought to
  know;
They say that the stranger was crazed with "hooch," and I'm
  not denying it's so.
I'm not so wise as the lawyer guys, but strictly between us
  two—
The woman that kissed him and—pinched his poke—was the
  lady that's known as Lou.

THE CREMATION OF SAM McGEE

There are strange things done in the midnight sun
  By the men who moil for gold;
The Arctic trails have their secret tales
  That would make your blood run cold;
The Northern Lights have seen queer sights,
  But the queerest they ever did see
Was that night on the marge of Lake Lebarge
  I cremated Sam McGee.

Now Sam McGee was from Tennessee, where the cotton
  blooms and blows.
Why he left his home in the South to roam round the Pole
  God only knows.
He was always cold, but the land of gold seemed to hold him
  like a spell;
Though he'd often say in his homely way that he'd "sooner
  live in hell."

On a Christmas Day we were mushing our way over the
  Dawson trail.
Talk of your cold! through the parka's fold it stabbed like a
  driven nail.

48

If our eyes we'd close, then the lashes froze, till sometimes we
    couldn't see;
It wasn't much fun, but the only one to whimper was Sam
    McGee.

And that very night as we lay packed tight in our robes beneath
    the snow,
And the dogs were fed, and the stars o'erhead were dancing
    heel and toe,
He turned to me, and, "Cap," says he, "I'll cash in this trip,
    I guess;
And if I do, I'm asking that you won't refuse my last request."

Well, he seemed so low that I couldn't say no: then he says
    with a sort of moan:
"It's the cursèd cold, and it's got right hold till I'm chilled
    clean through to the bone.
Yet 'taint being dead, it's my awful dread of the icy grave that
    pains:
So I want you to swear that, foul or fair, you'll cremate my
    last remains."

A pal's last need is a thing to heed, so I swore I would not fail;
And we started on at the streak of dawn, but God! he looked
    ghastly pale.
He crouched on the sleigh, and he raved all day of his home
    in Tennessee;

And before nightfall a corpse was all that was left of Sam
    McGee.

There wasn't a breath in that land of death, and I hurried,
    horror driven,
With a corpse half-hid that I couldn't get rid because of a
    promise given;
It was lashed to the sleigh, and it seemed to say: "You may tax
    your brawn and brains,
But you promised true, and it's up to you to cremate those last
    remains."

Now a promise made is a debt unpaid, and the trail has its own
    stern code.
In the days to come, though my lips were dumb, in my heart
    how I cursed that load.
In the long, long night, by the lone firelight, while the huskies,
    round in a ring,
Howled out their woes to the homeless snows—O God! how
    I loathed the thing!

And every day that quiet clay seemed to heavy and heavier
    grow;
And on I went, though the dogs were spent and the grub was
    getting low;
The trail was bad, and I felt half mad, but I swore I would
    not give in;

And I'd often sing to the hateful thing, and it hearkened with
    a grin.

Till I came to the marge of Lake Lebarge, and a derelict
    there lay;
It was jammed in the ice, but I saw in a trice it was called
    the "Alice May."
And I looked at it, and I thought a bit, and I looked at my
    frozen chum:
Then, "Here," said I, with a sudden cry, "is my cre-ma-tor-eum."

Some planks I tore from the cabin floor, and I lit the boiler
    fire;
Some coal I found that was lying around, and I heaped
    the fuel higher;
The flames just soared, and the furnace roared—such a
    blaze you seldom see;
And I burrowed a hole in the glowing coal, and I stuffed
    in Sam McGee.

Then I made a hike, for I didn't like to hear him sizzle so;
And the heavens scowled, and the huskies howled, and the
    wind began to blow.
It was icy cold, but the hot sweat rolled down my cheeks,
    and I don't know why;
And the greasy smoke in an inky cloak went streaking down
    the sky.

c

I do not know how long in the snow I wrestled with grisly
    fear;
But the stars came out and they danced about ere again I
    ventured near;
I was sick with dread, but I bravely said: "I'll just take a
    peep inside.
I guess he's cooked, and it's time I looked," . . . then the
    door I opened wide.

And there sat Sam, looking cool and calm, in the heart of
    the furnace roar;
And he wore a smile you could see a mile, and he said: "Please
    close that door.
It's fine in here, but I greatly fear you'll let in the cold and
    storm—
Since I left Plumtree, down in Tennessee, it's the first time
    I've been warm."

There are strange things done in the midnight sun
    By the men who moil for gold;
The Arctic trails have their secret tales
    That would make your blood run cold.
The Northern Lights have seen queer sights,
    But the queerest they ever did see
Was that night on the marge of Lake Lebarge
    I cremated Sam McGee.

MY MADONNA

I HALED me a woman from the street,
    Shameless, but, oh, so fair!
I bade her sit in the model's seat,
    And I painted her sitting there.

    I hid all trace of her heart unclean;
        I painted a babe at her breast;
    I painted her as she might have been
        If the Worst had been the Best.

She laughed at my picture, and went away.
    Then came, with a knowing nod,
A connoisseur, and I heard him say:
    "'Tis Mary, the Mother of God."

    So I painted a halo round her hair,
        And I sold her, and took my fee,
    And she hangs in the Church of Saint Hilaire,
        Where you and all may see.

UNFORGOTTEN

I KNOW a garden where the lilies gleam,
   And one who lingers in the sunshine there;
   She is than white-stoled lily far more fair,
And oh, her eyes are heaven-lit with dream.

   I know a garret, cold and dark and drear,
      And one who toils and toils with tireless pen,
      Until his brave, sad eyes grow weary—then
   He seeks the stars, pale, silent as a seer.

And ah, it's strange, for desolate and dim
   Between these two there rolls an ocean wide;
   Yet he is in the garden by her side,
And she is in the garret there with him.

THE RECKONING

It's fine to have a blow-out in a fancy restaurant,
With terrapin and canvas-back and all the wine you want;
To enjoy the flowers and music, watch the pretty women pass,
Smoke a choice cigar, and sip the wealthy water in your glass;
It's bully in a high-toned joint to eat and drink your fill,
But it's quite another matter when you
                              Pay the bill.

It's great to go out every night on fun or pleasure bent,
To wear your glad rags always, and to never save a cent;
To drift along regardless, have a good time every trip;
To hit the high spots sometimes, and to let your chances slip;
To know you're acting foolish, yet to go on fooling still,
Till Nature calls a show-down, and you
                              Pay the bill.

Time has got a little bill—get wise while yet you may,
For the debit side's increasing in a most alarming way;
The things you had no right to do, the things you should
      have done,
They're all put down: it's up to you to pay for every one.
So eat, drink, and be merry, have a good time if you will,
But God help you when the time comes, and you
                              Foot the bill.

QUATRAINS

One said: Thy life is thine to make or mar,
To flicker feebly, or to soar, a star;
It lies with thee—the choice is thine, is thine,
To hit the ties or drive thy auto-car.

I answer Her: The choice is mine—ah, no!
We all were made or marred long, long ago.
The parts are written: hear the super wail:
"Who is stage-managing this cosmic show?"

Blind fools of fate, and slaves of circumstance.
Life is a fiddler, and we all must dance.
From gloom where mocks that will-o'-wisp, Freewill,
I heard a voice cry: "Say, give us a chance."

Chance! Oh, there is no chance. The scene is set.
Up with the curtain! Man, the marionette,
Resumes his part. The gods will work the wires.
They've got it all down fine, you bet, you bet!

It's all decreed: the mighty earthquake crash;
The countless constellations' wheel and flash;
The rise and fall of empires, war's red tide,
The composition of your dinner hash.

There's no haphazard in this world of ours:
Cause and effect are grim, relentless powers.
They rule the world. (A king was shot last night.
Last night I held the joker and both bowers.)

From out the mesh of fate our heads we thrust.
We can't do what we would, but what we must.
Heredity has got us in a cinch.
(Consoling thought, when you've been on a "bust.")

Hark to the song where spheral voices blend:
"There's no beginning, never will be end."
It makes us nutty; hang the astral chimes!
The table's spread; come, let us dine, my friend.

THE MEN THAT DON'T FIT IN

THERE'S a race of men that don't fit in,
    A race that can't stay still;
So they break the hearts of kith and kin,
    And they roam the world at will.
They range the field and they rove the flood,
    And they climb the mountain's crest;
Theirs is the curse of the gipsy blood,
    And they don't know how to rest.

If they just went straight they might go far;
    They are strong and brave and true;
But they're always tired of the things that are,
    And they want the strange and new
They say: "Could I find my proper groove,
    What a deep mark I would make!"
So they chop and change, and each fresh move
    Is only a fresh mistake.

And each forgets, as he strips and runs,
    With a brilliant, fitful pace,

It's the steady, quiet, plodding ones
   Who win in the lifelong race.
And each forgets that his youth has fled,
   Forgets that his prime is past,
Till he stands one day with a hope that's dead
   In the glare of the truth at last.

He has failed, he has failed; he has missed his
      chance;
  He has just done things by half.
Life's been a jolly good joke on him,
   And now is the time to laugh.
Ha, ha! He is one of the Legion Lost;
  He was never meant to win;
He's a rolling stone, and it's bred in the bone;
  He's a man who won't fit in.

MUSIC IN THE BUSH

O'ER the dark pines she sees the silver moon,
  And in the west, all tremulous, a star,
And soothing sweet she hears the mellow tune
  Of cow-bells jangled in the fields afar.

Quite listless, for her daily stent is done,
  She stands, sad exile, at her rose-wreathed door,
And sends her love eternal with the sun
  That goes to gild the land she'll see no more.

The grave, gaunt pines imprison her sad gaze,
  And still the sky and darkling drearily;
She feels the chilly breath of dear, dead days
  Come sifting through the alders eerily.

Oh, how the roses riot in their bloom!
  The curtains stir as with an ancient pain;
Her old piano gleams from out the gloom,
  And waits and waits her tender touch in vain.

But now her hands like moonlight brush the keys
  With velvet grace, melodious delight;
And now a sad refrain from overseas
  Goes sobbing on the bosom of the night.

And now she sings. (O singer in the gloom,
  Voicing the sorrow we can ne'er express,
Here in the Farness where we few have room
  Unshamed to show our love and tenderness,

Our hearts will echo, till they beat no more,
  That song of sadness and of motherland;
And stretched in deathless love to England's shore,
  Some day she'll hearken and she'll understand.)

A prima-donna in the shining past,
  But now a mother growing old and grey,
She thinks of how she held a people fast
  In thrall, and gleaned the triumphs of a day.

She sees a sea of faces like a dream;
  She sees herself a queen of song once more;
She sees lips part in rapture, eyes agleam;
  She sings as never once she sang before.

She sings a wild, sweet song that throbs with pain,
    The added pain of life that transcends art,
A song of home, a deep, celestial strain,
    The glorious swan-song of a dying heart.

A lame tramp comes along the railway track,
    A grizzled dog whose day is nearly done:
He passes, pauses, then comes slowly back
    And listens there—an audience of one.

She sings—her golden voice is passion-fraught
    As when she charmed a thousand eager ears;
He listens trembling, and she knows it not,
    And down his hollow cheeks roll bitter tears.

She ceases and is still, as if to pray;
    There is no sound, the stars are all alight—
Only a wretch who stumbles on his way,
    Only a vagrant sobbing in the night.

THE RHYME OF THE REMITTANCE MAN

There's a four-pronged buck a-swinging in the shadow of
  my cabin,
  And it roamed the velvet valley till to-day;
But I tracked it by the river, and I trailed it in the cover,
  And I killed it on the mountain miles away.
Now I've had my lazy supper, and the level sun is gleaming
  On the water where the silver salmon play;
And I light my little corn-cob, and I linger softly dreaming,
  In the twilight, of a land that's far away.

Far away, so faint and far, is flaming London, fevered Paris,
  That I fancy I have gained another star;
Far away the din and hurry, far away the sin and worry,
  Far away—God knows they cannot be too far.
Gilded galley-slaves of Mammon—how my purse-proud brothers
  taunt me!
  I might have been as well-to-do as they
Had I clutched like them my chances, learned their wisdom,
  crushed my fancies,
  Starved my soul and gone to business every day.

Well, the cherry bends with blossom, and the vivid grass is
    springing,
  And the star-like lily nestles in the green;
And the frogs their joys are singing, and my heart in tune
    is ringing,
  And it doesn't matter what I might have been.
While above the scented pine-gloom, piling heights of golden
    glory,
  The sun-god paints his canvas in the west;
I can couch me deep in clover, I can listen to the story
  Of the lazy, lapping water—it is best.

While the trout leaps in the river, and the blue grouse thrills
    the cover,
  And the frozen snow betrays the panther's track,
And the robin greets the dayspring with the rapture of a
    lover,
  I am happy, and I'll nevermore go back.
For I know I'd just be longing for the little old log cabin,
  With the morning-glory clinging to the door,
Till I loathed the city places, cursed the care on all the faces,
  Turned my back on lazar London evermore.

So send me far from Lombard Street, and write me down a
    failure;
  Put a little in my purse and leave me free.

Say: "He turned from Fortune's offering to follow up a pale
  lure,
  He is one of us no longer—let him be."
I am one of you no longer: by the trails my feet have broken,
  The dizzy peaks I've scaled, the camp-fire's glow,
By the lonely seas I've sailed in—yea, the final word is spoken,
  I am signed and sealed to nature. Be it so.

THE LOW-DOWN WHITE

This is the pay-day up at the mines, when the bearded brutes
    come down;
There's money to burn in the streets to-night, so I've sent
    my klooch to town,
With a haggard face and a ribband of red entwined in her
    hair of brown.

And I know at the dawn she'll come reeling home with the
    bottles, one, two, three;
One for herself to drown her shame, and two big bottles for
    me,
To make me forget the thing I am and the man I used to be.

To make me forget the brand of the dog, as I crouch in this
    hideous place;
To make me forget once I kindled the light of love in a lady's
    face,
Where even the squalid Siwash now holds me a black disgrace.

Oh, I have guarded my secret well!   And who would dream
   as I speak
In a tribal tongue like a rogue unhung, 'mid the ranch-house
   filth and reek,
I could roll to bed with a Latin phrase, and rise with a verse
   of Greek?

Yet I was a senior prizeman once, and the pride of a college
   eight;
Called to the bar—my friends were true! but they could not
   keep me straight;
Then came the divorce, and I went abroad and "died" on the
   River Plate.

But I'm not dead yet; though with half a lung there isn't
   time to spare,
And I hope that the year will see me out, and, thank God,
   no one will care—
Save maybe the little slim Siwash girl with the rose of shame
   in her hair.

She will come with the dawn, and the dawn is near; I can
   see its evil glow,
Like a corpse-light seen through a frosty pane in a night of
   want and woe;
And yonder she comes, by the bleak bull-pines, swift staggering through the snow.

THE LITTLE OLD LOG CABIN

When a man gits on his uppers in a hard-pan sort of town,
    An' he ain't got nothin' comin', an' he can't afford ter eat.
An' he's in a fix fer lodgin', an' he wanders up an' down,
    An' you'd fancy he'd been boozin', he's so locoed 'bout
        the feet;
When he's feelin' sneakin' sorry, an' his belt is hangin' slack,
    An' his face is peaked an' grey-like, an' his heart gits down
        an' whines,
Then he's apt ter git a-thinkin' an' a-wishin' he was back
    In the little ol' log cabin in the shadder of the pines.

When he's on the blazin' desert, an' his canteen's sprung a leak,
    An' he's all alone an' crazy, an' he's crawlin' like a snail,
An' his tongue's so black an' swollen that it hurts him fer to
        speak,
    An' he gouges down fer water, an' the raven's on his trail;
When he's done with care and cursin', an' he feels more like
        to cry,
    An' he sees ol' Death a-grinnin', an' he thinks upon his
        crimes,
Then he's like ter hev' a vision, as he settles down ter die,
    Of the little ol' log cabin an' the roses an' the vines.

Oh, the little ol' log cabin, it's a solemn shinin' mark
    When a feller gits ter sinnin', an' a-goin' ter the wall,
An' folks don't understand him, an' he's gropin' in the dark,
    An' he's sick of bein' cursed at, an' he's longin' fer his call:
When the sun of life's a-sinkin' you can see it 'way above,
    On the hill from out the shadder in a glory 'gin the sky,
An' your mother's voice is callin', an' her arms are stretched
      in love,
    An' somehow you're glad you're goin', an' you ain't a-scared
      to die;
When you'll be like a kid again, an' nestle to her breast,
    An' never leave its shelter, an' forget, an' love, an' rest.

THE YOUNGER SON

If you leave the gloom of London and you seek a glowing land,
  Where all except the flag is strange and new,
There's a bronzed and stalwart fellow who will grip you by
    the hand,
  And greet you with a welcome warm and true;
For he's your younger brother, the one you sent away,
  Because there wasn't room for him at home;
And now he's quite contented, and he's glad he didn't stay,
  And he's building Britain's greatness o'er the foam.

When the giant herd is moving at the rising of the sun,
  And the prairie is lit with rose and gold;
And the camp is all a-bustle, and the busy day's begun,
  He leaps into the saddle sure and bold.
Through the round of heat and hurry, through the racket
    and the rout,
  He rattles at a pace that nothing mars;
And when the night-winds whisper, and camp-fires flicker out,
  He is sleeping like a child beneath the stars.

When the wattle-blossoms are drooping in the sombre she-oak
    glade,

And the breathless land is lying in a swoon,
He leaves his work a moment, leaning lightly on his spade,
And he hears the bell-bird chime the Austral noon.
The parakeets are silent in the gum-tree by the creek;
The ferny grove is sunshine-steeped and still;
But the dew will gem the myrtle in the twilight ere he seek
His little lonely cabin on the hill.

Around the purple, vine-clad slope the argent river dreams;
The roses almost hide the house from view;
A snow-peak of the Winterberg in crimson splendour gleams;
The shadow deepens down on the karroo.
He seeks the lily-scented dusk beneath the orange tree:
His pipe in silence glows and fades and glows,
And then two little maids come out and climb upon his knee,
And one is like the lily, one the rose.

He sees his white sheep dapple o'er the green New Zealand
plain,
And where Vancouver's shaggy ramparts frown,
When the sunlight threads the pine-gloom he is fighting might
and main
To clinch the rivets of an Empire down.
You will find him toiling, toiling, in the south or in the west,
A child of nature, fearless, frank and free:
And the warmest heart that beats for you is beating in his
breast,
And he sends you loyal greeting o'er the sea.

You've a brother in the Army, you've another in the Church;
   One of you is a diplomatic swell;
You've had the pick of everything and left him in the lurch;
   And yet I think he's doing very well.
I'm sure his life is happy, and he doesn't envy yours;
   I know he loves the land his pluck has won;
And I fancy in the years unborn, while England's fame endures,
   She will come to bless with pride—the Younger Son.

THE MARCH OF THE DEAD

THE cruel war was over--oh, the triumph was so sweet!
  We watched the troops returning, through our tears;
There was triumph, triumph, triumph down the scarlet glitter-
      ing street,
  And you scarce could hear the music for the cheers.
And you scarce could see the house-tops for the flags that
      flew between,
  The bells were pealing madly to the sky;
And every one was shouting for the Soldiers of the Queen,
  And the glory of an age was passing by.

And then there came a shadow, swift and sudden, dark and
      drear;
  The bells were silent, not an echo stirred.
The flags were drooping sullenly, the men forgot to cheer;
  We waited, and we never spoke a word.
The sky grew darker, darker, till from out the gloomy rack
  There came a voice that checked the heart with dread:
"Tear down, tear down your bunting now, and hang up sable
      black;
  They are coming--it's the Army of the Dead."

They were coming, they were coming, gaunt and ghastly, sad
     and slow;
    They were coming, all the crimson wrecks of pride;
With faces seared, and cheeks red smeared, and haunting eyes
     of woe,
    And clotted holes the khaki couldn't hide.
Oh, the clammy brow of anguish! the livid, foam-flecked lips!
    The reeling ranks of ruin swept along!
The limb that trailed, the hand that failed, the bloody finger-
     tips!
    And oh, the dreary rhythm of their song!

"They left us on the veldt-side, but we felt we couldn't stop,
    On this, our England's crowning festal day;
We're the men of Magersfontein, we're the men of Spion Kop,
    Colenso,—we're the men who had to pay.
We're the men who paid the blood-price. Shall the grave be
    all our gain?
    You owe us. Long and heavy is the score.
Then cheer us for our glory now, and cheer us for our pain,
    And cheer us as ye never cheered before."

The folks were white and stricken, and each tongue seemed
     weighed with lead;
    Each heart was clutched in hollow hand of ice;
And every eye was staring at the horror of the dead,
    The pity of the men who paid the price.

They were come, were come to mock us, in the first flush of
    our peace;
  Through writhing lips their teeth were all agleam;
They were coming in their thousands—oh, would they never
    cease!
  I closed my eyes, and then—it was a dream.

There was triumph, triumph, triumph down the scarlet gleam-
    ing street;
  The town was mad, a man was like a boy.
A thousand flags were flaming where the sky and city meet;
  A thousand bells were thundering the joy.
There was music, mirth and sunshine; but some eyes shone
    with regret:
  And while we stun with cheers our homing braves,
O God, in Thy great mercy, let us nevermore forget
  The graves they left behind, the bitter graves.

"FIGHTING MAC"

A LIFE TRAGEDY

A PISTOL-SHOT rings round and round the world:
  In pitiful defeat a warrior lies.
A last defiance to dark Death is hurled,
  A last wild challenge shocks the sunlit skies.
  Alone he falls with wide, wan, woeful eyes:
Eyes that could smile at death—could not face shame.

Alone, alone he paced his narrow room,
  In the bright sunshine of that Paris day;
Saw in his thought the awful hand of doom;
  Saw in his dream his glory pass away;
  Tried in his heart, his weary heart, to pray:
"O God! who made me, give me strength to face
The spectre of this bitter, black disgrace."

·　　·　　·　　·　　·　　·

The burn brawls darkly down the shaggy glen,
  The bee-kissed heather blooms around the door;

76

He sees himself a barefoot boy again,
  Bending o'er page of legendary lore.
He hears the pibroch, grips the red claymore,
Runs with the Fiery Cross a clansman true,
Sworn kinsman of Rob Roy and Roderick Dhu.

Eating his heart out with a wild desire,
  One day, behind his counter trim and neat,
He hears a sound that sets his brain afire—
  The Highlanders are marching down the street.
  Oh, how the pipes shrill out, the mad drums beat!
"On to the gates of Hell, my Gordons gay!"
He flings his hated yardstick far away.

He sees the sullen pass, high-crowned with snow,
  Where Afghans cower with eyes of gleaming hate;
He hurls himself against the hidden foe.
  They try to rally—ah, too late, too late!
  Again, defenceless, with fierce eyes that wait
For death, he stands, like baited bull at bay,
And flouts the Boers, that mad Majuba day.

He sees again the murderous Soudan,
  Blood-slaked and rapine swept. He seems to stand
Upon the gory plain of Omdurman.
  Then Magersfontein, and supreme command
  Over his Highlanders. To shake his hand

A King is proud, and princes call him friend,
And glory crowns his life—and now the end.

The awful end. His eyes are dark with doom;
   He hears the shrapnel shrieking overhead:
He sees the ravaged ranks, the flame-stabbed gloom.
   Oh, to have fallen! the battle-field his bed,
   With Wauchope and his glorious brother-dead.
Why was he saved for this, for this? And now
He raises the revolver to his brow.

                    .   .   .   .

In many a Highland home, framed with rude art,
   You'll find his portrait, rough-hewn, stern and square:
It's graven in the Fuyam fellah's heart;
   The Ghurka reads it at his evening prayer;
   The raw lands know it, where the fierce suns glare;
The Dervish fears it. Honour to his name,
Who holds aloft the shield of England's fame.

Mourn for our hero, men of Northern race!
   We do not know his sin; we only know
His sword was keen. He laughed death in the face,
   And struck, for Empire's sake, a giant blow.
   His arm was strong. Ah! well they learnt, the foe.
The echo of his deeds is ringing yet,
Will ring for aye. All else . . . let us forget.

THE WOMAN AND THE ANGEL

An angel was tired of heaven, as he lounged in the golden
    street;
His halo was tilted sideways, and his harp lay mute at his feet;
So the Master stooped in His pity, and gave him a pass to go,
For the space of a moon, to the earth-world, to mix with the
    men below.

He doffed his celestial garments, scarce waiting to lay them
    straight;
He bade goodbye to Peter, who stood by the golden gate;
The sexless singers of heaven chanted a fond farewell,
And the imps looked up as they pattered on the red-hot
    flags of hell.

Never was seen such an angel: eyes of a heavenly blue,
Features that shamed Apollo, hair of a golden hue;
The women simply adored him, his lips were like Cupid's
    bow;
But he never ventured to use them—and so they voted him
    slow.

Till at last there came One Woman, a marvel of loveliness,
And she whispered to him: "Do you love me?"
  And he answered that woman, "Yes."
And she said: "Put your arms around me, and kiss me, and
    hold me—so—"
But fiercely he drew back, saying: "This thing is wrong,
    and I know."

Then sweetly she mocked his scruples, and softly she him
    beguiled:
"You, who are verily man among men, speak with the tongue
    of a child.
We have outlived the old standards; we have burst, like an
    over-tight thong,
The ancient, outworn, puritanic traditions of Right and
    Wrong."

Then the Master feared for His angel, and called him again
    to His side,
For oh, the woman was wondrous, and oh, the angel was tried.
And deep in his hell sang the Devil, and this was the strain
    of his song:
"The ancient, outworn, puritanic traditions of Right and
    Wrong."

THE RHYME OF THE RESTLESS ONES

WE couldn't sit and study for the law;
  The stagnation of a bank we couldn't stand;
For our riot blood was surging, and we didn't need much
      urging
To excitements and excesses that are banned.
So we took to wine and drink and other things,
  And the devil in us struggled to be free;
Till our friends rose up in wrath, and they pointed out the
      path,
And they paid our debts and packed us o'er the sea.

Oh, they shook us off and shipped us o'er the foam,
To the larger lands that lure a man to roam;
        And we took the chance they gave
        Of a far and foreign grave,
And we bade goodbye for evermore to home.
And some of us are climbing on the peak,
  And some of us are camping on the plain;
By pine and palm you'll find us, with never claim to bind us,
By track and trail you'll meet us once again.

We are fated serfs to freedom—sky and sea;
  We have failed where slummy cities overflow;
But the stranger ways of earth know our pride and know
      our worth,
And we go into the dark as fighters go.

Yes, we go into the night as brave men go,
Though our faces they be often streaked with woe;
      Yet we're hard as cats to kill,
      And our hearts are reckless still,
And we've danced with death a dozen times or so.

And you'll find us in Alaska after gold,
  And you'll find us herding cattle in the South.
We like strong drink and fun; and when the race is run,
  We often die with curses in our mouth.
We are wild as colts unbroke, but never mean;
  Of our sins we've shoulders broad to bear the blame;
But we'll never stay in town, and we'll never settle down,
  And we'll never have an object or an aim.

No, there's that in us that time can never tame;
And life will always seem a careless game;
      And they'd better far forget—
      Those who say they love us yet—
Forget, blot out with bitterness our name.

NEW YEAR'S EVE

It's cruel cold on the water-front, silent and dark and drear;
  Only the black tide weltering, only the hissing snow;
And I, alone, like a storm-tossed wreck, on this night of the
    glad New Year,
  Shuffling along in the icy wind, ghastly and gaunt and slow.

They're playing a tune in McGuffy's saloon, and it's cheery and
    bright in there
  (God! but I'm weak—since the bitter dawn, and never a
    bite of food);
I'll just go over and slip inside—I mustn't give way to despair—
  Perhaps I can bum a little booze if the boys are feeling good.

They'll jeer at me, and they'll sneer at me, and they'll call me
    a whiskey soak;
  ("Have a drink? Well, thankee kindly, sir, I don't mind
    if I do.")
A drivelling, dirty gin-joint fiend, the butt of the bar-room joke;
  Sunk and sodden and hopeless—"Another? Well, here's to
    you!"

McGuffy is showing a bunch of the boys how Bob Fitzsim-
     mons hit;
   The barman is talking of Tammany Hall, and why the ward
        boss got fired;
I'll just sneak into a corner, and they'll let me alone a bit;
   The room is reeling round and round . . . O God, but I'm
        tired, I'm tired. . . .

.   .   .   .   .   .

Roses she wore on her breast that night. Oh, but their scent
        was sweet;
   Alone we sat on the balcony, and the fan-palms arched
        above;
The witching strain of a waltz by Strauss came up to our
        cool retreat,
   And I prisoned her little hand in mine, and I whispered
        my plea of love.

Then sudden the laughter died on her lips, and lowly she
        bent her head;
   And oh, there came in the deep, dark eyes a look that was
        heaven to see,
And the moments went, and I waited there, and never a word
        was said,
   And she plucked from her bosom a rose of red, and shyly
        gave it to me.

Then the music swelled to a crash of joy, and the lights blazed
        up like day;

And I held her fast to my throbbing heart, and I kissed her
bonny brow;
"She is mine, she is mine for evermore!" the violins seemed to
say.
And the bells were ringing the New Year in—O God! I can
hear them now.

Don't you remember that long, last waltz, with its sobbing,
sad refrain?
Don't you remember that last goodbye, and the dear eyes
dim with tears?
Don't you remember that golden dream, with never a hint
of pain,
Of lives that would blend like an angel-song in the bliss
of the coming year?

Oh, what have I lost! What have I lost! Ethel, forgive,
forgive!
The red, red rose is faded now, and it's fifty years ago.
'Twere better to die a thousand deaths than live each day
as I live!
I have sinned, I have sunk to the lowest depths—but oh,
I have suffered so!

Hark! Oh hark! I can hear the bells! . . . Look! I can see
her there,

Fair as a dream . . . but it fades . . . And now—I can hear
the dreadful hum
Of the crowded court . . . See! the Judge looks down . . .
NOT GUILTY, my Lord, I swear . . .
The bells, I can hear the bells again . . . Ethel, I come, I
come! . . .

.   .   .   .   .   .

"Rouse up, old man, it's twelve o'clock. You can't sleep here,
you know.
Say! ain't you got no sentiment? Lift up your muddled
head;
Have a drink to the glad New Year, a drop before you go—
You darned old dirty hobo . . . My God! Here, boy! He's
DEAD!"

COMFORT

SAY! You've struck a heap of trouble—
    Bust in business, lost your wife;
No one cares a cent about you,
    You don't care a cent for life;
Hard luck has of hope bereft you,
    Health is failing, wish you'd die—
Why, you've still the sunshine left you,
    And the big, blue sky.

    Sky so blue it makes you wonder
        If it's heaven shining through;
    Earth so smiling 'way out yonder,
        Sun so bright it dazzles you;
    Birds a-singing, flowers a-flinging
        All their fragrance on the breeze;
    Dancing shadows, green, still meadows—
        Don't you mope, you've still got these.

These, and none can take them from you;
    These, and none can weigh their worth.

What! you're tired and broke and beaten?—
  Why, you're rich—you've got the earth!
Yes, if you're a tramp in tatters,
  While the blue sky bends above,
You've got nearly all that matters,
  You've got God, and God is love.

PREMONITION

'Twas a year ago and the moon was bright
  (Oh, I remember so well, so well),
I walked with my love in a sea of light,
  And the voice of my sweet was a silver bell.

  And sudden the moon grew strangely dull,
    And sudden my love had taken wing;
  I looked on the face of a grinning skull,
    I strained to my heart a ghastly thing.

'Twas but fantasy, for my love lay still
  In my arms with her tender eyes aglow,
And she wondered why my lips were chill,
  Why I was silent and kissed her so.

A year has gone and the moon is bright,
  A gibbous moon like a ghost of woe:
I sit by a new-made grave to-night,
  And my heart is broken—it's strange, you know.

THE TRAMPS

Can you recall, dear comrade, when we tramped God's land
    together,
    And we sang the old, old Earth-song, for our youth was
        very sweet;
When we drank and fought and lusted, as we mocked at tie
    and tether,
    Along the road to Anywhere, the wide world at our feet.

Along the road to Anywhere, when each day had its story;
    When time was yet our vassal, and life's jest was still unstale;
When peace unfathomed filled our hearts as, bathed in amber
    glory,
    Along the road to Anywhere we watched the sunsets pale.

Alas! the road to Anywhere is pitfalled with disaster;
    There's hunger, want, and weariness, yet O we loved it so!
As on we tramped exultantly, and no man was our master,
    And no man guessed what dreams were ours, as swinging
        heel and toe,
We tramped the road to Anywhere, the magic road to Any-
    where,
    The tragic road to Anywhere, such dear, dim years ago.

L'ENVOI

You who have lived in the Land,
  You who have trusted the trail;
You who are strong to withstand,
  You who are swift to assail;
Songs have I sung to beguile,
  Vintage of desperate years
Hard as a harlot's smile,
  Bitter as unshed tears.

    Little of joy or mirth,
      Little of ease I sing;
    Sagas of men of earth,
      Humanly suffering,
    Such as you all have done;
      Savagely faring forth,
    Sons of the midnight sun,
      Argonauts of the North.

Far in the land God forgot
  Glimmers the lure of your trail;

Still in your lust are you taught
    Even to win is to fail.
Still must you follow and fight
    Under the vampire wing;
There in the long, long night,
    Hoping and vanquishing.

            Husbandmen of the Wild,
                Reaping a barren gain;
            Scourged by desire, reconciled
                Unto disaster and pain;
            These my songs are for you,
                You who are seared with the brand;
            God knows I have tried to be true;
                Please God you will understand.

BALLADS OF A CHEECHAKO

BALLADS OF A CHEECHAKO

TO THE MAN OF THE HIGH NORTH

My rhymes are rough, and often in my rhyming
  I've drifted, silver-sailed, on seas of dream,
Hearing afar the bells of Elfland chiming,
  Seeing the groves of Arcadie agleam.

I was the thrall of Beauty that rejoices
  From peak snow-diademed to regal star;
Yet to mine aerie ever pierced the voices,
  The pregnant voices of the Things That Are.

The Here, the Now, the vast Forlorn around us;
  The gold-delirium, the ferine strife;
The lusts that lure us on, the hates that hound us;
  Our red rags in the patch-work quilt of Life.

The nameless men who nameless rivers travel,
  And in strange valleys greet strange deaths alone;

The grim, intrepid ones who would unravel
  The mysteries that shroud the Polar Zone.

These will I sing, and if one of you linger
  Over my pages in the Long, Long Night,
And on some lone line lay a calloused finger,
  Saying: "It's human-true—it hits me right";
Then will I count this loving toil well spent;
Then will I dream awhile—content, content.

MEN OF THE HIGH NORTH

Men of the High North, the wild sky is blazing;
  Islands of opal float on silver seas;
Swift splendours kindle, barbaric, amazing;
  Pale ports of amber, golden argosies.
Ringed all around us the proud peaks are glowing;
  Fierce chiefs in council, their wigwam the sky;
Far, far below us the big Yukon flowing,
  Like threaded quicksilver, gleams to the eye.

Men of the High North, you who have known it;
  You in whose hearts its splendours have abode;
Can you renounce it, can you disown it?
  Can you forget it, its glory and its goad?
Where is the hardship, where is the pain of it?
  Lost in the limbo of things you've forgot;
Only remain the guerdon and gain of it;
  Zest of the foray, and God, how you fought!

You who have made good, you foreign faring;
  You money magic to far lands has whirled;

Can you forget those days of vast daring,
    There with your soul on Top o' the World?
Nights when no peril could keep you awake on
    Spruce boughs you spread for your couch in the snow;
Taste all your feasts like the beans and the bacon,
    Fried at the camp-fire at forty below?

Can you remember your huskies all going,
    Barking with joy and their brushes in air;
You in your parka, glad-eyed and glowing,
    Monarch, your subjects the wolf and the bear?
Monarch, your kingdom unravisht and gleaming;
    Mountains your throne, and a river your car;
Crash of a bull moose to rouse you from dreaming;
    Forest your couch, and your candle a star.

You who this faint day the High North is luring
    Unto her vastness, taintlessly sweet;
You who are steel-braced, straight-lipped, enduring,
    Dreadless in danger and dire in defeat:
Honour the High North ever and ever,
    Whether she crown you, or whether she slay;
Suffer her fury, cherish and love her—
    He who would rule he must learn to obey.

Men of the High North, fierce mountains love you;
    Proud rivers leap when you ride on their breast.

See, the austere sky, pensive above you,
    Dons all her jewels to smile on your rest.
Children of Freedom, scornful of frontiers,
    We who are weaklings honour your worth.
Lords of the wilderness, Princes of Pioneers,
    Let's have a rouse that will ring round the earth.

THE BALLAD OF THE NORTHERN LIGHTS

ONE of the Down and Out—that's me.   Stare at me well,
   ay, stare!
Stare and shrink—say! you wouldn't think that ı was a
   millionaire.
Look at my face, it's crimped and gouged—one of them
   death-mask things;
Don't seem the sort of man, do I, as might be the pal of
   kings?
Slouching along in smelly rags, a bleary-eyed, no-good bum;
À knight of the hollow needle, pard, spewed from the sodden
   slum.
Look me all over from head to foot; how much would you
   think I was worth?
A dollar? a dime? a nickel? • Why, *I'm the wealthiest man on
   earth.*

No, don't you think that I'm off my base.   You'll sing a
   different tune
If only you'll let me spin my yarn.   Come over to this saloon;
Wet my throat—it's as dry as chalk, and seeing as how it's you,
I'll tell the tale of a Northern trail, and so help me God, it's
   true.

I'll tell of the howling wilderness and the haggard Arctic
    heights,
Of a reckless vow that I made, and how *I staked the Northern
    Lights.*

Remember the year of the Big Stampede and the trail of
    Ninety-eight,
When the eyes of the world were turned to the North, and
    the hearts of men elate;
Hearts of the old dare-devil breed thrilled at the wondrous
    strike,
And to every man who could hold a pan came the message,
    "Up and hike."
Well, I was there with the best of them, and I knew I
    would not fail.
You wouldn't believe it to see me now; but wait till you've
    heard my tale.

You've read of the trail of Ninety-eight, but its woe no man
    may tell;
It was all of a piece and a whole yard wide, and the name
    of the brand was "Hell."
We heard the call and we staked our all; we were plungers
    playing blind,
And no man cared how his neighbour fared, and no man
    looked behind;

For a ruthless greed was born of need, and the weakling
    went to the wall,
And a curse might avail where a prayer would fail, and the
    gold lust crazed us all.

Bold were we, and they called us three the "Unholy Trinity";
There was Ole Olson, the Sailor Swede, and the Dago Kid
    and me.
We were the discards of the pack, the foreloopers of Unrest,
Reckless spirits of fierce revolt in the ferment of the West.
We were bound to win and we revelled in the hardships
    of the way.
We staked our ground and our hopes were crowned, and we
    hoisted out the pay.
We were rich in a day beyond our dreams, it was gold from
    the grass-roots down;
But were weren't used to such sudden wealth, and there was
    the siren town.
We were crude and careless frontiersmen, with much in us
    of the beast;
We could bear the famine worthily, but we lost our heads
    at the feast.
The town looked mighty bright to us, with a bunch of
    dust to spend,
And nothing was half too good them days, and every one
    was our friend.
Wining meant more than mining then, and life was a dizzy
    whirl,

Gambling and dropping chunks of gold down the neck of a
    dance-hall girl;
Till we went clean mad, it seems to me, and we squandered
    our last poke,
And we sold our claim, and we found ourselves one bitter
    morning—broke.

The Dago Kid he dreamed a dream of his mother's aunt who
    died—
In the dawn-light dim she came to him, and she stood by his
    bedside,
And she said: "Go forth to the highest North till a lonely
    trail ye find;
Follow it far and trust your star, and fortune will be kind."
But I jeered at him, and then there came the Sailor Swede
    to me,
And he said: "I dreamed of my sister's son, who croaked
    at the age of three.
From the herded dead he sneaked and said: 'Seek you an
    Arctic trail;
'Tis pale and grim by the Polar rim, but seek and ye shall
    not fail.'"
And lo! that night I too did dream of my mother's sister's son,
And he said to me: "By the Arctic Sea there's a treasure to
    be won.
Follow and follow a lone moose trail, till you come to a
    valley grim,

On the slope of the lonely watershed that borders the Polar
brim."

Then I woke my pals, and soft we swore by the mystic Silver
Flail,

'Twas the hand of Fate, and to-morrow straight we would
seek the lone moose trail.

We watched the groaning ice wrench free, crash on with a
hollow din;

Men of the wilderness were we, freed from the taint of sin.

The mighty river snatched us up and it bore us swift along;

The days were bright, and the morning light was sweet with
jewelled song.

We poled and lined up nameless streams, portaged o'er hill
and plain;

We burnt our boat to save the nails, and built our boat
again;

We guessed and groped, North, ever North, with many a
twist and turn;

We saw ablaze in the deathless days the splendid sunsets
burn.

O'er soundless lakes where the grayling makes a rush at the
clumsy fly;

By bluffs so steep that the hard-hit sheep falls sheer from
out the sky;

By lilied pools where the bull moose cools and wallows in
huge content;

By rocky lairs where the pig-eyed bears peered at our tiny tent.

Through the black canyon's angry foam we hurled to dreamy bars,

And round in a ring the dog-nosed peaks bayed to the mocking stars.

Spring and summer and autumn went; the sky had a tallow gleam,

Yet North and ever North we pressed to the land of our Golden Dream.

So we came at last to a tundra vast and dark and grim and lone;

And there was the little lone moose trail, and we knew it for our own.

By muskeg hollow and nigger-head it wandered endlessly;

Sorry of heart and sore of foot, weary men were we.

The short-lived sun had a leaden glare and the darkness came too soon,

And stationed there with a solemn stare was the pinched, anaemic moon.

Silence and silvern solitude till it made you dumbly shrink,

And you thought to hear with an outward ear the things you thought to think.

Oh, it was wild and weird and wan, and ever in camp o' nights

We would watch and watch the silver dance of the mystic Northern Lights.

And soft they danced from the Polar sky and swept in primrose
  haze;
And swift they pranced with their silver feet, and pierced
  with a blinding blaze.
They danced a cotillion in the sky; they were rose and silver
  shod;
It was not good for the eyes of man—'twas a sight for the eyes
  of God.
It made us mad and strange and sad, and the gold whereof
  we dreamed
Was all forgot, and our only thought was of the lights that
  gleamed.
Oh, the tundra sponge it was golden brown, and some was a
  bright blood-red;
And the reindeer moss gleamed here and there like the tomb-
  stones of the dead.
And in and out and around about the little trail ran clear,
And we hated it with a deadly hate and we feared with a
  deadly fear.
And the skies of night were alive with light, with a throbbing,
  thrilling flame;
Amber and rose and violet, opal and gold it came.
It swept the sky like a giant scythe, it quivered back to a
  wedge;
Argently bright, it cleft the night with a wavy golden edge.
Pennants of silver waved and streamed, lazy banners unfurled;
Sudden splendours of sabres gleamed, lightning javelins were
  hurled.

There in our awe we crouched and saw with our wild, uplifted
    eyes
Charge and retire the hosts of fire in the battlefield of the
    skies.

But all things come to an end at last, and the muskeg
    melted away,
And frowning down to bar our path a muddle of mountains
    lay.
And a gorge sheered up in granite walls, and the moose trail
    crept betwixt;
'Twas as if the earth had gaped too far and her stony jaws
    were fixt.
Then the winter fell with a sudden swoop, and the heavy
    clouds sagged low,
And earth and sky were blotted out in a whirl of driving
    snow.

We were climbing up a glacier in the neck of a mountain
    pass,
When the Dago Kid slipped down and fell into a deep
    crevasse.
When we got him out one leg hung limp, and his brow
    was wreathed with pain,
And he says: "'Tis badly broken, boys, and I'll never walk
    again.
It's death for all if ye linger here, and that's no cursèd lie;

Go on, go on while the trail is good, and leave me down to
    die."
He raved and swore, but we tended him with our uncouth,
    clumsy care.
The camp-fire gleamed and he gazed and dreamed with a
    fixed and curious stare.
Then all at once he grabbed my gun and he put it to his head,
And he says: "I'll fix it for you, boys!"—them are the words
    he said.

So we sewed him up in a canvas sack and we slung him
    to a tree;
And the stars like needles stabbed our eyes, and woeful men
    were we.
And on we went on our woeful way, wrapped in a daze of
    dream,
And the Northern Lights in the crystal nights came forth
    with a mystic gleam.
They danced and they danced the devil-dance over the naked
    snow;
And soft they rolled like a tide upshoaled with a ceaseless
    ebb and flow.
They rippled green with a wondrous sheen, they fluttered out
    like a fan;
They spread with a blaze of rose-pink rays never yet seen
    of man.
They writhed like a brood of angry snakes, hissing and
    sulphur pale;

Then swift they changed to a dragon vast, lashing a cloven
tail.
It seemed to us, as we gazed aloft with an everlasting stare,
They sky was a pit of bale and dread, and a monster revelled
there.
We climbed the rise of a hog-back range that was desolate
and drear,
When the Sailor Swede had a crazy fit, and he got to talking
queer.
He talked of his home in Oregon and the peach-trees all in
bloom,
And the fern head-high, and the topaz sky, and the forest's
scented gloom.
He talked of the sins of his misspent life, and then he seemed
to brood,
And I watched him there like a fox a hare, for I knew it
was not good.
And sure enough in the dim dawn-light I missed him from
the tent,
And a fresh trail broke through the crusted snow, and I knew
not where it went.
But I followed it o'er the seamless waste, and I found him
at shut of day,
Naked there as a new-born babe—so I left him where he lay.

Day after day was sinister, and I fought fierce-eyed despair,
And I clung to life, and I struggled on, I knew not why nor
where.

I packed my grub in short relays, and I cowered down in my
    tent,
And the world around was purged of sound like a frozen
    continent.
Day after day was dark as death, but ever and ever at nights,
With a brilliancy that grew and grew, blazed up the Northern
    Lights.
They rolled around with a soundless sound like softly bruiséd
    silk;
They poured into the bowl of the sky with the gentle flow
    of milk.
In eager, pulsing violet their wheeling chariots came,
Or they poised above the Polar rim like a coronal of flame.
From depths of darkness fathomless their lancing rays were
    hurled,
Like the all-combining searchlights of the navies of the world.
There on the roof-pole of the world as one bewitched I
    gazed,
And howled and grovelled like a beast as the awful splendours
    blazed.
My eyes were seared, yet thralled I peered through the parka
    hood nigh blind;
But I staggered on to the lights that shone, and never I
    looked behind.
There is a mountain round and low that lies by the Polar rim,
And I climbed its height in a whirl of light, and I peered o'er
    its jaggéd brim;
And there in a crater deep and vast, ungained, unguessed
    of men.

The mystery of the Arctic world was flashed into my ken.
For there these poor dim eyes of mine beheld the sight of
    sights—
That hollow ring was the source and spring of the mystic
    Northern Lights.

Then I staked that place from crown to base, and I hit the
    homeward trail.
Ah, God! it was good, though my eyes were blurred, and I
    crawled like a sickly snail.
In that vast white world where the silent sky communes
    with the silent snow,
In hunger and cold and misery I wandered to and fro.
But the Lord took pity on my pain, and He led me to the
    sea,
And some ice-bound whalers heard my moan, and they fed
    and sheltered me.
They fed the feeble scarecrow thing that stumbled out of
    the wild
With the ravaged face of a mask of death and the wandering
    wits of a child—
A craven, cowering bag of bones that once had been a man.
They tended me and they brought me back to the world, and
    here I am.

Some say that the Northern Lights are the glare of the Arctic
    ice and snow;

And some that it's electricity, and nobody seems to know.

But I'll tell you now—and if I lie, may my lips be stricken dumb—

It's a *mine,* a mine of the precious stuff that men call radium.

It's a million dollars a pound, they say, and there's tons and tons in sight.

You can see it gleam in a golden stream in the solitudes of night.

And it's mine, all mine—and say! if you have a hundred plunks to spare,

I'll let you have the chance of your life, I'll sell you a quarter share.

You turn it down? Well, I'll make it ten, seeing as you are my friend.

Nothing doing? Say! don't be hard—have you got a dollar to lend?

Just a dollar to help me out, I know you'll treat me white;

I'll do as much for you some day . . . God bless you, sir; good-night.

THE BALLAD OF THE BLACK FOX SKIN

I

THERE was Claw-fingered Kitty and Windy Ike living the
    life of shame,
When unto them in the Long, Long Night came the man-
    who-had-no-name;
Bearing his prize of a black fox pelt, out of the Wild he came.

His cheeks were blanched as the flume-head foam when the
    brown spring freshets flow;
Deep in their dark, sin-calcined pits were his sombre eyes
    aglow;
They knew him far for the fitful man who spat forth blood
    on the snow.

"Did ever you see such a skin?" quoth he; "there's nought
    in the world so fine—
Such fulness of fur as black as the night, such lustre, such
    size, such shine;
It's life to a one-lunged man like me; it's London, it's women,
    it's wine.

113

"The Moose-hides called it the devil-fox, and swore that no
    man could kill;
That he who hunted it, soon or late, must surely suffer some
    ill;
But I laughed at them and their old-squaw tales. Ha! Ha!
    I'm laughing still.

"For look ye, the skin—it's as smooth as sin, and black as
    the core of the Pit.
By gun or by trap, whatever the hap, I swore I would
    capture it;
By star and by star afield and afar, I hunted and would not
    quit.

"For the devil-fox, it was swift and sly, and it seemed to fleer
    at me;
I would wake in fright by the camp-fire light, hearing its
    evil glee;
Into my dream its eyes would gleam, and its shadow would
    I see.

"It sniffed and ran from the ptarmigan I had poisoned to
    excess;
Unharmed it sped from my wrathful lead ('twas as if I shot
    by guess);
Yet it came by night in the stark moonlight to mock at my
    weariness.

"I tracked it up where the mountains hunch like the vertebrae
    of the world;
I tracked it down to the death-still pits where the avalanche
    is hurled;
From the glooms to the sacerdotal snows, where the carded
    clouds are curled.

"From the vastitudes where the world protrudes through clouds
    like seas up-shoaled,
I held its track till it led me back to the land I had left of
    old—
The land I had looted many moons. I was weary and sick
    and cold.

"I was sick, soul-sick, of the futile chase, and there and then
    I swore
The foul fiend fox might scathless go, for I would hunt no
    more;
Then I rubbed mine eyes in a vast surprise—it stood by my
    cabin door.

"A rifle raised in the wraith-like gloom, and a vengeful shot
    that sped;
A howl that would thrill a cream-faced corpse—and the demon
    fox lay dead. . . .
Yet there was never a sign of wound, and never a drop he
    bled.

E

"So that was the end of the great black fox, and here is the
    prize I've won;
And now for a drink to cheer me up—I've mushed since the
    early sun;
We'll drink a toast to the sorry ghost of the fox whose race
    is run."

II

Now Claw-fingered Kitty and Windy Ike, bad as the worst
    were they;
In their road-house down by the river-trail they waited and
    watched for prey;
With wine and song they joyed night long, and they slept
    like swine by day.

For things were done in the Midnight Sun that no tongue
    will ever tell;
And men there be who walk earth free, but whose names are
    writ in hell—
Are writ in flames with the guilty names of Fournier and
    Labelle.

Put not your trust in a poke of dust would ye sleep the sleep
    of sin;
For there be those who would rob your clothes ere yet the
    dawn comes in;

And a prize likewise in a woman's eyes is a peerless black
    fox skin.

Put your faith in the mountain cat if you lie within his lair;
Trust the fangs of the mother-wolf, and the claws of the
    lead-ripped bear;
But oh, of the wiles and the gold-tooth smiles of a dance-hall
    wench beware!

Wherefore it was beyond all laws that lusts of man restrain,
A man drank deep and sank to sleep, never to wake again;
And the Yukon swallowed through a hole the cold corpse
    of the slain.

III

The black fox skin a shadow cast from the roof nigh to the
    floor;
And sleek it seemed and soft it gleamed, and the woman
    stroked it o'er;
And the man stood by with a brooding eye, and gnashed his
    teeth and swore.

When thieves and thugs fall out and fight there's fell arrears
    to pay;
And soon or late sin meets its fate, and so it fell one day
That Claw-fingered Kitty and Windy Ike fanged up like
    dogs at bay.

"The skin is mine, all mine," she cried; "I did the deed alone."
"It's share and share with a guilt-yoked pair," he hissed in a
    pregnant tone;
And so they snarled like malamutes over a mildewed bone.

And so they fought, by fear untaught, till haply it befell
One dawn of day she slipped away to Dawson town to sell
The fruit of sin, this black fox skin that had made their lives
    a hell.

She slipped away as still he lay, she clutched the wondrous fur;
Her pulses beat, her foot was fleet, her fear was as a spur;
She laughed with glee, she did not see him rise and follow
    her.

The bluffs uprear and grimly peer far over Dawson town;
They see its lights a blaze o' nights and harshly they look
    down;
They mock the plan and plot of man with grim, ironic frown.

The trail was steep; 'twas at the time when swiftly sinks
    the snow;
All honeycombed, the river ice was rotting down below;
The river chafed beneath its rind with many a mighty throe.

And up the swift and oozy drift a woman climbed in fear,
Clutching to her a black fox fur as if she held it dear;

And hard she pressed it to her breast—then Windy Ike drew
near.

She made no moan—her heart was stone—she read his smiling
face,
And like a dream flashed all her life's dark horror and disgrace;
A moment only—with a snarl he hurled her into space.

She rolled for nigh an hundred feet; she bounded like a ball;
From crag to crag she carromed down through snow and
timber fall; . . .
A hole gaped in the river ice; the spray flashed—that was all.

A bird sang for the joy of spring, so piercing sweet and frail;
And blinding bright the land was dight in gay and glittering
mail;
And with a wondrous black fox skin a man slid down the trail.

IV

A wedge-faced man there was who ran along the river bank,
Who stumbled through each drift and slough, and ever slipped
and sank,
And ever cursed his Maker's name, and ever "hooch" he drank.

He travelled like a hunted thing, hard harried, sore distrest;
The old grandmother moon crept out from her cloud-quilted
    nest;
The aged mountains mocked at him in their primeval rest.

Grim shadows diapered the snow; the air was strangely mild;
The valley's girth was dumb with mirth, the laughter of the
    wild;
The still, sardonic laughter of an ogre o'er a child.

The river writhed beneath the ice; it groaned like one in pain,
The yawning chasms opened wide, and closed, and yawned
    again;
And sheets of silver heaved on high until they split in twain.

From out the road-house by the trail they saw a man afar
Make for the narrow river-reach where the swift cross-currents
    are;
Where, frail and worn, the ice is torn and the angry waters jar.

But they did not see him crash and sink into the icy flow;
They did not see him clinging there, gripped by the undertow,
Clawing with bleeding finger-nails at the jagged ice and snow.

They found a note beside the hole where he had stumbled in;
"Here met his fate by evil luck a man who lived in sin,
And to the one who loves me least I leave this black fox skin."

And strange it is; for, though they searched the river all around,
No trace or sign of black fox skin was ever after found;
Though one man said he saw the tread of *hoofs* deep in the
   ground.

THE BALLAD OF PIOUS PETE

"The North has got him."—Yukonism.

I TRIED to refine that neighbour of mine, honest to God, I did.
I grieved for his fate, and early and late I watched over him like a kid.
I gave him excuse, I bore his abuse in every way that I could;
I swore to prevail; I camped on his trail; I plotted and planned for his good.
By day and by night I strove in men's sight to gather him into the fold,
With precept and prayer, with hope and despair, in hunger and hardship and cold.
I followed him into Gehennas of sin, I sat where the sirens sit;
In the shade of the Pole, for the sake of his soul, I strove with the powers of the Pit.

I shadowed him down to the scrofulous town; I dragged him from dissolute brawls;
But I killed the galoot when he started to shoot electricty into my walls.
God knows what I did he should seek to be rid of one who would save him from shame.

122

God knows what I bore that night when he swore and bade
    me make tracks from his claim.
I started to tell of the horrors of hell, when sudden his eyes
    lit like coals;
And "Chuck it," says he, "don't persecute me with your cant
    and your saving of souls."
I'll swear I was mild as I'd be with a child, but he called
    me the son of a slut;
And, grabbing his gun with a leap and a run, he threatened
    my face with the butt.
So what could I do (I leave it to you)? With curses he harried
    me forth;
Then he was alone, and I was alone, and over us menaced
    the North.

Our cabins were near; I could see, I could hear; but between
    us there rippled the creek;
And all summer through, with a rancour that grew, he would
    pass me and never would speak.
Then a shuddery breath like the coming of Death crept down
    from the peaks far away;
The water was still; the twilight was chill; the sky was a tatter
    of gray.
Swift came the Big Cold, and opal and gold the lights of the
    witches arose;
The frost-tyrant clinched, and the valley was cinched by the
    stark and cadaverous snows.

The trees were like lace where the star-beams could chase,
   each leaf with a jewel agleam.
The soft white hush lapped the Northland and wrapped us
   round in a crystalline dream;
So still I could hear quite loud in my ear the swish of the
   pinions of time;
So bright I could see, as plain as could be, the wings of God's
   angels ashine.

As I read in the Book I would oftentimes look to that cabin
   just over the creek.
Ah me, it was sad and evil and bad, two neighbours who
   never would speak!
I knew that full well like the devil in hell he was hatching
   out, early and late,
A system to bear through the frost-spangled air the warm,
   crimson waves of his hate.
I only. could peer and shudder and fear—'twas ever so ghastly
   and still;
But I knew over there in his lonely despair he was plotting
   me terrible ill.
I knew that he nursed a malice accurst, like the blast of a
   winnowing flame;
I pleaded aloud for a shield, for a shroud—Oh, God! then
   calamity came.

Mad! If I'm mad then you too are mad; but it's all in the
   point of view.

If you'd looked at them things gallivantin' on wings, all
    purple and green and blue;
If you'd noticed them twist, as they mounted and hissed like
    scorpions dim in the dark;
If you'd seen them rebound with a horrible sound, and spite-
    fully spitting a spark;
If you'd watched It with dread, as it hissed by your bed,
    that thing with the feelers that crawls—
You'd have settled the brute that attempted to shoot electricity
    into your walls.

Oh, some they were blue, and they slithered right through;
    they were silent and squashy and round;
And some they were green; they were wriggly and lean; they
    writhed with so hateful a sound.
My blood seemed to freeze; I fell on my knees; my face was
    a white splash of dread.
Oh, the Green and the Blue, they were gruesome to view;
    but the worst of them all were the Red.
They came through the door, they came through the floor,
    they came through the moss-creviced logs.
They were savage and dire; they were whiskered with fire;
    they bickered like malamute dogs.
They ravined in rings like iniquitous things; they gulped down
    the Green and the Blue.
I crinkled with fear whene'er they drew near, and nearer and
    nearer they drew.

And then came the crown of Horror's grim crown, the monster
so loathsomely red.

Each eye was a pin that shot out and in, as, squid-like, it oozed
to my bed;

So softly it crept with feelers that swept and quivered like
fine copper wire;

Its belly was white with a sulphurous light, its jaws were
a-drooling with fire.

It came and it came; I could breathe of its flame, but never
a wink could I look.

I thrust in its maw the Fount of the Law; I fended it off with
the Book.

I was weak—oh, so weak—but I thrilled at its shriek, as wildly
it fled in the night;

And deathlike I lay till the dawn of the day. (Was ever so
welcome the light?)

I loaded my gun at the rise of the sun; to his cabin so softly
I slunk.

My neighbour was there in the frost-freighted air, all wrapped
in a robe in his bunk.

It muffled his moans; it outlined his bones, as feebly he twisted
about;

His gums were so black, and his lips seemed to crack, and his
teeth all were loosening out.

'Twas a death's head that peered through the tangle of beard;
'twas a face I will never forget;

Sunk eyes full of woe, and they troubled me so with their
pleadings and anguish, and yet

As I rested my gaze in a misty amaze on the scurvy degenerate
wreck,

I thought of the Things with the dragon-fly wings, then laid I
my gun on his neck.

He gave out a cry that was faint as a sigh, like a perishing
malamute,

And he says unto me, "I'm converted," says he; "for Christ's
sake, Peter, don't shoot!"

They're taking me out with an escort about, and under a sergeant's care;

I am humbled indeed, for I'm 'cuffed to a Swede that thinks
he's a millionaire.

But it's all Gospel true what I'm telling to you—up there where
the Shadow falls—

That I settled Sam Noot when he started to shoot electricity
into my walls.

THE BALLAD OF BLASPHEMOUS BILL

I took a contract to bury the body of blasphemous Bill MacKie,
Whenever, wherever, or whatsoever the manner of death he
die—
Whether he die in the light o' day or under the peak-faced
moon;
In cabin or dance-hall, camp or dive, mucklucks or patent
shoon;
On velvet tundra or virgin peak, by glacier, drift or draw;
In muskeg hollow or canyon gloom, by avalanche, fang or
claw;
By battle, murder or sudden wealth, by pestilence, hooch or
lead—
I swore on the Book I would follow and look till I found my
tombless dead.

For Bill was a dainty kind of cuss, and his mind was mighty sot
On a dinky patch with flowers and grass in a civilised bone-
yard lot.
And where he died or how he died, it didn't matter a damn
So long as he had a grave with frills and a tombstone
"epigram."

So I promised him, and he paid the price in good cheechako
coin
(Which the same I blowed in that very night down in the
Tenderloin).
Then I painted a three-foot slab of pine: "Here lies poor Bill
MacKie,"
And I hung it up on my cabin wall and I waited for Bill to die.

Years passed away, and at last one day came a squaw with a
story strange,
Of a long-deserted line of traps 'way back of the Bighorn
range;
Of a little hut by the great divide, and a white man stiff and
still,
Lying there by his lonesome self, and I figured it must be
Bill.
So I thought of the contract I'd made with him, and I took
down from the shelf
The swell black box with the silver plate he'd picked out for
himself;
And I packed it full of grub and "hooch," and I slung it on
the sleigh;
Then I harnessed up my team of dogs and was off at dawn of
day.

You know what it's like in the Yukon wild when it's sixty-nine
below;

When the ice-worms wriggle their purple heads through the
crust of the pale blue snow;
When the pine-trees crack like little guns in the silence of the
wood,
And the icicles hang down like tusks under the parka hood;
When the stove-pipe smoke breaks sudden off, and the sky is
weirdly lit,
And the careless feel of a bit of steel burns like a red-hot spit;
When the mercury is a frozen ball, and the frost-fiend stalks
to kill—
Well, it was just like that that day when I set out to look for
Bill.

Oh, the awful hush that seemed to crush me down on every
hand,
As I blundered blind with a trail to find through that blank
and bitter land;
Half dazed, half crazed in the winter wild, with its grim
heart-breaking woes,
And the ruthless strife for a grip on life that only the sourdough knows!
North by the compass, North I pressed; river and peak and
plain
Passed like a dream I slept to lose and I waked to dream
again.

River and plain and mighty peak—and who could stand
unawed?

As their summits blazed, he could stand undazed at the foot
of the throne of God.
North, aye, North, through a land accurst, shunned by the
scouring brutes,
And all I heard was my own harsh word and the whine of
the malamutes,
Till at last I came to a cabin squat, built in the side of a hill,
And I burst in the door, and there on the floor, frozen to death,
lay Bill.

Ice, white ice, like a winding-sheet, sheathing each smoke-
grimed wall;
Ice on the stove-pipe, ice on the bed, ice gleaming over all;
Sparkling ice on the dead man's chest, glittering ice in his hair,
Ice on his fingers, ice in his heart, ice in his glassy stare;
Hard as a log and trussed like a frog, with his arms and legs
outspread.
I gazed at the coffin I'd brought for him, and I gazed at the
gruesome dead,
And at last I spoke: "Bill liked his joke; but still, goldarn his
eyes,
A man had ought to consider his mates in the way he goes
and dies."

Have you ever stood in an Arctic hut in the shadow of the
Pole,
With a little coffin six by three and a grief you can't control?

Have you ever sat by a frozen corpse that looks at you with a
     grin,
And that seems to say: "You may try all day, but you'll never
     jam me in?"
I'm not a man of the quitting kind, but I never felt so blue
As I sat there gazing at that stiff and studying what I'd do.
Then I rose and I kicked off the husky dogs that were nosing
     round about,
And I lit a roaring fire in the stove, and I started to thaw Bill
     out.

Well, I thawed and thawed for thirteen days but it didn't seem
     no good;
His arms and legs stuck out like pegs, as if they was made of
     wood.
Till at last I said: "It ain't no use—he's froze too hard to thaw;
He's obstinate, and he won't lie straight, so I guess I got to—
     saw."
So I sawed off poor Bill's arms and legs, and I laid him snug
     and straight
In the little coffin he picked hisself, with the dinky silver plate;
And I came nigh near to shedding a tear as I nailed him
     safely down;
Then I stowed him away in my Yukon sleigh, and I started
     back to town.

So I buried him as the contract was in a narrow grave and
     deep,

And there he's waiting the Great Clean-up, when the Judg-
    ment sluice-heads sweep;
And I smoke my pipe and I meditate in the light of the Mid-
    night Sun,
And sometimes I wonder if they *was*, the awful things I done.
And as I sit and the parson talks, expounding of the Law,
I often think of poor old Bill—*and how hard he was to saw.*

THE BALLAD OF ONE-EYED MIKE

*This is the tale that was told to me by the man with the crystal
eye,*
*As I smoked my pipe in the camp-fire light, and the Glories
swept the sky;*
*As the Northlights gleamed and curved and streamed, and the
bottle of "hooch" was dry.*

A man once aimed that my life be shamed, and wrought me a
deathly wrong;
I vowed one day I would well repay, but the heft of his hate
was strong.
He thonged me East and he thonged me West; he harried me
back and forth,
Till I fled in fright from his peerless spite to the bleak, bald-
headed North.

And there I lay, and for many a day I hatched plan after plan,
For a golden haul of the wherewithal to crush and to kill my
man;

And there I strove, and there I clove through the drift of icy
    streams;
And there I fought, and there I sought for the pay-streak of my
    dreams.

So twenty years, with their hopes and fears and smiles and tears
    and such,
Went by and left me long bereft of hope of the Midas touch;
About as fat as a chancel rat, and lo! despite my will,
In the weary fight I had clean lost sight of the man I sought
    to kill.

'Twas so far away, that evil day when I prayed the Prince of
    Gloom
For the savage strength and the sullen length of life to work
    his doom.
Nor sign nor word had I seen or heard, and it happed so long
    ago;
My youth was gone and my memory wan, and I willed it even
    so.

It fell one night in the waning light by the Yukon's oily flow,
I smoked and sat as I marvelled at the sky's port-winey glow;
Till it paled away to an absinthe gray, and the river seemed to
    shrink,
All wobbly flakes and wriggling snakes and goblin eye a-wink.
'Twas weird to see and it 'wildered me in a queer, hypnotic
    dream,

Till I saw a spot like an inky blot come floating down the
 stream;
It bobbed and swung; it sheered and hung; it romped round in
 a ring;
It seemed to play in a tricksome way; it sure was a merry thing.

In freakish flights strange oily lights came fluttering round its
 head,
Like butterflies of a monster size—then I knew it for the Dead.
Its face was rubbed and slicked and scrubbed as smooth as a
 shaven pate;
In the silver snakes that the water makes it gleamed like a
 dinner-plate.

It gurgled near, and clear and clear and large and large it grew;
It stood upright in a ring of light and it looked me through and
 through.
It weltered round with a woozy sound, and ere I could retreat,
With the witless roll of a sodden soul it wantoned to my feet.

And here I swear by this Cross I wear, I heard that "floater"
 say:
"I am the man from whom you ran, the man you sought to
 slay.
That you may note and gaze and gloat, and say 'Revenge is
 sweet,'

In the grit and grime of the river's slime I am rotting at your
  feet.

"The ill we rue we must e'en undo, though it rive us bone
  from bone;
So it came about that I sought you out, for I prayed I might
  atone.
I did you wrong, and for long and long I sought where you
  might live;
And now you're found, though I'm dead and drowned, I beg
  you to forgive."

So sad it seemed, and its cheek-bones gleamed, and its fingers
  flicked the shore;
And it lapped and lay in a weary way, and it hands met to
  implore;
That I gently said: "Poor, restless dead, I would never work
  you woe;
Though the wrong you rue you can ne'er undo, I forgave you
  long ago."

Then, wonder-wise, I rubbed my eyes and I woke from a horrid
  dream
The moon rode high in the naked sky, and something bobbed
  in the stream,
It held my sight in a patch of light, and then it sheered from
  the shore;
It dipped and sank by a hollow bank, and I never saw it more.

This was the tale he told to me, that man so warped and gray,
Ere he slept and dreamed, and the camp-fire gleamed in his eye
  in a wolfish way—
That crystal eye that raked the sky in the weird Auroral ray.

THE BALLAD OF THE BRAND

'Twas up in a land long famed for gold, where women were
    far and rare,
Tellus, the smith, had taken to wife a maiden amazingly fair;
Tellus, the brawny worker in iron, hairy and heavy of hand,
Saw her and loved her and bore her away from the tribe of a
    Southern land;
Deeming her worthy to queen his home and mother him little
    ones,
That the name of Tellus, the master smith, might live in his
    stalwart sons.

Now there was little of law in the land, and evil doings were
    rife,
And every man who joyed in his home guarded the fame of his
    wife;
For there were those of the silver tongue and the honeyed art
    to beguile,
Who would cozen the heart from a woman's breast and damn
    her soul with a smile.
And there were women too quick to heed a look or a whis-
    pered word,

And once in a while a man was slain, and the ire of the King
    was stirred;
So far and wide he proclaimed his wrath, and this was the law
    he willed:
"That whosoever killeth a man, even shall he be killed."

Now Tellus, the smith, he trusted his wife; his heart was
    empty of fear.
High on the hill was the gleam of their hearth, a beacon of
    love and cheer.
High on the hill they builded their bower, where the broom
    and the bracken meet;
Under a grove of oaks it was, hushed and drowsily sweet.
Here he enshrined her, his dearest saint, his idol, the light of
    his eye;
Her kisses rested upon his lips as brushes a butterfly.
The weight of her arms around his neck was light as the thistle
    down;
And sweetly she studied to win his smile, and gently she
    mocked his frown.

And when at the close of the dusty day his clangorous toil was
    done,
She hastened to meet him down the way all lit by the amber
    sun.
Their dove-cot gleamed in the golden light, a temple of stain-
    less love;

Like the hanging cup of a big blue flower was the topaz sky
above.
The roses and lilies yearned to her, as swift through their
throng she pressed;
A little white, fragile, fluttering thing that lay like a child on
his breast.
Then the heart of Tellus, the smith, was proud, and sang for
the joy of life.
And there in the bronzing summertide he thanked the gods for
his wife.

Now there was one called Philo, a scribe, a man of exquisite
grace,
Carved like the god Apollo in limb, fair as Adonis in face;
Eager and winning of manner, full of such radiant charm,
Womenkind fought for his favour and loved to their uttermost
harm.
Such was his craft and his knowledge, such was his skill at the
game.
Never was woman could flout him, so be he plotted her shame.
And so he drank deep of pleasure, and then it fell on a day
He gazed on the wife of Tellus and marked her out for his
prey.

Tellus, the smith, was merry, and the time of the year it was
June,
So he said to his stalwart helpers: "Shut down the forge at
noon.

Go ye and joy in the sunshine, rest in the coolth of the grove,
Drift on the dreamy river, every man with his love."
Then to himself: "Oh, Beloved, sweet will be your surprise;
To-day will we sport like children, laugh in each other's eyes;
Weave gay garlands of poppies, crown each other with flowers,
Pull plump carp from the lilies, rifle the ferny bowers.
To-day with feasting and gladness the wine of Cyprus will
    flow;
To-day is the day we were wedded only a twelve-month ago."

The larks trilled high in the heavens; his heart was lyric with
    joy;
He plucked a posy of lilies; he sped like a love-sick boy.
He stole up the velvety pathway—his cottage was sunsteeped
    and still;
Vines honeysuckled the window; softly he peeped o'er the sill.
The lilies dropped from his fingers; devils were choking his
    breath;
Rigid with horror, he stiffened; ghastly his face was as death.
Like a nun whose faith in the Virgin is met with a prurient
    jibe,
He shrank—'twas the wife of his bosom in the arms of Philo,
    the scribe.

Tellus went back to his smithy; he reeled like a drunken man;
His heart was riven with anguish; his brain was brooding a
    plan.

Straight to his anvil he hurried; started his furnace aglow;
Heated his iron and shaped it with savage and masterful blow.
Sparks showered over and round him; swiftly under his hand
There at last it was finished—a hideous and infamous Brand.

That night the wife of his bosom, the light of joy in her eyes,
Kissed him with words of rapture; but he knew that her words
     were lies.
Never was she so beguiling, never so merry of speech
(For passion ripens a woman as the sunshine ripens a peach).
He clenched his teeth into silence; he yielded up to her lure,
Though he knew that her breasts were heaving from the fire
     of her paramour.
"To-morrow," he said, "to-morrow"—he wove her hair in a
     strand,
Twisted it round his fingers and smiled as he thought of the
     Brand.

The morrow was come, and Tellus swiftly stole up the hill.
Butterflies drowsed in the noon-heat; coverts were sunsteeped
     and still.
Softly he padded the pathway unto the porch, and within
Heard he the low laugh of dalliance, heard he rapture of sin.
Knew he her eyes were mystic with light that no man should
     see,
No man kindle and joy in, no man on earth save he.
And never for him would it kindle. The blood-lust surged in
     his brain;

Through the senseless stone could he see them, wanton and
warily fain.
Horrible! Heaven he sought for, gained it and gloried and
fell—
Oh, it was sudden—headlong into the nethermost hell. . . .

Was this he, Tellus, this marble? Tellus . . . not dreaming a
dream?
Ah! sharp-edged as a javelin, was that a woman's scream?
Was it a door that shattered, shell-like, under his blow?
Was it his saint, that strumpet, dishevelled and cowering low?
Was it her lover, that wild thing, that twisted and gouged and
tore?
Was it a man he was crushing, whose head he beat on the
floor?
Laughing the while at its weakness, till sudden he stayed his
hand—
Through the red ring of his madness flamed the thought of the
Brand.

Then bound he the naked Philo with thongs that cut in the
flesh,
And the wife of his bosom, fear-frantic, he gagged with a
silken mesh,
Choking her screams into silence; bound her down by the hair;
Dragged her lover unto her under her frenzied stare
In the heat of the hearth-fire embers he heated the hideous
Brand;

Twisting her fingers open, he forced its haft in her hand.
He pressed it downward and downward; she felt the living
flesh sear;
She saw the throe of her lover; she heard the scream of his fear.
Once, twice and thrice he forced her, heedless of prayer and
shriek—
Once on the forehead of Philo, twice in the soft of his cheek.

Then (for the thing was finished) he said to the woman: "See
How you have branded your lover! Now will I let him go
free."
He severed the thongs that bound him, laughing "Revenge is
sweet,"
And Philo, sobbing in anguish, feebly rose to his feet.
The man who was fair as Apollo, god-like in woman's sight,
Hideous now as a satyr, fled to the pity of night.

*Then came they before the Judgment Seat, and thus spoke the
Lord of the Land:*
*"He who seeketh his neighbour's wife shall suffer the doom
of the Brand.*
*Brutish and bold on his brow be it stamped, deep in his cheek
let it sear,*
*That every man may look on his shame, and shudder and
sicken and fear.*
*He shall hear their mock in the market-place, their fleering jibe
at the feast,*

He shall seek the caves and the shroud of night, and the fellowship of the beast.
Outcast forever from homes of men, far and far shall he roam.
Such be the doom, sadder than death, of him who shameth a home."

THE BALLAD OF HARD-LUCK HENRY

Now wouldn't you expect to find a man an awful crank
That's staked out nigh three hundred claims, and every one a
    blank;
That's followed every fool stampede, and seen the rise and fall
Of camps where men got gold in chunks and he got none at all;
That's prospected a bit of ground and sold it for a song
To see it yield a fortune to some fool that came along;
That's sunk a dozen bed-rock holes, and not a speck in sight,
Yet sees them take a million from the claims to left and right?
Now aren't things like that enough to drive a man to booze?
But Hard-Luck Smith was hoodoo-proof—he knew the way to
    lose.

'Twas in the fall of nineteen four—leap-year I've heard them
    say—
When Hard-Luck came to Hunker Creek and took a hillside
    lay.
And lo! as if to make amends for all the futile past,
Late in the year he struck it rich, the real pay-streak at last.
The riffles of his sluicing-box were choked with speckled earth,
And night and day he worked that lay for all that he was
    worth.

And when in chill December's gloom his lucky lease expired
He found that he had made a stake as big as he desired.

One day while meditating on the waywardness of fate,
He felt the ache of lonely man to find a fitting mate;
A petticoated pard to cheer his solitary life,
A woman with soft, soothing ways, a confidant, a wife.
And while he cooked his supper on his little Yukon stove,
He wished that he had staked a claim in Love's rich treasure-
          trove;
When suddenly he paused and held aloft a Yukon egg,
For there in pencilled letters was the magic name of Peg.

You know these Yukon eggs of ours—some pink, some green,
          some blue—
A dollar per, assorted tints, assorted flavours too.
The supercilious cheechako might designate them high,
But one acquires a taste for them and likes them by-and-by.
Well, Hard-Luck Henry took this egg and held it to the light,
And there was more faint pencilling that sorely taxed his sight.
At last he made it out, and then the legend ran like this—
"Will Klondike miner write to Peg, Plumhollow, Squashville,
          Wis.?"

That night he got to thinking of this far-off, unknown fair;
It seemed so sort of opportune, an answer to his prayer.
She flitted sweetly through his dreams, she haunted him by
          day,

She smiled through clouds of nicotine, she cheered his weary
     way.
At last he yielded to the spell; his course of love he set—
Wisconsin his objective point; his object, Margaret.

With every mile of sea and land his longing grew and grew.
He practised all his pretty words, and these, I fear, were few.
At last, one frosty evening, with a cold chill down his spine,
He found himself before her house, the threshold of the shrine.
His courage flickered to a spark, then glowed with sudden
     flame—
He knocked; he heard a welcome word; she came—his goddess
     came.
Oh, she was fair as any flower, and huskily he spoke:
"I'm all the way from Klondike, with a mighty heavy poke.
I'm looking for a lassie, one whose Christian name is Peg,
Who sought a Klondike miner, and who wrote it on an egg."

The lassie gazed at him a space, her cheeks grew rosy red;
She gazed at him with tear-bright eyes, then tenderly she said:
"Yes, lonely Klondike miner, it is true my name is Peg.
It's also true I longed for you and wrote it on an egg.
My heart went out to some one in that land of night and cold;
But oh, I fear that Yukon egg must have been mighty old.
I waited long, I hoped and feared; you should have come
     before;
I've been a wedded woman now for eighteen months or more.
I'm sorry, since you've come so far, you ain't the one that wins;
But won't you take a step inside—*I'll let you see the twins.*"

THE MAN FROM ELDORADO

I

He's the man from Eldorado, and he's just arrived in town,
  In moccasins and oily buckskin shirt.
He's gaunt as any Indian, and pretty nigh as brown;
  He's greasy, and he smells of sweat and dirt.
He sports a crop of whiskers that would shame a healthy hog;
  Hard work has racked his joints and stooped his back;
He slops along the sidewalk followed by his yellow dog,
  But he's got a bunch of gold-dust in his sack.

He seems a little wistful as he blinks at all the lights,
  And maybe he is thinking of his claim
And the dark and dwarfish cabin where he lay and dreamed at
    nights,
  (Thank God, he'll never see the place again!)
Where he lived on tinned tomatoes, beef embalmed and sour-
    dough bread,
  On rusty beans and bacon furred with mould;
His stomach's out of kilter and his system full of lead,
  But it's over, and his poke is full of gold.

He has panted at the windlass, he has loaded in the drift,
  He has pounded at the face of oozy clay;
He has taxed himself to sickness, dark and damp and double
      shift,
  He has laboured like a demon night and day.
And now, praise God, it's over, and he seems to breathe again
  Of new-mown hay, the warm, wet, friendly loam;
He sees a snowy orchard in a green and dimpling plain,
  And a little vine-clad cottage, and it's—Home.

II

He's the man from Eldorado, and he's had a bite and sup,
  And he's met in with a drouthy friend or two;
He's cached away his gold-dust, but he's sort of bucking up,
  So he's kept enough to-night to see him through.
His eye is bright and genial, his tongue no longer lags;
  His heart is brimming o'er with joy and mirth;
He may be far from savoury, he may be clad in rags,
  But to-night he feels as if he owns the earth.

Says he: "Boys, here is where the shaggy North and I will
      shake;
  I thought I'd never manage to get free.
I kept on making misses; but at last I've got my stake;
  There's no more thawing frozen muck for me.

I am going to God's Country, where I'll live the simple life;
  I'll buy a bit of land and make a start;
I'll carve a little homestead, and I'll win a little wife,
  And raise ten little kids to cheer my heart."

They signified their sympathy by crowding to the bar;
  They bellied up three deep and drank his health.
He shed a radiant smile around and smoked a rank cigar;
  They wished him honour, happiness and wealth.
They drank unto his wife to be—that unsuspecting maid;
  They drank unto his children half a score;
And when they got through drinking, very tenderly they laid
  The man from Eldorado on the floor.

III

He's the man from Eldorado, and he's only starting in
  To cultivate a thousand-dollar jab.
His poke is full of gold-dust and his heart is full of sin,
  And he's dancing with a girl called Muckluck Mag.
She's as light as any fairy; she's as pretty as a peach;
  She's mistress of the witchcraft to beguile;
There's sunshine in her manner, there is music in her speech,
  And there's concentrated honey in her smile.

Oh, the fever of the dance-hall and the glitter and the shine,
    The beauty, and the jewels, and the whirl,
The madness of the music, the rapture of the wine,
    The languorous allurement of a girl!
She is like a lost madonna; he is gaunt, unkempt and grim;
    But she fondles him and gazes in his eyes;
Her kisses seek his heavy lips, and soon it seems to him
    He has staked a little claim in Paradise.

"Who's for a juicy two-step?" cries the master of the floor;
    The music throbs with soft, seductive beat.
There's glitter, gilt and gladness; there are pretty girls galore;
    There's a woolly man with moccasins on feet.
They know they've got him going; he is buying wine for all;
    They crowd around as buzzards at a feast,
Then when his poke is empty they boost him from the hall,
    And spurn him in the gutter like a beast.

He's the man from Eldorado, and he's painting red the town;
    Behind he leaves a trail of yellow dust;
In a whirl of senseless riot he is ramping up and down;
    There's nothing checks his madness and his lust.
And soon the word is passed around—it travels like a flame;
    They fight to clutch his hand and call him friend,
The chevaliers of lost repute, the dames of sorry fame;
    Then comes the grim awakening—the end.

IV

He's the man from Eldorado, and he gives a grand affair;
　　There's feasting, dancing, wine without restraint.
The smooth Beau Brummels of the bar, the faro men, are there;
　　The tinhorns and purveyors of red paint;
The sleek and painted women, their predacious eyes aglow—
　　Sure Klondike City never saw the like;
Then Muckluck Mag proposed the toast, "The giver of the
　　show,
　　The livest sport that ever hit the pike."

The "live one" rises to his feet; he stammers to reply—
　　And then there comes before his muddled brain
A vision of green vastitudes beneath an April sky,
　　And clover pastures drenched with silver rain.
He knows that it can never be, that he is down and out;
　　Life leers at him with foul and fetid breath;
And then amid the revelry, the song and cheer and shout,
　　He suddenly grows grim and cold as death.

He grips the table tensely, and he says: "Dear friends of mine,
　　I've let you dip your fingers in my purse;
I've crammed you at my table, and I've drowned you in my
　　wine,
　　And I've little left to give you but—my curse.

I've failed supremely in my plans; it's rather late to whine;
   My poke is mighty weasened up and small.
I thank you each for coming here; the happiness is mine—
   And now, you thieves and harlots, take it all."

He twists the thong from off his poke; he swings it o'er his
      head;
   The nuggets fall around their feet like grain.
They rattle over roof and wall; they scatter, roll and spread;
   The dust is like a shower of golden rain.
The guests a moment stand aghast, then grovel on the floor;
   They fight, and snarl, and claw, like beasts of prey;
And then, as everybody grabbed and everybody swore,
   The man from Eldorado slipped away.

v

He's the man from Eldorado, and they found him stiff and
      dead,
   Half covered by the freezing ooze and dirt.
A clotted Colt was in his hand, a hole was in his head,
   And he wore an old and oily buckskin shirt.
His eyes were fixed and horrible, as one who hails the end;
   The frost had set him rigid as a log;
And there, half lying on his breast, his last and only friend,
   There crouched and whined a mangy yellow dog.

MY FRIENDS

THE man above was a murderer, the man below was a thief;
And I lay there in the bunk between, ailing beyond belief;
A weary armful of skin and bone, wasted with pain and grief.

My feet were froze, and the lifeless toes were purple and green
    and grey;
The little flesh that clung to my bones, you could punch it in
    holes like clay;
The skin on my gums was a sullen black, and slowly peeling
    away.

I was sure enough in a direful fix, and often I wondered why
They did not take the chance that was left and leave me alone
    to die,
Or finish me off with a dose of dope—so utterly lost was I.

But no; they brewed me the green-spruce tea, and nursed me
    there like a child;
And the homicide he was good to me, and bathed my sores
    and smiled;
And the thief he starved that I might be fed, and his eyes
    were kind and mild.

156

Yet they were woefully wicked men, and often at night in
    pain
I heard the murderer speak of his deed and dream it over
    again;
I heard the poor thief sorrowing for the dead self he had slain.

I'll never forget that bitter dawn, so evil, askew and grey,
When they wrapped me round in the skins of beasts and they
    bore me to a sleigh,
And we started out with the nearest post an hundred miles
    away.

I'll never forget the trail they broke, with its tense, unutterable
    woe;
And the crunch, crunch, crunch, as their snow-shoes sank
    through the crust of the hollow snow;
And my breath would fail, and every beat of my heart was like
    a blow.

And oftentimes I would die the death, yet wake up to life
    anew;
The sun would be all ablaze on the waste, and the sky a
    blighting blue.
And the tears would rise in my snow-blind eyes and furrow
    my cheeks like dew.

And the camps we made when their strength outplayed and the
    day was pinched and wan;
And oh, the joy of that blessed halt, and how I did dread the
    dawn;
And how I hated the weary men who rose and dragged me on.

And oh, how I begged to rest, to rest—the snow was so sweet a
    shroud;
And oh, how I cried when they urged me on, cried and cursed
    them aloud;
Yet on they strained, all racked and pained, and sorely their
    backs were bowed.

And then it was all like a lurid dream, and I prayed for a swift
    release.
From the ruthless ones who would not leave me to die alone in
    peace;
Till I wakened up and I found myself at the post of the
    Mounted Police.

And there was my friend the murderer, and there was my
    friend the thief,
With bracelets of steel around their wrists, and wicked beyond
    belief:
But when they come to God's judgment seat—may I be allowed
    the brief.

THE PROSPECTOR

I strolled up old Bonanza, where I staked in Ninety-eight,
  A-purpose to revisit the old claim.
I kept thinking mighty sadly of the funny ways of Fate,
  And the lads who once were with me in the game.
Poor boys, they're down-and-outers, and there's scarcely one
    to-day
  Can show a dozen colours in his poke;
And me, I'm still prospecting, old and battered, gaunt and
    grey,
  And I'm looking for a grub-stake, and I'm broke.

I strolled up old Bonanza. The same old moon looked down;
  The same old landmarks seemed to yearn to me;
But the cabins all were silent, and the flat, once like a town,
  Was mighty still and lonesome-like to see.
There were piles and piles of tailings where we toiled with
    pick and pan,
  And turning round a bend I heard a roar,
And there a giant gold-ship of the very newest plan
  Was tearing chunks of pay-dirt from the shore.

159

It wallowed in its water-bed; it burrowed, heaved and swung;
    It gnawed its way ahead with grunts and sighs;
Its bill of fare was rock and sand; the tailings were its dung;
    It glared around with fierce electric eyes.
Full fifty buckets crammed its maw; it bellowed out for more;
    It looked like some great monster in the gloom.
With two to feed its sateless greed, it worked for seven score,
    And I sighed: "Ah, old-time miner, here's your doom!"

The idle windlass turns to rust; the sagging sluice-box falls;
    The holes you digged are water to the brim;
Your little sod-roofed cabins with the snugly moss-chinked
        walls
    Are deathly now and mouldering and dim.
The battle-field is silent where of old you fought it out;
    The claims you fiercely won are lost and sold;
But there's a little army that they'll never put to rout—
    The men who simply live to seek the gold.

The men who can't remember when they learned to swing
        a pack,
    Or in what lawless land the quest began;
The solitary seeker with his grub-stake on his back,
    The restless buccaneer of pick and pan.
On the mesas of the Southland, on the tundras of the North,
    You will find us, changed in face but still the same;
And it isn't need, it isn't greed that sends us faring forth—
    It's the fever, it's the glory of the game.

For once you've panned the speckled sand and seen the bonny
       dust,
  Its peerless brightness blinds you like a spell;
It's little else you care about; you go because you must,
  And you feel that you could follow it to hell.
You'd follow it in hunger, and you'd follow it in cold;
  You'd follow it in solitude and pain;
And when you're stiff and battened down let some one whisper
       "Gold,"
  You're lief to rise and follow it again.

Yet look you, if I find the stuff it's just like so much dirt;
  I fling it to the four winds like a child.
It's wine and painted women and the things that do me hurt,
  Till I crawl back, beggared, broken to the Wild.
Till I crawl back, sapped and sodden, to my grub-stake and
      my tent—
  There's a city, there's an army (hear them shout).
There's the gold in millions, millions, but I haven't got a cent;
  And oh, it's me, it's me that found it out.

It was my dream that made it good, my dream that made me go
  To lands of dread and death disprized of man;
But oh, I've known a glory that their hearts will never know,
  When I picked the first big nugget from my pan.
It's still my dream, my dauntless dream, that drives me forth
      once more

To seek and starve and suffer in the Vast;
That heaps my heart with eager hope, that glimmers on
        before—
    My dream that will uplift me to the last.

Perhaps I am stark crazy, but there's none of you too sane;
    It's just a little matter of degree.
My hobby is to hunt out gold; it's fortressed in my brain;
    It's life and love and wife and home to me.
And I'll strike it, yes, I'll strike it; I've a hunch I cannot fail;
    I've a vision, I've a prompting, I've a call;
I hear the hoarse stampeding of an army on my trail,
    To the last, the greatest gold camp of them all.

Beyond the shark-tooth ranges sawing savage at the sky
    There's a lowering land no white man ever struck;
There's gold, there's gold in millions, and I'll find it if I die,
    And I'm going there once more to try my luck.
Maybe I'll fail—what matter? It's a mandate, it's a vow;
    And when in lands of dreariness and dread
You seek the last lone frontier, far beyond your frontiers now,
    You will find the old prospector, silent, dead.

You will find a tattered tent-pole with a ragged robe below it;
    You will find a rusted gold-pan on the sod;
*You will find the claim I'm seeking, with my bones as stakes
        to show it;*
    But I've sought the last Recorder, and He's—God.

THE BLACK SHEEP

"The aristocratic ne'er-do-well in Canada frequently finds his way into the ranks of the Royal North-West Mounted Police."—*Extract*.

Hark to the ewe that bore him:
  "What has muddied the strain?
Never his brothers before him
  Showed the hint of a stain."
Hark to the tups and wethers;
  Hark to the old grey ram:
"We're all of us white, but he's black as night,
  And he'll never be worth a damn."

I'm up on the bally wood-pile at the back of the barracks yard;
"A damned disgrace to the force, sir," with a comrade standing
    guard;
Making the bluff I'm busy, doing my six months' hard.

"Six months' hard and dismissed, sir." Isn't that rather hell?
And all because of the liquor laws and the wiles of a native
    belle—
Some "hooch" I gave to a siwash brave who swore that he
    wouldn't tell.

163

At least they *say* that I did it.   It's so in the town report.
All that I can recall is a night of revel and sport,
When I woke with a "head" in the guard-room, and they
    dragged me sick into court.

And the O.C. said: "You are guilty," and I said never a word;
For, hang it, you see I couldn't—I didn't know *what* had
    occurred,
And, under the circumstances, denial would be absurd.

But the one that cooked my bacon was Grubbe, of the City
    Patrol.
He fagged for my room at Eton, and didn't I devil his soul!
And now he is getting even, landing me down in the hole.

Plugging away on the wood-pile; doing chores round the
    square.
There goes an officer's lady—gives me a haughty stare—
Me that's an earl's own nephew—that is the hardest to bear.

To think of the poor old mater awaiting her prodigal son.
Tho' I broke her heart with my folly, I was always the white-
    haired one.
(That fatted calf that they're cooking will surely be overdone.)
I'll go back and yarn to the Bishop; I'll dance with the village
    belle;

I'll hand round tea to the ladies, and everything will be well.
Where I have been won't matter; what I have seen I won't tell.

I'll soar to their ken like a comet.   They'll see me with never a
    stain;
But will they reform me?—far from it.   We pay for our pleasure
    with pain;
But the dog will return to his vomit, the hog to his wallow
    again.

I've chewed on the rind of creation, and bitter I've tasted the
    same.
Stacked up against hell and damnation, I've managed to stay
    in the game;
I've had my moments of sorrow; I've had my seasons of shame.

That's past; when one's nature's a cracked one, it's too jolly
    hard to mend.
So long as the road is level, so long as I've cash to spend,
I'm bound to go to the devil, and it's all the same in the end.

The bugle is sounding for stables; the men troop off through
    the gloom:
An orderly laying the tables sings in the bright mess-room.
(I'll wash in the prison bucket, and brush with the prison
    broom.)

I'll lie in my cell and listen; I'll wish that I couldn't hear
The laugh and the chaff of the fellows swigging the canteen
    beer;
The nasal tone of the gramophone playing "The Bandolier."

And it seems to me, though it's misty, that night of the flowing
    bowl,
That the man who potlatched the whiskey and landed me into
    the hole
*Was Grubbe, that unmerciful bounder, Grubbe, of the City
    Patrol.*

THE TELEGRAPH OPERATOR

I will not wash my face;
  I will not brush my hair;
I "pig" around the place—
  There's nobody to care.
Nothing but rock and tree;
  Nothing but wood and stone.
Oh, God, it's hell to be
  Alone, alone, alone!

Snow-peaks and deep-gashed draws
  Corral me in a ring.
I feel as if I was
  The only living thing
On all this blighted earth;
  And so I frowst and shrink,
And crouching by my hearth
  I hear the thoughts I think.

I think of all I miss—
  The boys I used to know;
The girls I used to kiss;
  The coin I used to blów;

167

The bars I used to haunt;
　　The racket and the row;
The beers I didn't want
　　(I wish I had 'em now).

Day after day the same,
　　Only a little worse;
No one to grouch or blame—
　　Oh, for a loving curse!
Oh, in the night I fear,
　　Haunted by nameless things,
Just for a voice to cheer,
　　Just for a hand that clings!

Faintly as from a star
　　Voices come o'er the line;
Voices of ghosts afar,
　　Not in this world of mine;
Lives in whose loom I grope;
　　Words in whose weft I hear
Eager the thrill of hope,
　　Awful the chill of fear.

I'm thinking out aloud;
　　I reckon that is bad;
(The snow is like a shroud)—
　　Maybe I'm going mad.
Say! wouldn't that be tough?
　　This awful hush that hugs

And chokes one is enough
   To make a man go "bugs."

There's not a thing to do;
   I cannot sleep at night;
No wonder I'm so blue;
   Oh, for a friendly fight!
The din and rush of strife;
   A music-hall aglow;
A crowd, a city, life—
   Dear God, I miss it so!

Here, you have moped enough!
   Brace up and play the game!
But say, it's awful tough—
   Day after day the same
(I've said that twice, I bet).
   Well, there's not much to say.
I wish I had a pet,
   Or something I could play.

Cheer up! don't get so glum
   And sick of everything;
The worst is yet to come;
   God help you till the Spring.
God shield you from the Fear;
   Teach you to laugh, not moan.
Ha! ha! it sounds so queer—
   Alone, alone, alone!

THE WOOD-CUTTER

The sky is like an envelope,
  One of those blue official things:
And, sealing it, to mock our hope,
  The moon, a silver wafer, clings.
What shall we find when death gives leave
To read—our sentence or reprieve?

I'm holding it down on God's scrap-pile, up on the fag-end of
    earth;
  O'er me a menace of mountains, a river that grits at my feet;
Face to face with my soul-self, weighing my life at its worth;
  Wondering what I was made for, here in my last retreat.

Last! Ah, yes, it's the finish. Have ever you heard a man
    cry?
  (Sobs that rake him and rend him, right from the base of
    the chest.)
That's how I've cried, oh, so often; and now that my tears
    are dry,
  I sit in the desolate quiet and wait for the infinite Rest.

Rest! Well, it's restful around me; it's quiet clean to the core.
  The mountains pose in their ermine, in golden the hills are
    clad;
The big, blue, silt-freighted Yukon seethes by my cabin door,
  And I think it's only the river that keeps me from going mad.

By day it's a ruthless monster, a callous, insatiate thing,
  With oily bubble and eddy, with sudden swirling of breast;
By night it's a writhing Titan, sullenly murmuring,
  Ever and ever goaded, and ever crying for rest.

It cries for its human tribute, but me it will never drown.
  I've learned the lore of my river; my river obeys me well.
I hew and I launch my cordwood, and raft it to Dawson town,
  Where wood means wine and women, and, incidentally,
    hell.

Hell and the anguish thereafter. Here as I sit alone
  I'd give the life I have left me to lighten some load of care:
(The bitterest part of the bitter is being denied to atone;
  Lips that mocked at Heaven lend themselves ill to prayer).

Impotent as a beetle pierced on the needle of Fate;
  A wretch in a cosmic death-cell, peaks for my prison bars;
'Whelmed by a world stupendous, lonely and listless I wait,
  Drowned in a sea of silence, strewn with confetti of stars.

See! from far up the valley a rapier pierces the night,
   The white search-ray of a steamer. Swiftly, serenely it nears;
A proud, white, alien presence, a glitering galley of light,
   Confident-poised, triumphant, freighted with hopes and
      fears.

I look as one looks on a vision I see it pulsating by;
   I glimpse joy-radiant faces; ı hear the thresh of the wheel.
Hoof-like my heart beats a moı ʼent; then silence swoops from
      the sky.
   Darkness is piled upon darkness.   God only knows how
      I feel.

Maybe you've seen me sometimes; maybe you've pitied me
      then—
   The lonely waif of the wood-camp, here by my cabin door.
Some day you'll look and see not; futile and outcast of men,
   I shall be far from your pity, resting forevermore.

My life was a problem in ciphers, a weary and profitless sum.
   Slipshod and stupid I worked it, dazed by negation and
      doubt.
Ciphers the total confronts me. Oh, Death, with thy moistened
      thumb,
   Stoop like a petulant schoolboy, wipe me forever out!

THE SONG OF THE MOUTH-ORGAN

(With apologies to the singer of the "Song of the Banjo.")

I'M a homely little bit of tin and bone;
   I'm beloved by the Legion of the Lost;
I haven't got a "vox humana" tone,
   And a dime or two will satisfy my cost.
I don't attempt your high-falutin' flights;
   I am more or less uncertain on the key;
But I tell you, boys, there's lots and lots of night
   When you've taken mighty comfort out of me.

I weigh an ounce or two, and I'm so small
   You can pack me in the pocket of your vest;
And when at night so wearily you crawl
   Into your bunk and stretch your limbs to rest,
You take me out and play me soft and low;
   The simple songs that trouble your heartstrings;
The tunes you used to fancy long ago,
   Before you made a rotten mess of things.

Then a dreamy look will come into your eyes,
　And you break off in the middle of a note;
And then, with just the dreariest of sighs,
　You drop me in the pocket of your coat.
But somehow I have bucked you up a bit;
　And, as you turn around and face the wall,
You don't feel quite so spineless and unfit—
　You're not so bad a fellow after all.

Do you recollect the bitter Arctic night;
　Your camp beside the canyon on the trail;
Your tent a tiny square of orange light;
　The moon above consumptive-like and pale;
Your supper cooked, your little stove aglow;
　You tired, but snug and happy as a child?
Then 'twas "Turkey in the Straw" till your lips were nearly
　　raw,
　And you hurled your bold defiance at the Wild.

Do you recollect the flashing, lashing pain;
　The gulf of humid blackness overhead;
The lightning making rapiers of the rain;
　The cattle-horns like candles of the dead;
You sitting on your bronco there alone,
　In your slicker, saddle-sore and sick with cold?
Do you think the silent herd did not hear "The Mocking
　　Bird,"
　Or relish "Silver Threads Among the Gold"?

Do you recollect the wild Magellan coast;
  The head-winds and the icy, roaring seas;
The nights you thought that everything was lost;
  The days you toiled in water to your knees;
The frozen ratlines shrieking in the gale;
  The hissing steeps and gulfs of livid foam:
When you cheered your messmates nine with "Ben Bolt" and
    "Clementine,"
  And "Dixie Land" and "Seeing Nellie Home"?

Let the jammy banjo voice the Younger Son,
  Who waits for his remittance to arrive;
I represent the grimy, gritty one,
  Who sweats his bones to keep himself alive;
Who's up against the real thing from his birth;
  Whose heritage is hard and bitter toil;
I voice the weary, smeary ones of earth,
  The helots of the sea and of the soil.

I'm the Steinway of strange mischief and mischance;
  I'm the Stradivarius of blank defeat;
In the down-world, when the devil leads the dance,
  I am simply and symbolically meet;
I'm the irrepressive spirit of mankind;
  I'm the small boy playing knuckle down with Death;
At the end of all things known, where God's rubbish-heap is
    thrown,
  I shrill impudent triumph at a breath.

I'm a humble little bit of tin and horn;
  I'm a byword, I'm a plaything, I'm a jest;
The virtuoso looks on me with scorn;
  But there's times when I am better than the best.
Ask the stoker and the sailor of the sea;
  Ask the mucker and the hewer of the pine;
Ask the herder of the plain, ask the gleaner of the grain—
  There's a lowly, loving kingdom—and it's mine.

THE TRAIL OF NINETY-EIGHT

I

Gold! We leapt from our benches. Gold! We sprang from
our stools.
Gold! We wheeled in the furrow, fired with the faith of fools.
Fearless, unfound, unfitted, far from the night and the cold,
Heard we the clarion summons, followed the master-lure—
Gold!

Men from the sands of the Sunland; men from the woods of
the West;
Men from the farms and the cities, into the Northland we
pressed.
Greybeards and striplings and women, good men and bad men
and bold,
Leaving our homes and our loved ones, crying exultantly—
"Gold!"

Never was seen such an army, pitiful, futile, unfit;
Never was seen such a spirit, manifold courage and grit;

Never has been such a cohort under one banner unrolled
As surged to the ragged-edged Arctic, urged by the arch-tempter·
   —Gold.

"Farewell!" we cried to our dearests; little we cared for their
   · tears.
"Farewell!" we cried to the humdrum and the yoke of the
      hireling years;
Just like a pack of school-boys, and the big crowd cheered us
      goodbye.
Never were hearts so uplifted, never were hopes so high.

The spectral shores flitted past us, and every whirl of the screw
Hurled us nearer to fortune, and ever we planned what we'd
      do—
Do with the gold when we got it—big, shiny nuggets like
      plums,
There in the sand of the river, gouging it out with our thumbs.

And one man wanted a castle, another a racing stud;
A third would cruise in a palace yacht like a red-necked prince
      of blood.
And so we dreamed and we vaunted, millionaires to a man,
Leaping to wealth in our visions long ere the trail began.

II

We landed in wind-swept Skagway. We joined the weltering
    mass,
Clamouring over their outfits, waiting to climb the Pass.
We tightened our girths and our pack-straps; we linked on the
    Human Chain,
Struggling up to the summit, where every step was a pain.

Gone was the joy of our faces, grim and haggard and pale;
The heedless mirth of the shipboard was changed to the care
    of the trail.
We flung ourselves in the struggle, packing our grub in relays,
Step by step to the summit in the bale of the winter days.

Floundering deep in the sump-holes, stumbling out again;
Crying with cold and weakness, crazy with fear and pain.
Then from the depths of our travail, ere our spirits were
    broke,
Grim, tenacious and savage, the lust of the trail awoke.

"Klondike or bust!" rang the slogan; every man for his own.
Oh, how we flogged the horses, staggering skin and bone!
Oh, how we cursed their weakness, anguish they could not
    tell,
Breaking their hearts in our passion, lashing them on till they
    fell!

G

For grub meant gold to our thinking, and all that could walk
    must pack;
The sheep for the shambles stumbled, each with a load on its
    back;
And even the swine were burdened, and grunted and squealed
    and rolled,
And men went mad in the moment, huskily clamouring
    "Gold!"

Oh, we were brutes and devils, goaded by lust and fear!
Our eyes were strained to the summit; the weaklings dropped
    to the rear,
Falling in heaps by the trail-side, heart-broken, limp and wan;
But the gaps closed up in an instant, and heedless the chain
    went on.

Never will I forget it, there on the mountain face,
Antlike, men with their burdens, clinging in icy space;
Dogged, determined and dauntless, cruel and callous and cold,
Cursing, blaspheming, reviling, and ever that battlecry—
    "Gold!"

Thus toiled we, the army of fortune, in hunger and hope and
    despair,
Till glacier, mountain and forest vanished, and, radiantly fair,

There at our feet lay Lake Bennett, and down to its welcome
we ran:
The trail of the land was over, the trail of the water began.

III

We built our boats and we launched them. Never has been
such a fleet;
A packing-case for a bottom, a mackinaw for a sheet.
Shapeless, grotesque, lopsided, flimsy, makeshift and crude,
Each man after his fashion builded as best he could.

Each man worked like a demon, as prow to rudder we raced;
The winds of the Wild cried "Hurry!" the voice of the waters,
"Haste!"
We hated those driving before us; we dreaded those pressing
behind;
We cursed the slow current that bore us; we prayed to the
God of the wind.

Spring! and the hillsides flourished, vivid in jewelled green;
Spring! and our hearts' blood nourished envy and hatred and
spleen.
Little cared we for the Spring-birth; much cared we to get on—
Stake in the Great White Channel, stake ere the best be gone.

The greed of the gold possessed us; pity and love were forgot.
Covetous visions obsessed us; brother with brother fought.
Partner with partner wrangled, each one claiming his due;
Wrangled and halved their outfits, sawing their boats in two.

Thuswise we voyaged Lake Bennett, Tagish, then Windy
    Arm,
Sinister, savage and baleful, boding us hate and harm.
Many a scow was shattered there on that iron shore;
Many a heart was broken straining at sweep and oar.

We roused Lake Marsh with a chorus, we drifted many a mile;
There was the canyon before us—cave-like its dark defile;
The shores swept faster and faster; the river narrowed to wrath;
Waters that hissed disaster reared upright in our path.

Beneath us the green tumult churning, above us the cavernous
    gloom;
Around us, swift twisting and turning, the black, sullen
    walls of a tomb.
We spun like a chip in a mill-race; our hearts hammered
    under the test;
Then—oh, the relief on each chill face!—we soared into
    sunlight and rest.

Hand sought for hand on the instant.   Cried we, "Our
    troubles are o'er!"
Then, like a rumble of thunder, heard we a canorous roar.
Leaping and boiling and seething, saw we a cauldron afume;
There was the rage of the rapids, there was the menace of
    ˙doom.

The river springs like a racer, sweeps through a gash in
    the rock;
Butts at the boulder-ribbed bottom, staggers and rears at
    the shock;
Leaps like a terrified monster, writhes in its fury and pain;
Then with the crash of a demon springs to the onset again.

Dared we that ravening terror; heard we its din in our ears;
Called on the Gods of our fathers, juggled forlorn with our
    fears;
Sank to our waists in its fury, tossed to the sky like a fleece;
Then, when our dread was the greatest, crashed into safety
    and peace.

But what of the others that followed, losing their boats by
    the score?
Well could we see them and hear them, strung down that
    desolate shore.

What of the poor souls that perished?   Little of them shall
    be said—
On to the Golden Valley, pause not to bury the dead.

Then there were days of drifting, breezes soft as a sigh;
Night trailed her robe of jewels over the floor of the sky.
The moonlit stream was a python, silver, sinuous, vast,
That writhed on a shroud of velvet—well, it was done at last.

There were the tents of Dawson, there the scar of the slide;
Swiftly we poled o'er the shallows, swiftly leapt o'er the side.
Fires fringed the mouth of Bonanza; sunset gilded the dome;
The test of the trail was over—thank God, thank God, we
    were Home!

THE BALLAD OF GUM-BOOT BEN

He was an old prospector with a vision bleared and dim.
He asked me for a grubstake, and the same I gave to him.
He hinted of a hidden trove, and when I made so bold
To question his veracity, this is the tale he told.

"I do not seek the copper streak, nor yet the yellow dust;
I am not fain for sake of gain to irk the frozen crust;
Let fellows gross find gilded dross, far other is my mark;
Oh, gentle youth, this is the truth—I go to seek the Ark.

"I prospected the Pelly bed, I prospected the White;
The Nordenscold for love of gold I piked from morn till night;
Afar and near for many a year I led the wild stampede,
Until I guessed that all my quest was vanity and greed.

"Then came I to a land I knew no man had ever seen,
A haggard land, forlornly spanned by mountains lank and lean;
The nitchies said 'twas full of dread, of smoke and fiery breath,
And no man dare put foot in there for fear of pain and death.

"But I was made all unafraid, so, careless and alone,
Day after day I made my way into that land unknown;
Night after night by camp-fire light I crouched in lonely
    thought;
Oh, gentle youth, this is the truth—I knew not what I sought.

"I rose at dawn; I wandered on. 'Tis somewhat fine and grand
To be alone and hold your own in God's vast awesome land;
Come woe or weal, 'tis fine to feel a hundred miles between
The trails you dare and pathways where the feet of men
    have been.

"And so it fell on me a spell of wander-lust was cast.
The land was still and strange and chill, and cavernous and
    vast;
And sad and dead, and dull as lead, the valleys sought the
    snows;
And far and wide on every side the ashen peaks arose.

"The moon was like a silent spike that pierced the sky right
    through;
The small stars popped and winked and hopped in vastitudes
    of blue;
And unto me for company came creatures of the shade,
And formed in rings and whispered things that made me
    half afraid.

"And strange though be, 'twas borne on me that land had
    lived of old,

And men had crept and slain and slept where now they
    toiled for gold;
Through jungles dim the mammoth grim had sought the oozy
    fen,
And on his track, all bent of back, had crawled the hairy men.

 And furthermore, strange deeds of yore in this dead place
    were done.
They haunted me, as wild and free I roamed from sun to sun;
Until I came where sudden flame uplit a terraced height,
A regnant peak that seemed to seek the coronal of night.

"I scaled the peak; my heart was weak, yet on and on I pressed.
Skyward I strained until I gained its dazzling silver crest;
And there I found, with all around a world supine and stark,
Swept clean of snow, a flat plateau, and on it lay—the Ark.

"Yes, there, I knew, by two and two the beasts did disembark,
And so in haste I ran and traced in letters on the Ark
My human name—Ben Smith's the same. And now I want
    to float
A syndicate to haul and freight to town that noble boat."

I met him later in a bar and made a gay remark
Anent an ancient miner and an option on the Ark.
He gazed at me reproachfully, as only topers can;
But what he said I can't repeat—he was a bad old man.

CLANCY OF THE MOUNTED POLICE

In the little Crimson Manual it's written plain and clear
That who would wear the scarlet coat shall say goodbye to
    fear;
Shall be a guardian of the right, a sleuth-hound of the trail—
In the little Crimson Manual there's no such word as "fail"—
Shall follow on though heavens fall, or hell's top-turrets freeze,
Half round the world, if need there be, on bleeding hands
    and knees.
It's duty, duty, first and last, the Crimson Manual saith;
The Scarlet Rider makes reply: "It's duty—to the death."
And so they sweep the solitudes, free men from all the earth;
And so they sentinel the woods, the wilds that know their
    worth;
And so they scour the startled plains and mock at hurt and
    pain,
And read their Crimson Manual, and find their duty plain.
Knights of the lists of unrenown, born of the frontier's need,
Disdainful of the spoken word, exultant in the deed;
Unconscious heroes of the waste, proud players of the game,
Props of the power behind the throne, upholders of the name;
For thus the Great White Chief hath said, "In all my lands
    be peace,"
And to maintain his word he gave his West the Scarlet Police.

Livid-lipped was the valley, still as the grave of God;
　Misty shadows of mountain thinned into mists of cloud;
Corpselike and stark was the land, with a quiet that crushed
　　and awed,
　And the stars of the weird sub-arctic glimmered over its
　　shroud.

Deep in the trench of the valley two men stationed the Post,
　Seymour and Clancy the reckless, fresh from the long patrol;
Seymour, the sergeant, and Clancy—Clancy who made his boast
　He could cinch like a bronco the Northland, and cling to
　　the prongs of the Pole.

Two lone men on detachment, standing for law on the trail;
　Undismayed in the vastness, wise with the wisdom of old—
Out of the night hailed a half-breed telling a pitiful tale,
　"White man starving and crazy on the banks of the
　　Nordenscold."

Up sprang the red-haired Clancy, lean and eager of eye;
　Loaded the long toboggan, strapped each dog at its post;
Whirled his lash at the leader; then, with a whoop and a cry,
　Into the Great White silence faded away like a ghost.

The clouds were a misty shadow, the hills were a shadowy mist;
　Sunless, voiceless and pulseless, the day was a dream of woe;
Through the ice-rifts the river smoked and bubbled and hissed;
　Behind was a trail fresh broken, in front the untrodden snow.

Ahead of the dogs ploughed Clancy, haloed by streaming
    breath;
  Through peril of open water, through ache of insensate cold;
Up rivers wantonly winding in a land affianced to death,
    Till he came to a cowering cabin on the banks of the
    Nordenscold.

Then Clancy loosed his revolver, and he strode through the
    open door;
    And there was the man he sought for, crouching beside
    the fire;
The hair of his beard was singeing, the frost on his back
    was hoar,
    And ever he crooned and chanted as if he never would tire:—

*"I panned and I panned in the shiny sand, and I sniped on the
    river bar;*
*But I know, I know, that it's down below that the golden
    treasures are;*
*So I'll wait and wait till the floods abate, and I'll sink a shaft
    once more,*
*And I'd like to bet that I'll go home yet with a brass band
    playing before."*

He was nigh as thin as a sliver, and he whined like a Moose-
    hide cur;
    So Clancy clothed him and nursed him as a mother nurses
    a child;

Lifted him on the toboggan, wrapped him in robes of fur,
  Then with the dogs sore straining started to face the wild.

Said the Wild, "I will crush this Clancy, so fearless and
      insolent;
  For him will I loose my fury, and bland and buffet and beat;
Pile up my snows to stay him; then when his strength is spent,
  Leap on him from my ambush and crush him under my feet.

"Him will I ring with my silence, compass him with my cold;
  Closer and closer clutch him unto mine icy breast;
Buffet him with my blizzards, deep in my snows enfold,
  Claiming his life as my tribute, giving my wolves the rest."

Clancy crawled through the vastness; o'er him the hate of the
      Wild;
  Full on his face fell the blizzard; cheering his huskies he ran;
Fighting, fierce-hearted and tireless, snows that drifted and
      piled,
  With ever and ever behind him singing the crazy man.

  "Sing hey, sing ho, for the ice and snow,
      And a heart that's ever merry;
  Let us trim and square with a lover's care
      (For why should a man be sorry?)
  A grave deep, deep, with the moon a-peep,
      A grave in the frozen mould.
  Sing hey, sing ho, for the winds that blow,

And a grave deep down in the ice and snow,
   A grave in the land of gold."

Day after day of darkness, the whirl of the seething snows;
   Day after day of blindness, the swoop of the stinging blast;
On through a blur of fury the swing of staggering blows;
   On through a world of turmoil, empty, inane and vast.

Night with its writhing storm-whirl, night despairingly black;
   Night with its hours of terror, numb and endlessly long;
Night with its weary waiting, fighting the shadows back,
   And ever the crouching madman singing his crazy song.

Cold with its creeping terror, cold with its sudden clinch;
   Cold so utter you wonder if 'twill ever again be warm;
Clancy grinned as he shuddered, "Surely it isn't a cinch
   Being wet-nurse to a looney in the teeth of an Arctic storm."

The blizzard passed and the dawn broke, knife-edged and
      crystal clear;
   The sky was a blue-domed iceberg, sunshine outlawed away;
Ever by snowslide and ice-rip haunted and hovered the Fear;
   Ever the Wild malignant poised and panted to slay.

The lead-dog freezes in harness—cut him out of the team!
   The lung of the wheel-dog's bleeding—shoot him and let him
      lie!

On and on with the others—lash them until they scream!
"Pull for your lives, you devils! On! To halt is to die."

There in the frozen vastness Clancy fought with his foes;
 The ache of the stiffened fingers, the cut of the snowshoe
  thong;
Cheeks black-raw through the hood-flap, eyes that tingled
 and closed,
 And ever to urge and cheer him quavered the madman's
  song.

Colder it grew and colder, till the last heat left the earth,
 And there in the great stark stillness the bale fires glinted
  and gleamed,
And the Wild all around exulted and shook with a devilish
 mirth,
 And life was far and forgotten, the ghost of a joy once
  dreamed.

Death! And one who defied it, a man of the Mounted Police;
 Fought it there to a standstill long after hope was gone;
Grinned through his bitter anguish, fought without let or
 cease,
 Suffering, straining, striving, stumbling, struggling on.

Till the dogs lay down in their traces, and rose and staggered
 and fell;

Till the eyes of him dimmed with shadows, and the trail
    was so hard to see;
Till the Wild howled out triumphant, and the world was a
    frozen hell—
Then said Constable Clancy: "I guess that it's up to me."

Far down the trail they saw him, and his hands they were
    blanched like bone;
His face was a blackened horror, from his eyelids the salt
    rheum ran;
His feet he was lifting strangely, as if they were made of stone,
But safe in his arms and sleeping he carried the crazy man.

So Clancy got into Barracks, and the boys made rather a scene;
    And the O.C. called him a hero, and was nice as a man
        could be;
But Clancy gazed down his trousers at the place where his
    toes had been,
    And then he howled like a husky, and sang in a shaky key:—

"When I go back to the old love that's true to the finger-tips,
I'll say: 'Here's bushels of gold, love,' and I'll kiss my girl
    on the lips;
'It's yours to have and to hold, love.' It's the proud, proud
    boy I'll be,
When I go back to the old love that's waited so long for me."

LOST

"Black is the sky, but the land is white—
  (O the wind, the snow and the storm!)—
Father, where is our boy to-night?
  Pray to God he is safe and warm."

"Mother, mother, why should you fear
  Safe is he, and the Arctic moon
Over his cabin shines so clear—
  Rest and sleep, 'twill be morning soon."

"It's getting dark awful sudden.   Say, this is mighty queer!
  Where in the world have I got to?   It's still and black as
    a tomb.
I reckoned the camp was yonder, I figured the trail was here—
  Nothing!   Just draw and valley packed with quiet and
    gloom;
Snow that comes down like feathers, thick and gobby and
    gray;
Night that looks spiteful ugly—seems that I've lost my way.

"The cold's got an edge like a jackknife—it must be forty
    below;

Leastways that's what it seems like—it cuts so fierce to the
    bone.
The wind's getting real ferocious; it's heaving and whirling
    the snow;
  It shrieks with a howl of fury, it dies away to a moan;
Its arms sweep round like a banshee's, swift and icily white,
And buffet and blind and beat me. Lord! it's a hell of a night.

"I'm all tangled up in a blizzard. There's only one thing
    to do—
  Keep on moving and moving; it's death, it's death if I rest.
Oh, God! if I see the morning, if only I struggle through,
  I'll say the prayers I've forgotten since I lay on my mother's
    breast.
I seem going round in a circle; maybe the camp is near.
  Say! did somebody holler? Was it a light I saw?
Or was it only a notion? I'll shout, and maybe they'll hear—
  No! the wind only drowns me—shout till my throat is raw.

"The boys are all round the camp-fire wondering when I'll be
    back.
  They'll soon be starting to seek me; they'll scarcely wait
    for the light.
What will they find, I wonder, when they come to the end of
    my track—
  A hand stuck out of a snowdrift, frozen and stiff and white.
That's what they'll strike, I reckon; that's how they'll find
    their pard,

A pie-faced corpse in a snowbank—curse you, don't be a
    fool!
Play the game to the finish; bet on your very last card;
    Nerve yourself for the struggle. Oh, you coward, keep cool!

"I'm going to lick this blizzard; I'm going to live the night.
    It can't down me with its bluster—I'm not the kind to be
        beat.
On hands and knees will I buck it; with every breath will I
        fight;
    It's life, it's life that I fight for—never it seemed so sweet.
I know that my face is frozen; my hands are numblike and
        dead;
    But oh, my feet keep a-moving, heavy and hard and slow;
They're trying to kill me, kill me, the night that's black
        overhead,
    The wind that cuts like a razor, the whipcord lash of the
        snow.

Keep a-moving, a-moving; don't, don't stumble, you fool!
    Curse this snow that's a-piling a-purpose to block my way.
It's heavy as gold in the rocker, it's white and fleecy as wool;
    It's soft as a bed of feathers, it's warm as a stack of hay.
Curse on my feet that slip so, my poor tired, stumbling feet—
    I guess they're a job for the surgeon, they feel so queerlike
        to lift—
I'll rest them just for a moment—oh, but to rest is sweet!
    The awful wind cannot get me, deep, deep down in the
        drift."

"Father, a bitter cry I heard,
  Out of the night so dark and wild.
Why is my heart so strangely stirred?
  'Twas like the voice of our erring child."

"Mother, mother, you only heard
  A waterfowl in the locked lagoon—
Out of the night a wounded bird—
  Rest and sleep, 'twill be morning soon."

Who is it talks of sleeping? I'll swear that somebody shook
  Me hard by the arm for a moment, but how on earth could
    it be?
See how my feet are moving—awfully funny they look—
  Moving as if they belonged to a some one that wasn't me.
The wind down the night's long alley bowls me down like a
    pin;
  I stagger and fall and stagger, crawl arm-deep in the snow.
Beaten back to my corner, how can I hope to win?
  And there is the blizzard waiting to give me the knockout
    blow.

Oh, I'm so warm and sleepy! No more hunger and pain.
  Just to rest for a moment; was ever rest such a joy?
Ha! what was that? I'll swear it, somebody shook me again;
  Somebody seemed to whisper: "Fight to the last, my boy."
Fight! That's right, I must struggle. I know that to rest
    means death;

Death, but then what does death mean?—ease from a world
    of strife.
Life has been none too pleasant; yet with my failing breath
    Still and still must I struggle, fight for the gift of life.

       *   *   *   *   *   *

Seems that I must be dreaming! Here is the old home trail!
    Yonder a light is gleaming; oh, I know it so well!
The air is scented with clover; the cattle wait by the rail;
    Father is through with the milking; there goes the supper-
    bell.

       *   *   *   *   *   *

Mother, your boy is crying, out in the night and cold;
    Let me in and forgive me, I'll never be bad any more:
I'm, oh, so sick and so sorry; please, dear mother, don't scold—
    It's just your boy, and he wants you. . . . Mother, open
    the door. . . .

      "Father, father, I saw a face
        Pressed just now to the window-pane!
      Oh, it gazed for a moment's space,
        Wild and wan, and was gone again!"
      "Mother, mother, you saw the snow
        Drifted down from the maple-tree
      (Oh, the wind that is sobbing so!
        Weary and worn and old are we)—
      Only the snow and a wounded loon—
        Rest and sleep, 'twill be morning soon."

L'ENVOI

We talked of yesteryears, of trails and treasure,
  Of men who played the game and lost or won;
Of mad stampedes, of toil beyond all measure,
  Of camp-fire comfort when the day was done.
We talked of sullen nights by moon-dogs haunted,
  Of bird and beast and tree, of rod and gun;
Of boat and tent, of hunting-trip enchanted
  Beneath the wonder of the midnight sun;
Of bloody-footed dogs that gnawed the traces,
  Of prisoned seas, wind-lashed and winter-locked.
The ice-grey dawn was pale upon our faces,
  Yet still we filled the cup and still we talked.

The city street was dimmed. We saw the glitter
  Of moon-picked brilliants on the virgin snow,
And down the drifted canyon heard the bitter,
  Relentless slogan of the winds of woe.
The city was forgot, and, parka-skirted,
  We trod that leagueless land that once we knew;
We saw stream past, down valleys glacier-girted,
  The wolf-worn legions of the caribou;

We smoked our pipes, o'er scenes of triumph dwelling;
  Of deeds of daring, dire defeats, we talked;
And other tales that lost not in the telling,
  Ere to our beds uncertainly we walked.

And so, dear friends, in gentler valleys roaming,
  Perhaps, when on my printed page you look,
Your fancies by the firelight may go homing
  To that lone land that haply you forsook.
And if perchance you hear the silence calling,
  The frozen music of star yearning heights,
Or, dreaming, see the seines of silver trawling
  Across the sky's abyss on vasty nights,
You may recall that sweep of savage splendour,
  That land that measures each man at his worth,
And feel in memory, half fierce, half tender,
  The brotherhood of men that know the North.

RHYMES OF A ROLLING STONE

I have no doubt at all the Devil grins
    As seas of ink I spatter;
Ye Gods, forgive my "literary" sins—
    The other kind don't matter.

PRELUDE

I sing no idle songs of dalliance days,
  No dreams Elysian inspire my rhyming;
I have no Celia to enchant my lays,
  No pipes of Pan have set my heart to chiming;
I am no wordsmith dripping gems divine
  Into the golden chalice of a sonnet;
If love songs witch you, close this book of mine,
            Waste no time on it.

Yet bring I to my work an eager joy,
  A lusty love of life and all things human;
Still in me leaps the wonder of the boy,
  A pride in man, a deathless faith in woman.
Still red blood calls, still rings the valiant fray;
  Adventure beacons through the summer gloaming;
Oh, long and long and long will be the day
            Ere I come homing!

This earth is ours to love: lute, brush and pen,
  They are but tongues to tell of life sincerely;
The thaumaturgic Day, the might of men,
  O God of Scribes, grant us to grave them clearly!
Grant heart that homes in heart, then all is well.
  Honey is honey-sweet, howe'er the hiving.
Each to his work, his wage at evening bell,
  The strength of striving.

RHYMES OF
A ROLLING STONE

A ROLLING STONE

There's sunshine in the heart of me,
  My blood sings in the breeze;
The mountains are a part of me,
  I'm fellow to the trees.
My golden youth I'm squandering,
  Sun-libertine am I;
A-wandering, a-wandering,
  Until the day I die.

I was once, I declare, a Stone Age man,
  And I roomed in the cool of a cave;
I have known, I will swear, in a new life-span,
  The fret and the sweat of a slave:
For far over all that folks hold worth,
  There lives and there leaps in me
A love of the lowly things of earth,
  And a passion to be free.

To pitch my tent with no prosy plan
    To range and to change at will;
To mock at the mastership of man,
    To seek Adventure's thrill.
Carefree to be, as a bird that sings,
    To go my own sweet way;
To reck not at all what may befall,
    But to live and to love each day.

To make my body a temple pure
    Wherein I dwell serene;
To care for the things that shall endure,
    The simple, sweet and clean.
To oust out envy and hate and rage,
    To breathe with no alarm;
For Nature shall be my anchorage,
    And none shall do me harm.

To shun all lures that debauch the soul,
    The orgied rites of the rich;
To eat my crust as a rover must
    With the rough-neck down in the ditch.
To trudge by his side whate'er betide;
    To share his fire at night;
To call him friend to the long trail-end,
    And to read his heart aright.

To scorn all strife, and to view all life
    With the curious eyes of a child;
From the plangent sea to the prairie,
    From the slum to the heart of the Wild.
From the red-rimmed star to the speck of sand,
    From the vast to the greatly small;
For I know that the whole for good is planned,
    And I want to see it all.

To see it all, the wide world-way,
    From the fig-leaf belt to the Pole;
With never a one to say me nay,
    And none to cramp my soul.
In belly-pinch I will pay the price,
    But God! let me be free;
For once I know in the long ago,
    They made a slave of me.

In a flannel shirt from earth's clean dirt,
    Here, pal, is my calloused hand!
Oh, I love each day as a rover may,
    Nor seek to understand.
To *enjoy* is good enough for me;
    The gipsy of God am I;
Then here's a hail to each flaring dawn!
And here's a cheer to the night that's gone!
And may I go a-roaming on
    Until the day I die!

Then every star shall sing to me
  Its song of liberty;
And every morn shall bring to me
  Its mandate to be free.
In every throbbing vein of me
  I'll feel the vast Earth-call:
O body, heart and brain of me,
  Praise Him who made it all!

THE SOLDIER OF FORTUNE

"DENY your God!" they ringed me with their spears;
  Blood-crazed were they, and reeking from the strife;
Hell-hot their hate, and venom-fanged their sneers,
  And one man spat on me and nursed a knife,
And there was I, sore wounded and alone,
  I, the last living of my slaughtered band.
Oh, sinister the sky, and cold as stone!
  In one red laugh of horror reeled the land.
And dazed and desperate I faced their spears,
  And like a flame out-leaped that naked knife,
And like a serpent stung their bitter jeers:
  "Deny your God, and we will give you life."

Deny my God! Oh, life was very sweet!
  And it is hard in youth and hope to die;
And there my comrades dear lay at my feet,
  And in that blear of blood soon must I lie.
And yet . . . I almost laughed—it seemed so odd,
  For long and long had I not vainly tried
To reason out and body forth my God,
  And prayed for light, and doubted—and *denied*.

Denied the Being I could not conceive,
　Denied a life-to-be beyond the grave. . . .
And now they ask me, who do not believe,
　Just to deny, to voice my doubt, to save
This life of mine that sings so in the sun,
　The bloom of youth yet red upon my cheek,
My only life!—O fools! 'tis easy done,
　I will deny . . . and yet I do not speak.

"Deny your God!" their spears are all agleam,
　And I can see their eyes with blood-lust shine;
Their snarling voices shrill into a scream,
　And, mad to slay, they quiver for the sign.
Deny my God! yes, I could do it well;
　Yet if I did, what of my race, my name?
How they would spit on me, these dogs of hell!
　Spurn me, and put on me the brand of shame.
A white man's honour! what of that, I say?
　Shall these black curs cry "Coward" in my face?

They who would perish for their gods of clay—
　Shall I defile my country and my race?
My country! what's my country to me now?
　Soldier of Fortune, free and far I roam;
All men are brothers in my heart, I vow;
　The wide and wondrous world is all my home.
My country! reverent of her splendid Dead,
　Her heroes proud, her martyrs pierced with pain:

For me her puissant blood was vainly shed;
  For me her drums of battle beat in vain,
And free I fare, half-heedless of her fate:
  No faith, no flag, I owe—then why not seek
This last loop-hole of life? Why hesitate?
  I will deny . . . and yet I do not speak.

"Deny your God!" their spears are poised on high,
  And tense and terrible they wait the word;
And dark and darker glooms the dreary sky,
  And in that hush of horror no thing stirred.
Then, through the ringing terror and sheer hate
  Leaped there a vision to me—Oh, how far!
A face, Her face . . . through all my stormy fate
  A joy, a strength, a glory and a star.

Beneath the pines, where lonely camp-fires gleam
  In seas forlorn, amid the deserts drear,
How I had gladdened to that face of dream!
  And never, never had it seemed so dear.
O silken hair that veils the sunny brow!
  O eyes of grey, so tender and so true!
O lips of smiling sweetness! must I now
  Forever and forever go from you?
Ah, yes, I must . . . for if I do this thing,
  How can I look into your face again?
Knowing you think me more than half a king.
  I with my craven heart, my honour slain.

No! no! my mind's made up. I gaze above,
  Into that sky insensate as a stone;
Not for my creed, my country, but my Love
  Will I stand up and meet my death alone.
Then, though it be to utter dark I sink,
  The God that dwells in me is not denied;
"Best" triumphs over "Beast"—and so I think
  Humanity itself is glorified. . . .

"And now, my butchers, I embrace my fate.
  Come! let my heart's blood slake the thirsty sod.
Curst be the life you offer! Glut your hate!
  Strike! Strike, you dogs! I'll *not* deny my God."
I saw the spears that seemed a-leap to slay,
  All quiver earthward at the headman's nod;
And in a daze of dream I heard him say:
  "Go, set him free who serves so well his God!"

THE GRAMOPHONE AT FOND-DU-LAC

Now Eddie Malone got a swell grammyfone, to draw all the
    trade to his store;
An' sez he: "Come along for a season of song, which the like
    ye had niver before."
Then Dogrib an' Slave, an' Yellow-knife brave, an' Cree in
    his dinky canoe,
Confluated near, to see an' to hear Ed's grammyfone make
    its dayboo.

Then Ed turned the crank, an' there on the bank they squatted
    like bumps on a log,
For acres around there wasn't a sound, not even the howl of
    a dog.
When out of the horn there sudden was born such a marvel-
    lous elegant tone;
An' then like a spell on that auddyence fell the voice of its
    first grammyfone.

"*Bad medicine!*" cried Old Tom, the One-eyed, an' made for
    to jump in the lake;
But no one gave heed to his little stampede, so he guessed
    he had made a mistake.
Then Roll-in-the-Mud, a chief of the blood, observed in choice
    Chippewayan:

215

"You've brought us canned beef, an' it's now my belief, that
    this here's a case of *'canned man.'* "

Well, though I'm not strong on the Dago in song, that sure
    got me goin' for fair.
There was Crusoe an' Scotty an' Ma'am Shoeman,
    Hank, an' Melber an' Bonchy was there.
'Twas silver an' gold, an' sweetness untold, to hear all them
    big guinneys sing;
An' thick all around an' inhalin' the sound, them Indians
    formed in a ring.

So solemn they˙ sat, an' they smoked an' they spat, but their
    eyes sort o' glistened an' shone:
Yet niver a word of approvin' occurred till that guy Harry
    Lauder came on.
Then hunter of moose an' squaw an' papoose jest laughed
    till their stummicks was sore;
Six times Eddie set back that record an' yet they hollered an'
    hollered for more.

I'll never forget that frame-up, you bet; them caverns of
    sunset agleam;
Them still peaks aglow, them shadders below, an' the lake
    like a petrified dream;
The teepees that stood by the edge of the wood; the evenin'
    star blinkin' alone;
The peace an' the rest, an' final an' best, the music of Ed's
    grammyfone.

Then sudden an' clear there rang on my ear a song mighty
    simple an' old;
Heart-hungry an' high it thrilled to the sky, all about "silver
    threads in the gold."
'Twas tender to tears, an' it brung back the years the mem'ries
    that hallow an' yearn;
'Twas home-love an' joy, 'twas the thought of my boy . . . an'
    right there I vowed I'd return.

Big Four-finger Jack was right at my back, an' I saw with a
    kind o' surprise,
He gazed at the lake with a heartful of ache, an' the tears
    irrigated his eyes.
An' sez he: "Cuss me, pard! but that there hits me hard; I've
    a mother does nuthin' but wait;
She's turned eighty-three, an' she's only got me, an' I'm scared
    it'll soon be too late."

      *   *   *   *   *   *

On Fond-du-lac's shore I'm hearin' once more that blessed old
    grammyfone play.
The summer's all gone, an' I'm still livin' on in the same old
    haphazardous way.
Oh, I cut out the booze, an' with muscles an' thews I corralled
    all the coin to go back;
But it wasn't to be—he'd a mother, you see—so I—*slipped it
    to Four-finger Jack.*

THE LAND OF BEYOND

HAVE ever you heard of the Land of Beyond,
　That dreams at the gates of the day?
Alluring it lies at the skirts of the skies,
　And ever so far away;
Alluring its calls: O ye the yoke galls,
　And. ye of the trail overfond,
With saddle and pack, by paddle and track,
　Let's go to the Land of Beyond!

Have ever you stood where the silences brood,
　And vast the horizons begin,
At the dawn of the day to behold far away
　The goal you would strive for and win?
Yet, ah! in the night when you gain to the height,
　With the vast pool of heaven star-spawned,
Afar and agleam, like a valley of dream,
　Still mocks you a Land of Beyond.

Thank God! there is always a Land of Beyond
　For us who are true to the trail;

A vision to seek, a beckoning peak,
  A farness that never will fail;
A pride in our soul that mocks at a goal,
  A manhood that irks at a bond,
And try how we will, unattainable still,
  Behold it, our Land of Beyond.

SUNSHINE

I

Flat as a drum-head stretch the haggard snows;
   The mighty skies are palisades of light;
The stars are blurred; the silence grows and grows;
   Vaster and vaster vaults the icy night.
Here in my sleeping-bag I cower and pray:
"Silence and night, have pity; stoop and slay."

I have not slept for many, many days.
   I close my eyes with weariness—that's all.
I still have strength to feed the drift-wood blaze
   That flickers weirdly on the icy wall.
I still have strength to pray: "God rest her soul,
Here in the awful shadow of the Pole."

There in the cabin's alcove low she lies,
   Still candles gleaming at her head and feet;
All snow-drop white, ash-cold, with closèd eyes,
   Lips smiling, hands at rest—O God, how sweet!
How all unutterably sweet she seems . . .
Not dead, not dead, indeed—she dreams, she dreams.

220

II

"Sunshine," I called her, and she brought, I vow,
  God's blessed sunshine to this life of mine.
I was a rover, of the breed who plough
  Life's furrow in a far-flung, lonely line;
The wilderness my home, my fortune cast
In a wild land of dearth, barbaric, vast.

When did I see her first? Long had I lain
  Groping my way to life through fevered gloom.
Sudden the cloud of darkness left my brain;
  A velvet bar of sunshine pierced the room,
And in that mellow glory aureoled
She stood, she stood, all golden in its gold.

Sunshine! O miracle! the earth grew glad;
  Radiant each blade of grass, each living thing.
What a huge strength, high hope, proud will I had!
  All the wide world with rapture seemed to ring.
Would she but wed me? *Yes:* then fared we forth
Into the vast, unvintageable North.

III

In Muskrat Land the conies leap,
  The wavies linger in their flight;
The jewelled, snake-like rivers creep;

The sun, sad rogue, is out all night;
The great wood-bison paws the sand,
In Muskrat Land, in Muskrat Land.

In Muskrat Land dim streams divide
The tundras belted by the sky.
How sweet in slim canoe to glide,
And dream, and let the world go by!
Build gay camp-fires on greening strand!
In Muskrat Land, in Muskrat Land.

IV

And so we dreamed and drifted, she and I;
And how she loved that free unfathomed life!
There, in the peach-bloom of the midnight sky,
The silence welded us, true man and wife.
Then North and North invincibly we pressed
Beyond the Circle, to the world's white crest.

And on the wind-flailed Arctic waste we stayed,
Dwelt with the Huskies by the Polar sea.
Fur had they, white fox, marten, mink, to trade
And we had food-stuff, bacon, flour and tea.
So we made snug, chummed up with all the band;
Sudden the Winter swooped on Husky Land.

V

What was that ill so sinister and dread,
    Smiting the tribe with sickness to the bone?
So that we waked one morn to find them fled;
    So that we stood and stared, alone, alone.
Bravely she smiled and looked into my eyes;
    Laughed at their troubled, stern, foreboding pain;
Gaily she mocked the menace of the skies,
    Turned to our cheery cabin once again,
Saying: "'Twill soon be over, dearest one,
The long, long night: then O the sun, the sun!"

VI

God made a heart of gold, of gold,
    Shining and sweet and true;
Gave it a home of fairest mould,
    Blest it, and called it—You.

God gave the rose its grace of glow,
    And the lark its radiant glee;
But, better than all, I know, I know,
    God gave you, Heart, to me.

VII

She was all sunshine in those dubious days;
    Our cabin beaconed with defiant light;

We chattered by the friendly drift-wood blaze;
   Closer and closer cowered the hag-like night.
A wolf-hound would have been a welcome sound,
   And there was none in all that stricken land;
Yet with such silence, darkness, death around,
   Learned we to love as few can understand.
Spirit with spirit fused, and soul to soul,
There in the sullen shadow of the Pole.

VIII

What was that haunting horror of the night?
   Brave was she; buoyant, full of sunny cheer.
Why was her face so small, so strangely white?
   Then did I turn from her, heart-sick with fear;
Sought in my agony the outcast snows;
   Prayed in my pain to that insensate sky;
Grovelled and sobbed and cursed, and then arose;
   "Sunshine! O heart of gold! to die! to die!"

IX

She died on Christmas Day—it seems so sad
   That one you love should die on Christmas Day.
Head-bowed I knelt by her; O God! I had
   No tears to shed, no moan, no prayer to pray.
I heard her whisper: "Call me, will you, dear?
   They say Death parts, but I won't go away.

I will be with you in the cabin here;
  Oh, I will plead with God to let me stay!
Stay till the Night is gone, till Spring is nigh,
Till sunshine comes . . . be brave . . . I'm tired . . . good-
    bye. . . ."

X

For weeks, for months I had not seen the sun;
  The minatory dawns are leprous pale;
The felon days malinger one by one;
  How like a dream Life is! how vain! how stale!
I, too, am faint; that vampire-like disease
  Has fallen on me; weak and cold am I,
Hugging a tiny fire in fear I freeze:
  The cabin must be cold, and so I try
To bear the frost, the frost that fights decay,
The frost that keeps her beautiful alway.

XI

She lies within an icy vault;
It glitters like a cave of salt.
All marble-pure and angel-sweet
With candles at her head and feet,
Under an ermine robe she lies.
I kiss her hands, I kiss her eyes:
"Come back, come back, O Love, I pray,

Into this house, this house of clay!
Answer my kisses soft and warm;
Nestle again within my arm.
Come! for I know that you are near;
Open your eyes and look, my dear.
Just for a moment break the mesh;
Back from the spirit leap to flesh.
Weary I wait; the night is black;
Love of my life, come back, come back!"

XII

Last night maybe I was a little mad,
　　For as I prayed despairful by her side,
Such a strange, antic visioning I had:
　　Lo! it did seem *her eyes were open wide.*
Surely I must have dreamed!   I stared once more . . .
　　No, 'twas a candle's trick, a shadow cast.
There were her lashes locking as before.
　　(Oh, but it filled me with a joy so vast!)
No, 'twas a freak, a fancy of the brain.
　　(Oh, but to-night I'll try again, again!)

XIII

It was no dream; now do I know that Love
　　Leapt from the starry battlements of Death;
For in my vigil as I bent above,

Calling her name with eager, burning breath,
Sudden there came a change; again I saw
    The radiance of the rose-leaf stain her cheek;
Rivers of rapture thrilled in sunny thaw;
    Cleft were her coral lips as if to speak;
Curved were her tender arms as if to cling,
    Open the flower-like eyes of lucent blue,
Looking at me with love so pitying
    That I could fancy Heaven shining through.
"Sunshine," I faltered, "stay with me, oh, stay!"
    Yet ere I finished, in a moment's flight,
There in her angel purity she lay—
    Ah! but I know she'll come again to-night.
Even as radiant sword leaps from the sheath,
Soul from the body leaps—we call it Death.

XIV

Even as this line I write,
    Do I know that she is near;
Happy am I, every night
    Comes she back to bid me cheer;
Kissing her, I hold her fast;
Win her into life at last.

Did I dream that yesterday
    On yon mountain ridge a glow
Soft as moonstone paled away,

Leaving less forlorn the snow?
Could it be the sun? Oh, fain
Would I see the sun again!

Oh, to see a coral dawn
    Gladden to a crocus glow!
Day's a spectre dim and wan,
    Dancing on the furtive snow;
Night's a cloud upon my brain:
Oh, to see the sun again!

You who find us in this place,
    Have you pity in your breast;
Let us in our last embrace
    Under earth sun-hallowed rest.
Night's a claw upon my brain:
Oh, to see the sun again!

XV

The Sun! at last the Sun! I write these lines,
    Here on my knees, with feeble, fumbling hand;
Look! in yon mountain cleft a radiance shines.
    Gleam of a primrose—see it thrill, expand,
Grow glorious. Dear God be praised! it streams
    Into the cabin in a gush of gold.
Look! there she stands, the angel of my dreams,

All in the radiant shimmer aureoled;
First as I saw her from my bed of pain;
  First as I loved her when the darkness passed.
Now do I know that Life is not in vain;
  Now do I know God cares, at last, at last!
Light outlives dark, joy grief, and Love's the sum:
Heart of my heart! Sunshine! I come . . . I come . . .

THE IDEALIST

Oh, you who have daring deeds to tell!
And you who have felt Ambition's spell!
Have you heard of the louse who longed to dwell
   In the golden hair of a queen?
He sighed all day and he sighed all night,
And no one could understand it quite,
For the head of a slut is a louse's delight,
   But he pined for the head of a queen.

So he left his kinsfolk in merry play,
And off by his lonesome he stole away,
From the home of his youth so bright and gay,
   And gloriously unclean.
And at last he came to the palace gate,
And he made his way in a manner straight
(For a louse may go where a man must wait)
   To the tiring-room of the queen.

The queen she spake to her tiring-maid:
"There's something the matter, I'm afraid.

To-night ere for sleep my hair ye braid,
    Just see what may be seen."
And lo, when they combed that shining hair,
They found him alone in his glory there,
And he cried: "I die, but I do not care,
    For I've lived in the head of a queen!"

ATHABASKA DICK

When the boys come out from Lac Labiche in the lure of the
   early Spring,
   To take the pay of the "Hudson's Bay," as their fathers did
      before,
They are all aglee for the jamboree, and they make the
   Landing ring
   With a whoop and a whirl, and a "Grab your girl," and a rip
      and a skip and a roar.
For the spree of Spring is a sacred thing, and the boys must
   have their fun;
   Packer and tracker and half-breed Cree, from the boat to
      the bar they leap;
And then when the long flotilla goes, and the last of their
   pay is done,
   The boys from the bank of Lac Labiche swing to the
      heavy sweep.
And oh, how they sigh! and their throats are dry, and sorry
   are they and sick:
Yet there's none so cursed with a lime-kiln thirst as that
   Athabaska Dick.

He was long and slim and lean of limb, but strong as a
   stripling bear;

And by the right of his skill and might he guided the Long
    Brigade.
All water-wise were his laughing eyes, and he steered with a
    careless care,
    And he shunned the shock of foam and rock, till they came
      to the Big Cascade.
And here they must make the long *portage*, and the boys
    sweat in the sun;
    And they heft and pack, and they haul and track, and each
      must do his trick;
But their thoughts are far in the Landing bar, where the
    founts of nectar run:
    And no man thinks of such gorgeous drinks as that Athabaska
      Dick.

'Twas the close of day, and his long boat lay just over the
    Big Cascade,
    When there came to him one Jack-pot Jim, with a wild
      light in his eye;
And he softly laughed, and he led Dick aft, all eager, yet half
    afraid,
    And snugly stowed in his coat he showed a pilfered flask
      of "rye."
And in haste he slipped, or in fear he tripped, but—Dick in
    warning roared—
    And there rang a yell, and it befell that Jim was overboard.

Oh, I heard a splash, and quick as a flash I knew he could
    not swim.

I saw him whirl in the river swirl, and thresh his arms
about.
In a queer, strained way I heard Dick say: "I'm going after
him,"
Throw off his coat, leap down the boat—and then I gave
a shout:
"Boys, grab him, quick! You're crazy, Dick: Far better
one than two!
Hell, man! You know you've got no show! It's sure and
certain death . . ."
And there we hung, and there we clung, with beef and brawn
and thew,
And sinews cracked and joints were racked, and panting
came our breath;
And there we swayed and there we prayed, still strength and
hope were spent—
Then Dick, he threw us off like rats and after Jim he went.

With a mighty urge amid the surge of river-rage he leapt,
And gripped his mate and desperate he fought to gain the
shore;
With teeth agleam he bucked the stream, yet swift and sure
he swept
To meet the mighty cataract that waited all aroar.
And there we stood like carven wood, our faces sickly white,
And watched him as he beat the foam, and inch by inch
he lost;

And nearer, nearer drew the fall, and fiercer grew the fight,
  Till on the very cascade crest a last farewell he tossed.
Then down and down and down they plunged into that pit
      of dread;
And mad we tore along the shore to claim our bitter dead.

And from that hell of frenzied foam, that crashed and fumed
      and boiled,
  Two little bodies bubbled up, and they were heedless then;
And oh, they lay like senseless clay! and bitter hard we toiled,
  Yet never, never gleam of hope, and we were weary men.
And moments mounted into hours, and black was our despair;
  And faint were we, and we were fain to give them up as
      dead,
When suddenly I thrilled with hope: "Back, boys! and give
      him air;
  I feel the flutter of his heart . . ." And, as the word I said,
Dick gave a sigh, and gazed around, and saw our breathless
      band;
  And saw the sky's blue floor above, all strewn with golden
      fleece;
And saw his comrade Jack-pot Jim, and touched him with his
      hand;
  And then there came into his eyes a look of perfect peace.
And as there, at his very feet, the thwarted river raved,
I heard him murmur low and deep: "Thank God! the *whiskey's*
      saved."

CHEER

It's a mighty good world, so it is, dear lass,
  When even the worst is said.
There's a smile and a tear, a sigh and a cheer,
  But better be living than dead;
A joy and a pain, a loss and a gain;
  There's honey and maybe some gall:
Yet still I declare, foul weather or fair,
  It's a mighty good world after all.

For look, lass! at night when I break from the fight,
  My Kingdom's awaiting for me;
There's comfort and rest, and the warmth of your breast,
  And little ones climbing my knee.
There's fire-light and song—Oh, the world may be wrong,
  Its empires may topple and fall:
My home is my care—if gladness be there,
  It's a mighty good world after all.

O heart of pure gold! I have made you a fold,
  It's sheltered, sun-fondled and warm.

236

O little ones, rest! I have fashioned a nest;
  Sleep on! you are safe from the storm.
For there's no foe like fear, and there's no friend like cheer,
  And sunshine will flash at our call;
So crown Love as King, and let us all sing—
  "It's a mighty good world after all."

THE RETURN

THEY turned him loose; he bowed his head,
  A felon, bent and grey.
His face was even as the Dead,
  He had no word to say.

He sought the home of his old love,
  To look on her once more;
And where her roses breathed above,
  He cowered beside the door.

She sat there in the shining room;
  Her hair was silver grey.
He stared and stared from out the gloom;
  He turned to go away.

Her roses rustled overhead.
  She saw, with sudden start.
"I knew that you would come," she said,
  And held him to her heart.

Her face was rapt and angel-sweet;
She touched his hair of grey;

*   *   *   *   *

But he, sob-shaken, at her feet,
Could only pray and pray.

THE JUNIOR GOD

Гне Junior God looked from his place
  In the conning-towers of heaven,
And he saw the world through the span of space
  Like a giant golf-ball driven.
And because he was bored, as some gods are,
  With high celestial mirth,
He clutched the reins of a shooting star,
  And he steered it down to earth.

The Junior God, 'mid leaf and bud,
  Passed on with a weary air,
Till lo! he came to a pool of mud,
  And some hogs were rolling there.
Then in he plunged with gleeful cries,
  And down he lay supine;
For they had no mud in paradise,
  And they likewise had no swine.

The Junior God forgot himself;
  He squelched mud through his toes;
With the careless joy of a wanton boy,
  His reckless laughter rose.

Till, tired at last, in a brook close by,
   He washed off every stain;
Then softly up to the radiant sky
   He rose, a god again.

The Junior God now heads the roll
   In the list of heaven's peers;
He sits in the House of High Control,
   And he regulates the spheres.
Yet does he wonder, do you suppose,
   If, even in gods divine,
The best and wisest may not be those
   Who have wallowed awhile with the swine?

THE NOSTOMANIAC

On the ragged edge of the world I'll roam,
And the home of the wolf shall be my home,
And a bunch of bones on the boundless snows
The end of my trail . . . who knows, who knows!

I'm dreaming to-night in the fire-glow, alone in my study tower,
   My books battalioned around me, my Kipling flat on my
      knee;
But I'm not in the mood for reading, I haven't moved for an
      hour;
   Body and brain I'm weary, weary the heart of me;
Weary of crushing a longing it's little I understand,
   For I thought that my trail was ended, I thought I had
      earned my rest;
But oh, its stronger than life is, the call of the hearthless land!
   And I turn to the North in my trouble, as a child to the
      mother-breast.

Here in my den it's quiet; the sea-wind taps on the pane;
   There's comfort and ease and plenty, the smile of the
      South is sweet.

All that a man might long for, fight for and seek in vain,
   Pictures and books and music, pleasure my last retreat.
Peace! I thought I had gained it, I swore that my tale was told;
   By my hair that is grey I swore it, by my eyes that are
      slow to see;
Yet what does it all avail me? to-night, to-night, as of old,
   Out of the dark I hear it—the Northland calling to me.

And I'm daring a rampageous river that runs the devil knows
      where;
   My hand is athrill on the paddle, the birch-bark bounds
      like a bird.
Hark to the rumble of rapids!   Here in my morris chair,
   Eager and tense I'm straining—isn't it most absurd?
Now in the churn and the lather, foam that hisses and stings,
   Leap I, keyed for the struggle, fury and fume and roar;
Rocks are spitting like hell-cats—Oh, it's a sport for kings,
   Life on a twist of the paddle . . . there's my "Kim" on the
      floor.

How I thrill and I vision!   Then my camp of a night;
   Red and gold of the fire-glow, net afloat in the stream;
Scent of the pines and silence, little "pal" pipe alight,
   Body a-purr with pleasure, sleep untroubled of dream:
Banquet of paystreak bacon! moment of joy divine,
   When the bannock is hot and gluey, and the teapot's nearing
      the boil!

I

Never was wolf so hungry, stomach cleaving to spine . .
 Ha! there's my servant calling, says that dinner will spoil.

What do I want with dinner? Can I eat any more?
 Can I sleep as I used to? . . . Oh, I abhor this life!
Give me the Great Uncertain, the Barren Land for a floor,
 The Milky Way for a roof-beam, splendour and space and
  strife:
Something to fight and die for—the limpid Lake of the Bear,
 The Empire of Empty Bellies, the dunes where the Dogribs
  dwell;
Big things, real things, live things . . . here in my morris
  chair,
 How I ache for the Northland! "Dinner and servants"—
  Hell!

Am I too old, I wonder? Can I take one trip more?
 Go to the granite-ribbed valleys, flooded with sunset wine,
Peaks that pierce the aurora, rivers I must explore,
 Lakes of a thousand islands, millioning hordes of the Pine?
Do they miss me, I wonder, valley and peak and plain?
 Whispering each to the other: "Many a moon has passed . . .
Where has he gone, our lover? Will he come back again?
 Star with his fires our tundra, leave us his bones at last?"

Yes, I'll go back to the Northland, back to the way of the bear,
 Back to the muskeg and mountain, back to the ice-leaguered
  sea.

Old am I! What does it matter? Nothing I would not dare;
  Give me a trail to conquer—Oh, it is "meat" to me!
I will go back to the Northland, feeble and blind and lame;
  Sup with the sunny-eyed Husky, eat moose-nose with the Cree;
Play with the Yellow-knife bastards, boasting my blood and
    my name:
    I will go back to the Northland, for the Northland is calling
      to me.

Then give to me paddle and whiplash, and give to me tumpline
      and gun;
  Give to me salt and tobacco, flour and a gunny of tea;
Take me up over the Circle, under the flamboyant sun;
  Turn me foot-loose like a savage—that is the finish of me.
I know the trail I am seeking, it's up by the Lake of the Bear;
  It's down by the Arctic Barrens, it's over to Hudson's Bay;
Maybe I'll get there—maybe: death is set by a hair . . .
    Hark! it's the Northland calling! now must I go away . . .

    Go to the Wild that waits for me;
    Go where the moose and the musk-ox be;
    Go to the wolf and the secret snows;
    Go to my fate . . . who knows, who knows!

AMBITION

THEY brought the mighty chief to town;
　　They showed him strange, unwonted sights;
Yet as he wandered up and down,
　　He seemed to scorn their vain delights.
His face was grim, his eye lacked fire,
　　As one who mourns a glory dead;
And when they sought his heart's desire:
　　"Me like-um tooth same gold," he said.

A dental place they quickly found,
　　He neither moaned nor moved his head.
They pulled his teeth so white and sound;
　　They put in teeth of gold instead.
Oh, never saw I man so gay,
　　His very being seemed to swell:
"Ha, ha!" he cried, "Now Injun say
　　Me heap big chief, *me look like hell!*"

TO SUNNYDALE

There lies the trail to Sunnydale,
  Amid the lure of laughter.
Oh, how can we unhappy be
  Beneath its leafy rafter!
Each perfect hour is like a flower,
  Each day is like a posy.
How can you say the skies are grey?
  You're wrong, my friend, they're rosy.

With right good will let's climb the hill,
  And leave behind all sorrow.
Oh, we'll be gay! a bright to-day
  Will make a bright to-morrow.
Oh, we'll be strong! the way is long
  That never has a turning;
The hill is high, but there's the sky,
  And how the West is burning!

And if through chance of circumstance
  We have to go bare-foot, sir,

247

We'll not repine—a friend of mine
   Has got no feet to boot, sir.
This Happiness a habit is,
   And Life is what we make it:
See! there's the trail to Sunnydale!
   Up, friend! and let us take it.

THE BLIND AND THE DEAD

She lay like a saint on her copper couch;
  Like an angel asleep she lay,
In the stare of the ghoulish folks that slouch
  Past the Dead and sneak away.

Then came old Jules of the sightless gaze,
  Who begged in the streets for bread.
Each day he had come for a year of days,
  And groped his way to the Dead.

"What's the Devil's Harvest to-day?" he cried;
  "A wanton with eyes of blue!
I've known too many a such," he sighed;
  "Maybe I know this . . . mon Dieu!"

He raised the head of the heedless Dead;
  He fingered the frozen face. . . .
Then a deathly spell on the watchers fell—
  God! it was still, that place!

He raised the head of the careless Dead;
   He fumbled a vagrant curl;
And then with his sightless smile he said:
   "It's only my little girl."

"Dear, my dear, did they hurt you so!
   Come to your daddy's heart . . ."
Aye, and he held so tight, you know,
   They were hard to force apart.

No! Paris isn't always gay;
   And the morgue has its stories, too:
You are a writer of tales, you say—
   Then there is a tale for you.

THE ATAVIST

WHAT are you doing here, Tom Thorne, on the white top-knot
of the world,
    Where the wind has the cut of a naked knife and the stars
are rapier keen?
Hugging a smudgy willow fire, deep in a lynx robe curled;
    You that's a lord's own son, Tom Thorne—what does your
madness mean?

Go home, go home to your clubs, Tom Thorne! home to
your evening dress!
    Home to your place of power and pride, and the feast
that waits for you!
Why do you linger all alone in the splendid emptiness,
    Scouring the Land of the Little Sticks on the trail of the
caribou?

Why did you fall off the Earth, Tom Thorne, out of our
social ken?
    What did your deep damnation prove? What was your
dark despair?

251

Oh, with the width of a world between, and years to the
count of ten,
If they cut out your heart to-night, Tom Thorne, *her*
name would be graven there.

And you fled afar for the thing called Peace, and you thought
you would find it here,
In the purple tundras vastly spread, and the mountains
whitely piled;
It's a weary quest and a dreary quest, but I think that the end
is near;
For they say that the Lord has hidden it in the secret heart
of the Wild.

And you know that heart as few men know, and your eyes are
fey and deep,
With a "something lost" come welling back from the raw,
red dawn of life:
With woe and pain have you greatly lain, till out of abysmal
sleep
The soul of the Stone Age leaps in you, alert for the ancient
strife.

And if you came to our feast again, with its pomp and glee and
glow,
I think you would sit stone-still, Tom Thorne, and see in a
daze of dream

A mad sun goading to frenzied flame the glittering gems of the
  snow,
  And a monster musk-ox bulking black against the blood-red
  gleam.

I think you would see berg-battling shores, and stammer and
  halt and stare
  With a sudden sense of the frozen void, serene and vast and
  still;
And the aching gleam and the hush of dream, and the track
  of a great white bear,
  And the primal lust that surged in you as you sprang to
  make your kill.

I think you would hear the bull-moose call, and the glutted
  river roar,
  And spy the hosts of the caribou shadow the shining plain;
And feel the pulse of the silences, and stand elate once more
  On the verge of the yawning vastitudes that call to you in
  vain.

For I think you are one with the stars and the sun, and the
  wind and the wave and the dew;
  And the peaks untrod that yearn to God and the valleys
  undefiled;

Men soar with wings, and they bridle kings, but what is it all
to you,
  Wise in the ways of the wilderness, and strong with the
  strength of the Wild?

You have spent your life, you have waged your strife where
never we play a part;
  You have held the throne of the Great Unknown, you have
  ruled a kingdom vast:

*   *   *   *   *   *

*But to-night there's a strange, new trail for you, and you go,
O weary heart!*
  *To the peace and rest of the Great Unguessed . . . at last,
  Tom Thorne, at last.*

THE SCEPTIC

My Father Christmas passed away
  When I was barely seven.
At twenty-one, alack a-day,
  I lost my hope of heaven.

Yet not in either lies the curse:
  The hell of it's because
I don't know which loss hurt the worse—
  My God or Santa Claus.

THE ROVER

OH, how good it is to be
Foot-loose and heart-free!
Just my dog and pipe and I, underneath the vast sky;
Trail to try and goal to win, white road and cool inn;
Fields to lure a lad afar, clear spring and still star;
Lilting feet that never tire, green dingle, faggot fire;
None to hurry, none to hold, heather hill and hushed fold;
Nature like a picture-book, laughing leaf and bright brook;
Every day a jewel bright, set serenely in the night;
Every night a holy shrine, radiant for a day divine.
Weathered cheek and kindly eye, let the wanderer go by.
Woman-love and wistful heart, let the gipsy one depart.
For the farness and the road are his glory and his goad.
Oh, the lilt of youth and Spring! Eyes laugh and lips sing.
Yea, but it is good to be
Foot-loose and heart-free!

II

Yet how good it is to come
Home at last, home, home!
On the clover swings the bee, overhead's the hale tree.
Sky of turquoise gleams through, yonder glints the lake's blue.
In a hammock let's swing, weary of wandering;
Tired of wild, uncertain lands, strange faces, faint hands.
Has the wondrous world gone cold? Am I growing old, old?
Grey and weary . . . let me dream, glide on the tranquil stream.
Oh, what joyous days I've had, full, fervid, gay, glad!
Yet there comes a subtle change, let the stripling rove, range.
From sweet roving comes sweet rest, after all, home's best.
And if there's a little bit of woman-love with it,
I will count my life content, God-blest and well spent . . .

Oh, but it is good to be
Foot-loose and heart-free!
Yet how good it is to come
Home at last, home, home!

BARB-WIRE BILL

At dawn of day the white land lay all gruesome-like and grim,
When Bill McGee he says to me: "We've *got* to do it, Jim.
We've got to make Fort Liard quick. I know the river's bad,
But, oh! the little woman's sick . . . why! don't you savvy, lad?"
And me! Well, yes, I must confess it wasn't hard to see
Their little family group of two would soon be one of three.
And so I answered, careless-like: "Why, Bill! you don't suppose
I'm scared of that there 'babbling brook'? Whatever you say —goes."

A real live man was Barb-wire Bill, with insides copper-lined;
For "barb-wire" was the brand of "hooch" to which he most inclined.
They knew him far; his igloos are on Kittiegazuit strand.
They knew him well, the tribes who dwell within the Barren Land.
From Koyokuk to Kuskoquim his fame was everywhere;
And he did love, all life above, that little Julie Claire,
The lithe, white slave-girl he had bought for seven hundred skins.
And taken to his wickiup to make his moccasins.

258

We crawled down to the river bank, and feeble folk were we,
That Julie Claire from God-knows-where, and Barb-wire Bill
and me.
From shore to shore we heard the roar the heaving ice-floes
make,
And loud we laughed, and launched our raft, and followed in
their wake.
The river swept and seethed and leapt, and caught us in its
stride;
And on we hurled amid a world that crashed on every side.
With sullen din the banks caved in; the shore-ice lanced the
stream;
The naked floes like spooks arose, all jigging and agleam.
Black anchor-ice of strange device shot upward from its bed,
As night and day we cleft our way, and arrow-like we sped.

But "Faster still!" cried Barb-wire Bill, and looked the live-long
day
In dull despair at Julie Claire, where white like death she lay,
And sometimes he would seem to pray and sometimes seem to
curse,
And bent above with eyes of love, yet ever she grew worse.
And as we plunged and leapt and lunged, her face was plucked
with pain,
And I could feel his nerves of steel a-quiver at the strain.
And in the night he gripped me tight as I lay fast asleep;
The river's kicking like a steer . . . run out the forward sweep!

That's Hell-gate Canyon right ahead; I know of old its roar,
And . . . I'll be damned! *the ice is jammed!* We've got to
make the shore."

With one wild leap I gripped the sweep.   The night was black
as sin.
The float-ice crashed and ripped and smashed, and stunned us
with its din.
And near and near, and clear and clear I heard the canyon
boom;
And swift and strong we swept along to meet our awful doom.
And as with dread I glimpsed ahead the death that waited
there,
My only thought was of the girl, the little Julie Claire;
And so, like demon mad with fear, I panted at the oar,
And foot by foot, and inch by inch, we worked the raft ashore.

The bank was staked with grinding ice, and as we scraped and
crashed,
I only knew one thing to do, and through my mind it flashed:
Yet while I groped to find the rope, I heard Bill's savage cry:
"That's my job, lad!   It's me that jumps.   I'll snub this raft or
die!"
I saw him leap, I saw him creep, I saw him gain the land;
I saw him crawl, I saw him fall, then run with rope in hand.
And then the darkness gulped him up, and down we dashed
once more,

And nearer, nearer drew the jam, and thunder-like its roar.
Oh, God! all's lost . . . from Julie Claire there came a wail of
    pain,
And then—the rope grew sudden taut, and quivered at the
    strain;
It slacked and slipped, it whined and gripped, and oh, I held
    my breath!
And there we hung and there we swung right in the jaws of
    death.

A little strand of hempen rope, and how I watched it there,
With all around a hell of sound, and darkness and despair;
A little strand of hempen rope, I watched it all alone,
And somewhere in the dark behind I heard a woman moan;
And somewhere in the dark ahead I heard a man cry out,
Then silence, silence, silence fell, and mocked my hollow
    shout.
And yet once more from out the shore I heard that cry of pain,
A moan of mortal agony, then all was still again.

That night was hell with all the frills, and when the dawn
    broke dim,
I saw a lean and level land, but never sign of him,
I saw a flat and frozen shore of hideous device,
I saw a long-drawn strand of rope that vanished through the
    ice.
And on that treeless, rockless shore I found my partner—dead.
No place was there to snub the raft, so—*he had served instead!*

And with the rope lashed round his waist, in last defiant
    fight,
He'd thrown himself beneath the ice, that closed and gripped
    him tight;
And there he'd held us back from death, as fast in death he
    lay . . .
Say, boy! I'm not the pious brand, but--I just tried to pray.

And then I looked to Julie Clare, and sore abashed was I,
For from the robes that covered her *I heard—a baby cry*. . . .

*   *   *   *   *   *

Thus was Love conqueror of death, and life for life was given;
And though no saint on earth, d'ye think Bill's squared hisself
    with Heaven?

" ? "

IF you had the choice of two women to wed,
  (Though of course the idea is quite absurd),
And the first from her heels to her dainty head
  Was charming in every sense of the word:
And yet in the past (I grieve to state)
She never had been exactly "straight."

And the second—she was beyond all cavil,
  A model of virtue, I must confess;
And yet, alas! she was dull as the devil,
  And rather a dowd in the way of dress;
Though what she was lacking in wit and beauty
She more than made up for in "sense of duty."

Now, suppose you must wed, and make no blunder,
  And either would love you, and let you win her—
Which of the two would you choose, I wonder,
  The stolid saint or the sparkling sinner?

JUST THINK!

Just think! some night the stars will gleam
    Upon a cold, grey stone,
And trace a name with silver beam,
    And lo! 'twill be your own.

That night is speeding on to greet
    Your epitaphic rhyme.
Your life is but a little beat
    Within the heart of Time.

A little gain, a little pain,
    A laugh, lest you may moan!
A little blame, a little fame,
    A star-gleam on a stone.

THE LUNGER

Jack would laugh an' joke all day:
Never saw a lad so gay;
Singin' like a medder lark,
Loaded to the Plimsoll mark
With God's sunshine was that boy;
Had a strangle-holt on Joy.
Held his head 'way up in air,
Left no callin'-cards on Care;
Breezy, buoyant, brave and true;
Sent his sunshine out to you;
Cheerfulest when clouds were black—
    Happy Jack! Oh, Happy Jack!

Sittin' in my shack alone
I could hear him in his own,
Singin' far into the night,
Till it didn't seem just right
One man should corral the fun,
Live his life so in the sun;
Didn't seem quite natural

Not to have a grouch at all;
Not a trouble, not a lack—
    Happy Jack! Oh, Happy Jack!

He was plumbful of good cheer
Till he struck that low-down year;
Got so thin, so little to him,
You could most see daylight through him.
Never was his eye so bright,
Never was his cheek so white.
Seemed as if somethin' was wrong,
Sort o' quaver in his song.
Same old smile, same hearty voice:
"Bless you, boys! let's all rejoice!"
But old Doctor shook his head;
"Half a lung" was all he said.
Yet that half was surely right,
For I heard him every night,
Singin', singin' in his shack—
    Happy Jack! Oh, Happy Jack!

Then one day a letter came
Endin' with a female name;
Seemed to get him in the neck,
Sort o' pile-driver effect;
Paled his lip and plucked his breath,
Left him starin' still as death.

Somethin' had gone awful wrong,
Yet that night he sang his song.
Oh, but it was good to hear!
For there clutched my heart a fear,
So that I quaked listenin'
Every night to hear him sing.
But each day he laughed with me,
An' his smile was full of glee.
Nothin' seemed to set him back—
   Happy Jack! Oh, Happy Jack!

Then oné night the singin' stopped.
Seemed as if my heart just flopped;
For I'd learned to love the boy
With his gilt-edged line of joy,
With his glorious gift of bluff,
With his splendid fightin' stuff.
Sing on, lad, and play the game!
O dear God! . . . no singin' came,
But there surged to me instead—
Silence, silence, deep and dread;
Till I shuddered, tried to pray,
Said: "He's maybe gone away."
Oh, yes, he had gone away,
Gone forever and a day.

But he'd left behind him there,
In his cabin, pinched and bare,

His poor body, skin and bone,
His sharp face, cold as a stone,
An' his stiffened fingers pressed
Somethin' bright upon his breast:
Locket with a silken curl,
Poor, sweet portrait of a girl.
Yet I reckon at the last
How defiant-like he passed;
For there sat upon his lips
Smile that death could not eclipse;
An' within his eyes lived still
Joy that dyin' could not kill.

An' now when the nights are long,
How I miss his cheery song!
How I sigh an' wish him back!
  Happy Jack! Oh, Happy Jack!

THE MOUNTAIN AND THE LAKE

I KNOW a mountain thrilling to the stars,
  Peerless and pure, and pinnacled with snow;
Glimpsing the golden dawn o'er coral bars,
  Flaunting the vanisht sunset's garnet glow;
Proudly patrician, passionless, serene;
  Soaring in silvered steeps where cloud-surfs break;
Virgin and vestal—Oh, a very Queen!
  And at her feet there dreams a quiet lake.

My lake adores my mountain—well I know,
  For I have watched it from its dawn-dream start,
Stilling its mirror to her splendid snow,
  Framing her image in its trembling heart;
Glassing her graciousness of greening wood.
  Kissing her throne, melodiously mad,
Thrilling responsive to her every mood,
  Gloomed with her sadness, gay when she is glad.

My lake has dreamed and loved since time was born;
  Will love and dream till time shall cease to be;

Gazing to Her in worship half forlorn,
  Who looks towards the stars and will not see—
My peerless mountain, splendid in her scorn. . . .
  Alas! poor little lake! Alas! poor me!

THE HEADLINER AND THE BREADLINER

Moko, the Educated Ape, is here,
  The pet of vaudeville, so the posters say,
  And every night the gaping people pay
To see him in his panoply appear;
To see him pad his paunch with dainty cheer,
  Puff his perfecto, swill champagne, and sway
  Just like a gentleman, yet all in play,
Then bow himself off stage with brutish leer.

And as to-night, with noble knowledge crammed,
  I 'mid this human compost take my place,
I, once a poet, now so dead and damned,
  The woeful tears half freezing on my face:
"O God!" I cry, "let me but take his shape,
  Moko's the Blest, the Educated Ape."

DEATH IN THE ARCTIC

I

I took the clock down from the shelf;
"At eight," said I, "I shoot myself,"
It lacked a *minute* of the hour,
And as I waited all a-cower,
A skinful of black, boding pain,
Bits of my life came back again. . . .

"Mother, there's nothing more to eat—
Why don't you go out on the street?
Always you sit and cry and cry;
Here at my play I wonder why.
Mother, when you dress up at night,
Red are your cheeks, your eyes are bright;
Twining a riband in your hair,
Kissing good-bye you go down-stair
Then I'm as lonely as can be.
Oh, how I wish you were with me!
Yet when you go out on the street,
Mother, there's always lots to eat." . . .

II

For days the igloo has been dark;
But now the rag wick sends a spark
That glitters in the icy air,
And wakes frost sapphires everywhere;
Bright, bitter flames, that adder-like
Dart here and there, yet fear to strike
The gruesome gloom wherein *they* lie,
My comrades, oh, so keen to die!
And I, the last—well, here I wait
The clock to strike the hour of eight. . . .

"Boy, it is bitter to be hurled
Nameless and naked on the world;
Frozen by night and starved by day,
Curses and kicks and clouts your pay.
But you must fight!   Boy, look on me!
Anarch of all earth-misery;
Beggar and tramp and shameless sot;
Emblem of ill, in rags that rot.
Would you be foul and base as I?
Oh, it is better far to die!
Swear to me now you'll fight and fight,
Boy, or I'll kill you here to-night." . . .

III

Curse this silence soft and black!
Sting, little light, the shadows back!

Dance, little flame with freakish glee!
Twinkle with brilliant mockery!
Glitter on ice-robed roof and floor!
Jewel the bear-skin of the door!
Gleam in my beard, illume my breath,
Blanch the clock face that times my death!
But do not pierce that murk so deep,
Where in their sleeping-bags they sleep!
But do not linger where they lie,
They who had all the luck to die! . . .

"There is nothing more to say;
Let us part and go our way.
Since it seems we can't agree,
I will go across the sea.
Proud of heart and strong am I;
Not for woman will I sigh;
Hold my head up gay and glad;
You can find another lad." . . .

IV

Above the igloo piteous flies
Our frayed flag to the frozen skies.
Oh, would you know how earth can be
A hell—go north of Eighty-three!
Go, scan the snows day after day,
And hope for help, and pray and pray;
Have seal-hide and sea-lice to eat;

Melt water with your body's heat;
Sleep all the fell, black winter through
Beside the dear, dead men you knew.
(The walrus blubber flares and gleams—
O God! how long a minute seems!) . . .

"Mary, many a day has passed,
    Since that morn of hot-head youth.
Come I back at last, at last,
    Crushed with knowing of the truth;
How through bitter, barren years
    You loved me, and me alone;
Waited, wearied, wept your tears—
    Oh, could I atone, atone,
I would pay a million-fold!
    Pay you for the love you gave.
Mary, look down as of old—
    I am kneeling by your grave." . . .

v

Olaf, the Blonde, was the first to go;
Bitten his eyes were by the snow;
Sightless and sealed his eyes of blue,
So that he died before I knew.
Here in these poor weak arms he died:
"Wolves will not get you, lad," I lied;
"For I will watch till Spring come round;

K

Slumber you shall beneath the ground."
Oh, how I lied! I scarce can wait:
Strike, little clock, the hour of eight! . . .

"Comrade, can you blame me quite?
The horror of the long, long night
Is on me, and I've borne with pain
So long, and hoped for help in vain.
So frail am I, and blind and dazed;
With scurvy sick, with silence crazed.
Beneath the Arctic's heel of hate,
Avid for Death I wait, I wait.
Oh, if I falter, fail to fight,
Can you, dear comrade, blame me quite?"

VI

Big Eric gave up months ago.
But seldom do men suffer so.
His feet sloughed off, his fingers died,
His hands shrunk up and mummified.
I had to feed him like a child;
Yet he was valiant, joked and smiled,
Talked of his wife and little one
(Thanks be to God that I have none),
Passed in the night without a moan,
Passed, and I'm here, alone, alone. . . .

"I've got to kill you, Dick.
  Your life for mine, you know.
Better to do it quick,
  A swift and sudden blow.
See! here's my hand to lick;
  A hug before you go—
God! but it makes me sick;
  Old dog, I love you so.
Forgive, forgive me, Dick—
  A swift and sudden blow."

VII

Often I start up in the dark,
  Thinking the sound of bells to hear.
Often I wake from sleep: "Oh, hark!
  Help . . . it is coming . . . near and near."
Blindly I reel toward the door;
  There the snow billows bleak and bare;
Blindly I seek my den once more,
  Silence and darkness and despair.
Oh, it is all a dreadful dream!
  Scurvy and cold and death and dearth;
I will awake to warmth and gleam,
  Silvery seas and greening earth.
Life is a dream, its wakening,
Death, gentle shadow of God's wing. . . .

"Tick, little clock, my life away!
Even a second seems a day.
Even a minute seems a year,
Peopled with ghosts that press and peer
Into my face so charnel white,
Lit by the devilish, dancing light.
Tick, little clock! mete out my fate:
Tortured and tense I wait, I wait." . . .

VIII

Oh, I have sworn! the hour is nigh:
When it strikes eight I die, I die.
Raise up the gun—it stings my brow—
When it strikes eight . . . all ready . . . *now*—

* * * * * *

Down from my hand the weapon dropped;
Wildly I stared . . .

THE CLOCK HAD STOPPED.

IX

Phantoms and fears and ghosts have gone.
 Peace seems to nestle in my brain.
Lo! the clock stopped, I'm living on;
 Heart-sick I was, and less than sane.

Yet do I scorn the thing I planned,
　　Hearing a voice: "O coward, fight!"
Then the clock stopped . . . whose was the hand?
　　Maybe 'twas God's—ah, well, all's right.
Heap on me darkness, fold on fold!
　　Pain! wrench and rack me!　What care I?
Leap on me, hunger, thirst and cold!
　　I will await my time to die;
Looking to Heaven that shines above;
Looking to God, and love . . . and love.

x

Hark! what is that?　Bells, dogs again!
　　Is it a dream?　I sob and cry.
See! the door opens, fur-clad men
　　Rush to my rescue; frail am I;
Feeble and dying, dazed and glad.
　　There is the pistol where it dropped.
"Boys, it was hard—but I'm not mad . . .
　　Look at the clock—it stopped, it stopped.
Carry me out.　The heavens smile.
　　See there's an arch of gold above.
Now, let me rest a little while—
　　Looking to God and love . . . and love."

DREAMS ARE BEST

I JUST think that dreams are best,
  Just to sit and fancy things;
Give your gold no acid test,
  Try not how your silver rings;
Fancy women pure and good,
  Fancy men upright and true:
Fortressed in your solitude,
  Let Life be a dream to you.

For I think that Thought is all;
  Truth's a minion of the mind;
Love's ideal comes at call;
  As ye seek so shall ye find.
But ye must not seek too far;
  Things are never what they seem:
Let a star be just a star,
  And a woman—just a dream.

O you Dreamers, proud and pure,
  You have gleaned the sweet of life!

Golden truths that shall endure
  Over pain and doubt and strife.
I would rather be a fool
  Living in my Paradise,
Than the leader of a school,
  Sadly sane and weary-wise.

O you Cynics with your sneers,
  Fallen brains and hearts of brass;
Tweak me by my foolish ears,
  Write me down a simple ass!
I'll believe the real "you"
  Is the "you" without a taint;
I'll believe each woman, too,
  But a slightly damaged saint.

Yes, I'll smoke my cigarette,
  Vestured in my garb of dreams,
And I'll borrow no regret;
  All is gold that golden gleams.
So I'll charm my solitude
  With the faith that Life is blest.
Brave and noble, bright and good . . .
  Oh, I think that dreams are best!

THE QUITTER

When you're lost in the Wild, and you're scared as a child,
   And Death looks you bang in the eye,
And you're sore as a boil, it's according to Hoyle
   To cock your revolver and . . . die.
But the Code of a Man says: "Fight all you can,"
   And self-dissolution is barred.
In hunger and woe, oh, it's easy to blow . . .
   It's the hell-served-for-breakfast that's hard.

"You're sick of the game!" Well, now, that's a shame.
   You're young and you're brave and you're bright.
"You've had a raw deal!" I know—but don't squeal,
   Buck up, do your damnedest, and fight.
It's the plugging away that will win you the day,
   So don't be a piker, old pard!
Just draw on your grit; it's so easy to quit:
   It's the keeping-your-chin-up that's hard.

It's easy to cry that you're beaten—and die;
   It's easy to crawfish and crawl;

But to fight and to fight when hope's out of sight—
  Why, that's the best game of them all!
And though you come out of each gruelling bout
  All broken and beaten and scarred,
Just .have one more try—it's dead easy to die.
  It's the keeping-on-living that's hard.

THE COW-JUICE CURE

THE clover was in blossom, an' the year was at the June,
When Flap-jack Billy hit the town, likewise O'Flynn's saloon.
The frost was on the fodder an' the wind was growin' keen,
When Billy got to seein' snakes in Sullivan's shebeen.

Then in meandered· Deep-hole Dan, once comrade of the cup:
"Oh, Billy, for the love of Mike, why don't ye sober up?
I've got the gorgus recipay, 'tis smooth an' slick as silk—
Jest quit yer strangle-holt on hooch, an' irrigate with milk.
Lackteeal flooid is the lubrication you require;
Yer nervus frame-up's like a bunch of snarled piano wire.
You want to get it coated up with addypose tishoo,
So's it will work elastic-like, an' milk's the dope for you."

Well, Billy was complyable, an' in a month, it's strange,
That cow-juice seemed to oppyrate a most amazin' change.
"Call up the water-wagon, Dan, an' book my seat," sez he.
"'Tis mighty queer,' sez Deep-hole Dan, "'twas just the same
    with me."

284

They shanghaied little Tom O'Shane, they cached him safe
away.
An' though he objurgated some, they "cured" him night an'
day;
An' pretty soon there came the change amazin' to explain:
"I'll never take another drink," sez Timothy O'Shane.
They tried it out on Spike Muldoon, that toper of renown;
They put it over Grouch McGraw, the terror of the town.
They roped in "tanks" from far and near, an' every test was
sure,
An' like a flame there ran the fame of Deep-hole's Cow-juice
Cure.

"It's mighty queer," sez Deep-hole Dan, "I'm puzzled through
and through;
It's only milk from Riley's ranch, no other milk will do."
An' it jest happened on that night, with no predictive plan,
He left some milk from Riley's ranch a'settin' in a pan;
An' picture his amazement when he poured that milk next
day—
There in the bottom of the pan a dozen "colours" lay.

"Well, what d'ye know 'bout that?" sez Dan; "Gosh-ding my
. dasted eyes,
We've been an' had the Gold Cure, Bill, an' none of us was
wise!
The milk's free-millin', that's a cinch: there's colours everywhere.

Now, let us figger this thing out—how does the dust git there?
'Gold from the grass-roots down,' they say—why, Bill! we've got
    it cold—
Them cows what nibbles up the grass, jest nibbles up the
    gold.
We're blasted, bloomin' millionaires; dissemble an' lie low:
We'll follow them gold-bearin' cows, an' prospect where they
    go."

An' so it came to pass, fer weeks them miners might be found
A-sneakin' round on Riley's ranch, an' snipin' at the ground;
Till even Riley stops an' stares, an' presently allows:
"Them boys appear to take a mighty interest in cows."
An' night an' day they shadowed each auriferous bovine,
An' panned the grass-roots on their trail, yet nivver gold they
    seen.
An' all that season, secret-like, they worked an' nothin' found;
An' there was colours in the milk, but none was in the ground.
An' mighty desperate was they, an' down upon their luck,
When sudden, inspiration-like, the source of it they struck.
An' where d'ye think they traced it to? It grieves my heart to
    tell—
In the black sand at the bottom of that wicked milkman's *well*.

WHILE THE BANNOCK BAKES

Light up your pipe again, old chum, and sit awhile with me;
  I've got to watch the bannock bake—how restful is the air!
You'd little think that we were somewhere north of Sixty-three.
  Though where I don't exactly know, and don't precisely
    care.
The man-size mountains palisade us round on every side;
  The river is a-flop with fish, and ripples silver-clear;
The midnight sunshine brims yon cleft—we think it's the
    Divide;
  We'll get there in a month, maybe, or maybe in a year.

It doesn't matter, does it, pal? We're of that breed of men
  With whom the world of wine and cards and women dis-
    agree;
Your trouble was a roofless game of poker now and then,
  And "raising up my elbow," that's what got away with me.
We're merely "Undesirables," artistic more or less;
  My horny hands are Chopin-wise; you quote your Browning
    well;
And yet we're fooling round for gold in this damned wilder-
    ness:
  The joke is, if we found it, we would both go straight to hell.

Well, maybe we won't find it—and at least we've got the "life."
  We're both as brown as berries, and could wrestle with a
      bear:
(That bannock's raising nicely, pal; just jab it with your knife.)
  Fine specimens of manhood they would reckon us out there.
It's the tracking and the packing and the poling in the sun;
  It's the sleeping in the open, it's the rugged, unfaked food;
It's the snow-shoe and the paddle, and the camp-fire and the
      gun,
  And when I think of what I was, I know that it is good.

Just think of how we've poled all day up this strange little
      stream;
  Since life began no eye of man has seen this place before;
How fearless all the wild things are! the banks with goose-
      grass gleam,
  And there's a bronzy muskrat sitting sniffing at his door.
A mother duck with brood of ten comes squattering along;
  The tawny, white-winged ptarmigan are flying all about;
And in that swirly, golden pool, a restless, gleaming throng,
  The trout are waiting till we condescend to take them out.

Ah, yes, it's good! I'll bet that there's no doctor like the Wild:
  (Just turn that bannock over there; it's getting nicely brown):
I might be in my grave by now, forgotten and reviled,
  Or rotting like a sickly cur in some far, foreign town.
I might be that vile thing I was—it all seems like a dream;
  I owed a man a grudge one time that only life could pay;

And yet it's half-forgotten now—how petty these things seem!
  (But that's "another story," pal; I'll tell it you some day.)

How strange two "irresponsibles" should chum away up here;
  But round the Arctic Circle friends are few and far between.
We've shared the same camp-fire and tent for nigh on seven
      year,
  And never had a word that wasn't cheering and serene.
We've halved the toil and split the spoil, and borne each
      other's pack;
  By all the Wild's freemasonry we're brothers, tried and true;
We've swept on danger side by side, and fought it back to back,
  And you would die for me, old pal, and I would die for you.

Now there was that time I got lost in Rory Bory Land,
  (How quick the blizzards sweep on one across that Polar sea!)
You formed a rescue crew of One, and saw a frozen hand
  That stuck out of a drift of snow—and, partner, it was Me.
But I got even, did I not, that day the paddle broke?
  White water on the Coppermine—a rock—a split canoe—
Two fellows struggling in the foam (one couldn't swim a
      stroke):
  A half-drowned man I dragged ashore . . . and, partner, it
      was You.

         *   *   *   *   *   *

In Rory Borealis Land the winter's long and black;
  The silence seems a solid thing, shot through with wolfish
      woe;

And rowelled by the eager stars the skies vault vastly back,
    And man seems but a little mite in that weird-lit plateau.
Nothing to do but smoke and yarn of wild and mis-spent lives,
    Beside the camp-fire there we sat—what tales you told to me
Of love and hate, and chance and fate, and temporary wives!
    In Rory Borealis Land, beside the Arctic Sea.

One yarn you told me in those days I can remember still;
    It seemed as if I visioned it, so sharp you sketched it in;
Bellona was the name, I think; a coast town in Brazil,
    Where nobody did anything but serenade and sin.
I saw it all—the jewelled sea, the golden scythe of sand,
    The stately pillars of the palms, the feathery bamboo,
The red-roofed houses and the swart, sun-dominated land,
    The people ever children, and the heavens ever blue.

You told me of that girl of yours, that blossom of old Spain,
    All glamour, grace and witchery, all passion, verve and
        glow.
How maddening she must have been! You made me see her
    plain,
    There by our little camp-fire, in the silence and the snow.
You loved her and she loved you. She'd a husband too, I
    think;
    A doctor chap, you told me, whom she treated like a dog,
A white man living on the beach, a hopeless slave to
    drink—
    (Just turn that bannock over there, that's propped against the
    log).

That story seemed to strike me, pal—it happens every day:
  You had to go away awhile, then somehow it befell
The doctor chap discovered, gave her up, and went away;
  You came back, tired of her in time . . . there's nothing more
    to tell.
Hist! see those willows silvering where swamp and river meet!
  Just reach me up my rifle, quick; that's Mister Moose, I
    know—
There now, *I've got him dead to rights* . . . but, hell! we've lots
    to eat!
  I don't believe in taking life—we'll let the beggar go.

Heigh-ho! I'm tired; the bannock's cooked; it's time we both
    turned in.
  The morning mist is coral-kissed, the morning sky is gold.
The camp-fire's a confessional—what funny yarns we spin!
  It sort of made me think a bit, that story that you told.
The fig-leaf belt and Rory Bory are such odd extremes,
  Yet after all how very small this old world seems to be . . .
Yes, that was quite a yarn, old pal, and yet to me it seems
  You missed the point: the point is that the "doctor chap"
    . . . was *me*.

THE LOST MASTER

"AND when I come to die," he said,
    "Ye shall not lay me out in state,
Nor leave your laurels at my head,
    Nor cause your men of speech orate;
No monument your gift shall be,
    No column in the Hall of Fame;
But just this line ye grave for me:
    'He played the game.'"

So when his glorious task was done,
    It was not of his fame we thought;
It was not of his battles won,
    But of the pride with which he fought;
But of his zest, his ringing laugh,
    His trenchant scorn of praise or blame:
And so we graved his epitaph,
    "He played the game."

And so we, too, in humbler ways
    Went forth to fight the fight anew,

And heeding neither blame nor praise,
   We held the course he set us true.
And we, too, find the fighting sweet;
   And we, too, fight for fighting's sake;
And though we go down in defeat,
   And though our stormy hearts may break,
We will not do our Master shame:
We'll play the game, please God,
     We'll play the game.

LITTLE MOCCASINS

Come out, O Little Moccasins, and frolic on the snow!
  Come out, O tiny beaded feet, and twinkle in the light!
I'll play the old Red River reel, you used to love it so:
  Awake, O Little Moccasins, and dance for me to-night!

Your hair was all a gleamy gold, your eyes a cornflower blue;
  Your cheeks were pink as tinted shells, you stepped light as
    a fawn,
Your mouth was like a coral bud, with seed pearls peeping
    through;
  As gladdening as Spring you were, as radiant as dawn.

Come out, O Little Moccasins! I'll play so soft and low,
  The songs you loved, the old heart-songs that in my mem'ry
    ring;
O child, I want to hear you now beside the camp-fire glow!
  With all your heart a-throbbing in the simple words you
    sing.

For there was only you and I, and you were all to me;
  And round us were the barren lands, but little did we fear;

Of all God's happy, happy folks the happiest were we . . .
　(Oh, call her, poor old fiddle mine, and maybe she will hear!)

Your mother was a half-breed Cree, but you were white all
　　　through;
　And I your father was—but, well, that's neither here nor
　　　there;
I only know, my little Queen, that all my world was you,
　And now that world can end to-night, and I will never care.

For there's a tiny wooden cross that pricks up through the
　　　snow:
　(Poor little Moccasins! you're tired, and so you lie at rest.)
And there's a grey-haired, weary man beside the camp-fire
　　　glow:
　(O fiddle mine! the tears to-night are drumming on your
　　　breast.)

THE WANDERLUST

THE Wanderlust has lured me to the seven lonely seas,
  Has dumped me on the tailing-piles of dearth:
The Wanderlust has haled me from the morris chairs of ease,
  Has hurled me to the ends of all the earth.
How bitterly I've cursed it, oh, the Painted Desert knows,
  The wraithlike heights that hug the pallid plain,
The all-but-fluid silence—yet the longing grows and grows,
  And I've got to glut the Wanderlust again.

          Soldier, sailor in what a plight I've been!
          Tinker, tailor, oh, what a sight I've seen!
          And I'm hitting the trail in the morning, boys,
              And you won't see my heels for dust;
            For it's "all day" with you
            When you answer the cue
              Of the Wan-der-lust.

The Wanderlust has got me . . . by the belly-aching fire,
  By the fever and the freezing and the pain;
By the darkness that just drowns you, by the wail of home
    desire,

296

I've tried to break the spell of it—in vain.
Life might have been a feast for me, now there are only crumbs;
  In rags and tatters, beggar-wise I sit;
Yet there's no rest or peace for me, imperious it drums,
  The Wanderlust, and I must follow it.

  Highway, by-way, many a mile I've done;
  Rare way, fair way, many a height I've won;
  But I'm pulling my freight in the morning, boys,
    And it's over the hills or bust!
    For there's never a cure
    When you list to the lure
    Of the Wan-der-lust.

The Wanderlust has taught me . . . it has whispered to my
    heart
  Things all you stay-at-homes will never know.
The white man and the savage are but three short days apart,
  Three days of cursing, crawling, doubt and woe.
Then it's down to chewing muclucs, to the water you can *eat*,
  To fish you bolt with nose held in your hand.
When you get right down to cases, it's King Grub that rules
    the races,
  And the Wanderlust will help you understand.

  Haunting, taunting, that is the spell of it;
  Mocking, baulking, that is the hell of it;

But I'll shoulder my pack in the morning, boys,
  And I'm going because I must;
    For it's so-long to all
    When you answer the call
      Of the Wan-der-lust.

The Wanderlust has blest me . . . in a ragged blanket curled,
  I've watched the gulf of Heaven foam with stars;
I've walked with eyes wide open to the wonder of the world,
  I've seen God's flood of glory burst its bars.
I've seen the gold a-blinding in the riffles of the sky,
  Till I fancied me a bloated plutocrat;
But I'm freedom's happy bond-slave ,and I will be till I die,
  And I've got to thank the Wanderlust for that.

    Wild heart, child heart, all of the world your home.
    Glad heart, mad heart, what can you do but roam?
    Oh, I'll beat it once more in the morning, boys,
      With a pinch of tea and a crust;
        For you cannot deny
        When you hark to the cry
          Of the Wan-der-lust.

The Wanderlust will claim me at the finish for its own.
  I'll turn my back on men and face the Pole.
Beyond the Arctic outposts I will venture all alone;
  Some Never-never Land will be my goal.

Thank God! there's none will miss me, for I've been a bird of
      flight;
  And in my moccasins I'll take my call;
    For the Wanderlust has ruled me,
    And the Wanderlust has schooled me,
  And I'm ready for the darkest trail of all.

    Grim land, dim land, oh, how the vastness calls!
    Far land, star land, oh, how the stillness falls!
    For you never can tell if it's heaven or hell,
       And I'm taking the trail on trust;
     But I haven't a doubt
     That my soul will leap out
       On its Wan-der-lust.

THE TRAPPER'S CHRISTMAS EVE

It's mighty lonesome-like and drear.
  Above the Wild the moon rides high,
And shows up sharp and needle-clear
  The emptiness of earth and sky;
No happy homes with love aglow;
  No Santa Claus to make believe:
Just snow and snow, and then more snow;
  It's Christmas Eve, it's Christmas Eve.

And here am I where all things end,
  And Undesirables are hurled;
A poor old man without a friend,
  Forgot and dead to all the world;
Clean out of sight and out of mind. . . .
  Well, maybe it is better so;
We all in life our level find,
  And mine, I guess is pretty low.

Yet as I sit with pipe alight
  Beside the cabin-fire, it's queer

This mind of mine must take to-night
  The backward trail of fifty year.
The school-house and the Christmas tree;
  The children with their cheeks aglow;
Two bright blue eyes that smile on me . . .
  Just half a century ago.

Again (it's maybe forty years),
  With faith and trust almost divine,
These same blue eyes, abrim with tears,
  Through depths of love look into mine.
A parting, tender, soft and low,
  With arms that cling and lips that cleave—
Ah me! it's all so long ago,
  Yet seems so sweet this Christmas Eve.

Just thirty years ago again . . .
  We say a bitter, *last* good-bye;
Our lips are white with wrath and pain;
  Our little children cling and cry.
Whose was the fault? It matters not,
  For man and woman both deceive;
It's buried now and all forgot.
  Forgiven, too, this Christmas Eve.

And she (God pity me) is dead;
  Our children men and women grown.

I like to think that they are wed,
   With little children of their own,
That crowd around their Christmas tree . . .
   I would not ever have them grieve,
Nor shed a single tear for me,
   To mar their joy this Christmas Eve.

Stripped to the buff and gaunt and still
   Lies all the land in grim distress.
Like lost soul wailing, long and shrill,
   A wolf-howl cleaves the emptiness.
Then hushed as Death is everything.
   The moon rides haggard and forlorn . . .
"O hark the herald angels sing!"
   God bless all men—it's Christmas morn

THE WORLD'S ALL RIGHT

Be honest, kindly, simple, true;
Seek good in all, scorn but pretence;
Whatever sorrow come to you,
Believe in Life's Beneficence!

The World's all right; serene I sit,
And cease to puzzle over it.
There's much that's mighty strange, no doubt;
But Nature knows what she's about;
And in a million years or so
We'll know more than to-day we know.
Old Evolution's under way—
What ho! the World's all right, I say.

Could things be other that they are?
All's in its place, from mote to star.
The thistledown that flits and flies
Could drift no hairsbreadth otherwise.
What is, must be; with rhythmic laws
All Nature chimes, Effect and Cause.
The sand-grain and the sun obey—
What ho! the World's all right, I say.

303

Just try to get the Cosmic touch,
The sense that "you" don't matter much.
A million stars are in the sky;
A million planets plunge and die.
A million million men are sped;
A million million wait ahead.
Each plays his part and has his day—
       What ho! the World's all right, I say.

Just try to get the Chemic view:
A million million lives made "you."
In lives a million you will be
Immortal down Eternity;
Immortal on this earth to range,
With never death, but ever change.
You always were, and will be aye—
       What ho! the World's all right, I say.

Be glad! And do not blindly grope
For Truth that lies beyond our scope;
A sober plot informeth all
Of Life's unroarious carnival.
Your day is such a little one,
A gnat that lives from sun to sun;
Yet gnat and you have parts to play—
       What ho! the World's all right, I say.

And though it's written from the start,
Just act your best your little part.
Just be as happy as you can,
And serve your kind, and die—a man.
Just live the good that in you lies,
And seek no guerdon of the skies;
Just make your Heaven here, to-day—
     What ho! the World's all right, I say.

Remember! in Creation's swing
The Race and not the man's the thing.
There's battle, murder, sudden death,
And pestilence, with poisoned breath.
Yet quick forgotten are such woes;
On, on the stream of Being flows.
Truth, Beauty, Love maintain their sway—
     What ho! the World's all right, I say.

The World's all right; serene I sit,
And joy that I am part of it;
And put my trust in Nature's plan.
And try to aid her all I can;
Content to pass, if in my place
I've served the uplift of the Race.
Truth! Beauty! Love! O Radiant Day—
     What ho! the World's all right, I say.

THE BALDNESS OF CHEWED-EAR

WHEN Chewed-ear Jenkins got hitched up to Guinneyveer McGee,
His flowin' locks, ye recollect, wuz frivolous an' free;
But in old Hymen's jack-pot, it's a most amazin' thing,
Them flowin' locks jest disappeared like snowballs in the Spring;
Jest seemed to wilt an' fade away like dead leaves in the Fall,
An' left old Chewed-ear balder than a whitewashed cannon ball.

Now Missis Chewed-ear Jenkins, that wuz Guinneyveer McGee,
  Wuz jest about as fine a draw as ever made a pair;
But when the boys got joshin' an' suggested it was she
    That must be inflooenshul for the old man's slump in hair—
    Why! Missis Chewed-ear Jenkins jest went clean up in the air.

"To demonstrate," sez she that night, "the lovin' wife I am,
I've bought a dozen bottles of Bink's Anty-Dandruff Balm.

306

'Twill make yer hair jest sprout an' curl like squash-vines in
  the sun,
An' I propose to sling it on till every drop is done."
That hit old Chewed-ear's funny side, so he lays back an'
  hollers:
"The day you raise a hair, old girl, you'll git a thousand
  dollars."

Now, whether 'twas the prize or not 'tis mighty hard to say,
But Chewed-ear didn't seem to have much comfort from that
  day.
With bottles of that dandruff dope she followed at his heels,
An' sprinkled an' massaged him even when he ate his meals.
She waked him from his beauty sleep with tender, lovin' care,
An' rubbed and scrubbed assiduous, yet never sign of hair.

Well, naturally all the boys soon tumbled to the joke,
An' at the Wow-wow's Social 'twas Cold-deck Davis spoke:
"The little woman's workin' mighty hard on Chewed-ear's
  crown;
Let's give her for a three-fifths share a hundred dollars down.
We stand to make five hundred clear—boys, drink in whiskey
  straight:
'The Chewed-ear Jenkins Hirsute Propagation Syndicate.'"

The boys wuz on, an' soon chipped in the necessary dust;
  They primed up a committy to negotiate the deal;

L

Then Missis Jenkins yielded, bein' rather in disgust,
   An' all wuz signed an' witnessed, an' invested with a seal.
They rounded up old Chewed-ear, an' they broke it what
    they'd done;
   Allowed they'd bought an interest in his chance of raisin
    hair;
They yanked his hat off anxious-like, opinin' one by one,
   Their magnifyin'-glasses showed fine prospects everywhere.
They bought Hairlene, an' Thatchem, an' Jay's Cappillery
    Juice,
   An' Seven Something Sisters, an' Macassar an' Bay Rum,
An' every one insisted on his speshul right to sluice
   His speshul line of lotion onto Chewed-ear's cranium.
They only got the merrier the more the old man roared,
An' shares in "Jenkins Hirsute" went sky-highin' on the board.

The Syndicate wuz hopeful that they'd demonstrate the pay,
An' Missis Jenkins laboured in her perseverin' way.
The boys discussed on "surface rights," an' "out-crops," an'
    so on,
An' planned to have it "crown" surveyed, an' blueprints of it
    drawn.
They ran a base line, sluiced an' yelled, an' every one wuz
    glad
Except the balance of the property, an' he wuz "mad."
"It gives me pain," he interjects, "to squash yer glowin' dream,
But you wuz fools when you got in on this here 'Hirsute'
    scheme.

You'll never raise a hair on me"—when lo! that very night,
Preparin' to retire, he got a most unpleasant fright:
For on that shinin' dome of his, so prominently bare,
He felt the baby outcrop of a second growth of hair.

A thousand dollars! Sufferin' Cæsar! Well, it must be saved!
He grabbed his razor recklesslike, an' shaved an' shaved an'
     shaved.
An' when his head wuz smooth again he gives a mighty sigh,
An' sneaks away, an' buys some Hair Destroyer on the sly.
So there wuz Missis Jenkins with "Restorer" wagin' fight,
An' Chewed-ear with "Destroyer" circumventin' her at night.
The battle wuz a mighty one; his nerves wuz on the strain,
An' yet in spite of all he did that hair began to gain.

The situation grew intense, so quietly one day,
He gave his shareholders the slip, an' made his get-away.
Jest like a criminal he skipped, an' aimed to defalcate
The Chewed-ear Jenkins Hirsute Propagation Syndicate.
His guilty secret burned him, an' he sought the city's din:
"I've got to get a wig," sez he, "to cover up my sin.
It's growin', growin', night an' day; it's most amazin' hair";
An' when he looked at it that night, he shuddered with despair.
He shuddered an' suppressed a cry at what his optics seen—
For on my word of honour, boys, that hair was growin' *green*.
At first he guessed he'd get some dye, an' try to dye it black;
An' then he saw 'twas Nemmysis wuz layin' on his track.

He must jest face the music, an' confess the thing he'd done,
An' pay the boys an' Guinneyveer the money they had won.
An' then there came a big idee—it thrilled him like a shock:
Why not control the Syndicate by buyin' up the stock?

An' so next day he hurried back with smoothly shaven pate,
An' for a hundred dollars he bought up the Syndicate.
'Twas mighty frenzied finance an' the boys set up a roar,
But "Hirsutes" from the market wuz withdrawn for evermore.
An' to this day in Nuggetsville they tell the tale how slick
The Syndicate sold out too soon, and Chewed-ear turned the
    trick.

THE MOTHER

THERE will be a singing in your heart,
  There will be a rapture in your eyes;
You will be a woman set apart,
  You will be so wonderful and wise.
You will sleep, and when from dreams you start,
  As of one that wakes in Paradise,
There will be a singing in your heart,
  There will be a rapture in your eyes.

There will be a moaning in your heart,
  There will be an anguish in your eyes;
You will see your dearest ones depart,
  You will hear their quivering good-byes.
Yours will be the heartache and the smart,
  Tears that scald and lonely sacrifice;
There will be a moaning in your heart,
  There will be an anguish in your eyes.

There will come a glory in your eyes,
  There will come a peace within your heart;

311

Sitting 'neath the quiet evening skies,
  Time will dry the tear and dull the smart.
You will know that you have played your part;
  Yours shall be the love that never dies:
You, with Heaven's peace within your heart,
  You, with God's own glory in your eyes.

THE DREAMER

THE lone man gazed and gazed upon his gold,
  His sweat, his blood, the wage of weary days;
But now how sweet, how doubly sweet to hold
  All gay and gleamy to the camp-fire blaze.
The evening sky was sinister and cold;
  The willows shivered, wanly lay the snow;
The uncommiserating land, so old,
  So worn, so grey, so niggard in its woe,
Peered through its ragged shroud. The lone man sighed,
  Poured back the gaudy dust into its poke,
Gazed at the seething river listless-eyed,
  Loaded his corn-cob pipe as if to smoke;
Then crushed with weariness and hardship crept
Into his ragged robe, and swiftly slept.

        *   *   *   *   *

Hour after hour went by; a shadow slipped
  From vasts of shadow to the camp-fire flame;
  Gripping a rifle with a deadly aim,
A gaunt and hairy man with wolfish eyes. . . .

        *   *   *   *   *

313

The sleeper dreamed, and lo! this was his dream:
  He rode a streaming horse across a moor.
Sudden 'mid pit-black night a lightning gleam
  Showed him a wayside inn, forlorn and poor.
A sullen host unbarred the creaking door,
  And led him to a dim and dreary room,
Wherein he sat and poked the fire a-roar,
  So that weird shadows jigged athwart the gloom.
He ordered wine. 'Od's blood! but he was tired.
  What matter! Charles was crushed and George was King;
His party high in power; how he aspired!
  Red guineas packed his purse, too tight to ring.
The firelight gleamed upon his silken hose,
  His silver buckles and his powdered wig.
What ho! more wine! He drank, he slowly rose
  What made the shadows dance that madcap jig?
He clutched the candle, steered his way to bed,
And in a trice was sleeping like the dead.

        *   *   *   *   *

Across the room there crept, so shadow soft,
  His sullen host, with naked knife agleam,
(A gaunt and hairy man with wolfish eyes.) . . .
  And as he lay, the sleeper dreamed a dream:

        *   *   *   *   *

'Twas in a ruder land, a wilder day.
  A rival princeling sat upon his throne,

Within a dungeon dark and foul he lay,
  With chains that bit and festered to the bone.
They haled him harshly to a vaulted room,
  Where One gazed on him with malignant eye;
And in that devil-face he read his doom,
  Knowing that ere the dawn-light he must die.
Well, he was sorrow-glutted; let them bring
  Their prize assassins to the bloody work.
His kingdom lost, yet would he die a King,
  Peerless and proud, as when he faced the Turk.
Ah, God! the glory of that great Crusade!
  The bannered pomp, the gleam, the splendid urge!
The crash of reeking combat, blade to blade!
  The reeling ranks, blood-avid and a-surge!
For long he thought; then feeling o'er him creep
Vast weariness, he fell into a sleep.

        *   *   *   *   *

The cell door opened; soft the headsman came,
  Within his hand a mighty axe agleam,
(A gaunt and hairy man with wolfish eyes.) . . .
  And as he lay, the sleeper dreamed a dream:

        *   *   *   *   *

'Twas in a land unkempt, of life's red dawn,
  Where in his sanded cave he dwelt alone;
Sleeping by day, or sometimes worked upon
  His flint-head arrows and his knives of stone;

By night stole forth and slew the savage boar,
  So that he loomed a hunter of loud fame,
And many a skin of wolf and wild-cat wore,
  And counted many a flint-head to his name;
Wherefore he walked the envy of the band,
  Hated and feared, but matchless in his skill
Till lo! one night deep in that shaggy land,
  He tracked a yearling bear and made his kill;
Then over-worn he rested by a stream,
And sank into a sleep too deep for dream.

*   *   *   *   *

Hunting his food a rival caveman crept
  Through those dark woods, and marked him where he lay;
Cowered and crawled upon him as he slept,
  Poising a mighty stone aloft to slay—
(A gaunt and hairy man with wolfish eyes.) . . .

*   *   *   *   *

The great stone crashed. The Dreamer shrieked and woke,
  And saw, fear-blinded, in his dripping cell,
A gaunt and hairy man, who with one stroke
  Swung a great axe of steel that flashed and fell. . . .

So that he woke amid his bedroom gloom,
  And saw, hair-poised, a naked, thirsting knife,
A gaunt and hairy man with eyes of doom—
  And then the blade plunged down to drink his life. . . .

So that he woke, wrenched back his robe, and looked,
  And saw beside his dying fire upstart
A gaunt and hairy man with finger crooked—
  A rifle rang, a bullet searched his heart. . . .

      *   *   *   *   *

The morning sky was sinister and cold.
  Grotesque the Dreamer sprawled, and did not rise,
For long and long there gazed upon some gold
  A gaunt and hairy man with wolfish eyes.

AT THIRTY-FIVE

THREE score and ten, the Psalmist saith,
  And half my course is well-nigh run;
I've had my flout at dusty death,
  I've had my whack of feast and fun.
I've mocked at those who prate and preach,
  I've laughed with any man alive;
But now with sobered heart I reach
  The Great Divide of Thirty-five.

And looking back I must confess
  I've little cause to feel elate.
I've played the mummer more or less;
  I fumbled fortune, flouted fate.
I've vastly dreamed and little done;
  I've idly watched my brothers strive:
Oh, I have loitered in the sun
  By primrose paths to Thirty-five!

And those who matched me in the race,
  Well, some are out and trampled down;

The others jog with sober pace;
    Yet one wins delicate renown.
O midnight feast and famished dawn!
    O gay, hard life, with hope alive!
O golden youth, forever gone,
    How sweet you seem at Thirty-five!

Each of our lives is just a book
    As absolute as Holy Writ;
We humbly read, and may not look
    Ahead, nor change one word of it.
And here are joys and here are pains;
    And here we fail and here we thrive;
O wondrous volume! What remains
    When we reach chapter Thirty-five?

The very best, I dare to hope.
    Ere Fate writes Finis to the tome;
A wiser head, a wider scope,
    And for the gipsy heart, a home;
A songful home, with loved ones near,
    With joy, with sunshine all alive:
Watch me grow younger every year—
    Old Age! thy name is Thirty-five!

THE SQUAW-MAN

The cow-moose comes to water, and the beaver's overbold,
  The net is in the eddy of the stream;
The tepee stars the vivid sward with russet, red and gold,
  And in the velvet gloom the fire's agleam.
The night is ripe with quiet, rich with incense of the pine;
  From sanctuary lake I hear the loon:
The peaks are bright against the blue, and drenched with
    sunset wine,
  And like a silver bubble is the moon.

Cloud-high I climbed but yesterday; a hundred miles around
  I looked to see a rival fire agleam.
As in a crystal lens it lay, a land without a bound.
  All lure, and virgin vastitude, and dream.
The great sky roared exultantly, the great earth bared its breast,
  All river-veined and patterned with the pine;
The heedless hordes of caribou were streaming to the West,
  A land of lustrous mystery—and mine.

Yea, mine to frame my Odyssey: Oh, little do they know
   My conquest and the kingdom that I keep!
The meadows of the musk-ox where the laughing grasses grow,
   The rivers where the careless conies leap.
Beyond the silent Circle, where white men are fierce and few,
   I lord it, and I mock at man-made law;
Like a flame upon the water is my little light canoe,
   And yonder in the fireglow is my squaw.

A squaw-man! yes, that's what I am; sneer at me if you will.
   I've gone the grilling pace that cannot last;
With bawdry, bridge and brandy—Oh, I've drunk enough
      to kill
   A dozen such as you, but that is past.
I've swung round to my senses, found the place where I
      belong;
   The City made a madman out of me;
But here beyond the Circle, where there's neither right nor
      wrong,
   I leap from life's strait-jacket, and I'm free.

Yet ever in the far forlorn, by trails of lone desire;
   Yet ever in the dawn's white leer of hate;
Yet ever by the dripping kill, beside the drowsy fire,
   There comes the fierce heart-hunger for a mate.
There comes the mad blood-clamour for a woman's clinging
      hand,

Love-humid eyes, the velvet of a breast:
And so I sought the Bonnet-plumes, and chose from out the
    band
  The girl I thought the sweetest and the best.

O wistful women I have loved before my dark disgrace!
  O women fair and rare in my home land!
Dear ladies, if I saw you now I'd turn away my face,
  Then crawl to kiss your footprints in the sand!
And yet—that day the rifle jammed—a wounded moose at bay—
  A roar, a charge . . . I faced it with my knife:
A shot from out the willow-scrub, and there the monster lay . . .
  Yes, little Laughing Eyes, you saved my life.

The man must have the woman, and we're all brutes more
    or less,
  Since first the male ape shinned the family tree;
And yet I think I love her with a husband's tenderness,
  And yet I know that she would die for me.
Oh, if I left you, Laughing Eyes, and nevermore came back,
  God help you, girl! I know what you would do . . .
I see the lake wan in the moon, and from the shadow black,
  There drifts a little *empty* birch canoe.

We're here beyond the Circle, where there's never wrong
    nor right;
  We aren't spliced according to the law;

But by the gods I hail you on this hushed and holy night
    As the mother of my children, and my squaw.
I see your little slender face set in the firelight glow;
    I pray that I may never make it sad;
I hear you croon a baby song, all slumber-soft and low—
    God bless you, little Laughing Eyes! I'm glad.

HOME AND LOVE

Just Home and Love! the words are small,
　　Four little letters unto each;
And yet you will not find in all
　　The wide and gracious range of speech
Two more so tenderly complete:
　　When angels talk in Heaven above,
I'm sure they have no words more sweet
　　　　Than Home and Love.

Just Home and Love! it's hard to guess
　　Which of the two were best to gain.
Home without Love is bitterness;
　　Love without home is often pain.
No! each alone will seldom do;
　　Somehow they travel hand and glove:
If you win one you must have two,
　　　　Both Home and Love.

And if you've both, well, then I'm sure
　　You ought to sing the whole day long;

It doesn't matter if you're poor
   With these to make divine your song.
And so I praisefully repeat,
   When angels talk in Heaven above,
There are no words more simply sweet
   Than Home and Love.

I'M SCARED OF IT ALL

I'M scared of it all, God's truth! so I am:
    It's too big and brutal for me.
My nerve's on the raw and I don't give a damn
    For all the "hoorah" that I see.
I'm pinned between subway and overhead train,
    Where automobillies swoop down;
Oh, I want to go back to the timber again—
    I'm scared of the terrible town.

I want to go back to my lean, ashen plains;
    My rivers that flash into foam;
My ultimate valleys where solitude reigns;
    My trail from Fort Churchill to Nome.
My forests packed full of mysterious gloom,
    My ice-fields agrind and aglare:
The city is deadfalled with danger and doom—
    I know that I'm safer up there.

I watch the wan faces that flash in the street:
    All kinds and all classes I see.

Yet never a one in the million I meet
  Has the smile of a comrade for me.
Just jaded and panting like dogs in a pack;
  Just tensed and intent on the goal:
O God! but I'm lonesome—I wish I was back,
  Up there in the land of the Pole.

I wish I was back on the Hunger Plateaus,
  And seeking the lost caribou;
I wish I was up where the Coppermine flows
  To the kick of my little canoe.
I'd like to be far on some weariful shore,
  In the land of the Blizzard and Bear:
Oh, I wish I was snug in the Arctic once more,
  For I know I am safer up there!

I prowl in the canyons of dismal unrest;
  I cringe—I'm so weak and so small.
I can't get my bearings, I'm crushed and oppressed
  With the haste and the waste of it all.
The slaves and the madmen, the lust and the sweat,
  The fear in the faces I see;
The getting, the spending, the fever, the fret—
  It's too bleeding cruel for me.

I feel it's all wrong, but I can't tell you why—
  The palace, the hovel next door;

The insolent towers that sprawl to the sky,
　The crush and the rush and the roar.
I'm trapped like a fox and I fear for my pelt;
　I cower in the crash and the glare;
Oh, I want to be back in the avalanche belt,
　For I know that it's safer up there!

I'm scared of it all. Oh, afar I can hear
　The voice of my solitudes call!
We're nothing but brute with a little veneer,
　And nature is best after all.
There's tumult and terror abroad in the street;
　There's menace and doom in the air;
I've got to get back to my thousand-mile beat;
The trail where the cougar and silver-tip meet;
The snows and the camp-fire, with wolves at my feet;
　Good-bye, for it's safer up there.

To be forming good habits up there;
To be starving on rabbits up there;
　In your hunger and woe,
　Though it's sixty below,
Oh, I know that it's safer up there!

A SONG OF SUCCESS

Ho! we were strong, we were swift, we were brave.
　　Youth was a challenge, and Life was a fight.
All that was best in us gladly we gave,
　　Sprang from the rally, and leapt for the height.
Smiling is Love in a foam of Spring flowers:
　　Harden our hearts to him—on let us press!
Oh, what a triumph and pride shall be ours!
　　See where it beacons, the star of success!

Cares seem to crowd on us—so much to do:
　　New fields to conquer. and time's on the wing.
Grey hairs are showing, a wrinkle or two;
　　Somehow our footstep is losing its spring.
Pleasure's forsaken us, Love ceased to smile:
　　Youth has been funeralled; Age travels fast.
Sometimes we wonder: Is it worth while?
　　There! we have gained to the summit at last.

Aye, we have triumphed! Now must we haste,
　　Revel in victory . . . why! what is wrong?
Life's choicest vintage is flat to the taste—
　　Are we too late?　Have we laboured too long?
Wealth, power, fame we hold . . . ah! but the truth:
　　Would we not give this vain glory of ours
For one mad, glad year of glorious youth,
　　Life in the Springtide, and Love in the flowers?

THE SONG OF THE CAMP-FIRE

I

HEED me, feed me, I am hungry, I am red-tongued with desire;
  Boughs of balsam, slabs of cedar, gummy faggots of the pine,
Heap them on me, let me hug them to my eager heart of fire,
  Roaring, soaring up to heaven as a symbol and a sign.
Bring me knots of sunny maple, silver birch and tamarack;
  Leaping, sweeping, I will lap them with my ardent wings
    of flame;
I will kindle them to glory, I will beat the darkness back;
  Streaming, gleaming, I will goad them to my glory and my
    fame.
Bring me gnarly limbs of live-oak, aid me in my frenzied fight;
  Strips of iron-wood, scaly blue-gum, writhing redly in
    my hold;
With my lunge of lurid lances, with my whips that flail the
    night,
  They will burgeon into beauty, they will foliate in gold.
Let me star the dim sierras, stab with light the inland seas;
  Roaming wind and roaring darkness! seek no mercy at my
    hands;
I will mock the marly heavens, lamp the purple prairies,
  I will flaunt my deathless banners down the far, unhouseled
    lands.

In the vast and vaulted pine-gloom where the pillared forests
    frown,
  By the sullen, brutish rivers running where God only knows,
On the starlit coral beaches when the combers thunder down,
  In the death-spell of the barrens, in the shudder of the snows;
In a blazing belt of triumph from the palm-leaf to the pine,
  As a symbol of defiance, lo! the wilderness I span;
And my beacons burnt exultant as an everlasting sign
  Of unending domination, of the mastery of Man;
I, the Life, the fierce Uplifter, I that weaned him from the
    mire;
  I, the angel and the devil; I, the tyrant and the slave;
I, the Spirit of the Struggle; I, the mighty God of Fire;
  I, the Maker and Destroyer; I, the Giver and the Grave.

II

Gather round me, boy and grey-beard, frontiersmen of every
    kind.
Few are you, and far and lonely, yet an army forms behind:
By your camp-fires shall they know you, ashes scattered
    to the wind.

Peer into my heart of solace, break your bannock at my blaze;
Smoking, stretched in lazy shelter, build your castles as
    you gaze;
Or, it may be, deep in dreaming, think of dim, unhappy days.

Let my warmth and glow caress you, for your trails are grim
    and hard;
Let my arms of comfort press you, hunger-hewn and battle-
    scarred:
O my lovers! how I bless you with your lives so madly marred!

For you seek the silent spaces, and their secret lore you glean;
For you win the savage races, and the brutish Wild you wean;
And I gladden desert places, where camp-fire has never been.

From the Pole unto the Tropics is there trail ye have not dared?
And because you hold death lightly, so by death shall you be
    spared,
(As the sages of the ages in their pages have declared.)

On the roaring Arkilinik in a leaky bark canoe;
Up the cloud of Mount McKinley, where the avalanche leaps
    through;
In the furnace of Death Valley, when the mirage glimmers
    blue.

Now a smudge of wiry willows on the weary Kuskoquim;
Now a flare of gummy pine-knots where Vancouver's scaur is
    grim;
Now a gleam of sunny ceiba, when the Cuban beaches dim.

Always, always God's Great Open: lo! I burn with keener light
In the corridors of silence, in the vestibules of night;
'Mid the ferns and grasses gleaming, was there ever gem so
   bright?

Not for weaklings, not for women, like my brother of the
   hearth;
Ring your songs of wrath around me, I was made for manful
   mirth,
In the lusty, gusty greatness, on the bald spots of the earth.

Men, my masters! Men, my lovers! ye have fought and ye
   have bled;
Gather round my ruddy embers, softly glowing is my bed;
By my heart of solace dreaming, rest ye and be comforted!

III

I am dying, O my masters! by my fitful flame ye sleep;
   My purple plumes of glory droop forlorn.
Grey ashes choke and cloak me, and above the pines there
   creep
   The stealthy silver moccasins of morn.
There comes a countless army; it's the Legion of the Light;
   It tramps in gleaming triumph round the world;
And before its jewelled lances all the shadows of the night
   Back in to abysmal darknesses are hurled.

Leap to life again, my lovers! ye must toil and never tire;
  The day of daring, doing, brightens clear,
When the bed of spicy cedar and the jovial camp-fire
  Must only be a memory of cheer.
There is hope and golden promise in the vast portentous dawn;
  There is glamour in the glad, effluent sky:
Go and leave me; I will dream of you and love you when
      you're gone;
  I have served you, O my masters! let me die.

A little heap of ashes, grey and sodden by the rain,
  Wind-scattered, blurred and blotted by the snow:
Let that be all to tell of me, and glorious again,
  Ye things of greening gladness, leap and glow!
A black scar in the sunshine by the palm-leaf or the pine,
  Blind to the night and dead to all desire;
Yet oh, of life and uplift what a symbol and a sign!
Yet oh, of power and conquest what a destiny is mine!
A little heap of ashes—Yea! a miracle divine
  The footprint of a god, all-radiant Fire.

HER LETTER

"I'm taking pen in hand this night, and hard it is for me;
  My poor old fingers tremble so, my hand is stiff and slow,
And even with my glasses on I'm troubled sore to see . . .
  You'd little know your mother, boy; you'd little, little know.
You mind how brisk and bright I was, how straight and trim
        and smart;
  'Tis weariful I am the now, and bent and frail and grey.
I'm waiting at the road's end, lad; and all that's in my heart,
  Is just to see my boy again before I'm called away.

"Oh, well I mind the sorry day you crossed the gurly sea;
  'Twas like the heart was torn from me, a waeful wife was I.
You said that you'd be home again in two years, maybe three;
  But nigh a score of years have gone, and still the years
        go by.
I know it's cruel hard for you, you've bairnies of your own;
  I know the siller's hard to win, and folks have used you ill:
But oh, think of your mother, lad, that's waiting by her lone!
  And even if you canna come—*just write and say you will.*

"Aye, even though there's little hope, just promise that you'll
    try.
  It's weary, weary waiting, lad; just say you'll come next year.
I'm thinking there will be no 'next'; I'm thinking soon I'll lie
    With all the ones I've laid away . . . but oh, the hope
    will cheer!
You know you're all that's left to me, and we are seas apart;
  But if you'll only *say* you'll come, then will I hope and pray.
I'm waiting by the grave-side, lad; and all that's in my heart
  Is just to see my boy again before I'm called away."

THE MAN WHO KNEW

THE Dreamer visioned Life as it might be,
  And from his dream forthright a picture grew,
A painting all the people thronged to see,
  And joyed therein—till came the Man Who Knew,
Saying: "'Tis bad. Why do ye gape, ye fools?
He painteth not according to the schools."

The Dreamer probed Life's mystery of woe,
  And in a book he sought to give the clue;
The people read, and saw that it was so,
  And read again—then came the Man Who Knew,
Saying: "Ye witless ones! this book is vile:
It hath not got the rudiments of style."

Love smote the Dreamer's lips, and silver-clear
  He sang a song so sweet, so tender true,
That all the market-place was thrilled to hear,
  And listened rapt—till came the Man Who Knew,
Saying: "His technique's wrong; he singeth ill.
Waste not your time." The singer's voice was still.

338

And then the people roused as if from sleep,
   Crying: "What care we if it be not Art!
Hath he not charmed us, made us laugh and weep?
   Come, let us crown him where he sits apart."
Then, with his picture spurned, his book unread,
.His song unsung, they found their Dreamer—*dead*.

M

THE LOGGER

In the moonless, misty night, with my little pipe alight,
    I am sitting by the camp-fire's fading cheer;
Oh, the dew is falling chill on the dim, deer-haunted hill,
    And the breakers in the bay are moaning drear.
The toilful hours are sped, the boys are long abed,
    And I alone a weary vigil keep;
In the sightless, sullen sky I can hear the night-hawk cry,
    And the frogs in frenzied chorus from the creek.

And somehow the ember's glow brings me back the long ago,
    The days of merry laughter and light song;
When I sped the hours away with the gayest of the gay
    In the giddy whirl of fashion's festal throng.
Oh, I ran a grilling race and I little recked the pace,
    For the lust of youth ran riot in my blood;
But at last I made a stand in this God-forsaken land
    Of the pine-tree and the mountain and the flood.

And now I've got to stay, with an overdraft to pay
    For pleasure in the past with future pain;

And I'm not the chap to whine, for if the chance were mine
    I know I'd choose the old life once again.
With its woman's eyes ashine, and its flood of golden wine;
    Its fever and its frolic and its fun;
The old life with its din, its laughter and its sin—
    And chuck me in the gutter when it's done.

Ah, well! it's past and gone, and the memory is wan,
    That conjures up each old familiar face;
And here by fortune hurled, I am dead to all the world,
    And I've learned to lose my pride and keep my place.
My ways are hard and rough, and my arms are strong and
    tough,
    And I hew the dizzy pine till darkness falls;
And sometimes I take a dive, just to keep my heart alive,
    Among the gay saloons and dancing-halls.

In the distant, dinful town just a little drink, to drown
    The cares that crowd and canker in my brain;
Just a little joy to still set my pulses all athrill,
    Then back to brutish labour once again.
And things will go on so until one day I shall know
    That Death has got me cinched beyond a doubt:
Then I'll crawl away from sight, and morosely in the night
    My weary, wasted life will peter out.

Then the boys will gather round, and they'll launch me in
      the ground,
  And pile on stones the timber wolf to foil;
And the moaning pine will wave overhead a nameless grave,
  Where the blacksnake in the sunshine loves to coil.
And they'll leave me there alone, and perhaps with softened
      tone
  Speak of me sometimes in the camp-fire's glow
As a played-out, broken chum, who has gone to Kingdom
      Come,
  And who went the pace in England long ago.

THE PASSING OF THE YEAR

My glass is filled, my pipe is lit,
  My den is all a cosy glow;
And snug before the fire I sit,
  And wait to *feel* the old year go.
I dedicate to solemn thought,
  Amid my too-unthinking days,
This sober moment, sadly fraught
  With much of blame, with little praise.

Old Year! upon the Stage of Time
  You stand to bow your last adieu;
A moment, and the prompter's chime
  Will ring the curtain down on you.
Your mien is sad, your step is slow;
  You falter as a Sage in pain;
Yet turn, Old Year, before you go,
  And face your audience again.

343

That sphynx-like face, remote, austere,
    Let us all read, whate'er the cost:
O Maiden! why that bitter tear?
    Is it for dear one you have lost?
Is it for fond illusion gone?
    For trusted lover proved untrue?
O sweet girl-face, so sad, so wan,
    What hath the Old Year meant to you?

And you, O neighbour on my right,
    So sleek, so prosperously clad!
What see you in that aged wight
    That makes your smile so gay and glad?
What opportunity unmissed?
    What golden gain, what pride of place?
What splendid hope? O Optimist!
    What read you in that withered face?

And you, deep shrinking in the gloom,
    What find you in that filmy gaze?
What menace of a tragic doom?
    What dark, condemning yesterdays?
What urge to crime, what evil done?
    What cold, confronting shape of fear?
O haggard, haunted, hidden One,
    What see you in the dying year?

And so from face to face I flit,
    The countless eyes that stare and stare;
Some are with approbation lit,
    And some are shadowed with despair.
Some show a smile and some a frown;
    Some joy and hope, some pain and woe:
Enough! Oh, ring that curtain down!
    Old weary year! it's time to go.

My pipe is out, my glass is dry;
    My fire is almost ashes too:
But once again, before you go,
    And I prepare to meet the New:
Old Year! a parting word that's true,
    For we've been comrades, you and I—
I *thank God for each day of you;*
    There! bless you now! Old Year, good-bye!

THE GHOSTS

Smith, great writer of stories, drank; found it immortalized
    his pen;
Fused in his brain-pan, else a blank, heavens of glory now
    and then;
Gave him the magical genius touch; God-given power to
    gouge out, fling
Flat in your face a soul-thought—Bing! Twiddle your heart-
    strings in his clutch.
"Bah!" said Smith, "let my body lie stripped to the buff in
    swinish shame,
If I can blaze in the radiant sky out of adoring stars my name.
Sober am I nonentitized; drunk am I more than half a god.
Well, let the flesh be sacrificed; spirit shall speak and shame
    the clod.
Who would not gladly, gladly give Life to do one thing that
    will live?"

Smith had a friend, we'll call him Brown; dearer than brothers
    were those two.
When in the wassail Smith would drown, Brown would rescue
    and pull him through.

When Brown was needful Smith would lend; so it fell as
    the years went by,
Each on the other would depend: then at the last Smith
    came to die.

There Brown sat in the sick man's room, still as a stone in
    his despair;
Smith bent on him his eyes of doom, shook back his lion
    mane of hair;
Said: "Is there one in my chosen line, writer of forthright
    tales, my peer?
Look in that little desk of mine; there is a package, bring
    it here.
Story of stories, gem of all; essence and triumph, key and clue;
Tale of a loving woman's fall; soul swept hellward, and God!
    it's true,
I was the man—Oh, yes, I've paid, paid with mighty and
    mordant pain.
Look! here's the masterpiece I've made out of my sin, my
    manhood slain.
Art supreme! yet the world would stare, know my mistress
    and blaze my shame.
I have a wife and daughter—there! take it and thrust it in
    the flame."

Brown answered: "Master, you have dipped pen in your
    heart, your phrases sear.

Ruthless, unflinching, you have stripped naked your soul and
    set it here.
Have I not loved you well and true? See! between us the
    shadows drift;
This bit of blood and tears means You—oh, let me have it,
    a parting gift.
Sacred I'll hold it, a trust divine; sacred your honour, her
    dark despair;
Never shall it see printed line: here, by the living God I swear."
Brown on a Bible laid his hand; Smith, great writer of stories,
    sighed:
"Comrade, I trust you, and understand. Keep my secret!"
    And so he died.

Smith was buried—upsoared his sales; lured you his books
    in every store;
Exquisite, whimsy, heart-wrung tales; men devoured them
    and craved for more.
So when it slyly got about Brown had a post-humous
    manuscript,
Jones, the publisher, sought him out, into his pocket deep
    he dipped.
"A thousand dollars?" Brown shook his head.
        "The story is not for sale," he said.

Jones went away, then others came. Tempted and taunted,
    Brown was true.

Guarded at friendship's shrine, the fame of the unpublished
story grew and grew.

It's a long, long lane that has no end, but some lanes end
in the Potter's field;

Smith to Brown had been more than friend: patron, protector,
spur and shield.

Poor, loving-wistful, dreamy Brown, long and lean, with a
smile askew,

Friendless he wandered up and down, gaunt as a wolf, as
hungry, too.

Brown with his lilt of saucy rhyme, Brown with his tilt of
tender mirth,

Garretless in the gloom and grime, singing his glad, mad
songs of earth:

So at last with a faith divine, down and down to the
Hunger-line.

There as he stood in a woeful plight, tears a-freeze on his
sharp cheek-bones,

Who should chance to behold his plight but the publisher,
the plethoric Jones;

Peered at him for a little while, held out a bill: "*Now,* will
you sell?"

Brown scanned it with his twisted smile: "A thousand dollars!
you go to hell!"

Brown enrolled in the homeless host, sleeping anywhere,
anywhen;

Suffered, strove, became a ghost, slave of the lamp for other
men;

For What's-his-name and So-and-so in the abyss his soul he
stripped,

Yet in his want, his worst of woe, held he fast to the manuscript.

Then one day as he chewed his pen, half in hunger and half
despair,

Creaked the door of his garret den; Dick, his brother, was
standing there.

Down on the pallet bed he sank, ashen his face, his voice a
wail:

"Save me, brother! I've robbed the bank, to-morrow it's
ruin, capture, gaol.

Yet there's a chance: I could to-day pay back the money, save
our name;

You have a manuscript, they say, worth a thousand—think
man! the shame. . . ."

Brown with his heart pain-pierced the while, with his stern,
starved face, and his lips stone-pale,

Shuddered and smiled his twisted smile: "Brother, I guess you
go to gaol."

While poor Brown in the leer of dawn wrestled with God for
the sacred fire,

Came there a woman weak and wan, out of the mob, the
murk, the mire;

Frail as a reed, a fellow ghost, weary with woe, with sorrowing;

Two pale souls in the legion lost; lo! Love bent with a tender
    wing,

Taught them a joy so deep, so true, it seemed that the whole
    world-fabric shook,

Thrilled and dissolved in radiant dew: then Brown made him
    a golden book,

Full of the faith that Life is good, that the earth is a dream
    divinely fair,

Lauding his gem of womanhood, in many a lyric rich and rare;

Took it to Jones, who shook his head: "I will consider it,"
    he said.

While he considered, Brown's wife lay clutched in the tentacles
    of pain;

Then came the doctor, grave and grey; spoke of decline, of
    nervous strain;

Hinted Egypt, the South of France—Brown with terror was
    tiger-gripped.

Where was the money? What the chance? Pitiful God! . . .
    the manuscript!

A thousand dollars—his only hope! He gazed and gazed at
    the garret wall . . .

Reached at last for the envelope, turned to his wife and told
    her all.

Told of his friend, his promise true; told like his very heart
    would break;

"Oh, my dearest! what shall I do? Shall I not sell it for your
    sake?"

Ghostlike she lay, as still as doom; turned to the wall her
    weary head;

Icy-cold in the pallid gloom, silent as death . . . at last she said:
"Do, my husband! Keep your vow! Guard his secret and
    let me die . . .
Oh, my dear, I must tell you now—*the woman he loved and
    wronged was I;*
Darling! I haven't long to live: I never told you—forgive,
    forgive!"

For a long, long time Brown did not speak; sat bleak-browed
    in the wretched room;
Slowly a tear stole down his cheek, and he kissed her hand
    in the dismal gloom.
To break his oath, to brand her shame; his well-loved friend,
    his worshipped wife;
To keep his vow, to save her name, yet at the cost of what?
    Her life!
A moment's space did he hesitate, a moment of pain and
    dread and doubt,
Then he broke the seals and, stern as fate, unfolded the sheets
    and spread them out . . .
On his knees by her side he limply sank, peering amazed—
    each page was blank.

(For oh, the supremest of our art are the stories we do not
    dare to tell,
Locked in the silence of the heart, for the awful records of
    Heav'n and Hell.)

Yet those two in the silence there seemed less weariful than
 before.

Hark! a step on the garret stair, a postman knocks at the
 flimsy door.

"Registered letter!" Brown thrills with fear; opens and reads,
 then bends above:

"Glorious tidings!   Egypt, dear!   The book is accepted—life
 and love!"

GOOD-BYE, LITTLE CABIN

O DEAR little cabin, I've loved you so long,
  And now I must bid you good-bye!
I've filled you with laughter, I've thrilled you with song,
  And sometimes I've wished I could cry.
Your walls they have witnessed a weariful fight,
  And rung to a won Waterloo:
But oh, in my triumph I'm dreary to-night—
  Good-bye, little cabin, to you!

Your roof is bewhiskered, your floor is aslant,
  Your walls seem to sag and to swing;
I'm trying to find just your faults, but I can't—
  You poor, tired, heart-broken old thing!
I've seen when you've been the best friend that I had,
  Your light like a gem on the snow;
You're sort of a part of me—Gee! but I'm sad;
  I hate, little cabin, to go.

Below your cracked window red raspberries climb;
  A hornet's nest hangs from a beam;

Your rafters are scribbled with adage and rhyme,
  And dimmed with tobacco and dream.
"Each day has its laugh," and "Don't worry, just work."
  Such mottoes reproachfully shine,
Old calendars dangle—what memories lurk
  About you, dear cabin of mine!

I hear the world-call and the clang of the fight;
  I hear the hoarse cry of my kind;
Yet well do I know, as I quit you to-night,
  It's Youth that I'm leaving behind.
And often I'll think of you, empty and black,
  Moose antlers nailed over your door:
Oh, if I should perish my ghost will come back
  To dwell in you, cabin, once more!

How cold, still and lonely, how weary you seem!
  A last wistful look and I'll go.
Oh, will you remember the lad with his dream!
  The lad that you comforted so.
The shadows enfold you, it's drawing to night;
  The evening star needles the sky:
And huh! but it's stinging and stabbing my sight—
  God bless you, old cabin, good-bye!

HEART O' THE NORTH

AND when I come to the dim trail-end,
I who have been Life's rover,
This is all I would ask, my friend,
Over and over and over:

A little space on a stony hill,
With never another near me,
Sky o' the North that's vast and still,
With a single star to cheer me;

Star that gleams on a moss-grey stone
Graven by those who love me—
There would I lie alone, alone,
With a single pine above me;

Pine that the north wind whinnies through—
Oh, I have been Life's lover,
But there I'd lie and listen to
Eternity passing over.

THE SCRIBE'S PRAYER

When from my fumbling hand the tired pen falls,
  And in the twilight weary droops my head;
While to my quiet heart a still voice calls,
  Calls me to join my kindred of the Dead;
Grant that I may, O Lord, ere rest be mine,
Write to Thy praise one radiant, ringing line.

For all of worth that in this clay abides,
  The leaping rapture and the ardent flame,
The hope, the high resolve, the faith that guides;
  All, all is Thine, and liveth in Thy name:
Lord, have I dallied with the sacred fire!
Lord, have I trailed Thy glory in the mire!

E'en as a toper from the dram-shop reeling,
  Sees in his garret's blackness, dazzling fair,
All that he might have been, and, heart-sick, kneeling,
  Sobs in the passion of a vast despair;
So my ideal self haunts me alway—
When the accounting comes, how shall I pay?

For in the dark I grope, nor understand;
  And in my heart fight selfishness and sin:
Yet, Lord, I do not seek Thy helping hand;
  Rather let me my own salvation win:
Let me through strife and penitential pain
Onward and upward to the heights attain.

Yea, let me live my life, its meaning seek;
  Bear myself fitly in the ringing fight;
Strive to be strong that I may aid the weak;
  Dare to be true—O God! the Light, the Light!
Cometh the Dark so soon?... I've mocked Thy word,
  Yet do I know Thy Love: have mercy, Lord.

THE RHYMES OF A RED-CROSS MAN

THE RHYMES OF A
RED-CROSS MAN

FOREWORD

I've tinkered at my bits of rhymes
In weary, woeful, waiting times;
In doleful hours of battle-din,
Ere yet they brought the wounded in;
Through vigils of the fateful night,
In lousy barns by candle-light;
In dug-outs, sagging and aflood,
On stretchers stiff and bleared with blood;
By ragged grove, by ruined road,
By hearths accurst where Love abode;
By broken altars, blackened shrines
I've tinkered at my bits of rhymes.

I've solaced me with scraps of song
The desolated ways along:
Through sickly fields all shrapnel-sown,
And meadows reaped by death alone;
By blazing cross and splintered spire,
By headless Virgin in the mire;

By gardens gashed amid their bloom,
By gutted grave, by shattered tomb;
Beside the dying and the dead
Where rocket green and rocket red
In trembling pools of poising light
With flowers of flame festoon the night.
Ah, me! by what dark ways of wrong
I've cheered my heart with scraps of song.

So here's my sheaf of war-won verse,
And some is bad, and some is worse.
And if at times I curse a bit,
You needn't read that part of it;
For through it all like horror runs
The red resentment of the guns.
And you yourself would mutter when
You took the things that once were men
And sped them through that zone of hate
To where the dripping surgeons wait;
And wonder too if in God's sight
War ever, ever can be right.

Yet may it not be, crime and war
But effort misdirected are?
And if there's good in war and crime,
There may be in my bits of rhyme,
My songs from out the slaughter mill:
So take or leave them as you will.

THE CALL

(France, August First, 1914.)

FAR and near, high and clear,
Hark to the call of War!
Over the gorse and the golden dells,
Ringing and swinging of clamorous bells,
Praying and saying in wild farewells:
　　War!　War!　War!

High and low, all must go:
Hark to the shout of War!
Leave to the women the harvest yield;
Gird ye, men, for the sinister field;
A sabre instead of a scythe to wield:
　　War!　Red War!

Rich and poor, lord and boor,
Hark to the blast of War!
Tinker and tailor and millionaire,
Actor in triumph and priest in prayer,
Comrades now in the hell out there,
　　Sweep to the fire of War!

Prince and page, sot and sage,
　　Hark to the roar of War!
Poet, professor and circus clown,
Chimney-sweeper and fop o' the town,
Into the pot and be melted down:
　　Into the pot of War!

Women all, hear the call,
　　The pitiless call of War!
Look your last on your dearest ones,
Brothers and husbands, fathers, sons;
Swift they go to the ravenous guns,
　　The gluttonous guns of War.

Everywhere thrill the air
　　The maniac bells of War.
There will be little of sleeping to-night;
There will be wailing and weeping to-night;
Death's red sickle is reaping to-night:
　　War! War! War!

THE FOOL

"But it isn't playing the game," he said,
And he slammed his books away;
"The Latin and Greek I've got in my head
Will do for a duller day."
"Rubbish!" I cried; "the bugle's call
Isn't for lads from school."
D'ye think he'd listen? Oh, not at all:
So I called him a fool, a fool.

Now there's his dog by his empty bed,
And the flute he used to play,
And his favourite bat . . . but Dick he's dead,
Somewhere in France, they say:
Dick with his rapture of song and sun,
Dick of the yellow hair,
Dicky whose life had but begun,
Carrion-cold out there.

Look at his prizes all in a row
Surely a hint of fame.
Now he's finished with, nothing to show:
Doesn't it seem a shame?
Look from the window! All you see
Was to be his one day:
Forest and furrow, lawn and lea,
And he goes and chucks it away.

Chucks it away to die in the dark.
Somebody saw him fall,
Part of him mud, part of him blood,
The rest of him—not at all.
And yet I'll bet he was never afraid,
And he went as the best of 'em go,
For his hand was clenched on his broken blade,
And his face was turned to the foe.

And I called him a fool . . . Oh, blind was I!
And the cup of my grief's abrim.
Will Glory o' England ever die
So long as we've lads like him?
So long as we've fond and fearless fools,
Who, spurning fortune and fame,
Turn out with the rallying cry of their schools
Just bent on playing the game.

A fool! Ah, no! He was more than wise.
His was the proudest part.
He died with the glory of faith in his eyes,
And the glory of love in his heart.
And though there's never a grave to tell,
Nor a cross to mark his fall,
Thank God! we know that he "batted well"
In the last great Game of all.

THE VOLUNTEER

SEZ I: My Country calls? Well, let it call.
I grins perlitely and declines with thanks.
Go, let 'em plaster every blighted wall,
'Ere's *one* they don't stampede into the ranks.
Them politicians with their greasy ways;
Them empire-grabbers—fight for 'em?   No fear!
I've seen this mess a-comin' from the days
Of Algyserious and Aggydear:
    I've felt me passion rise and swell,
    But . . . wot the 'ell, Bill? Wot the 'ell?

Sez I: My Country?   Mine?   I likes their cheek.
Me mud-bespattered by the cars they drive,
Wot makes me measly thirty bob a week,
And sweats red blood to keep meself alive!
Fight for the right to slave that they may spend,
Them in their mansions, me 'ere in my slum?
No, let 'em fight wot's something to defend:
But me, I've nothin',—let the Kaiser come.
    And so I cusses 'ard and well,
    But . . . wot the 'ell, Bill? Wot the 'ell?

370

Sez I: If they would do the decent thing,
And shield the missis and little 'uns,
Why, even *I* might shout God save the King,
And face the chances of them 'ungry guns.
But we've got three, another on the way;
It's that wot makes me snarl and set me jor:
The wife and nippers wot of 'em, I say,
If I gets knocked out in this blasted war?
 Gets proper busted by a shell,
 But . . . wot the 'ell, Bill? Wot the 'ell?

Ay, wot the 'ell's the use of all this talk?
To-day some boys in blue was passin' me,
And some of 'em they 'ad no legs to walk,
And some of 'em they 'ad no eyes to see.
And—well, I couldn't look 'em in the face,
And so I'm goin', goin' to declare
I'm under forty-one and take me place
To face the music with the bunch out there.
 A fool, you say! Maybe you're right.
 I'll have no peace unless I fight.
 I've ceased to think; I only know
 I've gotta go, Bill, gotta go.

THE CONVALESCENT

. . . So I walked among the willows very quietly all night;
There was no moon at all, at all; no timid star alight;
There was no light at all, at all; I wint from tree to tree,
And I called him as his mother called, but he nivver answered
    me.

Oh I called him all the night-time, as I walked the wood alone;
And I listened and I listened, but I nivver heard a moan;
Then I found him at the dawnin', when the sorry sky was red:
I was lookin' for the livin', but I only found the dead.

Sure I know that it was Shamus by the silver cross he wore;
But the bugles they were callin', and I heard the cannon roar.
Oh I had no time to tarry, so I said a little prayer,
And I clasped his hands together, and I left him lyin' there.

Now the birds are singin', singin', and I'm home in Donegal,
And it's Springtime, and I'm thinkin' that I only dreamed it all;
I dreamed about that evil wood, all crowded with its dead,
Where I knelt beside me brother when the battle-dawn was red.

Where I prayed beside me brother ere I wint to fight anew:
Such dreams as these are evil dreams; I can't believe it's true.
Where all is love and laughter, sure it's hard to think of
     loss. . . .
But mother's sayin' nothin', and she clasps—*a silver cross.*

THE MAN FROM ATHABASKA

Oh the wife she tried to tell me that 'twas nothing but the
    thrumming
Of a wood-pecker a-rapping on the hollow of a tree;
And she thought that I was fooling when I said it was the
    drumming
Of the mustering of legions, and 'twas calling unto me;
'Twas calling me to pull my freight and hop across the sea.

And a-mending of my fish-nets sure I started up in wonder,
For I heard a savage roaring and 'twas coming from afar;
Oh the wife she tried to tell me that 'twas only summer
    thunder,
And she laughed a bit sarcastic when I told her it was War;
'Twas the chariots of battle where the mighty armies are.

Then down the lake came Half-breed Tom with russet sail
    a-flying,
And the word he said was "War" again, so what was I to do?

Oh, the dogs they took to howling, and the missis took to
    crying,
As I flung my silver foxes in the little birch canoe:
Yes, the old girl stood a-blubbing till an island hid the view.

Says the factor: "Mike, you're crazy! They have soldier men
    a-plenty.
You're as grizzled as a badger, and you've sixty year or so."
"But I haven't missed a scrap," says I, "since I was one and
    twenty.
And shall I miss the biggest? You can bet your whiskers—no!"
So I sold my furs and started . . . and that's eighteen months
    ago.

For I joined the Foreign Legion, and they put me for a starter
In the trenches of the Argonne with the Boche a step away;
And the partner on my right hand was an *apache* from Mont-
    martre;
On my left there was a millionaire from Pittsburg, U.S.A.
(Poor fellow! They collected him in bits the other day.)

But I'm sprier than a chipmunk, save a touch of the lumbago,
And they calls me Old Methoosalah, and *blagues* me all the
    day.
I'm their exhibition sniper, and they work me like a Dago,
And laugh to see me plug a Boche a half a mile away.
Oh I hold the highest record in the regiment, they say.

And at night they gather round me, and I tell them of my
    roaming
In the Country of the Crepuscule beside the Frozen Sea;
Where the musk-ox runs unchallenged, and the caribou goes
    homing,
And they sit like little children, just as quiet as can be:
Men of every crime and colour, how they harken unto me!

And I tell them of the Furland, of the tumpline and the paddle,
Of secret rivers loitering, that no one will explore;
And I tell them of the ranges, of the pack-strap and the saddle,
And they fill their pipes in silence, and their eyes beseech
    for more;
While above the star-shells fizzle and the high explosives roar.

And I tell of lakes fish-haunted, where the big bull moose
    are calling,
And forests still as sepulchres with never trail or track;
And valleys packed with purple gloom, and mountain peaks
    appalling,
And I tell them of my cabin on the shore at Fond du Lac;
And I find myself a-thinking: Sure I wish that I was back.

So I brag of bear and beaver while the batteries are roaring,
And the fellows on the firing steps are blazing at the foe;
And I yarn of fur and feather when the *marmites* are a-soaring,

And they listen to my stories, seven *poilus* in a row,
Seven lean and lousy *poilus* with their cigarettes aglow.

And I tell them when it's over how I'll hike for Athabaska,
And those seven greasy *poilus* they are crazy to go too.
And I'll give the wife the "pickle-tub" I promised, and I'll
    ask her
The price of mink and marten, and the run of caribou,
And I'll get my traps in order, and I'll start to work anew.

For I've had my fill of fighting, and I've seen a nation scattered,
And an army swung to slaughter, and a river red with gore,
And a city all a-smoulder, and . . . as if it really mattered,
For the lake is yonder dreaming, and my cabin's on the shore;
And the dogs are leaping madly, and the wife is singing gladly,
And I'll rest in Athabaska, and I'll leave it nevermore.

THE RED RETREAT

Tramp, tramp, the grim road, the road from Mons to Wipers
(I've 'ammered out this ditty with me bruised and bleedin' feet);
Tramp, tramp, the dim road—we didn't 'ave no pipers,
And bellies that was 'oller was the drums we 'ad to beat.
Tramp, tramp, the bad road, the bits o' kiddies crying there.
The fell birds a-flyin' there, the 'ouses all aflame;
Tramp, tramp, the sad road, the pals I left a-lyin' there,
Red there, and dead there. . . . Oh, blimy, it's a shame!

A-singin' " 'Oo's Yer Lady Friend?" we started out from 'Arver,
A-singin' till our froats was dry—we didn't care a 'ang;
The Frenchies 'ow they lined the way, and slung us their
     palaver,
And all we knowed to arnser was the one word "vang";
They gave us booze and caporal, and cheered for us like crazy,
And all the pretty gels was out to kiss us as we passed;
And ow they all went dotty when we 'owled the Marcelaisey!
Oh, Gawd! Them was the 'appy days, the days too good
     to last.

We started out for God Knows Where, we started out a-roarin';
We 'ollered: "'Ere We Are Again," and 'struth! but we was
    dry.
The dust was gummin' up our ears, and 'ow the sweat was
    pourin';
The road was long, the sun was like a brazier in the sky,
We wondered where the 'Uns was—we wasn't long a-wonderin',
For down a scruff of 'ill-side they rushes like a flood;
Then oh! 'twas music 'eavenly, our batteries a thunderin';
And arms and legs went soarin' in the fountain of their blood.

For on they came like bee swarms, a-hochin' and a-singin';
We pumped the bullets into 'em; we couldn't miss a shot.
But though we mowed 'em down like grass, like grass was
    they a-springin',
And all our 'ands was blistered, for our rifles was so 'ot.
We roared with battle-fury, and we lammed the stuffin' out
    of 'em,
And then we fixed our bay'nets and we spitted 'em like meat.
You should 'ave 'eard the beggars squeal; you should 'ave
    seen the rout of 'em,
And 'ow we cussed and wondered when the word came:
    "Retreat!"

Retreat! That was the 'ell of it. It fair upset our 'abits,
A-runnin' from them blighters over 'alf the roads of France;
A-scurryin' before 'em like a lot of blurry rabbits,

And 'knowin' we could smash 'em if we just 'ad 'alf a chance.
Retreat!   That was the bitter bit, a-limpin' and a-blunderin';
All day and night a-hoofin' it and sleepin' on our feet;
A-fightin' rearguard actions for a bit of rest, and wonderin'
If sugar beets or mangels was the 'olesomest to eat.

Ho yus, there isn't many left that started out so cheerily;
There was no bands a-playin' and we 'ad no autmobeels.
Our tummies they was 'oller, and our 'eads was 'angin' wearily,
And if we stopped to light a fag the 'Uns was on our 'eels.
That rotten road!   I can't forget the kids and mothers flyin'
        there,
The bits of barns a-blazin' and the 'orrid sights I sor;
The stiffs that lined the wayside, me own pals a-lyin' there,
Their faces covered over wiv a little 'eap of stror.

Tramp, tramp, the red road, the wicked bullets 'ummin'
(I've panted out this ditty with me 'ot 'ard breath).
Tramp, tramp, the dread road, the Boches all a-comin',
The lootin' and the shootin' and the shrieks o' death.
Tramp, tramp, the fell road, the mad 'orde pursuin' there,
And 'ow we 'urled it back again, them grim, grey waves;
Tramp, tramp, the 'ell road, the 'orror and the ruin there,
The graves of me mateys there, the grim, sour graves.

THE HAGGIS OF PRIVATE McPHEE

"Hae ye heard whit ma auld mither's postit tae me?
It fair makes me hamesick," says Private McPhee.
"And whit did she send ye?" says Private McPhun,
As he cockit his rifle and bleezed at a Hun.
"A haggis! A *haggis!*" says Private McPhee;
"The brawest big haggis I ever did see.
And think! It's the morn when fond memory turns
Tae haggis and whuskey—the Birthday o' Burns.
We maun find a dram; then we'll ca' in the rest
O' the lads, and we'll hae a Burns' Nicht wi' the best."

"Be ready at sundoon," snapped Sergeant McCole;
"I want you two men for the List'nin' Patrol."
Then Private McPhee looked at Private McPhun:
"I'm thinkin', ma lad, we're confoundedly done."
Then Private McPhun looked at Private McPhee:
"I'm thinkin', auld chap, it's a' aff wi' oor spree."
But up spoke their crony, wee Wullie McNair:
"Jist lea' yer braw haggis for me tae prepare;
And as for the dram, if I search the camp roun',
We maun hae a drappie tae jist haud it doon.

Sae rin, lads, and think, though the nicht it be black,
O' the haggis that's waitin' ye when ye get back."

My! but it wis waesome on Naebuddy's Land,
And the deid they were rottin' on every hand.
And the rockets like corpse candles hauntit the sky,
And the winds o' destruction went shudderin' by.
There wis skelpin' o' bullets and skirlin' o' shells,
And breengin' o' bombs and a thoosand death-knells;
But cooryin' doon in a Jack Johnson hole
Little fashed the twa men o' the List'nin' Patrol.
For sweeter than honey and bricht as a gem
Wis the thocht o' the haggis that waitit for them.

Yet alas! in oor moments o' sunniest cheer
Calamity's aften maist cruelly near.
And while the twa talked o' their puddin' divine
The Boches below them were howkin' a mine.
And while the twa cracked o' the feast they would hae,
The fuse it was burnin' and burnin' away.
Then sudden a roar like the thunner o' doom,
A hell-leap o' flame . . . then the wheesht o' the tomb.

"Haw, Jock! Are ye hurtit?" says Private McPhun.
"Ay, Geordie, they've got me; I'm fearin' I'm done.
It's ma leg; I'm jist thinkin' it's aff at the knee.
Ye'd best gang and leave me," says Private McPhee.

"Oh leave ye I wunna," says Private McPhun;
"And leave ye I canna, for though I micht run,
It's no faur I wud gang, it's no muckle I'd see:
I'm blindit, and that's whit's the maitter wi' me."
Then Private McPhee sadly shakit his heid:
"If we bide here for lang, we'll be bidin' for deid.
And yet, Geordie lad, I could gang weel content
If I'd tasted that haggis ma auld mither sent."
"That's droll," says McPhun; "ye've jist speakit ma mind.
Oh I ken it's a terrible thing tae be blind;
And yet it's no' that that embitters ma lot—
It's missin' that braw muckle haggis ye've got."
For a while they were silent; then up once again
Spoke Private McPhee, though he whussilt wi' pain:
"And why should we miss it? Between you and me
We've legs for tae run, and we've eyes for tae see.
You lend me your shanks and I'll lend you ma sicht,
And we'll baith hae a kyte-fu' o' haggis the nicht."

Oh the sky it wis dourlike and dreepin' a wee,
When Private McPhun gruppit Private McPhee.
Oh the glaur it wis fylin' and crieshin' the grun',
When Private McPhee guidit Private McPhun.
"Keep clear o' them corpses—they're maybe no deid!
Haud on! There's a big muckle crater aheid.
Look oot! There's a sap; we'll be haein' a coup.
A staur-shell! For Godsake! Doun', lad, on yer daup.
Bear aff tae yer richt. . . . Aw yer jist daein' fine:
Before the nicht's feenished on haggis we'll dine."

There wis death and destruction on every hand;
There wis havoc and horror on Naebuddy's Land.
And the shells bickered doun wi' a crump and a glare,
And the hameless wee bullets were dingin' the air.
Yet on they went staggerin', cooryin' doun
When the stutter and cluck o' a Maxim crept roun'.
And the legs o' McPhun they were sturdy and stoot,
And McPhee on his back kept a bonnie look-oot.
"On, on, ma brave lad! We're no faur frae the goal
I can hear the braw sweerin' o' Sergeant McCole."

But strength has its leemit, and Private McPhun,
Wi' a sab and a curse fell his length on the grun'.
Then Private McPhee shoutit doon in his ear:
"Jist think o' the haggis! I smell it from here.
It's gushin' wi' juice, it's embaumin' the air;
It's steamin' for us, and we're—jist—aboot—there."
Then Private McPhun answers: "Dommit, auld chap!
For the sake o' the haggis I'll gang till I drap."
And he gets on his feet wi' a heave and a strain,
And onward he staggers in passion and pain.
And the flare and the glare and the fury increase,
Till you'd think they'd jist taken a' hell on a lease
And on they go reelin' in peetifu' plight,
And someone is shoutin' away on their right;
And someone is runnin', and noo they can hear
A sound like a prayer and a sound like a cheer;

And swift through the crash and the flash and the din,
The lads o' the Hielands are bringin them in.

"They're baith sairly woundit, but is it no' droll
Hoo they rave aboot haggis?" says Sergeant McCole.
When hirplin alang comes wee Wullie McNair,
And they a' wonnert why he wis greetin' sae sair.
And he says: "I'd jist liftit it oot o' the pot,
And there it lay steamin' and savoury hot,
When sudden I dooked at the fleech o' a shell,
And it *drapped on the haggis and dinged it tae hell*."

And oh, but the lads were fair taken aback;
Then sudden the order wis passed tae attack,
And up from the trenches like lions they leapt,
And on through the nicht like a torrent they swept
On, on, wi' their bayonets thirstin' before!
On, on tae the foe wi' a rush and a roar!
And wild to the welkin their battle-cry rang,
And doon on the Boches like tigers they sprang:
And there wisna a man but had death in his 'ee,
For he thocht o' the haggis o' Private McPhee.

THE LARK

FROM wrath-red dawn to wrath-red dawn,
The guns have brayed without abate;
And now the sick sun looks upon
The bleared, blood-boltered fields of hate
As if it loathed to rise again.
How strange the hush! Yet sudden, hark!
From yon down-trodden gold of grain,
The leaping rapture of a lark.

A fusillade of melody,
That sprays us from yon trench of sky;
A new amazing enemy
We cannot silence though we try;
A battery on radiant wings,
That from yon gap of golden fleece
Hurls at us hopes of such strange things
As joy and home and love and peace.

386

Pure heart of song! do you not know
That we are making earth a hell?
Or is it that you try to show
Life still is joy and all is well?
Brave little wings! Ah, not in vain
You beat into that bit of blue:
Lo! we who pant in war's red rain
Lift shining eyes, see Heaven too.

THE ODYSSEY OF 'ERBERT 'IGGINS

ME and Ed and a stretcher
Out on the nootral ground.
(If there's one dead corpse, I'll betcher
There's a 'undred smellin' around.)
Me and Eddie O'Brian,
Both of the R.A.M.C.
"It's a 'ell of a night
For a soul to take·flight,"
As Eddie remarks to me.
Me and Ed crawlin' 'omeward,
Thinkin' our job is done,
When sudden and clear,
Wot do we 'ear:
'Owl of a wounded 'Un.

"Got to take 'im," snaps Eddy;
"Got to take all we can.
'E may be a Germ
Wiv the 'eart of a worm,

But, blarst 'im! ain't 'e a man?"
So 'e sloshes out fixin' a dressin'
('E'd always a medical knack),
When that wounded 'Un
'E rolls to 'is gun,
And 'e plugs me pal in the back.

Now what would you do? I arst you.
There was me slaughtered mate,
There was that 'Un
(I'd collered 'is gun),
A-snarlin' 'is 'ymn of 'ate.
Wot did I do? 'Ere, whisper. . . .
'E'd a shiny bald top to 'is 'ead,
But when I got through,
Between me and you,
It was 'orrid and jaggy and red.

"'Ang on like a limpet, Eddy.
Thank God! you ain't dead after all."
It's slow and it's sure and it's steady
(Which is 'ard, for 'e's big and I'm small).
The rockets are shootin' and shinin',
It's rainin' a perishin' flood,
The bullets are buzzin' and whinin',
And I'm up to me stern in the mud.
There's all kinds of 'owlin' and 'ootin';
It's black as a bucket of tar:

Oh, I'm doin' my bit,
But I'm 'avin' a fit,
And I wish I was 'ome wiv Mar.
"Stick on like a plaster, Eddy.
Old sport, you're a-slakin' your grip."
Gord! But I'm crocky already;
My feet, 'ow they slither and slip!
There goes the biff of a bullet.
The Boches have got us for fair.
Another one—*Whut!*
The son of a slut!
'E managed to miss by a 'air.
'Ow! What was it jabbed at me shoulder?
Gave it a dooce of a wrench.
Is it Eddy or me
Wot's a-bleedin' so free?
Crust! but it's long to the trench.
I ain't just as strong as a Sandow,
And Ed ain't a flapper by far;
I'm blamed if I understand 'ow
We've managed to get where we are,
But 'ere's for a bit of a breather.
"Steady, there, Ed, 'arf a mo'.
Old pal, it's all right;
It's a 'ell of a fight,
But are we down-'earted? No-o-o."

Now war is a funny thing, ain't it?
It's the rummiest sort of a go.

For when it's most real,
It's then that you feel
You're a-watchin' a cinema show.
'Ere's me wot's a barber's assistant.
Hey presto! It's somewheres in France,
And I'm 'ere in a pit
Where a coal-box 'as 'it,
And it's all like a giddy romance.
The ruddy quick-firers are spittin',
The 'eavies are bellowin' 'ate,
And 'ere I am cashooly sittin'
And 'oldin' the 'ead of me mate.
Them gharstly green star-shells is beamin',
'Ot shrapnel is poppin' like rain,
And I'm sayin': "Bert 'Iggins, you're dreamin'
And you'll wake up in 'Ampstead again.
You'll wake up and 'ear yourself sayin':
'Would you like, sir, to 'ave a shampoo?'
'Stead of sheddin' yer blood
In the rain and the mud,
Which is some'ow the right thing to do;
Which is some'ow yer 'oary-eyed dooty,
Wot you're doin' the best wot you can,
For 'Ampstead and 'ome and beauty,
And you've been and you've slaughtered a man,
A feller wot punctured your partner;
Oh, you 'ammered 'im 'ard on the 'ead,
And you still see 'is eyes
Starin' bang at the skies,

And you ain't even sorry 'e's dead.
But you wish you was back in your diggin's
Asleep on your mouldy old stror.
Oh, you're doin' yer bit, 'Erbert 'Iggins,
But you ain't just enjoyin' the war."

"'Ang on like a hoctopus, Eddy.
It's us for the bomb-belt again.
Except for the shrap
Which 'as 'it me a tap,
I'm feelin' as right as the rain.
It's my silly old feet wot are slippin',
It's as dark as a 'ogs'ead o' sin,
But don't be oneasy, my pippin,
I'm goin' to pilot you in.
It's my silly old 'ead wot is reelin'.
The bullets is buzzin' like bees.
Me shoulder's red-'ot,
And I'm bleedin' a lot,
And me legs is on'inged at the knees.
But we're staggerin' nearer and nearer.
Just stick it, old sport, play the game.
I make 'em out clearer and clearer,
Our trenches a-snappin' with flame.
Oh, we're stumblin' closer and closer.
'Ang on there, lad!   Just one more try.
Did you say: Put you down?   Damn it, no, sir
I'll carry you in if I die.

By cracky! old feller, they've seen us.
They're sendin' out stretchers for two.
Let's give 'em the hoorah between us
('Anged lucky we aren't booked through).
My flipper is mashed to a jelly.
A bullet 'as tickled your spleen.
We've shed lots of gore
And we're leakin' some more,
But—wot a hoccasion it's been!
Ho! 'Ere comes the rescuin' party.
They're crawlin' out cautious and slow.
Come! Buck up and greet 'em, my 'earty,
Shoulder to shoulder—so.
They mustn't think we was down-'earted.
Old pal, we was never down-'earted.
If they arsts us if we was down-'earted
We'll 'owl in their fyces: 'No-o-o.' "

A SONG OF WINTER WEATHER

It isn't the foe that we fear;
It isn't the bullets that whine;
It isn't the business career
Of a shell, or the bust of a mine;
It isn't the snipers who seek
To nip our young hopes in the bud:
No, it isn't the guns,
And it isn't the Huns—
It's the Mud,

        Mud,

           Mud.

        It isn't the *mêlée* we mind.
        That often is rather good fun.
        It isn't the shrapnel we find
        Obtrusive when rained by the ton;
        It isn't the bounce of the bombs
        That gives us a positive pain:
        It's the strafing we get
        When the weather is wet—
        It's the Rain,

                Rain,

                    Rain.

It isn t because we lack grit
We shrink from the horrors of war.
We don't mind the battle a bit;
In fact that is what we are for;
It isn't the rum-jars and things
Make us wish we were back in the fold:
It's the fingers that freeze
In the boreal breeze—
It's the COLD,

        COLD,

            COLD.

        Oh, the rain, the mud, and the cold,
        The cold, the mud, and the rain;
        With weather at zero it's hard for a hero
        From language that's rude to refrain.
        With porridgy muck to the knees,
        With sky that's a-pouring a flood,
        Sure the worst of our foes
        Are the pains and the woes
        Of the RAIN,

                the COLD,

                      and the MUD.

TIPPERARY DAYS

Oн, weren't they the fine boys! You never saw the beat of
    them,
Singing all together with their throats bronze-bare;
Fighting-fit and mirth-mad, music in the feet of them,
Swinging on to glory and the wrath out there.
Laughing by and chaffing by, frolic in the smiles of them,
On the road, the white road, all the afternoon;
Strangers in a strange land, miles and miles and miles of them,
Battle-bound and heart-high, and singing this tune:

> It's a long way to Tipperary,
> It's a long way to go;
> It's a long way to Tipperary,
> And the sweetest girl I know.
> Good-bye, Piccadilly,
> Farewell, Leicester Square:
> It's a long, long way to Tipperary,
> But my heart's right there.

Come Yvonne and Juliette! Come Mimi and cheer for them!
Throw them flowers and kisses as they pass you by.
Aren't they the lovely lads! Haven't you a tear for them,
Going out so gallantly to dare and die?
What is it they're singing so? Some high hymn of Mother-
land?
Some immortal chanson of their Faith and King?
Marseillaise or Brabançon, anthem of that other land,
Dears, let us remember it, that song they sing:

> 'C'est un chemin long 'to Tepararee,'
> C'est un chemin long, c'est vrai;
> C'est un chemin long 'to Tepararee,'
> Et la belle fille qu'je connais;
> Bonjour, Peekadeely!
> Au revoir, Lestaire Squaire!
> C'est un chemin long 'to Tepararee,'
> Mais mon cœur 'ees zaire.' "

The gallant old "Contemptibles"! There isn't much remains
of them,
So full of fun and fitness, and a-singing in their pride;
For some are cold as clabber and the corby picks the brains of
them,
And some are back in Blighty, and a-wishing they had died.
Ah me! It seems but yesterday, that great, glad sight of them,

Swinging on to battle as the sky grew black and black;
Yet oh, their glee and glory, and the great, grim fight of them!—
Just whistle Tipperary and it all comes back:

> *It's a long way to Tipperary*
> *(Which means "'ome" anywhere);*
> *It's a long way to Tipperary*
> *(And the things wot make you care).*
> *Good-bye, Piccadilly*
> *('Ow I 'opes my folks is well);*
> *It's a long, long way to Tipperary—*
> *('R! Ain't War just 'ell?)*

FLEURETTE

(The Wounded Canadian speaks)

My leg? It's off at the knee.
Do I miss it? Well, some. You see
I've had it since I was born;
And lately a devilish corn.
(I rather chuckle with glee
To think how I've fooled that corn.)

But I'll hobble around all right.
It isn't that, it's my face.
Oh I know I'm a hideous sight,
Hardly a thing in place;
Sort of gargoyle, you'd say;
Nurse won't give me a glass,
But I see the folks as they pass
Shudder and turn away;
Turn away in distress . . .
Mirror enough I guess.

I'm gay! You bet I *am* gay;
But I wasn't a while ago.
If you'd seen me even to-day,
The darndest picture of woe,
With this Caliban mug of mine.
So ravaged and raw and red,
Turned to the wall—in fine,
Wishing that I was dead. . . .
What has happened since then,
Since I lay with my face to the wall,
The most despairing of men?
Listen! I'll tell you all.

That *poilu* across the way,
With the shrapnel wound in his head,
Has a sister: she came to-day
To sit awhile by his bed.
All morning I heard him fret:
"Oh, when will she come, Fleurette?"

Then sudden, a joyous cry;
The tripping of little feet;
The softest, tenderest sigh;
A voice so fresh and sweet;
Clear as a silver bell,
Fresh as the morning dews:
"*C'est toi, c'est toi, Marcel!*
Mon frère, comme je suis heureuse!"

So over the blanket's rim
I raised my terrible face,
And I saw—how I envied him!
A girl of such delicate grace;
Sixteen, all laughter and love;
As gay as a linnet, and yet
As tenderly sweet as a dove;
Half woman, half child—Fleurette.

Then I turned to the wall again.
(I was awfully blue, you see.)
And I thought with a bitter pain:
"Such visions are not for me."
So there like a log I lay,
All hidden, I thought, from view,
When sudden I heard her say:
"Ah!   Who is that *malheureux?*"
Then briefly I heard him tell
(However he came to know)
How I'd smothered a bomb that fell
Into the trench, and so
None of my men were hit,
Though it busted me up a bit.

Well, I didn't quiver an eye,
And he chattered and there she sat;
And I fancied I heard her sigh—
Though I wouldn't just swear to that.

And maybe she wasn't so bright,
Though she talked in a merry strain,
And I closed my eyes ever so tight,
Yet I saw her ever so plain:
Her dear little tilted nose,
Her delicate dimpled chin,
Her mouth like a budding rose,
And the glistening pearls within;
Her eyes like the violet:
Such a rare little queen—Fleurette.

And at last when she rose to go,
The light was a little dim,
And I ventured to peep, and so
I saw her, graceful and slim,
And she kissed him and kissed him, and oh
How I envied and envied him!

So when she was gone I said
In rather a dreary voice
To him of the opposite bed:
"Ah, friend, how you must rejoice!
But me, I'm a thing of dread.
For me nevermore the bliss,
The thrill of a woman's kiss."

Then I stopped, for lo! she was there,
And a great light shone in her eyes

And me! I could only stare,
I was taken so by surprise,
When gently she bent her head:
"May I kiss you, Sergeant?" she said.
Then she kissed my burning lips
With her mouth like a scented flower,
And I thrilled to the finger-tips,
And I hadn't even the power
To say: "God bless you, dear!"
And I felt such a precious tear
Fall on my withered cheek,
And darn it! I couldn't speak.

And so she went sadly away,
And I knew that my eyes were wet.
Ah, not to my dying day
Will I forget, forget!
Can you wonder now I am gay?
God bless her, that little Fleurette!

o

FUNK

WHEN your marrer bone seems 'oller,
And you're glad you ain't no taller,
And you're all a-shakin' like you 'ad the chills;
When your skin creeps like a pullet's,
And you're' duckin' all the bullets,
And you're green as gorgonzola round the gills;
When your legs seem made of jelly,
And you're squeamish in the belly,
And you want to turn about and do a bunk:
For Gawd's sake, kid, don't show it!
Don't let your mateys know it—
You're just sufferin' from funk, funk, funk.

Of course there's no denyin'
That it ain't so easy tryin'
To grin and grip your rifle by the butt,
When the 'ole world rips asunder,
And you sees yer pal go under,
As a bunch of shrapnel sprays 'im on the nut;

I admit it's 'ard contrivin',
When you' 'ears the shells arrivin',
To discover you're a bloomin' bit o' spunk;
But, my lad, you've got to do it,
And your God will see you through it,
For wot 'E 'ates is funk, funk, funk.

So stand up, son; look gritty,
And just 'um a lively ditty,
And only be afraid to be afraid;
Just 'old yer rifle steady,
And 'ave yer bay'nit ready,
For that's the way good soldier-men is made.
And if you 'as to die,
As it sometimes 'appens, why,
Far better die a 'ero than a skunk;
A'doin' of yer bit,
And so—to 'ell with it,
There ain't no bloomin' funk, funk, funk.

OUR HERO

"FLOWERS, only flowers—bring me dainty posies,
Blossoms for forgetfulness," that was all he said;
So we sacked our gardens, violets and roses,
Lilies white and bluebells laid we on his bed.
Soft his pale hands touched them, tenderly caressing;
Soft into his tired eyes came a little light;
Such a wistful love-look, gentle as a blessing;
There amid the flowers waited he the night.

"I would have you raise me; I can see the West then:
I would see the sun set once before I go."
So he lay a-gazing, seemed to be at rest then,
Quiet as a spirit in the golden glow.
So he lay a-watching rosy castles crumbling,
Moats of blinding amber, bastions of flame,
Rugged rifts of opal, crimson turrets tumbling;
So he lay a-dreaming till the shadows came.

"Open wide the window; there's a lark a-singing;
There's a glad lark singing in the evening sky.

How it's wild with rapture, radiantly winging:
Oh it's good to hear that when one has to die.
I am horror-haunted from the hell they found me;
I am battle-broken, all I want is rest.
Ah! It's good to die so, blossoms all around me,
And a kind lark singing in the golden West."

"Flowers, song and sunshine, just one thing is wanting,
Just the happy laughter of a little child."
So we brought out dearest, Doris all-enchanting;
Tenderly he kissed her; radiant he smiled.
"In the golden peace-time you will tell the story
How for you and yours, sweet, bitter deaths were ours. . . .
God bless little children!" So he passed to glory,
So we left him sleeping, still amid the flow'rs.

MY MATE

I'VE been sittin' starin', starin' at 'is muddy pair of boots,
And tryin' to convince meself it's 'im.
(Look out there, lad! That sniper—'e's a dysey when 'e shoots;
'E'll be layin' of you out the same as Jim.)
Jim as lies there in the dug-out wiv 'is blanket round 'is 'ead,
To keep 'is brains from mixin' wiv the mud;
And 'is face as white as putty, and his overcoat all red,
Like 'e's spilt a bloomin' paint-pot—but it's blood.

And I'm tryin' to remember of a time we wasn't pals.
'Ow often we've played 'ookey, 'im and me;
And sometimes it was music-'alls, and sometimes it was gals,
And even there we 'ad no disagree.
For when 'e copped Maria Jones, the one I liked the best,
I shook 'is 'and and loaned 'im 'arf a quid;
I saw 'im through the parson's job, I 'elped 'im make 'is nest,
I even stood god-farther to the kid.

So when the war broke out, sez 'e: "Well, wot abaht it, Joe?"
"Well, wot abaht it, lad?" sez I to 'im.

'Is missis made a awful fuss, but 'e was mad to go
('E always was 'igh-sperrited was Jim).
Well, none of it's been 'eaven, and the most of it's been 'ell,
But we've shared our baccy, and we've 'alved our bread.
We'd all the luck at Wipers, and we shaved through Noove
    Chapelle,
And . . . that snipin' barstard gits 'im on the 'ead.

Now wot I wants to know is, why it wasn't me was took?
I've only got meself, 'e stands for three.
I'm plainer than a louse, while 'e was 'andsome as a dook;
'E always *was* a better man than me.
'E was goin' 'ome next Toosday; 'e was 'appy as a lark,
And 'e'd just received a letter from 'is kid;
And 'e struck a match to show me, as we stood there in the
    dark,
When . . . that bleedin' bullet got 'im on the lid.

'E was killed so awful sudden that 'e 'adn't time to die
'E sorto jumped, and came down wiv a thud.
Them corpsy-lookin' star-shells kept a-streamin' in the sky,
And there 'e lay like nothin' in the mud.
And there 'e lay so quiet wiv no mansard to 'is 'ead,
And I'm sick, and blamed if I can understand:
The pots of 'alf and 'alf we've 'ad, and *zip!* like that—'e's dead,
Wiv the letter of 'is nipper in 'is 'and.

There's some as fights for freedom and there's some as fights
    for fun,
But me, my lad, I fights for bleedin' 'ate.
You can blame the war and blast it, but I 'opes it won't be
    done
Till I gets the bloomin' blood-price for me mate.
It'll take a bit o' bayonet to level up for Jim;
Then if I'm spared I think I'll 'ave a bid
Wiv 'er that was Maria Jones to take the place of 'im,
To sorter be a farther to 'is kid.

MILKING TIME

There's a drip of honeysuckle in the deep green lane;
There's old Martin jogging homeward on his worn old wain;
There are cherry petals falling, and a cuckoo calling, calling,
And a score of larks (God bless 'em) . . . but it's all pain, pain.
For you see I am not really there at all, not at all;
For you see I'm in the trenches where the crump-crumps fall;
And the bits o' shells are screaming and it's only blessed
    dreaming
That in fancy I am seeming back in old Saint Pol.

Oh I've thought of it so often since I've come down here;
And I never dreamt that any place could be so dear;
The silvered whinstone houses, and the rosy men in blouses,
And the kindly, white-capped women with their eyes spring-
    clear.
And mother's sitting knitting where her roses climb,
And the angelus is calling with a soft, soft chime,

And the sea-wind comes caressing, and the light's a golden
    blessing,
And Yvonne, Yvonne is guessing that it's milking time.

Oh it's Sunday, for she's wearing of her 'broidered gown;
And she draws the pasture pickets and the cows come down;
And their feet are powdered yellow, and their voices honey-
    mellow,
And they bring a scent of clover, and their eyes are brown.
And Yvonne is dreaming after, but her eyes are blue;
And her lips are made for laughter, and her white teeth too;
And her mouth is like a cherry, and a dimple mocking merry
Is lurking in the very cheek she turns to you.

So I walk beside her kindly, and she laughs at me;
And I heap her arms with lilac from the lilac tree;
And a golden light is welling, and a golden peace is dwelling,
And a thousand birds are telling how it's good to be.
And what are pouting lips for if they can't be kissed?
And I've filled her arms with blossom so she can't resist;
And the cows are sadly straying, and her mother must be saying
That Yvonne is long delaying . . . *God!   How close that missed!*

A nice polite reminder that the Boche are nigh;
That we're here to fight like devils, and if need be **die**;
That from kissing pretty wenches to the frantic firing-benches
Of the battered, tattered trenches is a far, far cry.

Yet still I'm sitting dreaming in the glare and grime;
And once again I'm hearing of them church-bells chime;
And how I wonder whether in the golden summer weather
We will fetch the cows together when it's milking time! . . .

English voice, months later:
"Ow, Bill! A rottin' Frenchy. Whew! 'E ain't 'arf
    prime. . . ."

YOUNG FELLOW MY LAD

"Where are you going, Young Fellow My Lad,
On this glittering morn of May?"
"I'm going to join the Colours, Dad;
They're looking for men, they say."
"But you're only a boy, Young Fellow My Lad;
You aren't obliged to go."
"I'm seventeen and a quarter, Dad,
And ever so strong, you know."

*　　　*　　　*　　　*　　　*　　　*

"So you're off to France, Young Fellow My Lad,
And you're looking so fit and bright."
"I'm terribly sorry to leave you, Dad,
But I feel that I'm doing right."
"God bless you and keep you, Young Fellow My Lad,
You're all of my life, you know."
"Don't worry.   I'll soon be back, dear Dad,
And I'm awfully proud to go."

*　　　*　　　*　　　*　　　*　　　*

"Why don't you write, Young Fellow My Lad!
I watch for the post each day;
And I miss you so, and I'm awfully sad,
And it's months since you went away.
And I've had the fire in the parlour lit,
And I'm keeping it burning bright
Till my boy comes home; and here I sit
Into the quiet night."

* * * * * *

"What is the matter, Young Fellow My Lad?
No letter again to-day,
Why did the postman look so sad,
And sigh as he turned away?
I hear them tell that we've gained new ground,
But a terrible price we've paid:
God grant, my boy, that you're safe and sound;
But oh I'm afraid, afraid."

* * * * * *

"They've told me the truth, Young Fellow My Lad:
You'll never come back again.
(Oh God! the dreams and the dreams I've had,
And the hopes I've nursed in vain!)
For you passed in the night, Young Fellow My Lad,
And you proved in the cruel test
Of the screaming shell and the battle hell
That my boy was one of the best."

"So you'll live, you'll live, Young Fellow My Lad,
In the gleam of the evening star,
In the woodnote wild and the laugh of the child,
In all sweet things that are.
And you'll never die, my wonderful boy,
While life is noble and true;
For all our beauty and hope and joy
We will owe to our lads like you."

A SONG OF THE SANDBAGS

No, Bill, I'm not a-spooning out no patriotic tosh
(The cove be'ind the sandbags ain't a death-or-glory cuss).
And though I strafes 'em good and 'ard I doesn't 'ate the Boche,
I guess they're mostly decent, just the same as most of us.
I guess they loves their 'omes and kids as much as you or me;
And just the same as you or me they'd rather shake than fight;
And if we'd 'appened to be born at Berlin-on-the-Spree,
We'd be out there, with 'Ans and Fritz, dead sure that we was
    right.

      A-standin' up to the sandbags,
      It's funny the thoughts wot come;
      Starin' into the darkness,
      'Earin' the bullets 'um;
      (Zing! Zip! Ping! Rip!
      'Ark 'ow the bullets 'um!)
      A-leanin' against the sandbags
      Wiv me rifle under me ear,
      Oh, I've 'ad more thoughts on a sentry-go
      Than I used to 'ave in a year.

I wonder, Bill, if 'Ans and Fritz is wonderin' like me
Wot's at the bottom of it all?   Wot all the slaughter's for?
'E thinks 'e's right (of course 'e ain't), but this we both agree,
If them as made it 'ad to fight, there wouldn't be no war.
If them as lies in feather beds while we kips in the mud;
If them as makes their fortoons while we fights for 'em like 'ell;
If them as slings their pots of ink just 'ad to sling their blood:
By Crust!   I'm thinkin' there'ud be another tale to tell.

Shiverin' up to the sandbags,
With a hicicle 'stead of a spine,
Don't it seems funny the things you think
'Ere in the firin' line:
(*Wee! Whut! Ziz! Zut!*
Lord! 'Ow the bullets whine!)
Hunkerin' down when a star-shell
Cracks in a sputter of light,
You can jaw to yer soul by the sandbags
Most any old time o' night.

They talks o' England's glory and a-'oldin' of our trade,
Of Empire and 'igh destiny until we're fair flim-flammed;
But if it's for the likes o' that that bloody war is made,
Then wot I say is: Empire and 'igh destiny be damned!
There's only one good cause, Bill, for poor blokes like us to
        fight:

That's self-defence, for 'earth and 'ome, and them that bears
   our name;
And that's wot I'm a-doin' by the sandbags 'ere to-night. . . .
But Fritz out there will tell you 'e's a-doin' of the same.

      Starin' over the sandbags,
      Sick of the 'ole damn thing;
      Firin' to keep meself awake,
      'Earin' the bullets sing
      (Hiss! Twang! Tsing! Pang!
      Saucy the bullets sing.)
      Dreamin' 'ere by the sandbags
      Of a day when war will cease,
      When 'Ans and Fritz and Bill and me
      Will clink our mugs in fraternity,
      And the Brotherhood of Labour will be
      The Brotherhood of Peace.

ON THE WIRE

Oh God, take the sun from the sky!
It's burning me, scorching me up.
God, can't You hear my cry?
Water! A poor, little cup!
It's laughing, the cursed sun!
See how it swells and swells
Fierce as a hundred hells!
God, will it never have done?
It's searing the flesh on my bones;
It's beating with hammers red
My eyeballs into my head;
It's parching my very moans.
See! It's the size of the sky,
And the sky is a torrent of fire,
Foaming on me as I lie
Here on the wire . . . the wire. . . .

Of the thousands that wheeze and hum
Heedlessly over my head,
Why can't a bullet come,

Pierce to my brain instead,
Blacken for ever my brain,
Finish for ever my pain?
Here in the hellish glare
Why must I suffer so?
Is it God doesn't care?
Is it God doesn't know?
Oh, to be killed outright,
Clean in the clash of the fight!
That is a golden death,
That is a boon; but this . . .
Drawing an anguished breath
Under a hot abyss,
Under a stooping sky
Of seething, sulphurous fire,
Scorching me up as I lie
Here on the wire . . . the wire. . . .

Hasten, Oh God, Thy night!
Hide from my eyes the sight
Of the body I stare and see
Shattered so hideously.
I can't believe that it's mine.
My body was white and sweet,
Flawless and fair and fine,
Shapely from head to feet;
Oh no, I can never be
The thing of horror I see

Under the rifle fire,
Trussed on the wire . . . the wire. . . .

Of night and of death I dream;
Night that will bring me peace,
Coolness and starry gleam,
Stillness and death's release.
Ages and ages have passed—
Lo! it is night at last.
Night! but the guns roar out.
Night! but the hosts attack.
Red and yellow and black
Geysers of doom upspout.
Silver and green and red
Star-shells hover and spread.
Yonder off to the right
Fiercely kindles the fight;
Roaring near and more near,
Thundering now in my ear;
Close to me, close . . . Oh, hark!
Someone moans in the dark.
I hear, but I cannot see,
I hear as the rest retire,
Someone is caught like me,
Caught on the wire . . . the wire. . . .

Again the shuddering dawn,
Weird and wicked and wan;

Again, and I've not yet gone.
The man whom I heard is dead.
Now I can understand:
A pistol gripped in his hand.
Well, he knew what to do,—
Yes, and now I know too. . . .

Hark the resentful guns!
Oh, how thankful am I
To think my beloved ones
Will never know how I die!
I've suffered more than my share;
I'm shattered beyond repair;
I've fought like a man the fight,
And now I demand the right
(God! how his fingers cling!)
To do without shame this thing.
Good! there's a bullet still;
Now I am ready to fire;
Blame me, God, if You will,
Here on the wire . . . the wire. . . .

BILL'S GRAVE

I'M gatherin' flowers by the wayside to lay on the grave of Bill;
I've sneaked away from the billet, 'cause Jim wouldn t under-
    stand;
'E'd call me a silly fat'ead, and larf till it made 'im ill,
To see me 'ere in the cornfield, wiv a big bookay in me 'and.

For Jim and me we are rough 'uns, but Bill was one o' the
    best;
We 'listed and learned together to larf at the wust wot comes;
Then Bill copped a packet proper, and took 'is departure West,
So sudden 'e 'adn't a minit to say good-bye to 'is chums.

And they took me to where 'e was planted, a sort of a measly
    mound,
And, thinks I, 'ow Bill would be tickled, bein' so soft and
    queer,
If I gathered a bunch o' them wild-flowers, and sort of ar-
    ranged them round
Like a kind of a bloody head-piece . . . and that's the reason
    I'm 'ere.

But not for the love of glory I wouldn't 'ave Jim to know.
'E'd call me a slobberin' Cissy, and larf till 'is sides was sore;
I'd 'ave larfed at meself meself too, it isn't so long ago;
But some'ow it changes a feller, 'avin' a taste of war.

It 'elps a man to be 'elpful, to know wot 'is pals is worth
(Them golden poppies is blazin' like lamps some fairy 'as lit);
I'm fond o' them big white dysies. . . . Now Jim's o' the salt
      o' the earth;
But 'e 'as got a tongue wot's a terror, and 'e ain't sentimental
      a bit.

I likes them blue chaps wot's 'idin' so shylike among the corn.
Won't Bill be glad! We was allus thicker 'n thieves, us three.
Why! 'Oo's that singin' so 'earty? *Jim!* And as sure as I'm
      born,
'E's there in the giddy cornfields, a-gatherin' flowers like me.

Quick! Drop me posy be'ind me. I watches 'im for a while,
Then I says: "Wot o', there, Chummy! Wot price the little
      bookay?"
And 'e starts like a bloke wot's guilty, and 'e says with a
      sheepish smile:
"She's a bit of orl right, the widder wot keeps the estaminay."

So 'e goes away in a 'urray, and I wishes 'im best 'o luck,
And I picks up me bunch o' wild-flowers, and the light's
      gettin' sorto dim,

When I makes me way to the boneyard, and . . . I stares like
 a man wot's stuck,
For wot do I see? *Bill's grave-mound strewn with the flowers
 of Jim.*

Of course I won't never tell 'im, bein' a tactical lad;
And Jim parley-voos to the widder: "Trez beans, lamoor;
 compree?"
Oh, 'e'd die of shame if 'e knew I knew; but say! won't Bill
 be glad
When 'e stares through the bleedin' clods and sees the blossoms
 of Jim and me!

JEAN DESPREZ

Oh ye whose hearts are resonant, and ring to War's romance,
Hear ye the story of a boy, a peasant boy of France;
A lad uncouth and warped with toil, yet who, when trial came,
Could feel within his soul upleap and soar the sacred flame;
Could stand upright, and scorn and smite, as only heroes may:
Oh, harken! Let me try to tell the tale of Jean Desprez.

With fire and sword the Teuton horde was ravaging the land,
And there was darkness and despair, grim death on every
    hand;
Red fields of slaughter sloping down to ruin's black abyss;
The wolves of war ran evil-fanged, and little did they miss.
And on they came with fear and flame, to burn and loot and
    slay.
Until they reached the red-roofed croft, the home of Jean
    Desprez.

"Rout out the village, one and all!" the Uhlan Captain said.
"Behold! Some hand has fired a shot. My trumpeter is dead.

Now shall they Prussian vengeance know; now shall they rue
  the day,
For by this sacred German slain, ten of these dogs shall pay."
They drove the cowering peasants forth, women and babes and
  men,
And from the last, with many a jeer, the Captain chose he ten;
Ten simple peasants, bowed with toil; they stood, they knew
  not why,
Against the grey wall of the church, hearing their children cry;
Hearing their wives and mothers wail, with faces dazed they
  stood.
A moment only. . . . *Ready! Fire!* They weltered in their
  blood.

But there was one who gazed unseen, who heard the frenzied
  cries,
Who saw these men in sabots fall before their children's eyes;
A Zouave wounded in a ditch, and knowing death was nigh,
He laughed with joy: "Ah! here is where I settle ere I die."
He clutched his rifle once again, and long he aimed and
  well. . . .
A shot! Beside his victims ten the Uhlan Captain fell.

They dragged the wounded Zouave out; their rage was like a
  flame.
With bayonets they pinned him down, until their Major came.
A blonde, full-blooded man he was, and arrogant of eye;
He stared to see with shattered skull his favourite Captain lie.

"Nay, do not finish him so quick, this foreign swine," he cried;
"Go nail him to the big church door: he shall be crucified."

With bayonets through hands and feet they nailed the Zouave
    there,
And there was anguish in his eyes, and horror in his stare;
"Water! A single drop!" he moaned; but how they jeered at
    him,
And mocked him with an empty cup, and saw his sight grow
    dim;
And as in agony of death with blood his lips were wet,
The Prussian Major gaily laughed, and lit a cigarette.

But 'mid the white-faced villagers who cowered in horror by,
Was one who saw the woeful sight, who heard the woeful cry:
"Water! One little drop, I beg! For love of Christ who
    died. . . ."
It was the little Jean Desprez who turned and stole aside;
It was the little bare-foot boy who came with cup abrim,
And walked up to the dying man, and gave the drink to him.

A roar of rage! They seize the boy; they tear him fast away.
The Prussian Major swings around; no longer is he gay.
His teeth are wolfishly a-gleam; his face all dark with spite:
"Go, shoot the brat," he snarls, "that dare defy our Prussian
    might.
Yet stay! I have another thought. I'll kindly be, and spare;

Quick; give the lad a rifle charged, and set him squarely there,
And bid him shoot, and shoot to kill. Haste! Make him
    understand.
The dying dog he fain would save shall perish by his hand.
And all his kindred they shall see, and all shall curse his name,
Who bought his life at such a cost, the price of death and
    shame."

They brought the boy, wild-eyed with fear; they made him
    understand;
They stood him by the dying man, a rifle in his hand.
"Make haste!" said they; "the time is short, and you must kill or
    die."
The Major puffed his cigarette, amusement in his eye.
And then the dying Zouave heard, and raised his weary head:
"Shoot, son, 'twill be the best for both; shoot swift and straight,"
    he said.
"Fire first and last, and do not flinch; for lost to hope am I;
And I will murmur: *Vive La France!* and bless you ere I die."

Half-blind with blows the boy stood there; he seemed to swoon
    and sway;
Then in that moment woke the soul of little Jean Desprez.
He saw the woods go sheening down; the larks were singing
    clear;

And oh! the scents and sounds of spring, how sweet they were!
   how dear!
He felt the scent of new-mown hay, a soft breeze fanned his
   brow;
Oh, God! the paths of peace and toil! ' How precious were
   they now!
The summer days and summer ways, how bright with hope
   and bliss!
The autumn such a dream of gold . . . and all must end in
   this:
This shining rifle in his hand, that shambles all around;
The Zouave there with dying glare; the blood upon the
   ground;
The brutal faces round him ringed, the evil eyes aflame;
That Prussian bully standing by, as if he watched a game.
"Make haste and shoot," the Major sneered; "a minute more I
   give;
A minute more to kill your friend, if you yourself would live."

They only saw a bare-foot boy, with blanched and twitching
   face;
They did not see within his eyes the glory of his race;
The glory of a million men who for fair France have died,
The splendour of self-sacrifice that will not be denied.
Yet . . . he was but a peasant boy, and oh! but life was
   sweet. . . .
"Your minute's nearly gone, my lad," he heard a voice repeat.

"Shoot! Shoot!" the dying Zouave moaned; "Shoot! Shoot!"
the soldiers said.
Then Jean Desprez reached out· and shot . . . *the Prussian
Major dead!*

GOING HOME

I'm goin' 'ome to Blighty—ain't I glad to 'ave the chance!
I'm loaded up wiv fightin', and I've 'ad my fill o' France;
I'm feelin' so excited-like, I want to sing and dance,
      For I'm goin' 'ome to Blighty in the mawnin'.

I'm goin' 'ome to Blighty: can you wonder as I'm gay?
I've got a wound I wouldn't sell for 'alf a year o' pay;
A harm that's mashed to jelly in the nicest sort o' way,
      For it takes me 'ome to Blighty in the mawnin'.

'Ow everlastin' keen I was on gettin' to the front!
I'd ginger for a dozen, and I 'elped to bear the brunt;
But Cheese and Crust! I'm crazy, now I've done me little stunt,
      To sniff the air of Blighty in the mawnin'.

I've looked upon the wine that's white, and on the wine that's red;

433

I've looked on cider flowin', till it fairly turned me 'ead;
But oh, the finest scoff will be, when all is done and said,
      A pint o' Bass in Blighty in the mawnin'!

I'm goin' back to Blighty, which I left to strafe the 'Un;
I've fought in bloody battles, and I've 'ad a 'eap of fun;
But now me flipper's busted, and I fink me dooty's done,
      And I'll kiss me gel in Blighty in the mawnin'.

Oh, there be furrin' lands to see, and some of 'em be fine;
And there be furrin' gels to kiss, and scented furrin' wine;
But there's no land like England, and no other gel like mine:
      Thank Gawd for dear old Blighty in the mawnin'.

COCOTTE

When a girl's sixteen, and as poor as she's pretty,
And she hasn't a friend and she hasn't a home,
Heigh-ho! She's as safe in Paris city
As a lamb night-strayed where the wild wolves roam;
And that was I; oh, it's seven years now
(Some water's run down the Seine since then),
And I've almost forgotten the pangs and the tears now,
And I've almost taken the measure of men.

Oh, I found me a lover who loved me only,
Artist and poet, and almost a boy.
And my heart was bruised, and my life was lonely,
And him I adored with a wonderful joy.
If he'd come to me with his pockets empty,
How we'd have laughed in a garret gay!
But he was rich, and in radiant plenty
We lived in a villa at Viroflay.

435

Then came the War, and of bliss bereft me;
Then came the call, and he went away;
All that he had in the world he left me,
With the rose-wreathed villa at Viroflay.
Then came the news and the tragic story:
My hero, my splendid lover was dead,
Sword in hand on the field of glory,
And he died with my name on his lips, they said.

So here am I in my widow's mourning,
The weeds I've really no right to wear;
And women fix me with eyes of scorning,
Call me "cocotte," but I do not care.
And men look at me with eyes that borrow
The brightness of love, but I turn away;
Alone, say I, I will live with Sorrow,
In my little villa at Viroflay.

And lo! I'm living alone with *Pity*,
And they say that pity from love's not far;
Let me tell you all: last week in the city
I took the metro at Saint Lazare;
And the carriage was crowded to overflowing,
And when there entered at Chateaudun
Two wounded *poilus* with medals showing,
I eagerly gave my seat to one.

You should have seen them: they'd slipped death's clutches,
But sadder a sight you will rarely find;
One had a leg off and walked on crutches,
The other, a bit of a boy, was blind.
And they both sat down, and the lad was trying
To grope his way as a blind man tries;
And half of the women around were crying,
And some of the men had tears in their eyes.

How he stirred me, this blind boy, clinging
Just like a child to his crippled chum.
But I did not cry. Oh no; a singing
Came to my heart for a year so dumb.
Then I knew that at three-and-twenty
There is wonderful work to be done,
Comfort and kindness and joy in plenty,
Peace and light and love to be won.

Oh, thought I, could mine eyes be given
To one who will live in the dark alway!
To love and to serve—'twould make life Heaven
Here in my villa at Viroflay.
So I left my *poilus:* and now you wonder
Why to-day I am so elate. . . .
Look! In the glory of sunshine yonder
They're bringing my blind boy in at the gate.

MY BAY'NIT

WHEN first I left Blighty they gave me a bay'nit,
And told me it 'ad to be smothered wiv gore;
But blimey! I 'aven't been able to stain it,
So far as I've gone, wiv the vintage of war.
For ain't it a fraud! When a Boche and yours truly
Gits into a mix in the grit and the grime,
'E jerks up 'is 'ands wiv a yell, and 'e's duly
        Part of me outfit every time.

    Left, right, Hans and Fritz!
    Goose step, keep up yer mits!
    Oh my, ain't it a shyme!
    Part of me outfit every time.

At toastin' a biscuit me bay'nit's a dandy;
I've used it to open a bully beef can;
For pokin' the fire it comes in werry 'andy;
For any old thing but for stickin' a man.

'Ow often I've said: " 'Ere, I'm goin' to press you
Into a 'Un till you're seasoned for prime,"
And fiercely I rushes to do it, but bless you!
          Part of me outfit every time.

          Lor, yus; *don't* they look glad?
          Right O!   'Owl Kamerad!
          Oh my, always the syme!
          Part of me outfit every time.

I'm 'untin' for someone to christen me bay'nit,
Some nice juicy Chewton wot's fightin' in France;
I'm fairly down'earted—'ow *can* yer explain it?
I keeps gettin' prisoners every chance.
As soon as they sees me they·ups and surrenders,
Extended like monkeys wot's tryin' to climb;
And I uses me bay'nit—to slit their suspenders—
          Part of me outfit every time.

          Four 'Uns; lor, wot a bag!
          'Ere, Fritz, sample a fag!
          Oh my, ain't it a gyme!
          Part of me outfit every time.

CARRY ON!

It's easy to fight when everything's right,
And you're mad with the thrill and the glory;
It's easy to cheer when victory's near,
And wallow in fields that are gory.
It's a different song when everything's wrong,
When you're feeling infernally mortal;
When it's ten against one, and hope there is none,
Buck up, little soldier, and chortle:

Carry on! Carry on!
There isn't much punch in your blow.
You're glaring and staring and hitting out blind;
You're muddy and bloody, but never you mind.
Carry on! Carry on!
You haven't the ghost of a show.
It's looking like death, but while you've a breath,
Carry on, my son! Carry on!

And so in the strife of the battle of life
It's easy to fight when you're winning;
It's easy to slave, and starve and be brave,
When the dawn of success is beginning.
But the man who can meet despair and defeat
With a cheer, there's the man of God's choosing;
The man who can fight to Heaven's own height
Is the man who can fight when he's losing.

Carry on! Carry on!
Things never were looming so black;
But show that you haven't a cowardly streak,
And though you're unlucky you never are weak.
Carry on! Carry on!
Brace up for another attack.
It's looking like hell, but—you never can tell:
Carry on, old man! Carry on!

There are some who drift out in the deserts of doubt,
And some who in brutishness wallow;
There are others, I know, who in piety go,
Because of a Heaven to follow.
But to labour with zest, and to give of your best,
For the sweetness and joy of the giving;
To help folks along with a hand and a song:
Why, there's the real sunshine of living.

Carry on! Carry on!
Fight the good fight and true;
Believe in your mission, greet life with a cheer;
There's big work to do and that's why you are here.
Carry on! Carry on!
Let the world be the better for you;
And at last when you die, let this be your cry:
Carry on, my soul! Carry on!

OVER THE PARAPET

All day long when the shells sail over
I stand at the sandbags and take my chance;
But at night, at night I'm a reckless rover,
And over the parapet gleams Romance.
Romance! Romance! How I've dreamed it, writing
Dreary old records of money and mart,
Me with my head chuckful of fighting
And the blood of vikings to thrill my heart.

But little I thought that my time was coming,
Sudden and splendid, supreme and soon;
And here I am with the bullets humming
As I crawl and I curse the light of the moon.
Out alone, for adventure thirsting,
Out in mysterious No Man's Land;
Prone with the dead when a star-shell, bursting,
Flares on the horrors on every hand.

There are ruby stars and they drip and wiggle;
And the grasses gleam in a light blood-red;

There are emerald stars, and their tails they wriggle,
And ghastly they glare on the face of the dead.
But the worst of all are the stars of whiteness,
That spill in a pool of pearly flame,
Pretty as gems in their silver brightness,
And etching a man for a bullet's aim.

Yet oh, it's great to be here with danger,
Here in the weird, death-pregnant dark,
In the devil's pasture a stealthy ranger,
When the moon is decently hiding. Hark!
What was that? Was it just the shiver
Of an eerie wind or a clammy hand?
The rustle of grass, or the passing quiver
Of one of the ghosts of No Man's Land?

It's only at night when the ghosts awaken,
And gibber and whisper horrible things;
For to every foot of this God-forsaken
Zone of jeopard some horror clings.
Ugh! What was that? It felt like a jelly,
That flattish mound in the noisome grass;
You three big rats running free of its belly,
Out of my way and let me pass!

But if there's horror, there's beauty, wonder;
The trench lights gleam and the rockets play.

That flood of magnificent orange yonder
Is a battery blazing miles away.
With a rush and a singing a great shell passes;
The rifles resentfully bicker and brawl,
And here I crouch in the dew-drenched grasses,
And look and listen and love it all.

God! what a life!   But I must make haste now,
Before the shadow of night be spent.
It's little the time there is to waste now,
If I'd do the job for which I was sent.
My bombs are right and my clippers ready,
And I wriggle out to the chosen place,
When I hear a rustle. . . . Steady! . . . Steady!
Who am I staring slap in the face?

There in the dark I can hear him breathing,
A foot away, and as still as death;
And my heart beats hard, and my brain is seething,
And I know he's a Hun by the smell of his breath.
Then: "Will you surrender?" I whisper hoarsely,
For it's death, swift death to utter a cry.
"English schwein-hund!" he murmurs coarsely.
"Then we'll fight it out in the dark," say I.

So we grip and we slip and we trip and wrestle
There in the gutter of No Man's Land;

And I feel my nails in his wind-pipe nestle,
And he tries to gouge, but I bite his hand.
And he tries to squeal, but I squeeze him tighter:
"Now," I say, "I can kill you fine;
But tell me first, you Teutonic blighter!
Have you any children?"   He answers: "Nein."

Nine! Well, I cannot kill such a father,
So I tie his hands and I leave him there.
Do I finish my little job?   Well, rather;
And I get home safe with some light to spare.
Heigh-ho! by day it's just prosy duty,
Doing the same old song and dance;
But oh! with the night—joy, glory, beauty:
Over the parapet—Life, Romance!

THE BALLAD OF SOULFUL SAM

You want me to tell you a story, a yarn of the firin' line,
Of our thin red kharki 'eroes, out there where the bullets
     whine;
Out there where the bombs are bustin', and the cannons like
     'ell-doors slam—
Just order another drink, boys, and I'll tell you of Soulful Sam.

Oh, Sam, he was never 'ilarious, though I've 'ad some mates as
     was wus;
He 'adn't C.B. on his programme, he never was known to cuss.
For a card or a skirt or a beer-mug he 'adn't a friendly word;
But when it came down to Scriptures, say! wasn't he just a
     bird!

He always 'ad tracts in his pocket, the which he would haste
     to present,
And though the fellers would use them in ways that they
     never was meant,
I used to read 'em religious, and frequent I've been impressed
By some of them bundles of 'oly dope he carried around in
     his vest.

For I—and oh, 'ow I shudder at the 'orror the word conveys!
'Ave been—let me whisper it 'oarsely—a gambler 'alf of me
    days;
A gambler, you 'ear—a gambler. It makes me wishful to weep,
And yet 'ow it's true, my brethren!—I'd rather gamble than
    sleep.

I've gambled the 'ole world over, from Monte Carlo to Maine;
From Dawson City to Dover, from San Francisco to Spain.
Cards! They 'ave been me ruin. They've taken me pride and
    me pelf,
And when I'd no one to play with—why, I'd go and I'd play by
    meself.

And Sam 'e would sit and watch me, as I shuffled a greasy deck,
And 'e'd say: "You're bound to Perdition." And I'd answer:
    "Git off me neck!"
And that's 'ow we came to get friendly, though built on a
    different plan,
Me wot's a desprite gambler, 'im sich a good young man.

But on to me tale. Just imagine . . . Darkness! The battle-
    front!
The furious 'Uns attackin'! Us ones a-bearin' the brunt!
Me crouchin' be'ind a sandbag, tryin' 'ard to keep calm,
When I 'ears someone singin' a 'ymn toon; be'old! it is Soulful
    Sam.

Yes; right in the crash of the combat, in the fury of flash and
   flame,
'E was shootin' and singin' serenely as if 'e enjoyed the same.
And there in the 'eat of the battle, as the 'ordes of demons
   attacked,
He dipped down into 'is tunic, and 'e 'anded me out a tract.

Then a star-shell flared, and I read it: Oh, Flee From the
   Wrath to Come!
Nice cheerful subject, I tell yer, when you're 'earin' the bullets
   'um.
And before I 'ad time to thank 'im, just one of them bits of lead
Comes slingin' along in a 'urry, and it 'its my partner. . . .
   Dead?

No, siree! not by a long sight! For it plugged 'im 'ard on the
   chest,
Just where 'e'd tracts for a army corps stowed away in 'is vest.
On its mission of death that bullet 'ustled along, and it caved
A 'ole in them tracts to 'is 'ide, boys—but the life o' me pal
   was saved.

And there as 'e showed me in triumph, and 'orror was chokin'
   me breath,
On came another bullet on its 'orrible mission of death;
On through the night it cavorted, seekin' its 'aven of rest,
And it zipped through a crack in the sandbags, and it wolloped
   me bang in the breast.

Was I killed, do you ask? Oh no, boys. Why am I sittin' 'ere
Gazin' with mournful vision at a mug long empty of beer?
With a throat as dry as a—oh, thanky! I don't much mind if
    I do.
Beer with a dash of 'Ollands, that's my particular brew.

Yes, that was a terrible moment. It 'ammered me 'ard o'er
    the 'eart;
It bowled me down like a ninepin, and I looked for the gore to
    start;
And I saw in the flash of a moment, in that thunder of hate
    and strife,
Me wretched past like a pitchur—the sins of a gambler's life.

For I 'ad no tracts to save me, to thwart that mad missile's
    doom;
I 'ad no pious pamphlets to 'elp me to cheat the tomb;
I 'ad no 'oly leaflets to baffle a bullet's aim;
I'd only—a deck of cards, boys, but . . . *it seemed to do just
    the same.*

ONLY A BOCHE

We brought him in from between the lines: we'd better have
    let him lie;
For what's the use of risking one's skin for a *type* that's going
    to die?
What's the use of tearing him loose under a gruelling fire,
When he's shot in the head, and worse than dead, and all
    messed up on the wire?
However, I say, we brought him in. *Diable!* The mud was
    bad;
The trench was crooked and greasy and high, and oh, what a
    time we had!
And often we slipped, and often we tripped, but never he
    made a moan;
And how we were wet with blood and with sweat! But we
    carried him in like our own.

Now there he lies in the dug-out dim, awaiting the ambulance,
And the doctor shrugs his shoulders at him, and remarks: "He
    hasn't a chance."

And we squat and smoke at our game of bridge on the glisten-
    ing, straw-packed floor,
And above our oaths we can hear his breath deep drawn in a
    kind of snore.

For the dressing station is long and low, and the candles gutter
    dim,
And the mean light falls on the cold clay walls and our faces
    bristly and grim;
And we flap our cards on the lousy straw, and we laugh and
    jibe as we play,
And you'd never know that the cursed foe was less than a
    mile away.
As we con our cards in the rancid gloom, oppressed by that
    snoring breath,
You'd never dream that our broad roof-beam was swept by
    the broom of death.

Heigh-ho! My turn for the dummy hand; I rise and I stretch
    a bit;
The fetid air is making me yawn, and my cigarette's unlit,
So I go to the nearest candle flame, and the man we brought
    is there,
And his face is white in the shabby light, and I stand at his
    feet and stare.
Stand for awhile, and quietly stare: for strange though it seems
    to be,
The dying Boche on the stretcher there has a queer resem-
    blance to me.

It gives one a kind of a turn, you know, to come on a thing like that.

It's just as if I were lying there, with a turban of blood for a hat,

Lying there in a coat grey-green instead of a coat grey-blue,

With one of my eyes all shot away, and my brain half tumbling through;

Lying there with a chest that heaves like a bellows up and down,

And a cheek as white as snow on a grave, and lips that are coffee brown.

And confound him, too! He wears, like me, on his finger a wedding ring,

And around his neck, as around my own, by a greasy bit of string,

A locket hangs with a woman's face, and I turn it about to see:

Just as I thought . . . on the other side the faces of children three;

Clustered together cherub-like, three little laughing girls,

With the usual tiny rosebud mouths and the usual silken curls.

"Zut!" I say, "he has beaten me; for me, I have only two,"

And I push the locket beneath his shirt, feeling a little blue.

Oh, it isn't cheerful to see a man, the marvellous work of God,

Crushed in the mutilation mill, crushed to a smeary clod;

Oh, it isn't cheerful to hear him moan, but it isn't that I mind,
It isn't the anguish that goes with him, it's the anguish he
    leaves behind.
For his going opens a tragic door that gives on a world of pain,
And the death he dies, those who live and love will die again
    and again.

So here I am at my cards once more, but it's kind of spoiling
    my play
Thinking of those three brats of his so many a mile away.
War is war, and he's only a Boche, and we all of us take our
    chance;
But all the same I'll be mighty glad when I'm hearing the am-
    bulance.
One foe the less, but all the same I'm heartily glad I'm not
The man who gave him his broken head, the sniper who fired
    the shot. . . .
No trumps you make it, I think you said?   You'll pardon me
    if I err;
For a moment I thought of other things. . . . *Mon Dieu!*
    Quelle vache de guerre.

PILGRIMS

For oh, when the war will be over
We'll go and we'll look for our dead;
We'll go when the bee's on the clover,
And the plume of the poppy is red:
We'll go when the year's at its gayest,
When meadows are laughing with flow'rs;
And there where the crosses are greyest,
We'll seek for the cross that is ours.

For they cry to us: *Friends, we are lonely,*
A'weary the night and the day;
But come in the blossom-time only,
Come when our graves will be gay:
When daffodils all are a-blowing,
And larks are a'thrilling the skies,
Oh, come with the hearts of you glowing,
And the joy of the Spring in your eyes.

But never, oh, never come sighing,
For ours was the Splendid Release;

And oh, but 'twas joy in the dying
To know we were winning you Peace!
So come when the valleys are sheening,
And fledged with the promise of grain;
And here where our graves will be greening,
Just smile and be happy again.

And so, when the war will be over,
We'll seek for the Wonderful One;
And maiden will look for her lover,
And mother will look for her son;
And there will be end to our grieving,
And gladness will gleam over loss,
As—glory beyond all believing!
We point . . . to a name on a cross.

MY PRISONER

WE was in a crump-'ole, 'im and me;
Fightin' wiv our bayonets was we;
Fightin' 'ard as 'ell we was,
Fightin' fierce as fire because
It was 'im or me as must be downed;
'E was twice as big as me;
I was 'arf the weight of 'e;
We was like a terryer and a 'ound.

'Struth! But 'e was sich a 'andsome bloke,
Me—I'm 'andsome as a chunk o' coke.
Did I give it 'im? Not 'arf!
Why, it fairly made me laugh,
'Cos 'is bloomin' bellows wasn't sound.
Couldn't fight for monkey nuts.
Soon I gets 'im in the guts,
There 'e lies a-floppin' in the ground.

In I goes to finish up the job.
Quick 'e throws 'is 'ands above 'is nob;

Speakin' English good as me:
"'Tain't no use to kill," says 'e;
"Can't yer tyke me prisoner instead?"
"Why, I'd like to, sir," says I;
"But—yer knows the reason why:
If we pokes our noses out we're dead.

"Sorry, sir. Then, on the other 'and
(As a gent like you must understand),
If I 'olds you longer 'ere,
Wiv yer pals so werry near,
It's me 'oo'll 'ave a free trip to Berlin;
If I lets yer go away,
Why, you'll fight another day:
See the sitooation I am in.

"Anyway I'll tell you wot I'll do,
Bein' kind and seein' as it's you,
Knowin' 'ow it's cold, the feel
Of a 'alf a yard o' steel,
I'll let yer 'ave a rifle ball instead;
Now, just think yerself in luck. . . .
'Ere, ol' man! You keep 'em stuck,
Them saucy dooks o' yours, above yer 'ead."

'Ow 'is mits shot up, it made me smile!
'Ow 'e seemed to ponder for a while!

Then 'e says: "It seems a shyme,
Me, a man wot's known ter Fyme;
Give me blocks of stone, I'll give yer gods.
Whereas, pardon me, I'm sure
You, my friend, are still obscure. . . ."
"In war," says I, "that makes no blurry odds."

Then says 'e: "I've painted picters too. . . .
Oh, dear God! the work I planned to do,
And to think this is the end!"
"'Ere," says I, "my hartist friend,
Don't you give yeself no friskin' airs,
Picters, statoos, is that why
You should be let off to die?
That the best ye done?   Just say yer prayers."

Once again 'e seems ter think awhile,
Then 'e smiles a werry 'aughty smile;
"Why, no, sir, it's not the best;
There's a locket next me breast,
Picter of a gel 'oo's eyes are blue.
That's the best I've done," says 'e.
"That's me darter, aged three. . . ."
"Blimey!" says I.   "I've a nipper, too."

Straight I chucks my rifle to one side;
Shows 'im wiv a lovin' father's pride

Me own little Mary Jane.
Proud 'e shows me 'is Elaine,
And we talks as friendly as can be;
Then I 'elps 'im on 'is way,
'Opes 'e's sife at 'ome to-day,
Wonders—*'ow would 'e 'ave treated me!*

TRI-COLOUR

Poppies, you try to tell me, glowing there in the wheat;
Poppies! Ah no! You mock me: it's blood, I tell you, it's
   blood.
It's gleaming wet in the grasses; it's glist'ning warm in the
   wheat;
It dabbles the ferns and the clover; it brims in an angry flood;
It leaps to the startled heavens; it smothers the sun; it cries
With scarlet voices of triumph from blossom and bough and
   blade.
See the bright horror of it! It's roaring out of the skies,
And the whole red world is a-welter. . . . Oh God! I'm
   afraid! I'm afraid!

Cornflowers, you say, just cornflowers, gemming the golden
   grain;
Ah no! You can't deceive me. Can't I believe my eyes?
Look! It's the dead, my comrades, stark on the dreadful plain,
All in their dark-blue blouses, staring up at the skies.

Comrades of canteen laughter, dumb in the yellow wheat.
See how they sprawl and huddle! See how their brows are
white!
Goaded on to the shambles, there in death and defeat. . . .
Father of Pity, hide them! Hasten, O God, Thy night!

Lilies (the light is waning), only lilies you say,
Nestling and softly shining there where the spear-grass waves.
No, my friend, I know better; brighter I see than day:
It's the poor little wooden crosses over their quiet graves.
Oh, how they're gleaming, gleaming! See! each cross has a
crown.
Yes, it's true I am dying; little will be the loss. . . .
Darkness . . . but look! In Heaven a light, and it's shining
down. . . .
God's accolade! Lift me up, friends. I'm going to win *my*
Cross.

A POT OF TEA

You make it in your mess-tin by the brazier's rosy gleam;
You watch it cloud, then settle amber clear;
You lift it with your bay'nit and you sniff the fragrant steam;
The very breath of it is ripe with cheer.
You're awful cold and dirty, and a-cursin' of your lot;
You scoff the blushin' 'alf of it, so rich and rippin' 'ot;
It bucks you up like anythink, just seems to touch the spot:
      God Bless the man that first discovered Tea!

Since I came out to fight in France, which ain't the other day,
I think I've drunk enough to float a barge;
All kinds of fancy foreign dope, from caffy and doo lay,
To rum they serves you out before a charge.
In back rooms of estaminays I've gurgled pints of cham;
I've swilled down mugs of cider till I've felt a bloomin' dam;
But 'struth! they all ain't in it with the vintage of Assam:
      God bless the man that first invented Tea!

I think them lazy lumps o' gods wot kips on asphodel,
Swigs nectar that's a flavour of Oolong;

I only wish them sons o' guns a-grillin' down in 'ell,
Could 'ave their daily ration of Suchong.
Hurrah! I'm off to battle, which is 'ell and 'eaven too;
And if I don't give some poor bloke a sexton's job to do,
To-night, by Fritz's camp-fire, won't I 'ave a gorgeous brew
      (For fightin' mustn't interfere with Tea).
To-night we'll all be tellin' of the Boches that we slew,
      As we drink the giddy victory in Tea.

THE REVELATION

The same old sprint in the morning, boys, to the same old
*   din and smut;*
Chained all day to the same old desk, down in the same old
*   rut;*
Posting the same old greasy books, catching the same old train:
Oh, how will I manage to stick it all, if I ever get back again?

We've bidden good-bye to life in a cage, we're finished with
    pushing a pen;
They're pumping us full of bellicose rage, they're showing us
    how to be men.
We're only beginning to find ourselves; we're wonders of
    brawn and thew;
But when we go back to our Cissy jobs—oh, what are we
    going to do?

For shoulders curved with the counter stoop will be carried
    erect and square;
And faces white from the office light will be bronzed by the
    open air;

465

And we'll walk with the stride of a new-born pride, with a
new-found joy in our eyes,
Scornful men who have diced with death under the naked
skies.

And when we get back to the dreary grind, and the bald-
headed boss's call,
Don't you think that the dingy window-blind, and the dingier
office wall,
Will suddenly melt to a vision of space, of violent, flame-
scarred night?
Then . . . oh, the joy of the danger-thrill, and oh, the roar
of the fight!

Don't you think as we peddle a card of pins the counter will
fade away,
And again we'll be seeing the sand-bag rims, and the barb-
wire's misty grey?
As a flat voice asks for a pound of tea, don't you fancy we'll
hear instead
The night-wind moan and the soothing drone of the packet
that's overhead?

Don't you guess that the things we're seeing now will haunt
us through all the years;
Heaven and hell rolled into one, glory and blood and tears;
Life's pattern picked with a scarlet thread, where once we
wove with a grey,

To remind us all how we played our part in the shock of an
    epic day?

Oh, we're booked for the Great Adventure now we're pledged
    to the Real Romance;
We'll find ourselves or we'll lose ourselves somewhere in giddy
    old France;
We'll know the zest of the fighter's life; the best that we have
    we'll give;
We'll hunger and thirst; we'll die . . . but first—we'll live;
    by the gods, we'll live!

We'll breathe free air and we'll bivouac under the starry sky;
We'll march with men, and we'll fight with men, and we'll see
    men laugh and die;
We'll know such joy as we never dreamed; we'll fathom
    the deeps of pain:
But the hardest bit of it all will be—when we come back
    home again.

For some of us smirk in a chiffon shop, and some of us teach
    in a school;
Some of us help with the seat of our pants to polish an office
    stool;
The merits of somebody's soap or jam some of us seek to explain,
But all of us wonder what we'll do when we have to go back
    again.

Ω

GRAND-PERE

AND so when he reached my bed
The General made a stand:
"My brave young fellow," he said,
    "I would shake your hand."

So I lifted my arm, the right,
With never a hand at all;
Only a stump, a sight
    Fit to appal.

"Well, well. Now that's too bad!
That's sorrowful luck," he said;
"But there! You give me, my lad,
    The left instead."

So from under the blanket's rim
I raised and showed him the other,
A snag as ugly and grim
    As its ugly brother.

He looked at each jagged wrist;
He looked but he did not speak;
And then he bent down and kissed
    Me on either cheek.

You wonder now I don't mind
I hadn't a hand to offer. . . .
They tell me (you know I'm blind)
    'Twas Grand-père Joffre.

SON

He hurried away, young heart of joy, under our Devon sky!
And I watched him go, my beautiful boy, and a weary woman
    was I.
For my hair is grey, and his was gold; he'd the best of his
    life to live;
And I'd loved him so, and I'm old, I'm old; and he's all I had
    to give.

Ah yes, he was proud and swift and gay, but oh how my eyes
    were dim!
With the sun in his heart he went away, but he took the
    sun with him.
For look! How the leaves are falling now, and the winter
    won't be long. . . .
Oh boy, my boy, with the sunny brow, and the lips of love
    and of song!

How we used to sit at the day's sweet end, we two by the fire-
    light's gleam,
And we'd drift to the Valley of Let's Pretend, on the beautiful
    river of Dream.

Oh dear little heart! All wealth untold would I gladly, gladly
  pay
Could I just for a moment closely hold that golden head to
  my grey.

For I gaze in the fire, and I'm seeing there a child, and he
  waves to me;
And I run and I hold him up in the air, and he laughs and
  shouts with glee;
A little bundle of love and mirth, crying: "Come, Mumsie
  dear!"
Ah me! If he called from the ends of the earth I know that
  my heart would hear.

          *   *   *   *   *   *

Yet the thought comes thrilling through all my pain: how
  worthier could he die?
Yea, a loss like that is a glorious gain, and pitiful proud am I.
For Peace must be bought with blood and tears, and the boys
  of our hearts must pay;
And so in our joy of the after-years, let us bless them every day.

And though I know there's a hasty grave with a poor little
  cross at its head,
And the gold of his youth he so gladly gave, yet to me he'll
  never be dead.

And the sun in my Devon lane will be gay, and my boy will
    be with me still,
So I'm finding the heart to smile and say: "Oh God, if it be
    Thy Will!"

THE BLACK DUDEEN

Humping it here in the dug-out,
Sucking me black dudeen,
I'd like to say in a general way
There's nothing like Nickyteen;
There's nothing like Nickyteen, me boys,
Be it pipes or snipes or cigars;
So be sure that a bloke
Has plenty to smoke,
If you wants him to fight your wars.

When I've eat my fill and my belt is snug,
I begin to think of my baccy plug.
I whittle a fill in my horny palm,
And the bowl of me old clay pipe I cram.
I trim the edges, I tamp it down,
I nurse a light with an anxious frown;
I begin to draw, and my cheeks tuck in,
And all my face is a blissful grin;
And up in a cloud the good smoke goes,
And the good pipe glimmers and fades and glows;

In its throat it chuckles a cheery song,
For I likes it hot and I likes it strong.
Oh, it's good is grub when you're feeling hollow,
But the best of a meal's the smoke to follow.

There was Micky and me on a night patrol,
Having to hide in a fizz-bang hole;
And sure I thought I was worse than dead
Wi' them crump-crumps hustlin' over me head.
Sure I thought 'twas the dirty spot,
Hammer and tongs till the air was hot.
And, mind you, water up to your knees.
And cold!   A monkey of brass would freeze.
And if we ventured our noses out
A "typewriter" clattered its pills about.
The field of glory!   Well, I don't think!
I'd sooner be safe and snug in clink.

Then Micky, he goes and he cops one bad,
He always was having ill-luck, poor lad.
Says he: "Old chummy, I'm booked right through;
Death and me 'as a wrongday voo.
But . . . 'aven't you got a pinch of shag?—
I'd sell me perishin' soul for a fag."
And there he shivered and cussed his luck,
So I gave him me old black pipe to suck:

And he heaves a sigh, and he takes to it
Like a babby takes to his mammy's tit;
Like an infant takes to his mother's breast,
Poor little Micky! he "travelled West."
But the dawn was near, though the night was black,
So I left him there and I started back.
And I laughed as the silly old bullets came,
For the bullet ain't made wot's got me name.
Yet some of 'em buzzed onhealthily near,
And one little blighter just chipped me ear.
But there! I got to the trench all right,
When sudden I jumped wi' a start o' fright,
And a word that doesn't look well in type:
I'd clean forgotten me old clay pipe.

So I had to do it all over again,
Crawling out on that filthy plain.
Through shells and bombs and bullets and all—
Only this time—I do not crawl.
I run like a man wot's missing a train,
Or a tom-cat caught in a plump of rain.
I hear the spit of a quick-fire gun
Tickle my heels, but I run, I run.
Through crash and crackle, and flicker and flame,
(Oh, the packet ain't issued wot's got me name!)
I run like a man that's no ideer
Of hunting around for a sooveneer.

I run bang into a German chap,
And he stares like an owl, so I bash his map.
And just to show him that I'm his boss,
I gives him a kick on the parados.
And I marches him back with me all serene,
With, *tucked in me gub, me old dudeen.*

Sitting here in the trenches
Me heart's a-splittin' with spleen,
For a parcel o' lead comes missing me head,
But it smashes me old dudeen.
God blast that red-headed sniper!
I'll give him somethin' to snipe;
Before the war's through
Just see how I do
That blighter that smashed me pipe.

THE LITTLE PIOU-PIOU

Oh, some of us lolled in the château,
And some of us slinked in the slum;
But now we are here with a song and a cheer
To serve at the sign of the drum.
They put us in trousers of scarlet,
In big sloppy ulsters of blue;
In boots that are flat, a box of a hat,
And they call us the little piou-piou,
      Piou-piou,
The laughing and quaffing piou-piou;
The swinging and singing piou-piou;
And so with a rattle we march to the battle,
The weary but cheery piou-piou.

Encore un petit verre de vin,
Pour nous mettre en route;
Encore un petit verre de vin
Pour nous mettre en train.

They drive us head-on for the slaughter;
We haven't got much of a chance;

The issue looks bad, but we're awfully glad
To battle and die for La France.
For some must be killed, that is certain:
There's only one's duty to do;
So we leap to the fray in the glorious way
They expect of the little piou-piou.
            En avant!
The way of the gallant piou-piou;
The dashing and smashing piou-piou;
The way grim and gory that leads us to glory
Is the way of the little piou-piou.

            Allons, enfants de la Patrie,
            Le jour de gloire est arrivé.

To-day you would scarce recognize us,
Such veterans warwise are we;
So grimy and hard, so calloused and scarred,
So "crummy," yet gay as can be.
We've finished with trousers of scarlet,
They're giving us breeches of blue,
With a helmet instead of a cap on our head,
Yet still we're the little piou-piou.
            Nous les aurons!

The jesting, unresting piou-piou;
The cheering, unfearing piou-piou;
The keep-your-head-level and fight-like-the-devil,
The dying, defying piou-piou.

À la bayonette! Jusqu'a la mort!
Sonnez la charge, clairons!

BILL THE BOMBER

THE poppies gleamed like bloody pools through cotton-woolly
    mist;
The Captain kept a-lookin' at the watch upon his wrist;
And there we smoked and squatted, as we watched the
    shrapnel .flame;
'Twas wonnerful, I'm tellin' you, how fast them bullets came.
'Twas weary work the waiting, though; I tried to sleep a wink,
For waitin' means a-thinkin', and it doesn't do to think.
So I closed my eyes a little, and I had a niceish dream
Of a-standin' by a dresser with a dish of Devon cream;
But I hadn't time to sample it, for suddenlike I woke:
"Come on, me lads!" the Captain says, 'n I climbed out
    through the smoke.

We spread out in the open: it was like a bath of lead;
But the boys they cheered and hollered fit to raise the bloody
    dead,
Till a beastly bullet copped 'em, then they lay without a sound,
And it's odd—we didn't seem to heed them corpses on the
    ground.

And I kept on thinkin', thinkin' as the bullets faster flew,
How they picks the werry best men, and they lets the rotters
    through;
So indiscriminatin' like, they spares a man of sin,
And a rare lad wot's a husband and a father gets done in.
And while havin' these reflections and advancin' on the run,
A bullet biffs me shoulder, and says I: "That's number one."

Well, it downed me for a jiffy, but I didn't lose me calm,
For I knew that I was needed: I'm a bomber, so I am.
I 'ad lost me cap and rifle, but I "carried on" because
I 'ad me bombs and knew that they was needed, so they was.
We didn't 'ave no singin' now, nor many men to cheer;
Maybe the shrapnel drowned 'em, crashin' out so werry near;
And the Maxims got us sideways, and the bullets faster flew,
And I copped one on me flipper, and says I: "That's number
    two."

I was pleased it was the left one, for I 'ad me bombs, ye see,
And 'twas 'ard if they'd be wasted like, and all along o' me.
And I'd lost me 'at and rifle—but I told you that before,
So I packed me mit inside me coat and "carried on" once
    more.
But the rumpus it was wicked, and the men were scarcer yet,
And I felt me ginger goin', but me jaws I kind o' set,
And we passed the Boche first trenches, which was 'eapin'
    'igh with dead,

And we started for their second, which was fifty feet ahead;
When something like a 'ammer smashed me savage on the knee,
And down I came all muck and blood: Says I: "That's number
    three."

So there I lay all 'elpless like, and bloody sick at that,
And worryin' like anythink, because I'd lost me 'at;
And thinkin' of me missis, and the partin' words she said:
"If you gets killed, write quick, ol' man, and tell me as
    you're dead."
And lookin' at me bunch o' bombs—that was the 'ardest blow,
To think I'd never 'ave the chance to 'url them at the foe.
And there was all our boys in front, a-fightin' there like mad,
And me as could 'ave 'elped 'em wiv the lovely bombs I 'ad.
And so I cussed and cussed, and then I struggled back again,
Into that bit of battered trench, packed solid with its slain.

Now as I lay a-lyin' there and blastin' of me lot,
And wishin' I could just dispose of all them bombs I'd got.
I sees within the doorway of a shy, retirin' dug-out
Six Boches all a-grinnin', and their Captain stuck 'is mug out;
And they 'ad a nice machine gun, and I twigged what they
    was at;
And they fixed it on a tripod, and I watched 'em like a cat;
And they got it in position, and they seemed so werry glad,
Like they'd got us in a death-trap, which, condemn their souls!
    they 'ad.

For there our boys was fightin' fifty yards in front, and 'ere
This lousy bunch of Boches they 'ad got us in the rear.

Oh it set me blood a-boilin', and I quite forgot me pain,
So I started crawlin', crawlin' over all them mounds of slain;
And them barstards was so busy-like they'd 'ad no eyes for me,
And me bleedin' leg was draggin', but me right arm it was
  free. . . .
And now they 'ave it all in shape, and swingin' sweet and clear;
And now they're all excited like, but—I am drawin' near;
And now they 'ave it loaded up, and now they're takin' aim. . . .
Rat-tat-tat-tat! Oh here, says I, is where I join the game.
And my right arm it goes swingin', and a bomb it goes a-slingin',
And that "typewriter" goes wingin' in a thunderbolt of flame.

Then these Boches, wot was left of 'em, they tumbled down
  their 'ole,
And up I climbed a mound of dead, and down on them I stole.
And oh that blessed moment when I heard their frightened yell,
And I laughed down in that dug-out, ere I bombed their souls
  to hell.
And now I'm in the hospital, surprised that I'm alive;
We started out a thousand men, we came back thirty-five.
And I'm minus of a trotter, but I'm most amazin' gay,
For me bombs they wasn't wasted, though, you might say,
  "thrown away."

THE WHISTLE OF SANDY McGRAW

You may talk o' your lutes and your dulcimers fine,
Your harps and your tabors and cymbals and a',
But here in the trenches jist gie me for mine
The wee penny whistle o' Sandy McGraw.
Oh it's: "Sandy, ma lad, will you lilt us a tune?"
And Sandy is willin' and trillin' like mad;
Sae silvery sweet that we a' throng aroun',
And some o' it's gay, but the maist o' it's sad.
Jist the wee simple airs that sink intae your hert,
And grup ye wi' love and wi' longin' for hame;
And ye glour like an owl till you're feelin' the stert
O' a tear, and you blink wi' a feelin' o' shame.
For his song's o' the heather, and here in the dirt
You listen and dream o' a land that's sae braw,
And he mak's you forget a' the harm and the hurt.
For he pipes like a laverock, does Sandy McGraw.

*   *   *   *   *   *

At Eepers I mind me when rank upon rank
We rose from the trenches and swept like the gale,

484

Till the rapid-fire guns got us fell on the flank
And the murderin' bullets came swishin' like hail:
Till a' that were left o' us faltered and broke;
Till it seemed for a moment a panicky rout,
When shrill through the fume and the flash and the smoke
The wee valiant voice o' a whistle piped out
The Campbells are comin': then into the fray
We bounded wi' bayonets reekin' and raw,
And oh we fair revelled in glory that day,
Jist thanks to the whistle o' Sandy McGraw.

*   *   *   *   *   *

At Loose, it wis after a sconnersome fecht,
On the field o' the slain I wis crawlin' aboot;
And the rockets were burnin' red holes in the nicht,
And the guns they were veciously thounderin' oot.
When sudden I heard a bit sound like a sigh,
And there in a crump-hole a kiltie I saw:
"Whit ails ye, ma lad? Are ye woundit?" says I.
"I've lost ma wee whustle," says Sandy McGraw.
" 'Twas oot by yon bing where we pressed the attack,
It drapped frae ma pooch, and between noo and dawn
There isna much time, so I'm jist crawlin' back . . ."
"Ye're daft, man!" I telt him, but Sandy wis gone.
Weel, I waited a wee, then I crawled oot masel,
And the big stuff wis gorin' and roarin' around,
And I seemed tae be under the oxter o' hell,
And Creation wis crackin' tae bits by the sound.

And I says in ma mind: "Gang ye back, ye auld fule!"
When I thrilled tae a note that wis saucy and sma';
And there in a crater, collected and cool,
Wi' his wee penny whistle, wis Sandy McGraw.
Ay, there he wis playin' as gleg as could be,
And listenin' hard wis a spectacled Boche;
Then Sandy turned roon' and he noddit tae me,
And he says: "Dinna blab on me, Sergeant McTosh.
The auld chap is deein'. He likes me tae play;
It's makin' him happy. Jist see his een shine!"
And thrillin' and sweet in the hert o' the fray
Wee Sandy wis playin' *The Watch on the Rhine*.

*   *   *   *   *   *

The last scene o' a'—'twas the day that we took
That bit o' black ruin they ca' Labbiesell.
It seemed the hale hillside jist shivered and shook,
And the red skies were roarin' and spewin' oot shell.
And the Sergeants were cursin' tae keep us in hand,
And hard on the leash we were strainin' like dugs,
When upward we shot at the word o' command,
And the bullets were dingin' their songs in oor lugs.
And onward we swept wi' a yell and a cheer,
And a' wis destruction, confusion and din,
And we knew that the trench o' the Boches wis near,
And it seemed jist the safest bit hole tae be in.
So we a' tumbled doon, and the Boches were there,
And they held up their hands, and they yelled: "Kamarad!"

And I merched aff wi' ten, wi' their palms in the air,
And my! I wis prood-like, and my! I wis glad.
And I thocht: if ma lassie could see me jist then. . . .
When sudden I sobered at somethin' I saw,
And I stopped and I stared, and I halted ma men,
For there on a stretcher wis Sandy McGraw.
Weel, he looks in ma face, jist as game as ye please:
"Ye ken hoo I hate tae be workin'," says he;
"But noo I can play in the street for bawbees,
Wi' baith o' ma legs taken aff at the knee."
And though I could see he wis rackit wi' pain,
He reached for his whistle and stertit tae play,
And quaverin' sweet wis the pensive refrain:
The flo'oers o' the forest are a' wede away.
Then sudden he stoppit: "Man, wis it no grand
Hoo we took a' them trenches?" . . . He shakit his heid. . . .
"I'll—no—play—nae—mair——" feebly doon frae his hand
Slipped the wee penny whistle and . . . *Sandy wis deid.*

*   *   *   *   *   *

And so ye may talk o' your Steinways and Strads,
Yer wunnerfu' organs and brasses sae braw;
But oot in the trenches jist gie me, ma lads,
Yon wee penny whistle o' Sandy McGraw.

THE STRETCHER-BEARER

My stretcher is one scarlet stain,
And as I tries to scrape it clean,
I tell you wot—I'm sick with pain
For all I've 'eard, for all I've seen;
Around me is the 'ellish night,
And as the war's red rim I trace,
I wonder if in 'Eaven's height
Our God don't turn away 'Is Face.

I don't care 'ose the Crime may be;
I 'olds no brief for kin or clan;
I 'ymns no 'ate: I only see
As man destroys his brother man;
I waves no flag: I only know,
As 'ere beside the dead I wait,
A million 'earts is weighed with woe,
A million 'omes is desolate.

488

In drippin' darkness, far and near,
All night I've sought them woeful ones.
Dawn shudders up and still I 'ear
The crimson chorus of the guns.
Look, like a ball of blood the sun
'Angs o'er the scene of wrath and wrong. . . .
"Quick! Stretcher-bearers on the run!"
O Prince of Peace! 'Ow long, 'ow long?

WOUNDED

Is it not strange? A year ago to-day,
With scarce a thought beyond the humdrum round,
I did my decent job and earned my pay;
Was averagely happy, I'll be bound.
Ay, in my little groove I was content,
Seeing my life run smoothly to the end,
With prosy days in stolid labour spent,
And jolly nights, a pipe, a glass, a friend.
In God's good time a hearth fire's cosy gleam,
A wife and kids, and all a fellow needs;
When presto! like a bubble goes my dream:
I leap upon the Stage of Splendid Deeds.
I yell with rage; I wallow deep in gore:
I, that was clerk in a drysalter's store.

Stranger than any book I've ever read,
Here on the reeking battlefield I lie,
Under the stars, propped up with smeary dead,

Like too, if no one takes me in, to die.
Hit on the arms, legs, liver, lungs and gall;
Damn glad there's nothing more of me to hit;
But calm, and feeling never pain at all,
And full of wonder at the turn of it.
For of the dead around me three are mine,
Three foemen vanquished in the whirl of fight;
So if I die I have no right to whine,
I feel I've done my little bit all right.
I don't know how—but there the beggars are,
As dead as herrings pickled in a jar.

And here am I, worse wounded than I thought;
For in the fight a bullet bee-like stings;
You never heed; the air is metal-hot,
And all alive with little flicking wings.
But on you charge. You see the fellows fall;
Your pal was by your side, fair fighting-mad,
You turn to him, and lo! no pal at all;
You wonder vaguely if he's copped it bad.
But on you charge. The heavens vomit death;
And vicious death is besoming the ground.
You're blind with sweat; you're dazed, and out of breath
And though you yell, you cannot hear a sound.
But on you charge. Oh, War's a rousing game!
Around you smoky clouds like ogres tower;

The earth is rowelled deep with spurs of flame,
And on your helmet stones and ashes shower.
But on you charge. It's odd! You have no fear.
Machine-gun bullets whip and lash your path;
Red, yellow, black the smoky giants rear;
The shrapnel rips, the heavens roar in wrath.
But on you charge. Barbed wire all trampled down;

The ground all gored and rent as by a blast;
Grim heaps of grey where once were heaps of brown;
A ragged ditch—the Hun first line at last,
All smashed to hell. Their second right ahead,
So on you charge. There's nothing else to do.
More reeking holes, blood, barbed wire, gruesome dead
(Your puttee strap's undone—that worries you).
You glare around. You think you're all alone.
But no; your chums come surging left and right.
The nearest chap flops down without a groan,
His face still snarling with the rage of fight.
Ha! here's the second trench—just like the first,
Only a little more so, more "laid out";
More pounded, flame-corroded, death-accurst;
A pretty piece of work, beyond a doubt.

Now for the third, and there your job is done,
So on you charge. You never stop to think.

Your cursed puttee's trailing as you run;
You feel you'd sell your soul to have a drink.
The acrid air is full of cracking whips.
You wonder how it is you're going still.
You foam with rage. Oh, God! to be at grips
With someone you can rush and crush and kill.
Your sleeve is dripping blood; you're seeing red;
You're battle-mad; your turn is coming now.
See! there's the jagged barbed wire straight ahead,
And there's the trench—you'll get there anyhow.
Your puttee catches on a strand of wire,
And down you go; perhaps it saves your life,
For over sandbag rims you see 'em fire,
Crop-headed chaps, their eyes ablaze with strife.
You crawl, you cower; then once again you plunge
With all your comrades roaring at your heels.
Have at 'em, lads! You stab, you jab, you lunge;
A blaze of glory, then the red world reels.
A crash of triumph, then . . . you're faint a bit . . .
That cursed puttee! Now to fasten it. . . .

Well, that's the charge. And now I'm here alone.
I've built a little wall of Hun on Hun,
To shield me from the leaden bees that drone
(It saves me worry, and it hurts 'em none).
The only thing I'm wondering is when
Some stretcher-men will stroll along my way?

It isn't much that's left of me, but then
Where life is, hope is, so at least they say.
Well, if I'm spared I'll be the happy lad.
I tell you I won't envy any king.
I've stood the racket, and I'm proud and glad;
I've had my crowning hour. Oh, War's the thing!
It gives us common, working chaps our chance,
A taste of glory, chivalry, romance.

Ay, War, they say, is hell; it's heaven, too.
It lets a man discover what he's worth.
It takes his measure, shows what he can do,
Gives him a joy like nothing else on earth.
It fans in him a flame that otherwise
Would flicker out, these drab, discordant days;
It teaches him in pain and sacrifice
Faith, fortitude, grim courage past all praise.
Yes, War is good. So here beside my slain,
A happy wreck, I wait amid the din;
For even if I perish mine's the gain. . . .
Hi there, you fellows! *Won't* you take me in?
Give me a fag to smoke upon the way. . . .
We've taken La Boiselle! The hell, you say!
Well, that would make a corpse sit up and grin. . . .
Lead on! I'll live to fight another day.

FAITH

Since all that is was ever bound to be;
Since grim, eternal laws our Being bind;
And both the riddle and the answer find,
And both the carnage and the calm decree;
Since plain within the Book of Destiny
Is written all the journey of mankind
Inexorably to the end; since blind
And mortal puppets playing parts are we:

Then let's have faith; good cometh out of ill;
The power that shaped the strife shall end the strife;
Then let's bow down before the Unknown Will;
Fight on, believing all is well with life;
Seeing within the worst of War's red rage
The gleam, the glory of the Golden Age.

THE COWARD

'AVE you seen Bill's mug in the Noos to-day?
'E's gyned the Victoriar Cross, they say;
Little Bill wot would grizzle and run away,
    If you 'it 'im a swipe on the jawr.
'E's slaughtered the Kaiser's men in tons;
'E's captured one of their quick-fire guns,
And 'e 'adn't no practice in killin' 'Uns
    Afore 'e went off to the war.

Little Bill wot I nussed in 'is by-by clothes;
Little Bill wot told me 'is childish woes;
'Ow often I've tidied 'is pore little nose
    Wiv the 'em of me pinnyfore.
And now all the papers 'is praises ring,
And 'e's been and 'e's shaken the 'and of the King,
And I sawr 'im to-day in the ward, pore thing,
    Where they're patching 'im up once more.

And 'e says: "Wot d'ye think of it, Lizer Ann?"
And I says: "Well, I can't make it out, old man;
You'd 'ook it as soon as a scrap began,
    When you was a bit of a kid."
And 'e whispers: " 'Ere, on the quiet, Liz,
They're makin' too much of the 'ole damn biz,
And the papers is printin' me ugly phiz,
    But . . . I'm 'anged if I know wot I did.

"Oh, the Captain comes and 'e says: 'Look, 'ere!
They're far too quiet out there: it's queer.
They're up to somethin'—'oo'll volunteer
    To crawl in the dark and see?'
Then I felt me 'eart like a 'ammer go,
And up jumps a chap and 'e says: 'Right O!'
But I chips in straight, and I says, 'Oh no!
    'E's a missis and kids—take me.'

     "And the next I knew I was sneakin' out,
    And the oozy corpses was all about,
    And I felt so scared I wanted to shout,
        And my skin fair prickled wiv fear;
    And I sez: 'You coward! You 'ad no right
    To take on the job of a man this night.'
    Yet still I kept creepin' till ('orrid sight!)
        The trench of the 'Uns was near.

"It was all so dark, it was all so still;
Yet somethin' pushed me against me will;
'Ow I wanted to turn!   Yet I crawled until
    I was seein' a dim light shine.
Then thinks I: 'I'll just go a little bit,
And see wot the doose I can make of it,'
And it seemed to come from the mouth of a pit:
    'Christmas!' sez I, 'a *mine*.'

"Then 'ere's the part wot I can't explain:
I wanted to make for 'ome again,
But somethin' was blazin' inside me brain,
    So I crawled to the trench instead;
Then I saw the bullet 'ead of a 'Un,
And 'e stood by a rapid-firer gun,
And I lifted a rock and I 'it 'im one,
    And 'e dropped like a chunk o' lead.

"Then all the 'Uns that was underground
Comes up with a rush and on with a bound,
And I swings that giddy old Maxim round
    And belts 'em solid and square.
You see I was off me chump wiv fear:
'If I'm sellin' me life,' sez I, 'it's dear.'
And the trench was narrow and they was near,
    So I peppered the brutes for fair.

"So I 'eld 'em back and I yelled with fright,
And the boys attacked and we 'ad a fight,
And we 'captured a section o' trench' that night
    Which we didn't expect to get;
And they found me there with me Maxim gun,
And I'd laid out a score if I'd laid out one,
And I fainted away when the thing was done,
    And I 'aven't got over it yet."

So that's the 'istory Bill told me.
Of course it's all on the strict Q.T.;
It wouldn't do to get out, you see,
    As 'e hacted against 'is will.
But 'e's convalescin' wiv all 'is might,
And 'e 'opes to be fit for another fight—
Say! Ain't 'e a bit of the real all right!
    Wot's the matter with Bill!

R

MISSIS MORIARTY'S BOY

Missis Moriarty called last week, and says she to me, says she:
"Sure the heart of me's broken entirely now—it's the fortunate
  woman you are;
You've still got your Dinnis to cheer up your home, but me
  Patsy boy where is he?
Lyin' alone, cold as a stone, kilt in the weariful wahr.
Oh, I'm seein' him now as I looked on him last, wid his hair
  all curly and bright,
And the wonderful, tenderful heart he had, and his eyes as
  he wint away,
Shinin' and lookin' down on me from the pride of his proper
  height:
Sure I'll remember me boy like that if I live to me dyin' day."

And just as she spoke them very same words me Dinnis came
  in at the door,
Came in from McGonigle's ould shebeen, came in from
  drinkin' his pay;
And Missis Moriarty looked at him, and she didn't say anny
  more,

But she wrapped her head in her ould black shawl, and she
quietly wint away.

And what was I thinkin', I ask ye now, as I put me Dinnis to
bed,

Wid him ravin' and cursin' one half o' the night, as cold by
his side I sat;

Was I thinkin' the poor ould woman she was, wid her Patsy
slaughtered and dead?

Was I weepin' for Missis Moriarty? I'm not so sure about that.

Missis Moriarty goes about wid a shinin' look on her face;

Wid her grey hair under her ould black shawl, and the eyes
of her mother-mild;

Some say she's a little bit off her head; but annyway it's the
case

Her timper's so swate that you nivver would tell she'd be
losin' her only child.

And I think, as I wait up ivery night for me Dinnis to come
home blind,

And I'm hearin' his stumblin' foot on the stair along about
half-past three:

Sure there's many a way of breakin' a heart, and I haven't
made up me mind—

Would I be Missis Moriarty, or Missis Moriarty me?

MY FOE

A Belgian Priest-Soldier speaks:

Gurr! you *cochon!* Stand and fight!
Show your mettle! Snarl and bite!
Spawn of an accursed race,
Turn and meet me face to face!
Here amid the wreck and rout
Let us grip and have it out!
Here where ruins rock and reel
Let us settle, steel to steel!
Look! Our houses, how they spit
Sparks from brands your friends have lit.
See! Our gutters running red,
Bright with blood your friends have shed.
Hark! Amid your drunken brawl
How our maidens shriek and call.
Why have *you* come here alone,
To this hearth's blood-spattered stone?
Come to ravish, come to loot,
Come to play the ghoulish brute.

Ah, indeed! We well are met,
Bayonet to bayonet.
God! I never killed a man:
Now I'll do the best I can.
Rip you to the evil heart,
Laugh to see the life-blood start.
Bah! you swine! I hate you so.
Show you mercy? No! . . . and no! . . .

There! I've done it. See! he lies
Death a-staring from his eyes;
Glazing eyeballs, panting breath,
How it's horrible, is Death!
Plucking at his bloody lips
With his trembling finger-tips;
Choking in a dreadful way
As if he would something say
In that uncouth tongue of his. . . .
Oh, how horrible Death is!

How I wish that he would die!
So unnerved, unmanned am I.
See! His twitching face is white!
See! His bubbling blood is bright.
Why do I not shout with glee?
What strange spell is over me?
There he lies; the fight was fair;
Let me toss my cap in air.

Why am I so silent? Why
Do I pray for him to die?
Where is all my vengeful joy?
Ugh! *My foe is but a boy.*

I'd a brother of his age
Perished in the war's red rage;
Perished in the Ypres hell:
Oh, I loved my brother well.
And though I be hard and grim,
How it makes me think of him!
He had just such flaxen hair
As the lad that's lying there.
Just such frank blue eyes were his. . . .
God! How horrible war is!

I have reason to be gay:
There is one less foe to slay.
I have reason to be glad:
Yet—my foe is such a lad.
So I watch in dull amaze,
See his dying eyes a-glaze,
See his face grow glorified,
See his hands outstretched and wide
To that bit of ruined wall
Where the flames have ceased to crawl,
Where amid the crumbling bricks
Hangs *a blackened crucifix.*

Now, oh now I understand.
Quick I press it in his hand,
Close his feeble finger-tips,
Hold it to his faltering lips.
As I watch his welling blood
I would stem it if I could.
God of Pity, let him live!
God of Love, forgive, forgive.

*   *   *   *   *   *

His face looked strangely, as he died,
Like that of One they crucified.
And in the pocket of his coat
I found a letter; thus he wrote:
The things I've seen! Oh mother, dear,
I'm wondering can God be here?
To-night amid the drunken brawl
I saw a Cross hung on a wall;
I'll seek it out, and there alone,
Perhaps I may atone, atone. . . .

Ah no! 'tis I who must atone,
No other saw but God alone;
Yet how can I forget the sight
Of that face so woeful white!
Dead I kissed him as he lay,
Knelt by him and tried to pray;

Left him lying there at rest,
Crucifix upon his breast.

Not for him the pity be.
Ye who pity, pity me,
Crawling now the ways I trod,
Blood-guilty in the sight of God.

MY JOB

I'VE got a little job on 'and, the time is drawin' nigh;
At seven by the Captain's watch I'm due to go and do it;
I wants to 'ave it nice and neat, and pleasin' to the eye,
And I 'opes the God of soldier men will see me safely through
   it.
Because, you see, it's somethin' I 'ave never done before;
And till you 'as experience noo stunts is always tryin';
The chances is I'll never 'ave to do it any more:
At seven by the Captain's watch my little job is . . . *dyin'*.

I've got a little note to write; I'd best begin it now.
I ain't much good at writin' notes, but here goes: "Dearest
   Mother,
I've been in many 'ot old 'do's'; I've scraped through safe
   some'ow,
But now I'm on the very point of tacklin' another.
A little job of hand-grenades; they called for volunteers.
They picked me out; I'm proud of it; it seems a trifle dicky.
If anythin' should 'appen, well, there ain't no call for tears,
And so . . . I 'opes this finds you well.—Your werry lovin'
   Micky."

I've got a little score to settle wiv them swine out there.
I've 'ad so many of me pals done in it's quite upset me.
I've seen so much of bloody death I don't seem for to care,
If I can only even up, how soon the blighters get me.
I'm sorry for them perishers that corpses in a bed;
I only 'opes mine's short and sweet, no linger-longer-lyin';
I've made a mess of life, but now I'll try to make instead . . .
It's seven sharp. Good-bye, old pals! . . . *a decent job in dyin'*.

THE SONG OF THE PACIFIST

WHAT do they matter, our headlong hates, when we take the
    toll of our Dead?
Think ye our glory and gain will pay for the torrent of blood
    we have shed?
By the cheers of our Victory will the heart of the mother be
    comforted?

If by the Victory all we mean is a broken and brooding foe;
Is the pomp and power of a glitt'ring hour, and a truce for an
    age or so:
By the clay-cold hand on the broken blade we have smitten a
    bootless blow!

If by the Triumph we only prove that the sword we sheathe
    is bright;
That justice and truth and love endure; that freedom's throned
    on the height;
That the feebler folks shall be unafraid; that Might shall
    never be Right;

If this be all: by the blood-drenched plains, by the havoc of
fire and fear,
By the rending roar of the War of Wars, by the Dead so
doubly dear. . . .
Then our Victory is a vast defeat, and it mocks us as we cheer.

Victory! there can be but one, hallowed in every land:
When by the graves of our common dead we who were foemen
stand;
And in the hush of our common grief hand is tendered to hand.

Triumph! Yes, when out of the dust in the splendour of
their release
The spirits of those who fell go forth and they hallow our
hearts to peace,
And, brothers in pain, with world-wide voice, we clamour
that War shall cease.

Glory! Ay, when from blackest loss shall be born most radiant
gain;
When over the gory fields shall rise a star that never shall wane:
Then, and then only, our Dead shall know that they have not
fall'n in vain.

When our children's children shall talk of War as a madness
that may not be;

When we thank our God for our grief to-day, and blazon from
    sea to sea

In the name of the Dead the banner of Peace . . . *that will be*
    Victory.

THE TWINS

THERE were two brothers, John and James,
And when the town went up in flames,
To save the house of James dashed John,
Then turned, and lo! his own was gone.

And when the great World War began,
To volunteer John promptly ran;
And while he learned live bombs to lob,
James stayed at home and—sneaked his job.

John came home with a missing limb;
That didn't seem to worry him;
But oh, it set his brain awhirl
To find that James had—sneaked his girl!

Time passed. John tried his grief to drown:
To-day James owns one-half the town;
His army contracts riches yield;
And John? Well, *search the Potter's Field*.

THE SONG OF THE SOLDIER-BORN

Give me the scorn of the stars and a peak defiant;
Wail of the pines and a wind with the shout of a giant;
Night and a trail unknown and a heart reliant.

Give me to live and love in the old; bold fashion;
A soldier's billet at night and a soldier's ration;
A heart that leaps to the fight with a soldier's passion.

For I hold as a simple faith there's no denying:
The trade of a soldier's the only trade worth plying;
The death of a soldier's the only death worth dying.

So let me go and leave your safety behind me;
Go to the spaces of hazard where nothing shall bind me;
Go till the word is War—and then you will find me.

Then you will call me and claim me because you will need me;
Cheer me and gird me and into the battle-wrath speed me. . . .
And when it's over, spurn me and no longer heed me.

For guile and a purse gold-greased are the arms you carry;
With deeds of paper you fight and with pens you parry;
You call on the hounds of the law your foes to harry.

You with your "Art for its own sake," posing and prinking;
You with your "Live and be merry," eating and drinking;
You with your "Peace at all hazard," from bright blood
    shrinking.

Fools! I will tell you now: though the red rain patters,
And a million of men go down, it's little it matters. . . .
There's the Flag upflung to the stars, though it streams in
    tatters.

There's a glory gold never can buy to yearn and to cry for;
There's a hope that's as old as the sky to suffer and sigh for;
There's a faith that out-dazzles the sun to martyr and die for.

Ah no! it's my dream that War will never be ended;
That men will perish like men, and valour be splendid;
That the Flag by the sword will be served, and honour
    defended.

That the tale of my fights will never be ancient story;
That though my eye may be dim and my beard be hoary,
I'll die as a soldier dies on the Field of Glory.

So give me a strong right arm for a wrong's swift righting;
Stave of a song on my lips as my sword is smiting;
Death in my boots maybe, but fighting, fighting.

AFTERNOON TEA

As I was saying . . . (No, thank you; I never take cream with
    my tea;
Cows weren't allowed in the trenches—got out of the habit,
    y'see.)
As I was saying, our Colonel leaped up like a youngster
    of ten:
"Come on, lads!" he shouts, "and we'll show 'em." And he
    sprang to the head of the men.
Then some bally thing seemed to trip him, and he fell on
    his face with a slam. . . .
Oh, he died like a true British soldier, and the last word he
    uttered was "Damn!"
And hang it! I loved the old fellow, and something just burst
    in my brain,
And I cared no more for the bullets than I would for a shower
    of rain.
'Twas an awf'ly funny sensation (I say, this is jolly nice tea);
I felt as if something had broken; by gad! I was suddenly free.
Free for a glorified moment, beyond regulations and laws,
Free just to wallow in slaughter, as the chap of the Stone Age
    was.

516

So on I went joyously nursing a Berserker rage of my own,
And though all my chaps were behind me, feeling most
    frightf'ly alone;
With the bullets and shells ding-donging, and the "krock" and
    the swish of the shrap;
And I found myself humming "Ben Bolt" . . . (Will you pass
    me the sugar, old chap?
Two lumps, please). . . . What was I saying?   Oh yes, the
    jolly old dash;
We simply ripped through the barrage, and on with a roar
    and a crash.
My fellows—Old Nick couldn't stop 'em.   On, on they went
    with a yell,
Till they tripped on the Boches' sand-bags—nothing much
    left to tell.
A trench so tattered and battered that even a rat couldn't live;
Some corpses tangled and mangled, wire you could pass
    through a sieve.
The jolly old guns had bilked us, cheated us out of our show,
And my fellows were simply yearning for a red mix-up with
    the foe.
So I shouted to them to follow, and on we went roaring
    again,
Battle-tuned and exultant, on in the leaden rain.
Then all at once a machine gun barks from a bit of a bank,
And our Major roars in a fury: "We've got to take it on flank."
He was running like fire to lead us, when down like a stone
    he comes,
As full of "typewriter" bullets as a pudding is full of plums.

So I took his job and we got 'em. . . . By gad! we got 'em
    like rats;

Down in a deep shell crater we fought like Kilkenny cats.

'Twas pleasant just for a moment to be sheltered and out of
    range,

With some one you *saw* to go for—it made an agreeable change.

And the Boches that missed my bullets, my chaps gave the
    bayonet jolt,

And all the time, I remember, I whistled and hummed "Ben
    Bolt."

Well, that little job was over, so hell for leather we ran,

On to the second line trenches—that's where the fun began.

For though we had strafed 'em like fury, there still were
    some Boches about,

And my fellows, teeth set and eyes glaring, like terriers routed
    'em out.

Then I stumbled on one of their dug-outs, and I shouted: "Is
    any one there?"

And a voice, "Yes, one; but I'm wounded," came faint up
    the narrow stair;

And my man was descending before me, when sudden a cry!
    a shot!

(I say, this cake is delicious. You make it yourself, do you not?)

My man? Oh, they killed the poor devil; for if there was
    one there was ten;

So after I'd bombed 'em sufficient I went down at the head
    of my men;

And four tried to sneak from a bunk-hole, but we cornered
    the rotters all right;

I'd rather not go into details, 'twas messy, that bit of the
fight.

But all of it's beastly messy; let's talk of pleasanter things:

The skirts that the girls are wearing, ridiculous fluffy
things,

So short that they show. . . . Oh, hang it! Well, if I must,
I must.

We cleaned out the second trench line, bomb and bayonet
thrust;

And on we went to the third one, quite calloused to crumping
by now;

And some of our fellows who'd passed us were making a deuce
of a row;

And my chaps—well, I just couldn't hold 'em. (It's strange
how it is with gore;

In some ways its just like whisky: if you taste it you must
have more.)

Their eyes were like beacons of battle; by gad, sir! they
couldn't be calmed,

So I headed 'em bang for the bomb-belt, racing like billy-be-
damned.

Oh, it didn't take long to arrive there, those who arrived at all;

The machine guns were certainly chronic, the shindy enough
to appal.

Oh yes, I omitted to tell you, I'd wounds on the chest and
the head,

And my shirt was torn to a gun-rag, and my face blood-
gummy and red.

I'm thinking I looked like a madman; I fancy I felt one too,

Half naked and swinging a rifle. . . . God! what a glorious
    "do."
As I sit here in old Piccadilly, sipping my afternoon tea,
I see a blind, bullet-chipped devil, and it's hard to believe
    that it's me;
I see a wild, war-damaged demon, smashing out left and
    right,
And humming "Ben Bolt" rather loudly, and hugely enjoying
    the fight.
And as for my men, may God bless 'em! I've loved 'em ever
    since then:
They fought like the shining angels; they're the pick o' the
    land, my men.
And the trench was a reeking shambles, not a Boche to be
    seen alive—
So I thought; but on rounding a traverse I came on a covey
    of five;
And four of 'em threw up their flippers, but the fifth chap,
    a sergeant, was game,
And though I'd a bomb and revolver he came at me just the
    same.
A sporty thing that, I tell you; I just couldn't blow him to
    hell,
So I swung to the point of his jaw-bone, and down like a
    ninepin he fell.
And then when I'd brought him to reason, he wasn't half
    bad, that Hun;
He bandaged my head and my short-rib as well as the Doc
    could have done.

So back I went with my Boches, as gay as a two-year-old colt,
And it suddenly struck me as rummy, I still was a-humming
"Ben Bolt."
And now, by Jove! how I've bored you. You've just let me
babble away;
Let's talk of the things that *matter*—your car or the newest
play. . . .

THE MOURNERS

I LOOK into the aching womb of night;
I look across the mist that masks the dead;
The moon is tired and gives but little light,
    The stars have gone to bed.

The earth is sick and seems to breathe with pain;
A lost wind whimpers in a mangled tree;
I do not see the foul, corpse-cluttered plain,
    The dead I do not see.

The slain I *would* not see . . . and so I lift
My eyes from out the shambles where they lie;
When lo! a million woman-faces drift
    Like pale leaves through the sky.

The cheeks of some are channelled deep with tears;
But some are tearless, with wild eyes that stare
Into the shadow of the coming years
    Of fathomless despair.

And some are young, and some are very old;
And some are rich, some poor beyond belief;
Yet all are strangely like, set in the mould
    Of everlasting grief.

They fill the vast of Heaven, face on face;
And then I see one weeping with the rest,
Whose eyes beseech me for a moment's space. . . .
    Oh, eyes I love the best!

Nay, I but dream. The sky is all forlorn,
And there's the plain of battle writhing red;
God pity them, the womenfolk who mourn!
    How happy are the dead!

L'ENVOI

My job is done; my rhymes are ranked and ready,
My word-battalions marching verse by verse;
Here stanza-companies are none too steady;
There print-platoons are weak, but might be worse,
And as in marshalled order I review them,
My type-brigades, unfearful of the fray.
My eyes that seek their faults are seeing through them
Immortal visions of an epic day.

It seems I'm in a giant bowling-alley;
The hidden heavies round me crash and thud;
A spire snaps like a pipe-stem in the valley;
The rising sun is like a ball of blood.
Along the road the "fantassins" are pouring,
And some are gay as fire, and some steel-stern. . . .
Then back again I see the red tide pouring,
Along the reeking road from Hebuterne.

And once again I seek Hill Sixty-Seven,
The Hun lines grey and peaceful in my sight;
When suddenly the rosy air is riven—
A "coal-box" blots the "boyou" on my right.
Or else to evil Carnoy I am stealing,
Past sentinels who hail with bated breath;
Where not a cigarette spark's dim revealing
May hint our mission in that zone of death.

I see across the shrapnel-seeded meadows
The jagged rubble-heap of La Boiselle;
Blood-guilty Fricourt brooding in the shadows,
And Thiepval's château empty as a shell.
Down Albert's riven streets the moon is leering:
The Hanging Virgin takes its bitter ray;
And all the road from Hamel I am hearing
The silver rage of bugles over Bray.

Once more within the sky's deep sapphire hollow
I sight a swimming Taube, a fairy thing;
I watch the angry shell flame flash and follow
In feather puffs that flick a tilted wing;
And then it fades, with shrapnel mirror's flashing;
The flashes bloom to blossoms lily gold;
The batteries are rancorously crashing,
And life is just as full as it can hold.

Oh spacious days of glory and of grieving!
Oh sounding hours of lustre and of loss!
Let us be glad we lived you, still believing
The God who gave the cannon gave the Cross.
Let us be sure amid the seething passions,
The lusts of blood and hate our souls abhor,
The Power that Order out of Chaos fashions
Smites fiercest in the wrath-red forge of War. . . .
Have faith! Fight on! Amid the battle-hell
Love triumphs, Freedom beacons, all is well.

BALLADS OF A BOHEMIAN

BALLADS OF A BOHEMIAN

PRELUDE

Alas! upon some starry height,
The Gods of Excellence to please,
This hand of mine will never smite
The Harp of High Serenities.
Mere minstrel of the street am I,
To whom a careless coin you fling;
But who, beneath the bitter sky,
Blue-lipped, yet insolent of eye,
Can shrill a song of Spring; .
A song of merry mansard days,
The cheery chimney-tops among;
Of rolics and of roundelays
When we were young . . . when we were young!
A song of love and lilac nights,
Of wit, of wisdom and of wine;
Of Folly whirling on the Heights,
Of hunger and of hope divine;
Of Blanche, Suzette and Celestine,
And all that gay and tender band
Who shared with us the fat, the lean,
The hazard of Illusion-land;

When scores of Philistines we slew
As mightily with brush and pen
We sought to make the world anew,
And scorned the gods of other men;
When we were fools divinely wise,
Who held it rapturous to strive;
When Art was sacred in our eyes,
And it was Heav'n to be alive. . . .

O days of glamour, glory, truth,
To you to-night I raise my glass;
O freehold of immortal youth,
Bohemia, the lost, alas!
O laughing lads who led the romp,
Respectable you've grown, I'm told:
Your heads you bow to power and pomp,
You've learned to know the worth of gold.
O merry maids who shared our cheer,
Your eyes are dim, your locks are grey;
And as you scrub I sadly fear
Your daughters speed the dance to-day.
O windmill land and crescent moon!
O Columbine and Pierrette!
To you my old guitar I tune
Ere I forget, ere I forget. . . .

So come, good men who toil and tire,
Who smoke and sip the kindly cup,

Ring round about the tavern fire
Ere yet you drink your liquor up;
And hear my simple songs of earth,
Of youth and truth and living things;
Of poverty and proper mirth,
Of rags and rich imaginings;
Of cock-a-hoop, blue-heavened days,
Of hearts elate and eager breath,
Of wonder, worship, pity, praise,
Of sorrow, sacrifice and death;
Of lusting, laughter, passion, pain,
Of lights that lure and dreams that thrall . . .
And if a golden word I gain,
Oh, kindly folks, God save you all!
And if you shake your heads in blame . . .
Good friends, God love you all the same.

PART ONE

SPRING

I

All day the sun has shone into my little attic, a bitter sunshine that brightened yet did not warm. And so as I toiled and toiled doggedly enough, many were the looks I cast at the three faggots I had saved to cook my evening meal. Now, however, my supper is over, my pipe alight, and as I stretch my legs before the embers I have at last a glow of comfort, a glimpse of peace.

MY GARRET

Here is my Garret up five flights of stairs;
Here's where I deal in dreams and ply in fancies
Here is the wonder-shop of all my wares,
My sounding sonnets and my red romances.
Here's where I challenge Fate and ring my rhymes,
And grope at glory—aye, and starve at times.

Here is my Stronghold: stout of heart am I,
Greeting each dawn as songful as a linnet;
And when at night on yon poor bed I lie
(Blessing the world and every soul that's in it),
Here's where I thank the Lord no shadow bars
My skylight's vision of the valiant stars.

MY GARRET

Here is my Palace tapestried with dreams.
Ah! though to-night ten *sous* are all my treasure,
While in my gaze immortal beauty gleams,
Am I not dowered with wealth beyond all measure?
Though in my ragged coat my songs I sing,
King of my soul, I envy not the king.

Here is my Heaven: it's so quiet here;
Only the scratch of pen, the candle's flutter;
Shabby and bare and small, but O how dear!
Mark you— my table with my work a-clutter,
My shelf of tattered books along the wall,
My bed, my broken chair—that's nearly all.

Only four faded walls, yet mine, all mine.
Oh, you fine folks, a pauper scorns your pity.
Look, where above me stars of rapture shine
See, where below me gleams the siren city . . .
Am I not rich?—a millionaire no less,
If wealth be told in terms of Happiness.

Ten *sous*. . . . I think one can sing best of poverty when one is holding
it at arm's-length. I'm sure that when I wrote these lines, fortune had
for a moment tweaked me by the nose. To-night, however, I am truly
down to ten sous. It is for that I have stayed in my room all day,
rolled in my blankets and clutching my pen with clammy fingers. For
I must work, work, work. I must finish my book before poverty
crushes me. I am not only writing for my living, but for my life.
Even to-day my Muse was mutinous. For hours and hours anxiously I

stared at a paper that was blank; nervously I paced up and down my garret; bitterly I flung myself on my bed. Then suddenly it all came. Line after line I wrote with hardly a halt. So I made another of my Ballads of the Boulevards. Here it is:

JULOT THE *APACHE*

You've heard of Julot the *apache,* and Gigolette, his *môme.* . . .
Montmartre was their hunting-ground, but Belville was their home.
A little chap just like a boy, with smudgy black moustache,—
Yet there was nothing juvenile in Julot the *apache.*
From head to heel as tough as steel, as nimble as a cat,
With every trick of twist and kick, a master of *savate.*
And Gigolette was tall and fair, as stupid as a cow,
With three combs in the greasy hair she banged upon her brow.
You'd see her on the Place Pigalle on any afternoon,
A primitive and strapping wench as brazen as the moon.
And yet there is a tale that's told of Clichy after dark,
And two *gendarmes* who swung their arms with Julot for a mark.
And oh, but they'd have got him too; they banged and blazed away,
When like a flash a woman leapt between them and their prey.
She took the medicine meant for him; she came down with a crash . . .
"Quick now, and make your get-away, O Julot the *apache!*" . . .

But no! He turned, ran swiftly back, his arms around her
    met;
They nabbed him sobbing like a kid, and kissing Gigolette.

Now I'm a reckless painter chap who loves a jamboree,
And one night in Cyrano's bar I got upon a spree;
And there were trollops all about, and crooks of every kind,
But though the place was reeling round I didn't seem to mind.
Till down I sank, and all was blank when in the bleary dawn
I woke up in my studio to find—my money gone;
Three hundred francs I'd scraped and squeezed to pay my
    quarter's rent.
"Someone has pinched my wad," I wailed; "it never has been
    spent."
And as I racked my brains to seek how I could raise some more,
Before my cruel landlord kicked me cowering from the door:
A knock . . . "Come in," I gruffly groaned; I did not raise my
    head,
Then lo! I heard a husky voice, a swift and silky tread:
"You got so blind, last night, *mon vieux,* I collared all your
    cash—
Three hundred francs. . . . There! *Nom de Dieu!*" said Julot
    the *apache.*

And that was how I came to know Julot and Gigolette,
And we would talk and drink a *bock,* and smoke a cigarette.
And I would meditate upon the artistry of crime,
And he would tell of cracking cribs and cops and doing time;

Or else when he was flush of funds he'd carelessly explain
He'd biffed some bloated *bourgeois* on the border of the Seine.
So gentle and polite he was, just like a man of peace,
And not a desperado and the terror of the police.

Now one day in a *bistro* that's behind the Place Vendôme
I came on Julot the *apache,* and Gigolette his *môme.*
And as they looked so very grave, says I to them, says I,
"Come on and have a little glass, it's good to rinse the eye.
You both look mighty serious; you've something on the heart."
"Ah, yes," said Julot the *apache,* "we've something to impart.
When such things come to folks like us, it isn't very gay . . .
It's Gigolette—she tells me that a *gosse* is on the way."
Then Gigolette, she looked at me with eyes like stones of gall:
"If we were honest folks," said she, "I wouldn't mind at all.
But then . . . you know the life we lead; well, anyway I mean
(That is, providing it's a girl) to call her Angeline."
"Cheer up," said I; "it's all in life. There's gold within the
      dross.
Come on, we'll drink another *verre* to Angeline the *gosse.*"

And so the weary winter passed, and then one April morn
The worthy Julot came at last to say the babe was born.
"I'd like to chuck it in the Seine," he sourly snarled, "and yet
I guess I'll have to let it live, because of Gigolette."
I only laughed, for sure I saw his spite was all a bluff,
And he was prouder than a prince behind his manner gruff.
Yet every day he'd blast the brat with curses deep and grim,
And swear to me that Gigolette no longer thought of *him.*

And then one night he dropped the mask; his eyes were sick
   with dread,
And when I offered him a smoke he groaned and shook his
   head:
"I'm all upset; it's Angeline . . . she's covered with a rash . . .
She'll maybe die, my little *gosse*," cried Julot the *apache*.

But Angeline, I joy to say, came through the test all right,
Though Julot, so they tell me, watched beside her day and
   night.
And when I saw him next, says he: "Come up and dine with
   me.
We'll buy a beefsteak on the way, a bottle and some *brie*."
And so I had a merry night within his humble home,
And laughed with Angeline the *gosse* and Gigolette the *môme*.
And every time that Julot used a word the least obscene,
How Gigolette would frown at him and point to Angeline:
Oh, such a little innocent, with hair of silken floss,
I do not wonder they were proud of Angeline the *gosse*.
And when her arms were round his neck, then Julot says to
   me:
"I must work harder now, *mon vieux*, since I've to work for
   three."
He worked so very hard indeed, the police dropped in one day,
And for a year behind the bars they put him safe away.

So dark and silent now, their home; they'd gone—I wondered
   where,
Till in a laundry near I saw a child with shining hair;

And o'er the tub a strapping wench, her arms in soapy foam;
Lo! it was Angeline the *gosse*, and Gigolette the *môme*.
And so I kept an eye on them and saw that all went right,
Until at last came Julot home, half crazy with delight.
And when he'd kissed them both, says he: "I've had my fill
    this time.
I'm on the honest now, I am; I'm all fed up with crime.
You mark my words, the page I turn is going to be clean,
I swear it on the head of her, my little Angeline."

And so, to finish up my tale, this morning as I strolled
Along the boulevard I heard a voice I knew of old.
I saw a rosy little man with walrus-like moustache . . .
I stopped, I stared. . . . By all the gods! 'twas Julot the *apache*.
"I'm in the garden way," he said, "and doing mighty well;
I've half an acre under glass, and heaps of truck to sell.
Come out and see. Oh come, my friend, on Sunday, wet or
    shine . . .
Say!—*it's the First Communion of that little girl of mine.*

II

Chez Moi, Montparnasse,
The same evening.

To-day is an anniversary. A year ago to-day I kicked over an office
stool and came to Paris, thinking to make a living by my pen. I was
twenty then, and in my pocket I had twenty pounds. Of that, my ten
sous are all that remain. And so to-night I am going to spend them,
not prudently on bread, but prodigally on beer.

As I stroll down the Boul' Mich' the lingering light has all the exquisite tenderness of violet; the trees are in their first translucent green; beneath them the lamps are lit with purest gold, and from the Little Luxembourg comes a silver jangle of tiny voices. Taking the gay side of the street, I enter a café. Although it isn't its true name, I choose to call my café

L'ESCARGOT D'OR

O Tavern of the Golden Snail!
Ten *sous* have I, so I'll regale;
Ten *sous* your amber brew to sip
(Eight for the *bock* and two the tip),
And so I'll sit the evening long,
And smoke my pipe and watch the throng.
The giddy crowd that drains and drinks
I'll watch it quiet as a sphinx;
And who among them all shall buy
For ten poor *sous* such joy as I?
As I who, snugly tucked away,
Look on it all as on a play,
A frolic scene of love and fun,
To please an audience of One.

O Tavern of the Golden Snail!
You've stuff indeed for many a tale.
All eyes, all ears, I nothing miss:
Two lovers lean to clasp and kiss;
The merry students sing and shout,

The nimble *garçons* dart about;
Lo! here come Mimi and Musette
With: *"S'il vous plait, une cigarette?"*
Marcel and Rudolf, Schaunard too,
Behold the old rapscallion crew,
With flowing tie and shaggy head . . .
Who says Bohemia is dead?
Oh shades of Murger! prank and clown,
And I will watch and write it down.

O Tavern of the Golden Snail!
What crackling throats have gulped your ale!
What sons of Fame from far and near
Have glowed and mellowed in your cheer!
Within this corner where I sit
Banville and Coppée clashed their wit;
And hither, too, to dream and drain,
And drown despair, came poor Verlaine.
Here Wilde would talk and Synge would muse,
Maybe like me with just ten *sous*.
Ah! one is lucky, is one not?
With ghosts so rare to drain a pot!
So may your custom never fail,
O Tavern of the Golden Snail!

There! my pipe is out. Let me light it again and consider. I have
no illusions about myself. I am not fool enough to think I am a poet,
but I have a knack of rhyme and I love to make verses. Mine is a
tootling, tin-whistle music. Humbly and afar I follow in the footsteps

of Praed and Lampson, of Field and Riley, hoping that in time my
Muse may bring me bread and butter. So far, however, it has been
all kicks and no coppers. And to-night I am at the end of my tether.
I wish I knew where to-morrow's breakfast was coming from. Well,
since rhyming's been my ruin, let me rhyme to the bitter end.

IT IS LATER THAN YOU THINK

Lone amid the café's cheer,
Sad of heart am I to-night;
Dolefully I drink my beer,
But no single line I write.
There's the wretched rent to pay,
Yet I glower at pen and ink:
Oh, inspire me, Muse, I pray,
It is later than you think!

Hello! there's a pregnant phrase.
Bravo! let me write it down;
Hold it with a hopeful gaze,
Gauge it with a fretful frown.
Tune it to my lyric lyre . . .
Ah! upon starvation's brink,
How the words are dark and dire:
It is later than you think.

Weigh them well. . . . Behold yon band,
Students drinking by the door,

Madly merry, *bock* in hand,
Saucers stacked to mark their score.
Get you gone, you jolly scamps;
Let your parting glasses clink;
Seek your long neglected lamps:
It is later than you think.

Look again: yon dainty blonde,
All allure and golden grace,
Oh so willing to respond
Should you turn a smiling face.
Play your part, poor pretty doll;
Feast and frolic, pose and prink;
There's the Morgue to end it all,
And it's later than you think.

Yon's a playwright—mark his face,
Puffed and purple, tense and tired;
Pasha-like he holds his place,
Hated, envied and admired.
How you gobble life, my friend;
Wine, and woman soft and pink!
Well, each tether has its end:
Sir, it's later than you think.

See yon living scarecrow pass
With a wild and wolfish stare
At each empty absinthe glass,
As if he saw Heaven there.

Poor damned wretch, to end your pain
There is still the Greater Drink.
Yonder waits the sanguine Seine . . .
It is later than you think.

Lastly, you who read; aye, you,
Who this very line may scan:
Think of all you planned to do . . .
Have you done the best you can?
See! the tavern lights are low;
Black's the night, and how you shrink
God; and is it time to go!
Ah! the clock is always slow;
It is later than you think;
Sadly later than you think;
Far, far later than you think.

Scarcely do I scribble that last line on the back of an old envelope when
a voice hails me. It is a fellow free-lance, a short-story man called
MacBean. He is having a feast of *Marennes* and he asks me to join
him.

MacBean is a Scotsman with the soul of an Irishman. He has a
keen, lean, spectacled face, and if it were not for his grey hair
he might be taken for a student of theology. However, there is
nothing of the Puritan in MacBean. He loves wine and women, and
money melts in his fingers.

He has lived so long in the Quarter he looks at life from the Parisian
angle. His knowledge of literature is such that he might be a Professor, but he would rather be a vagabond of letters. We talk shop. We
discuss the American short story, but MacBean vows they do these

things better in France. He says that some of the *contes* printed every day in the *Journal* are worthy of Maupassant. After that he buys more beer, and we roam airily over the fields of literature, plucking here and there a blossom of quotation. A fine talk, vivid and eager. It puts me into a kind of glow.

MacBean pays the bill from a handful of big notes, and the thought of my own empty pockets for a moment damps me. However, when we rise to go, it is well after midnight, and I am in a pleasant daze. The rest of the evening may be summed up in the following jingle:

NOCTAMBULE

Zut! it's two o'clock.
See! the lights are jumping.
Finish up your *bock,*
Time we all were humping.
Waiters stack the chairs,
Pile them on the tables;
Let us to our lairs
Underneath the gables.

Up the old Boul' Mich'
Climb with steps erratic.
Steady . . . how I wish
I was in my attic!
Full am I with cheer;
In my heart the joy stirs;
Couldn't be the beer,
Must have been the oysters.

In obscene array
Garbage cans spill over;
How I wish that they
Smelled as sweet as clover!
Charing women wait;
Cafés drop their shutters;
Rats perambulate
Up and down the gutters.

Down the darkened street
Market carts are creeping;
Horse with wary feet,
Red-faced driver sleeping.
Loads of vivid greens,
Carrots, leeks, potatoes,
Cabbages and beans,
Turnips and tomatoes.

Pair of dapper chaps,
Cigarettes and sashes,
Stare at me, perhaps
Desperate *apaches*.
"Needn't bother me,
Jolly well you know it;
Parceque je suis
Quartier Latin poète.

"Give you villanelles
Madrigals and lyrics

Ballades and rondels,
Odes and panegyrics.
Poet pinched and poor,
Pricked by cold and hunger;
Trouble's troubadour,
Misery's balladmonger."

Think how queer it is!
Every move I'm making,
Cosmic gravity's
Centre I am shaking;
Oh, how droll to feel
(As I now am feeling),
Even as I reel,
All the world is reeling.

Reeling too the stars,
Neptune and Uranus,
Jupiter and Mars,
Mercury and Venus;
Suns and moons with me,
As I'm homeward straying,
All in sympathy
Swaying, swaying, swaying.

Lord! I've got a head.
Well, it's not surprising.
I must gain my bed
Ere the sun be rising;

When the merry lark
In the sky is soaring,
I'll refuse to hark,
I'll be snoring, snoring.

Strike a sulphur match . . .
Ha! at last my garret.
Fumble at the latch,
Close the door and bar it.
Bed, you graciously
Wait, despite my scorning . . .
So, bibaciously
Mad old world, good morning.

III

MY GARRET, MONTPARNASSE,

April.

INSOMNIA

HEIGH HO! to sleep I vainly try;
Since twelve I haven't closed an eye,
And now it's three, and as I lie,
From Notre Dame to St. Denis
The bells of Paris chime to me;
"You're young," they say, "and strong and free."

I do not turn with sighs and groans
To ease my limbs, to rest my bones,
As if my bed were stuffed with stones.
No peevish murmur tips my tongue—
Ah no! for every sound upflung
Says: "Lad, you're free and strong and young."

And so beneath the sheet's caress
My body purrs with happiness;
Joy bubbles in my veins. . . . Ah yes,
My very blood that leaps along
Is chiming in a joyous song,
Because I'm young and free and strong.

Maybe it is the springtide. I am so happy I am afraid. The sense
of living fills me with exultation. I want to sing, to dance; I am dithy-
rambic with delight.

I think the moon must be to blame:
It fills the room with fairy flame;
It paints the wall, it seems to pour
A dappled flood upon the floor.
I rise and through the window stare . . .
Ye gods! how marvellously fair!
From Montrouge to the Martyr's Hill,
A silver city rapt and still;
Dim, drowsy deeps of opal haze,
And spire and dome in diamond blaze;

The little lisping leaves of spring
Like sequins softly glimmering;
Each roof a plaque of argent sheen,
A gauzy gulf the space between;
Each chimney-top a thing of grace,
Where merry moonbeams prank and chase;
And all that sordid was and mean,
Just Beauty, deathless and serene.

O magic city of a dream!
From glory unto glory gleam;
And I will gaze and pity those
Who on their pillows drowse and doze
And as I've nothing else to do,
Of tea I'll make a rousing brew,
And coax my pipes until they croon,
And chant a ditty to the moon.

There! my tea is black and strong. Inspiration comes with every
sip. Now for the moon.

The moon peeped out behind the hill
As yellow as an apricot;
Then up and up it climbed until
Into the sky it fairly got;
The sky was vast and violet;
The poor moon seemed to faint in fright,
And pale it grew and paler yet,
Like fine old silver, rinsed and bright.

And yet it climbed so bravely on
Until it mounted heaven-high;
Then earthward it serenely shone,
A silver sovereign of the sky,
A bland sultana of the night,
Surveying realms of lily light.

MOON SONG

A CHILD saw in the morning skies
The dissipated-looking moon,
And opened wide her big blue eyes,
And cried: "Look, look, my lost balloon
And clapped her rosy hands with glee:
"Quick, mother! Bring it back to me."

A poet in a lilied pond
Espied the moon's reflected charms,
And ravished by that beauty blonde,
Leapt out to clasp her in his arms.
And as he'd never learnt to swim,
Poor fool! that was the end of him.

A rustic glimpsed amid the trees
The bluff moon caught as in a snare.
"They say it do be made of cheese,"
Said Giles, "and that a chap bides there. . . .

That Blue Boar ale be strong, I vow—
The lad's a-winkin' at me now."

Two lovers watched the new moon hold
The old moon in her bright embrace.
Said she: "There's mother, pale and old,
And drawing near her resting place."
Said he: "Be mine, and with me wed,"
Moon-high she stared . . . she shook her head.

A soldier saw with dying eyes
The bleared moon like a ball of blood,
And thought of how in other skies,
So pearly bright on leaf and bud
Like peace its soft white beams had lain;
Like Peace! . . . He closed his eyes again.

Child, lover, poet, soldier, clown,
Ah yes, old Moon, what things you've seen!
I marvel now, as you look down,
How can your face be so serene?
And tranquil still you'll make your round,
Old Moon, when we are underground.

"And now, blow out your candle, lad, and get to bed. See, the dawn
is in the sky. Open your window and let its freshness rouge your
cheek. You've earned your rest. Sleep."
Aye, but before I do so, let me read again the last of my *Ballads*.

THE SEWING-GIRL

THE humble garret where I dwell
Is in that Quarter called the Latin;
It isn't spacious—truth to tell,
There's hardly room to swing a cat in.
But what of that! It's there I fight
For food and fame, my Muse inviting,
And all the day and half the night
You'll find me writing, writing, writing.

Now, it was in the month of May
As, wrestling with a rhyme rheumatic,
I chanced to look across the way,
And lo! within a neighbour attic,
A hand drew back the window shade,
And there, a picture glad and glowing,
I saw a sweet and slender maid,
And she was sewing, sewing, sewing.

So poor the room, so small, so scant,
Yet somehow oh, so bright and airy.
There was a pink geranium plant,
Likewise a very pert canary.
And in the maiden's heart it seemed
Some fount of gladness must be springing,
For as alone I sadly dreamed
I heard her singing, singing, singing.

God love her! how it cheered me then
To see her there so brave and pretty;
So she with needle, I with pen,
We slaved and sang above the city.
And as across my streams of ink
I watched her from a poet's distance,
She stitched and sang . . . I scarcely think
She was aware of my existence.

And then one day she sang no more.
That put me out, there's no denying.
I looked—she laboured as before,
But, bless me! she was crying, crying.
Her poor canary chirped in vain;
Her pink geranium drooped in sorrow;
"Of course," said I, "she'll sing again.
Maybe," I sighed, "she will to-morrow."

Poor child! 'twas finished with her song:
Day after day her tears were flowing;
And as I wondered what was wrong
She pined and peaked above her sewing.
And then one day the blind she drew,
Ah! though I sought with vain endeavour
To pierce the darkness, well I knew
My sewing-girl had gone for ever.

And as I sit alone to-night
My eves unto her room are turning . . .

I'd give the sum of all I write
Once more to see her candle burning,
Once more to glimpse her happy face,
And while my rhymes of cheer I'm ringing,
Across the sunny sweep of space
To hear her singing, singing, singing.

Heigh ho! I realize I am very weary. It's nice to be so tired, and
to know one can sleep as long as one wants. The morning sunlight
floods in at my window, so I draw the blind and throw myself on my
bed. . . .

IV

My Garret, Montparnasse,

April.

Hurrah! As I opened my eyes this morning to a hard, unfeeling
world, little did I think what a surprise awaited me. A big blue envelope had been pushed under my door. Another rejection, I thought,
and I took it up distastefully. The next moment I was staring at my
first cheque.

It was an express order for two hundred francs, in payment of a bit
of verse. . . . So to-day I will celebrate. I will lunch at the D'Harcourt,
I will dine on the Grand Boulevard, I will go to the theatre.

Well, here's the thing that has turned the tide for me. It is somewhat in the vein of "Sourdough" Service, the Yukon bard. I don't
think much of his stuff, but they say he makes heaps of money. I can
well believe it, for he drives a Hispano-Suiza in the Bois every afternoon. The other night he was with a crowd at the Dome Café, a
chubby chap who sits in a corner and seldom speaks. I was dis-

appointed. I thought he was a big, hairy man who swore like a trooper and mixed brandy with his beer. He only drank Vichy, poor fellow!

LUCILLE

OF course you've heard of the *Nancy Lee,* and how she sailed
    away
On her famous quest of the Arctic flea, to the wilds of Hudson's
    Bay?
For it was a foreign Prince's whim to collect this tiny cuss,
And a golden quid was no more to him than a copper to coves
    like us.
So we sailed away and our hearts were gay as we gazed on the
    gorgeous scene;
And we laughed with glee as we caught the flea of the wolf
    and the wolverine;
Yea, our hearts were light as the parasite of the ermine rat we
    slew,
And the great musk ox, and the silver fox, and the moose and
    the caribou.
And we laughed with zest as the insect pest of the marmot
    crowned our zeal,
And the wary mink and the wily "link," and the walrus and the
    seal.
And with eyes aglow on the scornful snow we danced a riga-
    doon,
Round the lonesome lair of the Arctic hare, by the light of the
    silver moon.

But the time was nigh to homeward hie, when, imagine our
      despair!
For the best of the lot we hadn't got—the flea of the polar
      bear.

Oh, his face was long and his breath was strong, as the Skipper
      he says to me:
"I wants you to linger 'ere, my lad, by the shores of the Hartic
      Sea;
I wants you to 'unt the polar bear the perishin' winter through,
And if flea ye find of its breed and kind, there's a 'undred quid
      for you."
But I shook my head: "No, Cap," I said; "it's yourself I'd like
      to please,
But I tells ye flat I wouldn't do that if ye went on yer bended
      knees."
Then the Captain spat in the seething brine, and he says:
      "Good luck to you,
If it can't be did for a 'undred quid, supposin' we call it two?"
So that was why they said good-bye, and they sailed and left
      me there—
Alone, alone in the Arctic Zone to hunt for the polar bear.

Oh, the days were slow and packed with woe, till I thought
      they would never end;
And I used to sit when the fire was lit, with my pipe for my
      only friend.
And I tried to sing some rollicky thing, but my song broke off
      in a prayer,

And I'd drowse and dream by the driftwood gleam: I'd dream
    of a polar bear;
I'd dream of a cloudlike polar bear that blotted the stars on
    high,
With ravenous jaws and flenzing claws, and the flames of hell
    in his eye.
And I'd trap around on the frozen ground, as a proper hunter
    ought,
And beasts I'd find of every kind, but never the one I sought.
Never a track in the white ice-pack that humped and heaved
    and flawed,
Till I came to think: "Why, strike me pink! if the creature ain't
    a fraud."
And then one night in the waning light, as I hurried home to
    sup,
I hears a roar by the cabin door, and a great white hulk heaves
    up.
So my rifle flashed, and a bullet crashed; dead, dead as a stone
    fell he,
And I gave a cheer, for there in his ear—Gosh ding me!—a tiny
    flea.

At last, at last! Oh, I clutched it fast, and I gazed on it with
    pride;
And I thrust it into a biscuit-tin, and I shut it safe inside;
With a lid of glass for the light to pass, and space to leap and
    play;
Oh, it kept alive; yea, seemed to thrive, as I watched it night
    and day.

And I used to sit and sing to it, and I shielded it from harm,
And many a feed it had at need on the heft of my hairy arm.
For you'll never know in that land of snow how lonesome a
    man can feel;
So I made a fuss of the little cuss, and I christened it "Lucille."

But the longest winter has its end, and the ice went out to sea,
And I saw one day a ship in the bay, and there was the *Nancy
    Lee.*
So a boat was lowered and I went aboard, and they opened
    wide their eyes—
Yes, they gave a cheer when the truth was clear, and they saw
    my precious prize.
And then it was all like a giddy dream; but to cut my story
    short,
We sailed away on the fifth of May to the foreign Prince's
    court;
To a palmy land and a palace grand, and the little Prince was
    there,
And a fat Princess in a satin dress with a crown of gold on her
    hair.
And they showed me into a shiny room, just him and her and
    me,
And the Prince he was pleased and friendly-like, and he calls
    for drinks for three.
And I shows them my battered biscuit-tin, and I makes my
    modest spiel,
And they laughed, they did, when I opened the lid, and out
    there popped Lucille.

Oh, the Prince was glad, I could soon see that, and the Princess
    she was too;
And Lucille waltzed round on the tablecloth as she often used
    to do.
And the Prince pulled out a purse of gold, and he put it in
    my hand;
And he says: "It was worth all that, I'm told, to stay in that
    nasty land."
And then he turned with a sudden cry, and he clutched at his
    royal beard;
And the Princess screamed, and well she might—for Lucille had
    disappeared.

"She must be here," said his Noble Nibbs, so we hunted all
    around;
Oh, we searched that place, but never a trace of the little beast
    we found.
So I shook my head, and I glumly said: "Gol darn the saucy
    cuss!
It's mighty queer, but she isn't here; so . . . she must be on one
    of us.
You'll pardon me if I make so free, but—there's just one thing
    to do:
If you'll kindly go for a half a mo' I'll search me garments
    through."
Then all alone on the shiny throne I stripped from head to
    heel;
In vain, in vain; it was very plain that I hadn't got Lucille.

So I garbed again, and I told the Prince, and he scratched his
    august head;
"I suppose if she hasn't selected you, it must be me," he said.
So *he* retired; but he soon came back, and his features showed
    distress:
"Oh, it isn't you and it isn't me." . . . Then we looked at the
    Princess.
So *she* retired; and we heard a scream, and she opened wide
    the door;
And her fingers twain were pinched to pain, but a radiant
    smile she wore:
"It's here," she cries, "our precious prize. Oh, I found it right
    away. . . ."
Then I ran to her with a shout of joy, but I choked with a wild
    dismay.
I clutched the back of the golden throne, and the room began
    to reel . . .
What she held to me was, ah yes! a flea, but . . . *it wasn't my
    Lucille.*

    After all, I did not celebrate. I sat on the terrace of the Café Napoli-
tain on the Grand Boulevard, half hypnotized by the passing crowd.
And as I sat I fell into conversation with a god-like stranger who sipped
some golden ambrosia. He told me he was an actor and introduced me
to his beverage, which he called a "Suze-Anni." He soon left me, but
the effect of the golden liquid remained, and there came over me a
desire to write. *C'était plus fort que moi.* So instead of going to the
Folies Bergère I spent all evening in the Omnium Bar near the Bourse,
and wrote the following:

ON THE BOULEVARD

Oh, it's pleasant sitting here,
Seeing all the people pass;
You beside your *bock* of beer,
I behind my *demi-tasse*.
Chatting of no matter what.
You the Mummer, I the Bard;
Ah, it's jolly, is it not?—
Sitting on the Boulevard.

More amusing than a book,
If a chap has eyes to see;
For, no matter where I look,
Stories, stories jump at me.
Moving tales my pen might write;
Poems plain on every face;
Monologues you could recite
With inimitable grace.

(Ah! Imagination's power)
See yon *demi-mondaine* there,
Idly toying with a flower,
Smiling with a pensive air . . .

Well, her smile is but a mask,
For I saw within her muff
Such a wicked little flask:
Vitriol—ugh! the beastly stuff.

Now look back beside the bar.
See yon curled and scented *beau*,
Puffing at a fine cigar—
Sale espèce de maquereau.
Well (of course, it's all surmise),
It's for him she holds her place;
When he passes she will rise,
Dash the vitriol in his face.

Quick they'll carry him away,
Pack him in a Red Cross car;
Her they'll hurry, so they say,
To the cells of St. Lazare.
What will happen then, you ask?
What will all the sequel be?
Ah! Imagination's task
Isn't easy . . . let me see . . .

She will go to gaol, no doubt,
For a year, or maybe two;
But as soon as she gets out
Start her bawdy life anew.

He will lie within a ward,
Harmless as a man can be,
With his face grotesquely scarred,
And his eyes that cannot see.

Then amid the city's din
He will stand against a wall,
With around his neck a tin
Into which the pennies fall.
She will pass (I see it plain,
Like a cinematograph),
She will halt and turn again,
Look and look, and maybe laugh.

Well, I'm not so sure of that—
Whether she will laugh or cry.
He will hold a battered hat
To the lady passing by.
He will smile a cringing smile,
And into his grimy hold,
With a laugh (or sob) the while,
She will drop a piece of gold.

"Bless you, lady," he will say,
And get grandly drunk that night.
She will come and come each day,
Fascinated by the sight.

Then somehow he'll get to know
(Maybe by a kindly friend)
Who she is, and so . . . and so
Bring my story to an end.

How his heart will burst with hate!
He will curse and he will cry.
He will wait and wait and wait,
Till again she passes by.
Then like tiger from its lair
He will leap from out his place,
Down her, clutch her by the hair,
Smear the vitriol on her face.

(Ah! Imagination rare)
See . . . he takes his hat to go;
Now he's level with her chair;
Now she rises up to throw. . . .
God! and she has done it too . . .
Oh, those screams! those hideous screams!
I imagined and . . . it's true:
How his face will haunt my dreams!

What a sight! It makes me sick
Seems I am to blame somehow.
Garçon, fetch a brandy quick . . .
There! I'm feeling better now.

Let's collaborate, we two,
You the Mummer, I the Bard;
Oh, what stunning stuff we'll do,
Sitting on the Boulevard!

It is strange how one works easily at times. I wrote this so quickly that I might almost say I had reached the end before I had come to the beginning. In such a mood I wonder why everybody does not write poetry. Get a Roget's *Thesaurus,* a rhyming dictionary; sit before your typewriter with a strong glass of coffee at your elbow, and just click the stuff off.

FACILITY

So easy 'tis to make a rhyme,
That did the world but know it,
Your coachman might Parnassus climb,
Your butler be a poet.

Then, oh, how charming it would be
If, when in haste hysteric
You called the page, you learned that he
Was grappling with a lyric.

Or else what rapture it would yield,
When cook sent up the salad,
To find within its depths concealed
A touching little ballad.

Or if for tea and toast you yearned,
What joy to find upon it
The chambermaid had coyly laid
A palpitating sonnet.

Your baker could the fashion set;
Your butcher might respond well;
With every tart a triolet,
With every chop a rondel.
Your tailor's bill . . . well, I'll be blowed!
Dear chap! I never knowed him . . .
He's gone and written me an ode,
Instead of what I *owed* him.

So easy 'tis to rhyme . . . yet stay!
Oh, terrible misgiving!
Please do not give the game away . . .
I've got to make my living.

V

My Garret,
May, 1914.

GOLDEN DAYS

Another day of toil and strife,
Another page so white,
Within that fateful Log of Life
That I and all must write;

Another page without a stain
To make of as I may,
That done, I shall not see again
Until the Judgment Day.

Ah, could I, could I backward turn
The pages of that Book,
How often would I blench and burn!
How often loathe to look!
What pages would be meanly scrolled;
What smeared as if with mud;
A few, maybe, might gleam like gold,
Some scarlet seem as blood.

O Record grave, God guide my hand
And make me worthy be,
Since what I write to-day shall stand
To all eternity;
Aye, teach me, Lord of Life, I pray,
As I salute the sun,
To bear myself that every day
May be a Golden One.

I awoke this morning to see the bright sunshine flooding into my
garret. No chamber in the palace of a king could have been more
fair. How I sang as I dressed! How I lingered over my coffee, savour-
ing every drop! How carefully I packed my pipe, gazing serenely over
the roofs of Paris.

Never is the city so lovely as in this month of May, when all the trees are in the fulness of their foliage. As I look, I feel a freshness of vision in my eyes. Wonder wakes in me. The simplest things move me to delight.

THE JOY OF LITTLE THINGS

It's good the great green earth to roam,
Where sights of awe the soul inspire;
But oh, it's best, the coming home,
The crackle of one's own hearth-fire!
You've hob-nobbed with the solemn Past;
You've seen the pageantry of kings;
Yet oh, how sweet to gain at last
The peace and rest of Little Things!

Perhaps you're counted with the Great;
You strain and strive with mighty men;
Your hand is on the helm of State;
Colossus-like you stride . . . and then
There comes a pause, a shining hour,
A dog that leaps, a hand that clings:
O Titan, turn from pomp and power;
Give all your heart to Little Things.

Go couch you childwise in the grass,
Believing it's some jungle strange,
Where mighty monsters peer and pass,

Where beetles roam and spiders range.
Mid gloom and gleam of leaf and blade,
What dragons rasp their painted wings!
O magic world of shine and shade!
O beauty land of Little Things!

I sometimes wonder, after all,
Amid this tangled web of fate,
If what is great may not be small,
And what is small may not be great.
So wondering I go my way,
Yet in my heart contentment sings . . .
O may I ever see, I pray,
God's grace and love in Little Things.

So give to me, I only beg,
A little roof to call my own,
A little cider in the keg,
A little meat upon the bone;
A little garden by the sea,
A little boat that dips and swings . . .
Take wealth, take fame, but leave to me,
O Lord of Life, just Little Things.

Yesterday I finished my tenth ballad. When I have done about a score I will seek a publisher. If I cannot find one, I will earn, beg or steal the money to get them printed. Then if they do not sell I will hawk them from door to door. Oh, I'll succeed, I know I'll succeed. And yet I don't want an easy success; give me the joy of the fight, the thrill of the adventure. Here's my last ballad:

THE ABSINTHE DRINKERS

H<small>E</small>'s yonder, on the terrace of the Café de la Paix,
The little wizened Spanish man, I see him every day.
He's sitting with his Pernod on his customary chair;
He's staring at the passers with his customary stare.
He never takes his piercing eyes from off that moving throng,
That current cosmopolitan meandering along:
Dark diplomats from Martinique, pale Rastas from Peru,
An Englishman from Bloomsbury, a Yank from Kalmazoo;
A poet from Montmartre's heights, a dapper little Jap,
Exotic citizens of all the countries on the map;
A tourist horde from every land that's underneath the sun—
That little wizened Spanish man, he misses never one.
Oh, foul or fair he's always there, and many a drink he buys,
And there's a fire of red desire within his hollow eyes,
And sipping of my Pernod, and a-knowing what I know,
Sometimes I want to shriek aloud and give away the show.
I've lost my nerve; he's haunting me; he's like a beast of prey,
That Spanish man that's watching at the Café de la Paix.

Say! Listen and I'll tell you all . . . the day was growing dim,
And I was with my Pernod at the table next to him;
And he was sitting soberly as if he were asleep,
When suddenly he seemed to tense, like tiger for a leap.
And then he swung around to me, his hand went to his hip,
My heart was beating like a gong—my arm was in his grip;

His eyes were glaring into mine; aye, though I shrank with fear,
His fetid breath was on my face, his voice was in my ear:
"Excuse my *brusquerie*," he hissed; "but, sir, do you suppose—
That portly man who passed us had a *wen upon his nose?*"

And then at last it dawned on me, the fellow must be mad;
And when I soothingly replied: "I do not think he had,"
The little wizened Spanish man subsided in his chair,
And shrouded in his raven cloak resumed his owlish stare.
But when I tried to slip away he turned and glared at me,
And oh, that fishlike face of his was sinister to see:
"Forgive me if I startled you; of course you think I'm queer;
No doubt you wonder who I am, so solitary here;
You question why the passers-by I piercingly review . . .
Well, listen, my bibacious friend, I'll tell my tale to you.

"It happened twenty years ago, and in another land:
A maiden young and beautiful, two suitors for her hand.
My rival was the lucky one; I vowed I would repay;
Revenge has mellowed in my heart, it's rotten ripe to-day.
My happy rival skipped away, vamoosed, he left no trace;
And so I'm waiting, waiting here to meet him face to face;
For has it not been ever said that all the world one day
Will pass in pilgrimage before the Café de la Paix?"

"But, sir," I made remonstrance, "if it's twenty years ago,
You'd scarcely recognize him now, he must have altered so."

The little wizened Spanish man he laughed a hideous laugh,
And from his cloak he quickly drew a faded photograph.
"You're right," said he; "but there are traits (oh, this you must
    allow)
That never change; Lopez was fat, he must be fatter now.
His paunch is senatorial, he cannot see his toes,
I'm sure of it; and then, behold! that wen upon his nose.
I'm looking for a man like that. I'll wait and wait until . . ."
"What will you do?" I sharply cried; he answered me: "Why,
    kill!
He robbed me of my happiness—nay, stranger, do not start;
I'll firmly and politely put—a bullet in his heart."

And then that little Spanish man, with big cigar alight,
Uprose and shook my trembling hand and vanished in the
    night.
And I went home and thought of him and had a dreadful
    dream
Of portly men with each a wen, and woke up with a scream.
And sure enough, next morning, as I prowled the Boulevard,
A portly man with wenny nose roamed into my regard;
Then like a flash I ran to him and clutched him by the arm:
"Oh, sir," said I, "I do not wish to see you come to harm;
But if your life you value aught, I beg, entreat and pray—
Don't pass before the terrace of the Café de la Paix."

That portly man he looked at me with such a startled air,
Then bolted like a rabbit down the rue Michaudière.

"Ha! ha! I've saved a life," I thought; and laughed in my relief,
And straightway joined the Spanish man o'er his *apéritif.*
And thus each day I dodged about and kept the strictest guard
For portly men with each a wen upon the Boulevard.
And then I hailed my Spanish pal, and sitting in the sun,
We ordered many Pernods and we drank them every one.
And sternly he would stare and stare until my hand would
        shake,
And grimly he would glare and glare until my heart would
        quake.
And I would say: "Alphonso, lad, I must expostulate;
Why keep alive for twenty years the furnace of your hate?
Perhaps his wedded life was hell; and you, at least are free . . ."
"That's where you've got it wrong," he snarled; "the fool she
        took was *me.*
My rival sneaked, threw up the sponge, betrayed himself a
        churl:
'Twas he who got the happiness, I only got—the girl."
With that he looked so devil-like he made me creep and shrink,
And there was nothing else to do but buy another drink.

Now yonder like a blot of ink he sits across the way,
Upon the smiling terrace of the Café de la Paix;
That little wizened Spanish man, his face is ghastly white,
His eyes are staring, staring like a tiger's in the night.
I know within his evil heart the fires of hate are fanned.
I know his automatic's ready waiting to his hand,
I know a tragedy is near, I dread, I have no peace . . .

Oh, don't you think I ought to go and call upon the police?
Look there . . . he's rising up . . . my God!   He leaps from
    out his place . . .
Yon millionaire from Argentine . . . the two are face to face . . .
A shot! A shriek! A heavy fall! A huddled heap!   Oh, see
The little wizened Spanish man is dancing in his glee. . . .
I'm sick . . . I'm faint . . . I'm going mad. . . . Oh, please
    take me away . . .
There's BLOOD upon the terrace of the Café de la Paix. . . .

And now I'll leave my work and sally forth.   The city is *en fête*.
I'll join the crowd and laugh and sing with the best.

> The sunshine seeks my little room
> To tell me Paris streets are gay;
> That children cry the lily bloom
> All up and down the leafy way;
> That half the town is mad with May,
> With flame of flag and boom of bell:
> For Carnival is King to-day;
> So pen and page, awhile farewell.

PART TWO

EARLY SUMMER

I

THE RELEASE

To-day within a grog-shop near
I saw a newly captured linnet,
Who beat against his cage in fear,
And fell exhausted every minute;
And when I asked the fellow there
If he to sell the bird were willing,
He told me with a careless air
That I could have it for a shilling.

And so I bought it, cage and all
(Although I went without my dinner),
And where some trees were fairly tall
And houses shrank and smoke was thinner,
The tiny door I open threw,
As down upon the grass I sank me:
Poor little chap! How quick he flew . . .
He didn't even wait to thank me.

Life's like a cage; we beat the bars,
We bruise our breasts, we struggle vainly;

Up to the glory of the stars
We strain with flutterings ungainly.
And then—God opens wide the door;
Our wondrous wings are arched for flying;
We poise, we part, we sing, we soar . . .
Light, freedom, love. . . . Fools call it—Dying.

Yes, that wretched little bird haunted me. I had to let it go. Since I have seized my own liberty I am a fanatic for freedom. It is now a year ago I launched on my great adventure. I have had hard times, been hungry, cold, weary. I have worked harder than ever I did and discouragement has slapped me on the face. Yet the year has been the happiest of my life.

And all because I am free. By reason of filthy money no one can say to me: Do this, or do that. "Master" doesn't exist in my vocabulary. I can look any man in the face and tell him to go to the devil. I belong to myself. I am not for sale. It's glorious to feel like that. It sweetens the dry crust and warms the heart in the icy wind. For that I will hunger and go threadbare; for that I will live austerely and deny myself all pleasure. After health, the best thing in life is freedom.

Here is the last of my ballads. It is by way of being an experiment. Its theme is commonplace, its language that of every day. It is a bit of realism in rhyme.

THE WEE SHOP

SHE risked her all, they told me, bravely sinking
The pinched economies of thirty years;
And there the little shop was, meek and shrinking,
The sum of all her dreams and hopes and fears.

Ere it was opened I would see them in it,
The grey-haired dame, the daughter with her crutch;
So fond, so happy, hoarding every minute,
Like artists, for the final tender touch.

The opening day! I'm sure that to their seeming
Was never shop so wonderful as theirs;
With pyramids of jam-jars rubbed to gleaming;
Such vivid cans of peaches, prunes and pears;
And chocolate, and biscuits in glass cases,
And bon-bon bottles, many-hued and bright;
Yet nothing half so radiant as their faces,
Their eyes of hope, excitement and delight.

I entered: how they waited all a-flutter!
How awkwardly they weighed my acid-drops!
And then with all the thanks a tongue could utter
They bowed me from the kindliest of shops.
I'm sure that night their customers they numbered;
Discussed them all in happy, breathless speech;
And though quite worn and weary, ere they slumbered,
Sent heavenward a little prayer for each.

And so I watched with interest redoubled
That little shop, spent in it all I had;
And when I saw it empty I was troubled,
And when I saw them busy I was glad.
And when I dared to ask how things were going,
They told me, with a fine and gallant smile:

"Not badly . . . slow at first . . . There's never knowing . . .
'Twill surely pick up in a little while."

I'd often see them through the winter weather.
Behind the shutters by a light's faint speck,
Poring o'er books, their faces close together,
The lame girl's arm around her mother's neck.
They dressed their window not one time but twenty,
Each change more pinched, more desperately neat;
Alas! I wondered if behind that plenty
The two who owned it had enough to eat.

Ah, who would dare to sing of tea and coffee?
The sadness of a stock unsold and dead;
The petty tragedy of melting toffee,
The sordid pathos of stale gingerbread.
Ignoble themes! And yet—those haggard faces!
Within that little shop. . . . Oh, here I say
One does not need to look in lofty places
For tragic themes, they're round us every day.

And so I saw their agony, their fighting,
Their eyes of fear, their heartbreak, their despair;
And there the little shop is, black and blighting,
And all the world goes by and does not care.
They say she sought her old employer's pity,
Content to take the pittance he would give.
The lame girl? yes, she's working in the city;
She coughs a lot—she hasn't long to live.

Last night MacBean introduced me to Saxon Dane the Poet. Truly, he is more like a blacksmith than a Bard—a big, bearded man whose black eyes brood sombrely or flash with sudden fire. We talked of Walt Whitman, and then of others.

"The trouble with poetry," he said, "is that it is too exalted. It has a phraseology of its own; it selects themes that are quite outside of ordinary experience. As a medium of expression it fails to reach the great mass of the people."

Then he added: "To hell with the great mass of the people! What have they got to do with it? Write to please yourself, as if not a single reader existed. The moment a man begins to be conscious of an audience he is artistically damned. You're not a Poet, I hope?"

I meekly assured him I was a mere maker of verse.

"Well," said he, "better good verse than middling poetry. And maybe even the humblest of rhymes has its uses. Happiness is happiness, whether it be inspired by a Rossetti sonnet or a ballad by G. R. Sims. Let each one who has something to say, say it in the best way he can, and abide the result. . . . After all," he went on, "what does it matter? We are living in a pigmy day. With Tennyson and Browning the line of great poets passed away, perhaps for ever. The world to-day is full of little minstrels, who echo one another and who pipe away tunefully enough. But with one exception they do not matter."

I dared to ask who was his one exception. He answered, "Myself, of course."

Here's a bit of light verse which it amused me to write to-day, as I sat in the sun on the terrace of the Closerie de Lilas:

THE PHILISTINE AND THE BOHEMIAN

SHE was a Philistine spick and span,
He was a bold Bohemian.
She had the *mode*, and the last at that;
He had a cape and a brigand hat.

She was so *riante* and *chic* and trim;
He was so shaggy, unkempt and grim.
On the rue de la Paix she was wont to shine;
The rue de la Gaîté was more his line.
She doted on Barclay and Dell and Caine;
He quoted Malarmé and Paul Verlaine.
She was a triumph at Tango teas;
At Vorticist's suppers he sought to please.
She thought that Franz Lehar was utterly great;
Of Strauss and Stravinski he'd piously prate.
She loved elegance, he loved art;
They were as wide as the poles apart:
Yet—Cupid and Caprice are hand and glove—
They met at a dinner, they fell in love.

Home he went to his garret bare,
Thrilling with rapture, hope, despair.
Swift he gazed in his looking-glass,
Made a grimace and murmured: "Ass!"
Seized his scissors and fiercely sheared,
Severed his buccaneering beard;
Grabbed his hair, and clip! clip! clip!
Off came a bunch with every snip.
Ran to a tailor's in startled state,
Suits a dozen commanded straight;
Coats and overcoats, pants in pairs,
Everything that a dandy wears;
Socks and collars, and shoes and ties,
Everything that a dandy buys.

Chums looked at him with wondering stare,
Fancied they'd seen him before somewhere;
A Brummell, a D'Orsay, a *beau* so fine,
A shining, immaculate Philistine.

Home she went in a raptured daze,
Looked in a mirror with startled gaze,
Didn't seem to be pleased at all;
Savagely muttered: "Insipid Doll!"
Clutched her hair and a pair of shears,
Cropped and bobbed it behind the ears;
Aimed at a wan and willowy-necked
Sort of a Holman Hunt effect;
Robed in subtile and sage-green tones,
Like the dames of Rossetti and F. B. Jones;
Girdled her garments billowing wide,
Moved with an undulating glide;
All her frivolous friends forsook,
Cultivated a soulful look;
Gushed in a voice with a creamy throb
Over some weirdly Futurist daub—
Did all, in short, that a woman can
To be a consummate Bohemian.

A year went past with its hopes and fears,
A year that seemed like a dozen years.
They met once more. . . . Oh, at last!   At last
They rushed together, they stopped aghast.

They looked at each other with blank dismay,
They simply hadn't a word to say.
He thought with a shiver: "Can this be she?"
She thought with a shudder: "This can't be he?"
This simpering dandy, so sleek and spruce;
This languorous lily in garments loose;
They sought to brace from the awful shock:
Taking a seat, they tried to talk.
She spoke of Bergson and Pater's prose,
He prattled of dances and ragtime shows;
She purred of pictures, Matisse, Cezanne,
His tastes to the girls of Kirchner ran;
She raved of Tschaikowsky and Cæsar Franck,
He owned that he was a jazz-band crank!
They made no headway. Alas! alas!
He thought her a bore, she thought him an ass.
And so they arose and hurriedly fled;
Perish Illusion, Romance, you're dead.
He loved elegance, she loved art,
Better at once to part, to part.

And what is the moral of all this rot?
Don't try to be what you know you're not.
And if you're made on a muttonish plan,
Don't seek to seem a Bohemian;
And if to the goats your feet incline,
Don't try to pass for a Philistine.

A Small Cafe in a Side Street,
June, 1914.

THE BOHEMIAN DREAMS

Because my overcoat's in pawn,
I choose to take my glass
Within a little *bistro* on
The rue du Montparnasse;
The dusty bins with bottles shine,
The counter's lined with zinc,
And there I sit and drink my wine,
And think and think and think.

I think of hoary old Stamboul,
Of Moslem and of Greek,
Of Persian in coat of wool,
Of Kurd and Arab sheikh;
Of all the types of weal and woe,
And as I raise my glass,
Across Galata bridge I know
They pass and pass and pass.

I think of citron-trees aglow,
Of fan-palms shading down,

Of sailors dancing heel and toe
With wenches black and brown;
And though it's all an ocean far
From Yucatan to France,
I'll bet beside the old bazaar
They dance and dance and dance.

I think of Monte Carlo, where
The pallid croupiers call,
And in the gorgeous, guilty air
The gamblers watch the ball;
And as I flick away the foam
With which my beer is crowned,
The wheels beneath the gilded dome
Go round and round and round.

I think of vast Niagara,
Those gulfs of foam a-shine,
Whose mighty roar would stagger a
More prosy bean than mine;
And as the hours I idly spend
Against a greasy wall,
I know that green the waters bend
And fall and fall and fall.

I think of Nijni Novgorod
And Jews who never rest;
And womenfolk with spade and hod
Who slave in Buda Pest;

Of squat and sturdy Japanese
Who pound the paddy soil,
And as I loaf and smoke at ease
They toil and toil and toil.

I think of shrines in Hindustan,
Of cloistral glooms in Spain,
Of minarets in Ispahan,
Of St. Sophia's fane,
Of convent towers in Palestine,
Of temples in Cathay,
And as I stretch and sip my wine
They pray and pray and pray.

And so my dreams I dwell within,
And visions come and go,
And life is passing like a Cin-
Ematographic Show;
Till just as surely as my pipe
Is underneath my nose,
Amid my visions rich and ripe
I doze and doze and doze.

Alas! it is too true. Once more I am counting the coppers, living
on the ragged edge. My manuscripts come back to me like boomerangs,
and I have not the postage, far less the heart, to send them out again.

MacBean seems to take an interest in my struggles. I often sit in
his room in the rue Saint-Julien-le-Pauvre, smoking and sipping whisky
into the small hours. He is an old hand, who knows the market and
frankly manufactures for it.

"Give me short pieces," he says; "things of three verses that will fill a blank half-page of a magazine. Let them be sprightly, and, if possible, have a snapper at the end. Give me that sort of article. I think I can place it for you."

Then he looked through a lot of my verse: "This is the kind of stuff I might be able to sell," he said:

A DOMESTIC TRAGEDY

CLORINDA met me on the way
As I came from the train:
Her face was anything but gay,
In fact, suggested pain.
"Oh hubby, hubby dear!" she cried,
"I've awful news to tell. . . ."
"What is it, darling?" I replied;
"Your mother—is she well?"

"Oh no! oh no! it is not that,
It's something else," she wailed.
My heart was beating pit-a-pat,
My ruddy visage paled.
Like lightning flash in heaven's dome
The fear within me woke:
"Don't say," I cried, "our little home
Has all gone up in smoke!"

She shook her head. Oh, swift I clasped
And held her to my breast;
"The children! Tell me quick," I gasped,
"Believe me, it is best."

Then, then she spoke; mid sobs I caught
These words of woe divine:
"It's coo-coo-cook has gone and bought
A new hat just like mine."

At present I am living on bread and milk. By doing this I can
rub along for another ten days. The thought pleases me. As long as I
have a crust I am master of my destiny. Some day, when I am rich
and famous, I shall look back on all this with regret. Yet I think I
shall always remain a Bohemian. I hate regularity. The clock was
never made for me. I want to eat when I am hungry, sleep when I
am weary, drink—well, any old time.

I prefer to be alone. Company is a constraint on my spirit. I never
make an engagement if I can avoid it. To do so is to put a mortgage
on my future. I like to be able to rise in the morning with the thought
that the hours before me are all mine, to spend in my own way—to
work, to dream, to watch the unfolding drama of life.

Here is another of my ballads. It is longer than most, and gave me
more trouble, though none the better for that.

THE PENCIL SELLER

A PENCIL, sir; a penny—won't you buy?
I'm cold and wet and tired, a sorry plight;
Don't turn your back, sir; take one just to try;
I haven't made a single sale to-night.
Oh, thank you, sir; but take the pencil too;
I'm not a beggar, I'm a business man.
Pencils I deal in, red and black and blue;
It's hard, but still I do the best I can.

Most days I make enough to pay for bread,
A cup o' coffee, stretching room at night.
One needs so little—to be warm and fed,
A hole to kennel in—oh, one's all right . . .
Excuse me, you're a painter, are you not?
I saw you looking at that dealer's show,
The *croûtes* he has for sale, a shabby lot—
What do I know of Art? What do I know . . .
Well, look! That David Strong so well displayed,
"White Sorcery" it's called, all gossamer,
And pale moon-magic and a dancing maid
(You like the little elfin face of her?)—
That's good; but still, the picture as a whole,
The values.—Pah! He never painted worse;
Perhaps because his fire was lacking coal,
His cupboard bare, no money in his purse.
Perhaps . . . they say he laboured hard and long,
And see now, in the harvest of his fame,
When round his pictures people gape and throng,
A scurvy dealer sells this on his name.
A wretched rag, wrung out of want and woe;
A soulless daub, not David Strong a bit,
Unworthy of his art. . . . How should I know?
How should I know? I'm *Strong*—I painted it.

There now, I didn't mean to let that out.
It came in spite of me—aye, stare and stare.
You think I'm lying, crazy, drunk, no doubt—
Think what you like, it's neither here nor there.

It's hard to tell so terrible a truth,
To gain to glory, yet be such as I.
It's true; that picture's mine, done in my youth,
Up in a garret near the Paris sky.
The child's my daughter; aye, she posed for me,
That's why I come and sit here every night.
The painting's bad, but still—oh, still I see
Her little face all laughing in the light.

So now you understand.—I live in fear
Lest one like you should carry it away;
A poor, pot-boiling thing, but oh, how dear!
"Don't let them buy it, pitying God!" I pray!
And hark ye, sir—sometimes my brain's awhirl.
Some night I'll crash into that window pane
And snatch my picture back, my little girl,
And run and run. . . .
                    I'm talking wild again;
A crab can't run. I'm crippled, withered, lame,
Palsied, as good as dead all down one side.
No warning had I when the evil came:
It struck me down in all my strength and pride.
Triumph was mine, I thrilled with perfect power;
Honour was mine, Fame's laurel touched my brow;
Glory was mine—within a little hour
I was a god and . . . what you find me now.

My child, that little, laughing girl you see,
She was my nurse for all ten weary years;

Her joy, her hope, her youth she gave for me;
Her very smiles were masks to hide her tears.
And I, my precious art, so rich, so rare,
Lost, lost to me—what could my heart but break!
Oh, as I lay and wrestled with despair,
I would have killed myself but for her sake. . . .

By luck I had some pictures I could sell,
And so we fought the wolf back from the door;
She painted too, aye, wonderfully well.
We often dreamed of brighter days in store,
And then quite suddenly she seemed to fail;
I saw the shadows darken round her eyes.
So tired she was, so sorrowful, so pale,
And oh, there came a day she could not rise.
The doctor looked at her; he shook his head,
And spoke of wine and grapes and Southern air:
"If you can get her out of this," he said,
"She'll have a fighting chance with proper care."

"With proper care!" When he had gone away,
I sat there, trembling, twitching, dazed with grief.
Under my old and ragged coat she lay,
Our room was bare and cold beyond belief.
"Maybe," I thought, "I still can paint a bit,
Some lilies, landscape, anything at all."
Alas! My brush, I could not steady it.
Down from my fumbling hand I let it fall.

"With proper care"—how could I give her that,
Half of me dead? . . . I crawled down to the street.
Cowering beside the wall, I held my hat
And begged of everyone I chanced to meet.
I got some pennies, bought her milk and bread,
And so I fought to keep the Doom away;
And yet I saw with agony of dread
My dear one sinking, sinking day by day.
And then I was awakened in the night:
"Please take my hands, I'm cold," I heard her sigh;
And soft she whispered, as she held me tight:
"Oh, daddy, we've been happy, you and I!"
I do not think she suffered any pain,
She breathed so quietly . . . but though I tried,
I could not warm her little hands again:
And so there in the icy dark she died. . . .

The dawn came groping in with fingers grey
And touched me, sitting silent as a stone;
I kissed those piteous lips, as cold as clay—
I did not cry, I did not even moan.
At last I rose, groped down the narrow stair;
An evil fog was oozing from the sky;
Half-crazed I stumbled on, I knew not where,
Like phantoms were the folks that passed me by.
How long I wandered thus I do not know,
But suddenly I halted, stood stock-still—
Beside a door that spilled a golden glow
I saw a name, *my name,* upon a bill.

"A Sale of Famous Pictures," so it read,
"A Notable Collection, each a gem,
Distinguished Works of Art by painters dead."
The folks were going in, I followed them.
I stood upon the outskirts of the crowd,
I only hoped that none might notice me.
Soon, soon I heard them call my name aloud:
"A 'David Strong,' his *Fête in Brittany*."
(A brave big picture that, the best I've done,
It glowed and kindled half the hall away,
With all its memories of sea and sun,
Of pipe and bowl, of joyous work and play.
I saw the sardine nets blue as the sky,
I saw the nut-brown fisher-boats put out.)
"Five hundred pounds!" rapped out a voice near by;
"Six hundred!" "Seven!" "Eight!" And then a shout:
"A thousand pounds!" Oh, how I thrilled to hear!
Oh, how the bids went up by leaps, by bounds!
And then a silence; then the auctioneer:
"It's going! Going! Gone! *Three thousand pounds!*"

Three thousand pounds! A frenzy leapt in me.
"That picture's mine," I cried; "I'm David Strong.
I painted it, this famished wretch you see;
I did it, I, and sold it for a song.
And in a garret three small hours ago
My daughter died for want of Christian care.
Look, look at me! . . . Is it to mock my woe
You pay three thousand for my picture there?" . . .

U

O God! I stumbled blindly from the hall;
The city crashed on me, the fiendish sounds
Of cruelty and strife, but over all
"Three thousand pounds!" I heard; "Three thousand
        pounds!"

There, that's my story, sir; it isn't gay.
Tales of the Poor are never very bright . . .
You'll look for me next time you pass this way . . .
I hope you'll find me, sir; good-night, good-night.

III

THE LUXEMBOURG,
June, 1914.

On a late afternoon, when the sunlight is mellow on the leaves, I
often sit near the Fontaine de Medicis, and watch the children at their
play. Sometimes I make bits of verse about them, such as:

FI-FI IN BED

Up into the sky I stare;
All the little stars I see;
And I know that God is there
O, how lonely He must be!

Me, I laugh and leap all day,
Till my head begins to nod;
He's so great, He cannot play:
I am glad I am not God.

> Poor kind God upon His throne,
> Up there in the sky so blue,
> Always, always all alone . . .
> *"Please, dear God, I pity You."*

Or else, sitting on the terrace of a café on the Boul' Mich', I sip slowly a Dubonnet or a Byrrh, and the charm of the Quarter possesses me. I think of men who have lived and loved there, who have grovelled and gloried, who have drunk deep and died. And then I scribble things like this:

GODS IN THE GUTTER

I DREAMED I saw three demi-gods who in a café sat;
And one was lean and satyr-like, and one was large and fat;
And one was eaten up with vice and verminous at that.
The first he spoke of secret sins, and gems and perfumes rare;
And velvet cats and courtesans voluptuously fair:
"Who is the Sybarite?" I asked. They answered: "Baudelaire."

The second talked in tapestries, by fantasy beguiled;
As frail as bubbles, hard as gems, his pageantries he piled;
"This Lord of Language, who is he?" They whispered "Oscar Wilde."

The third was staring at his glass from out abysmal pain;
With tears his eyes were bitten in beneath his bulbous brain.
"Who is the derelict?" said I. They told me: "Paul Verlaine."

Oh Wilde, Verlaine and Baudelaire, their lips were wet with
    wine;
Oh poseur, pimp and libertine! Oh cynic, sot and swine!
Oh votaries of velvet vice! . . . Oh gods of light divine!

Oh Baudelaire, Verlaine and Wilde, they knew the sinks
    of shame;
Their sun-aspiring wings they scorched at passion's altar flame;
Yet lo! enthroned, enskied they stand, Immortal Sons of Fame.

I dreamed I saw three demi-gods who walked with feet of clay,
With cruel crosses on their backs, along a miry way;
Who climbed and climbed the bitter steep . . . to which men
    turn and pray.

And while I am on the subject of the Quarter, let me repeat this,
which is included in my Ballads of the Boulevards:

THE DEATH OF MARIE TORO

WE'RE taking Marie Toro to her home in Père-La-Chaise;
We're taking Marie Toro to her last resting-place.
Behold! her hearse is hung with wreaths till everything is hid
Except the blossoms heaping high upon her coffin lid.

A week ago she roamed the street, a draggle and a slut,
A by-word of the Boulevard and everybody's butt;
A week ago she haunted us, we heard her whining cry,
We brushed aside the broken blooms she pestered us to buy;
A week ago she had not where to rest her weary head . . .
But now, oh, follow, follow on, for Marie Toro's dead.

Oh Marie, she was once a queen—ah yes, a queen of queens.
High-throned above the Carnival she held her splendid sway.
For four-and-twenty crashing hours she knew what glory means,
The cheers of half a million throats, the *délire* of a day.
Yet she was only one of us, a little sewing-girl,
Though far the loveliest and best of all our laughing band;
Then Fortune beckoned; off she danced, amid the dizzy whirl,
And we who once might kiss her cheek were proud to kiss
    her hand.
For swiftly as a star she soared; she had her every wish;
We saw her roped with pearls of price, with princes at her call;
And yet, and yet I think her dreams were of the old Boul' Mich',
And yet I'm sure within her heart she loved us best of all.
For one night in the Purple Pig, upon the rue Saint-Jacques,
We laughed and quaffed . . . a limousine came swishing to the
    door;
Then Raymond Jolicœur cried out: "It's Queen Marie come
    back,
In satin clad to make us glad, and witch our hearts once more."
But no, her face was strangely sad, and at the evening's end:
"Dear lads," she said; "I love you all, and when I'm far away,
Remember, oh, remember, little Marie is your friend,

And though the world may lie between, I'm coming back
    some day."
And so she went, and many a boy who's fought his way to
    Fame,
Can look back on the struggle of his garret days and bless
The loyal heart, the tender hand, the Providence that came
To him and all in hour of need, in sickness and distress.
Time passed away. She won their hearts in London, Moscow,
    Rome;
They worshiped her in Argentine, adored her in Brazil;
We smoked our pipes and wondered when she might be
    coming home,
And then we learned the luck had turned, the things were
    going ill.
Her health had failed, her beauty paled, her lovers fled away;
And someone saw her in Peru, a common drab at last.
So years went by, and faces changed; our beards were sadly
    grey,
And Marie Toro's name became an echo of the past.

You know that old and withered man, that derelict of art,
Who for a paltry franc will make a crayon sketch of you?
In slouching hat and shabby coat he looks and is the part,
A sodden old Bohemian, without a single *sou*.
A boon companion of the days of Rimbaud and Verlaine,
He broods and broods, and chews the cud of bitter souvenirs;
Beneath his mop of grizzled hair, his cheeks are gouged with
    pain,
The saffron sockets of his eyes are hollowed out with tears.

Well, one night in the D'Harcourt's din I saw him in his place,
When suddenly the door was swung, a woman halted there;
A woman cowering like a dog, with white and haggard face,
A broken creature, bent of spine, a daughter of Despair.
She looked and looked, as to her breast she held some withered
bloom;
"Too late! Too late! . . . they all are dead and gone," I heard
her say.
And once again her weary eyes went round and round the
room;
"Not one of all I used to know . . ." she turned to go away . . .
But quick I saw the old man start: "Ah no!" he cried, "Not all.
Oh, Marie Toro, queen of queens, don't you remember Paul?"

"Oh, Marie, Marie Toro, in my garret next the sky,
Where many a day and night I've crouched with not a crust
to eat,
A picture hangs upon the wall a fortune couldn't buy,
A portrait of a girl whose face is pure and angel-sweet."
Sadly the woman looked at him: "Alas! it's true," she said;
"That little maid, I knew her once. It's long ago—she's dead."
He went to her; he laid his hand upon her wasted arm:
"Oh, Marie Toro, come with me, though poor and sick am I.
For old times' sake I cannot bear to see you come to harm;
Ah! there are memories, God knows, that never, never die. . . ."
"Too late!" she sighed; "I've lived my life of splendour and
of shame;
I've been adored by men of power, I've touched the highest
height;

I've squandered gold like heaps of dirt—oh, I have played the
    game;
I've had my place within the sun . . . and now I face the night.
Look! look! you see I'm lost to hope; I live no matter how . . .
To drink and drink and so forget . . . that's all I care for now."

And so she went her heedless way, and all our help was vain.
She trailed along with tattered shawl and mud-corroded skirt;
She gnawed a crust and slept beneath the bridges of the Seine,
A garbage thing, a composite of alcohol and dirt.
The students learned her story and the cafés knew her well,
The Pascal and the Panthéon, the Sufflot and Vachette
She shuffled round the tables with the flowers she tried to sell,
A living mask of misery that no one will forget.
And then last week I missed her, and they found her in the
    street
One morning early, huddled down, for it was freezing cold;
But when they raised her ragged shawl her face was still and
    sweet;
Some bits of broken bloom were clutched within her icy hold.
That's all. . . . Ah yes, they say that saw: her blue, wide-open
    eyes
Were beautiful with joy again, with radiant surprise. . . .

A week ago she begged for bread: we've bought for her a stone,
And a peaceful place in Père-La-Chaise where she'll be well
    alone.

She cost a king his crown, they say; oh, wouldn't she be proud
If she could see the wreaths to-day, the coaches and the crowd!
So follow, follow, follow on with slow and sober tread,
For Marie Toro, gutter waif and queen of queens, is dead.

IV

THE CAFE DE DEUX MAGOTS,
June, 1914.

THE BOHEMIAN

UP in my garret bleak and bare
I tilted back on my broken chair,
And my three old pals were with me there,
        Hunger and Thirst and Cold;
Hunger scowled at his scurvy mate:
Cold cowered down by the hollow grate,
And I hated them with a deadly hate
        As old as life is old.

So up in my garret that's near the sky
I smiled a smile that was thin and dry:
"You've roomed with me twenty year," said I,
        "Hunger and Thirst and Cold;
But now, begone down the broken stair!
I've suffered enough of your spite . . . so there!"
Bang! Bang! I slapped on the table bare
        A glittering heap of gold.

"Red flames will jewel my wine to-night;
I'll loose my belt that you've lugged so tight;
Ha! Ha! Dame Fortune is smiling bright;
        The stuff of my brain I've sold;
Canaille of the gutter, up! Away!
You've battened on me for a bitter-long day;
But I'm driving you forth, and forever and aye,
        Hunger and Thirst and Cold."

So I kicked them out with a scornful roar;
Yet, oh, they turned at the garret door;
Quietly there they spoke once more:
        "The tale is not all told.
It's *au revoir*, but it's not good-bye;
We're yours, old chap, till the day you die;
Laugh on, you fool! Oh, you'll never defy
        Hunger and Thirst and Cold."

Hurrah! The crisis in my financial career is over. Once more I
have weathered the storm, and never did money jingle so sweetly
in my pocket. It was MacBean who delivered me. He arrived at the
door of my garret this morning, with a broad grin of pleasure on his face.

"Here," said he; "I've sold some of your rubbish. They'll take more
too, of the same sort."

With that, he handed me three crisp notes. For a moment I thought
that he was paying the money out of his own pocket, as he knew I
was desperately hard up; but he showed me the letter enclosing the
cheque he had cashed for me.

So we sought the Grand Boulevard, and I had a Pernod, which
rose to my head in delicious waves of joy. I talked ecstatic nonsense,
and seemed to walk like a god on clouds of gold. We dined on frogs'

legs and Vouvray, and then went to see the Revue at the Marigny.
A very merry evening.

Such is the life of Bohemia, up and down, fast and feast; its very
uncertainty its charm.

Here is my latest ballad, another attempt to express the sentiment
of actuality:

THE AUCTION SALE

HER little head just topped the window-sill;
She even mounted on a stool, maybe;
She pressed against the pane, as children will,
And watched us playing, oh so wistfully!
And then I missed her for a month or more,
And idly thought: "She's gone away, no doubt,"
Until a hearse drew up beside the door . . .
I saw a tiny coffin carried out.

And after that, towards dusk I'd often see
Behind the blind another face that looked:
Eyes of a young wife watching anxiously,
Then rushing back to where her dinner cooked.
She often gulped it down alone, I fear,
Within her heart the sadness of despair,
For near to midnight I would vaguely hear
A lurching step, a stumbling on the stair.

These little dramas of the common day!
A man weak-willed and fore-ordained to fail . . .

The window's empty now, they've gone away,
And yonder, see, their furniture's for sale.
To all the world their door is open wide,
And round and round the bargain-hunters roam,
And peer and gloat, like vultures avid-eyed,
Above the corpse of what was once a home.

So reverent I go from room to room,
And see the patient care, the tender touch,
The love that sought to brighten up the gloom,
The woman-courage tested overmuch.
Amid those things so intimate and dear,
Where now the mob invades with brutal tread,
I think: "What happiness is buried here,
What dreams are withered and what hopes are dead!"

Oh, woman dear, and were you sweet and glad
Over the lining of your little nest!
What ponderings and proud ideas you had!
What visions of a shrine of peace and rest!
For there's his easy-chair upon the rug,
His reading-lamp, his pipe-rack on the wall,
All that you could devise to make him snug--
And yet you could not hold him with it all.

Ah, patient heart, what homelike joys you planned
To stay him by the dull domestic flame!
Those silken cushions that you worked by hand
When you had time, before the baby came.

Oh, how you wove around him cosy spells,
And schemed so hard to keep him home of nights!
Aye, every touch and turn some story tells
Of sweet conspiracies and dead delights.

And here upon the scratched piano stool,
Tied in a bundle, are the songs you sung;
That cosy that you worked in coloured wool,
The Spanish lace you made when you were young,
And lots of modern novels, cheap reprints,
And little dainty knick-knacks everywhere;
And silken bows and curtains of gay chintz . . .
And oh, her tiny crib, her folding chair!

Sweet woman dear, and did your heart not break,
To leave this precious home you made in vain?
Poor shabby things! so prized for old times' sake,
With all their memories of love and pain.
Alas! while shouts the raucous auctioneer,
And rat-faced dames are prying everywhere,
The echo of old joy is all I hear,
All, all I see just heartbreak and despair.

Imagination is the great gift of the gods. Given it, one does not need
to look afar for subjects. There is a romance in every face.

Those who have Imagination live in a land of enchantment which
the eyes of others cannot see. Yet if it brings marvellous joy it also
brings exquisite pain. Who lives a hundred lives must die a hundred
deaths.

I do not know any of the people who live around me. Sometimes I pass them on the stairs. However, I am going to give my imagination rein, and string some rhymes about them.

Before doing so, having money in my pocket and seeing the prospect of making more, let me blithely chant about:

THE JOY OF BEING POOR

I

LET others sing of gold and gear, the joy of being rich;
But oh, the days when I was poor, a vagrant in a ditch!
When every dawn was like a gem, so radiant and rare,
And I had but a single coat, and not a single care;
When I would feast right royally on bacon, bread and beer,
And dig into a stack of hay and doze like any peer;
When I would wash beside a brook my solitary shirt,
And though it dried upon my back I never took a hurt;
When I went romping down the road contemptuous of care,
And slapped Adventure on the back—by Gad! we were a pair;
When, though my pockets lacked a coin, and though my coat
was old,
The largess of the stars was mine, and all the sunset gold;
When time was only made for fools, and free as air was I,
And hard I hit and hard I lived beneath the open sky;
When all the roads were one to me, and each had its allure . . .
Ye Gods! these were the happy days, the days when I was poor.

II

Or else, again, old pal of mine, do you recall the times
You struggled with your storyettes, I wrestled with my rhymes;
Oh, we were happy, were we not?—we used to live so "high"
(A little bit of broken roof between us and the sky);
Upon the forge of art we toiled with hammer and with tongs;
You told me all your ripping yarns, I sang to you my songs.
Our hats were frayed, our jackets patched, our boots were down
     at heel,
But oh, the happy men were we, although we lacked a meal.
And if I sold a bit of rhyme, or if you placed a tale,
What feasts we had of tenderloins and apple-tarts and ale!
And yet how often we would dine as cheerful as you please,
Beside our little friendly fire on coffee, bread and cheese.
We lived upon the ragged edge, and grub was never sure,
But oh, these were the happy days, the days when we were poor.

III

Alas! old man, we're wealthy now, it's sad beyond a doubt;
We cannot dodge prosperity, success has found us out.
Your eye is very dull and drear, my brow is creased with care,
We realize how hard it is to be a millionaire.
The burden's heavy on our backs—you're thinking of your rents,
I'm worrying if I'll invest in five or six per cents.

We've limousines, and marble halls, and flunkeys by the score,
We play the part . . . but say, old chap, oh, isn't it a bore?
We work like slaves, we eat too much, we put on evening dress;
We've everything a man can want, I think . . . but happiness.

Come, let us sneak away, old chum; forget that we are rich,
And earn an honest appetite, and scratch an honest itch.
Let's be two jolly garreteers, up seven flights of stairs,
And wear old clothes and just pretend we aren't millionaires;
And wonder how we'll pay the rent, and scribble ream on ream,
And sup on sausages and tea, and laugh and loaf and dream.

And when we're tired of that, my friend, oh, you will come
     with me;
And we will seek the sunlit roads that lie beside the sea.
We'll know the joy the gipsy knows, the freedom nothing mars,
The golden treasure-gates of dawn, the mintage of the stars.
We'll smoke our pipes and watch the pot, and feed the crackling
     fire,
And sing like two old jolly boys, and dance to heart's desire;
We'll climb the hill and ford the brook and camp upon the
     moor . . .
Old chap, let's haste, I'm mad to taste the Joy of Being Poor.

V

My Garret, Montparnasse,
June, 1914.

MY NEIGHBOURS

To rest my fagged brain now and then,
When wearied of my proper labours,
I lay aside my lagging pen
And get to thinking on my neighbours;
For, oh, around my garret den
There's woe and poverty a-plenty,
And life's so interesting when
A lad is only two-and-twenty.

Now, there's that artist gaunt and wan,
A little card his door adorning;
It reads: "Je ne suis pour personne,"
A very frank and fitting warning.
I fear he's in a sorry plight;
He starves, I think, too proud to borrow
I hear him moaning every night:
Maybe they'll find him dead to-morrow.

611

Room 4

THE PAINTER CHAP

HE gives me such a bold and curious look,
That young American across the way,
As if he'd like to put me in a book
(Fancies himself a poet, so they say).
Ah well! He'll make no "document" of me.
I lock my door. Ha! ha! Now none shall see. . . . .

Pictures, just pictures piled from roof to floor,
Each one a bit of me, a dream fulfilled,
A vision of the beauty I adore,
My own poor glimpse of glory, passion-thrilled . . .
But now my money's gone, I paint no more.

For three days past I have not tasted food;
The jewelled colours run . . . I reel, I faint;
They tell me that my pictures are no good,
Just crude and childish daubs, a waste of paint.
I burned to throw on canvas all I saw—
Twilight on water, tenderness of trees,
Wet sands at sunset and the smoking seas,
The peace of valleys and the mountain's awe:
Emotion swayed me at the thought of these.
I sought to paint ere I had learned to draw,
And that's the trouble. . . .

Ah well! here am I,

Facing my failure after struggle long;
And there they are, my *croûtes* that none will buy
(And doubtless they are right and I am wrong);
Well, when one's lost one's faith it's time to die. . . .

This knife will do . . . and now to slash and slash;
Rip them to ribands, rend them every one,
My dreams and visions—tear and stab and gash,
So that their crudeness may be known to none;
Poor, miserable daubs! Ah! there, it's done. . . .

And now to close my little window tight.
Lo! in the dusking sky, serenely set,
The evening star is like a beacon bright.
And see! to keep her tender tryst with night
How Paris veils herself in violet. . . .

Oh, why does God create such men as I?—
All pride and passion and divine desire,
Raw, quivering nerve-stuff and devouring fire,
Foredoomed to failure though they try and try;
Abortive, blindly to destruction hurled;
Unfound, unfit to grapple with the world. . . .

And now to light my wheezy jet of gas;
Chink up the window-crannies and the door,
So that no single breath of air may pass;
So that I'm sealed air-tight from roof to floor.
There, there, that's done; and now there's nothing more. . . .

Look at the city's myriad lamps a-shine;
See, the calm moon is launching into space . . .
There will be darkness in these eyes of mine
Ere it can climb to shine upon my face.
Oh, it will find such peace upon my face! . . .

City of Beauty, I have loved you well,
A laugh or two I've had, but many a sigh;
I've run with you the scale from Heav'n to Hell.
Paris, I love you still . . . good-bye, good-bye.
Thus it all ends—unhappily, alas!
It's time to sleep, and now . . . *blow out the gas*. . . .

*   *   *   *   *

> *Now there's that little midinette*
> *Who goes to work each morning daily;*
> *I choose to call her Blithe Babette,*
> *Because she's always humming gaily;*
> *And though the Goddess "Comme-il-faut"*
> *May look on her with prim expression,*
> *It's Pagan Paris where, you know,*
> *The queen of virtues is Discretion.*

Room 6

THE LITTLE WORKGIRL

Three gentlemen live close beside me—
A painter of pictures bizarre,

A poet whose virtues might guide me
A singer who plays the guitar;
And there on my lintel is Cupid;
I leave my door open, and yet
These gentlemen, aren't they stupid,
They never make love to Babette.

I go to the shop every morning;
I work with my needle and thread
Silk, satin and velvet adorning,
Then luncheon on coffee and bread.
Then sewing and sewing till seven;
Or else, if the order I get,
I toil and I toil till eleven—
And such is the day of Babette.

It doesn't seem cheerful, I fancy;
The wage is unthinkably small;
And yet there is one thing I can say:
I keep a bright face through it all.
I chaff though my head may be aching;
I sing a gay song to forget;
I laugh though my heart may be breaking—
It's all in the life of Babette.

That gown, O my lady of leisure,
You begged to be "finished in haste."
It gives you an exquisite pleasure,
Your lovers remark on its taste.

Yet . . . oh, the poor little white faces,
The tense midnight toil and the fret . . .
I fear that the foam of its laces
Is salt with the tears of Babette.

It takes a brave heart to be cheery
With no gleam of hope in the sky;
The future's so utterly dreary,
I'm laughing—in case I should cry.
And if, where the gay lights are glowing,
I dine with a man I have met,
And snatch a bright moment—who's going
To blame a poor little Babette?

And you, Friend beyond all the telling,
Although you're an ocean away,
Your pictures, they tell me, are selling,
You're married and settled, they say.
Such happiness one wouldn't barter;
Yet, oh, do you never regret
The Springtide, the roses, Montmartre,
Youth, poverty, love and—Babette?

*　　*　　*　　*　　*

That blond-haired chap across the way
With sunny smile and voice so mellow,
He sings in some cheap cabaret,
Yet what a gay and charming fellow!

His breath with garlic may be strong,
What matters it? his laugh is jolly;
His day he gives to sleep and song;
His night's made up of song and folly.

ROOM 5

THE CONCERT-SINGER

I'M one of these haphazard chaps
Who sits in cafés drinking;
A most improper taste, perhaps,
Yet pleasant, to my thinking.
For, oh, I hate discord and strife;
I'm sadly, weakly human;
And I do think the best of life
Is wine and song and woman.

Now, there's that youngster on my right
Who thinks himself a poet,
And so he toils from morn to night
And vainly hopes to show it;
And there's that dauber on my left,
Within his chamber shrinking—
He looks like one of hope bereft;
He lives on air, I'm thinking.

But me, I love the things that are,
My heart is always merry;
I laugh and tune my old guitar:
Sing ho! and hey-down-derry.
Oh, let them toil their lives away
To gild a tawdry era,
But I'll be gay while yet I may:
Sing tira-lira-lira.

I'm sure you know that picture well,
A monk, all else unheeding,
Within a bare and gloomy cell
A musty volume reading;
While through the window you can see
In sunny glade entrancing,
With cap and bells beneath a tree
A jester dancing, dancing.

Which is the fool and which the sage
I cannot quite discover;
But you may look in learning's page
And I'll be laughter's lover.
For this our life is none too long,
And hearts were made for gladness;
Let virtue lie in joy and song,
The only sin be sadness.

So let me troll a jolly air,
Come what come will to-morrow;

I'll be no *cabotin* of care,
No *souteneur* of sorrow.
Let those who will indulge in strife,
To my most merry thinking,
The true philosophy of life
Is laughing, loving, drinking.

*   *   *   *   *

And there's that weird and ghastly hag
Who walks head bent, with lips a-mutter;
With twitching hands and feet that drag,
And tattered skirts that sweep the gutter,
An outworn harlot, lost to hope,
With staring eyes and hair that's hoary
I hear her gibber, dazed with dope:
I often wonder what's her story.

ROOM 7

THE COCO-FIEND

I LOOK at no one, me;
I pass them on the stair;
Shadows! I don't see;
Shadows! everywhere.
Haunting, taunting, staring, glaring,
Shadows! I don't care.
Once my room I gain
Then my life begins

Shut the door on pain;
How the Devil grins!
Grin with might and main;
Grin and grin in vain;
Here's where Heav'n begins:
Cocaine!   Cocaine!

A whiff! Ah, that's the thing.
How it makes me gay!
Now I want to sing,
Leap, laugh, play.
Ha! I've had my fling!
Mistress of a king
In my day.
Just another snuff . . .
Oh, the blessed stuff!
How the wretched room
Rushes from my sight;
Misery and gloom
Melt into delight;
Fear and death and doom
Vanish in the night.
No more cold and pain,
I am young again,
Beautiful again,
Cocaine!   Cocaine!

Oh, I was made to be good, to be good,
For a true man's love and a life that's sweet;

Fireside blessings and motherhood,
Little ones playing around my feet.
How it all unfolds like a magic screen,
Tender and glowing and clear and glad,
The wonderful mother I might have been,
The beautiful children I might have had;
Romping and laughing and shrill with glee,
Oh, I see them now and I see them plain.
Darlings! Come nestle up close to me,
You comfort me so, and you're just . . . Cocaine.

It's Life that's all to blame:
We can't do what we will;
She robes us with her shame,
She crowns us with her ill.
I do not care, because
I see with bitter calm,
Life made me what I was,
Life makes me what I am.
Could I throw back the years,
It all would be the same;
Hunger and cold and tears
Misery, fear and shame,
And then the old refrain,
Cocaine! Cocaine!

A love-child I, so here my mother came,
Where she might live in peace with none to blame.

And how she toiled! Harder than any slave,
What courage! patient, hopeful, tender, brave.
We had a little room at Lavilette,
So small, so neat, so clean, I see it yet.
Poor mother! sewing, sewing late at night,
Her wasted face beside the candlelight,
This Paris crushed her. How she used to sigh!
And as I watched her from my bed I knew
She saw red roofs against a primrose sky,
And glistening fields and apples dimmed with dew.
Hard times we had. We counted every *sou,*
We sewed sacks for a living. I was quick . . .
Four busy hands to work instead of two.
Oh, we were happy there, till she fell sick. . . .

My mother lay, her face turned to the wall,
And I, a girl of sixteen, fair and tall,
Sat by her side, all stricken with despair,
Knelt by her bed and faltered out a prayer.
A doctor's order on the table lay,
Medicine for which, alas! I could not pay;
Medicine to save her life, to soothe her pain.
I sought for something I could sell, in vain . . .
All, all was gone! The room was cold and bare;
Gone blankets and the cloak I used to wear;
Bare floor and wall and cupboard, every shelf—
Nothing that I could sell . . . except myself.

I sought the street, I could not bear
To hear my mother moaning there.
I clutched the paper in my hand.
'Twas hard. You cannot understand . . .
I walked as martyr to the flame,
Almost exalted in my shame.
They turned, who heard my voiceless cry,
"For Sale, a virgin, who will buy?"
And so myself I fiercely sold,
And clutched the price, a piece of gold.

Into a pharmacy I pressed;
I took the paper from my breast.
I gave my money . . . how it gleamed!
How precious to my eyes it seemed!
And then I saw the chemist frown,
Quick on the counter throw it down,
Shake with an angry look his head:
"Your *louis d'or* is bad," he said.

Dazed, crushed, I went into the night,
I clutched my gleaming coin so tight.
No, no, I could not well believe
That anyone could so deceive.
I tried again and yet again—
Contempt, suspicion and disdain;
Always the same reply I had:
"Get out of this. Your money's bad."

Heart-broken to the room I crept,
To mother's side.   All still . . . she slept . . .
I bent, I sought to raise her head . . .
"Oh, God have pity!" she was dead.

> That's how it all began.
> Said I: Revenge is sweet.
> So in my guilty span
> I've ruined many a man.
> They've grovelled at my feet,
> I've pity had for none;
> I've bled them every one.
> Oh, I've had interest for
> That worthless *louis d'or.*

> But now it's over; see
> I care for no one, me;
> Only at night sometimes
> In dreams I hear the chimes
> Of wedding-bells and see
> A woman without stain,
> With children at her knee.
> Ah, how you comfort me,
> Cocaine! . . .

PART THREE

LATE SUMMER

I

THE OMNIUM BAR, NEAR THE BOURSE,
Late July, 1914.

MACBEAN, before he settled down to the manufacture of mercantile fiction, had ideas of a nobler sort, which bore their fruit in a slender book of poems. In subject they are either erotic, mythologic, or descriptive of nature. So polished are they that the mind seems to slide over them; so faultless in form that the critics hailed them with highest praise, and as many as a hundred copies were sold.

Saxon Dane, too, has published a book of poems, but he, on the other hand, defies tradition to an eccentric degree. Originality is his sin. He strains after it in every line. I must confess I think much of the free verse he writes is really prose, and a good deal of it blank verse chopped up into odd lengths. He talks of assonance and colour, of stress and pause and accent, and bewilders me with his theories.

He and MacBean represent two extremes, and at night, as we sit in the Café du Dôme, they have the hottest of arguments. As for me, I listen with awe, content that my medium is verse, and that the fashions of Hood, Thackeray and Bret Harte are the fashions of to-day.

Of late I have been doing light stuff, "fillers" for MacBean. Here are three of my specimens:

THE PHILANDERER

OH, have you forgotten those afternoons
With riot of roses and amber skies,

626

When we thrilled to the joy of a million Junes,
And I sought for your soul in the deeps of your eyes?
I would love you, I promised, for ever and aye,
And I meant it too; yet, oh, isn't it odd?
When we met in the Underground to-day
I addressed you as Mary instead of as Maude.

Oh, don't you remember that moonlit sea,
With us on a silver trail afloat,
When I gracefully sank on my bended knee
At the risk of upsetting our little boat?
Oh, I vowed that my life was blighted then,
As friendship you proffered with mournful mien;
But now as I think of your children ten,
I'm glad you refused me, Evangeline.

Oh, is that moment eternal still
When I breathed my love in your shell-like ear,
And you plucked at your fan as a maiden will,
And you blushed so charmingly, Guinevere?
Like a worshipper at your feet I sat;
For a year and a day you made me mad;
But now, alas! you are forty, fat,
And I think: What a lucky escape I had!

Oh, maidens I've set in a sacred shrine,
Oh, Rosamond, Molly and Mignonette,

x

I've deemed you in turn the most divine,
In turn you've broken my heart . . . and yet
It's easily mended. What's past is past.
To-day on Lucy I'm going to call;
For I'm sure that I know true love at last,
And *She* is the fairest girl of all.

THE *PETIT VIEUX*

"Sow your wild oats in your youth," so we're always told;
But I say with deeper sooth: "Sow them when you're old."
I'll be wise till I'm about seventy or so:
Then, by Gad! I'll blossom out as an ancient *beau*.

I'll assume a dashing air, laugh with loud Ha! ha! . . .
How my grandchildren will stare at their grandpapa!
Their perfection aurioled I will scandalize:
Won't I be a hoary old sinner in their eyes!

Watch me, how I'll learn to chaff barmaids in a bar;
Scotches daily, gaily quaff, puff a fierce cigar.
I will haunt the Tango teas, at the stage-door stand;
Wait for Dolly Dimpleknees, bouquet in my hand.

Then at seventy I'll take flutters at roulette;
While at eighty hope I'll make good at poker yet;

And in fashionable togs to the races go,
Gayest of the gay old dogs, ninety years or so.

"Sow your wild oats while you're young," that's what you are
    told;
Don't believe the foolish tongue—sow 'em when you're old.
Till you've threescore years and ten, take my humble tip,
Sow your nice tame oats and then . . . Hi, boys! Let 'er rip.

MY MASTERPIECE

It's slim and trim and bound in blue;
Its leaves are crisp and edged with gold;
Its words are simple, stalwart too;
Its thoughts are tender, wise and bold.
Its pages scintillate with wit;
Its pathos clutches at my throat:
Oh, how I love each line of it!
That Little Book I Never Wrote.

In dreams I see it praised and prized
By all, from ploughman unto peer;
It's pencil-marked and memorized,
It's loaned (and not returned, I fear);
It's worn and torn and travel-tossed,
And even dusky natives quote
That classic that the world has lost,
The Little Book I Never Wrote.

Poor ghost! For homes you've failed to cheer,
For grieving hearts uncomforted,
Don't haunt me now. . . . Alas! I fear
The fire of Inspiration's dead.
A humdrum way I go to-night,
From all I hoped and dreamed remote;
Too late . . . a better man must write
That Little Book I Never Wrote.

Talking about writing books, there is a queer character who shuffles
up and down the little streets that neighbour the Place Maubert,
and who, they say, has been engaged on one for years. Sometimes I
see him cowering in some cheap *bouge,* and his wild eyes gleam at
me through the tangle of his hair. But I do not think he ever sees
me. He mumbles to himself, and moves like a man in a dream. His
pockets are full of filthy paper, on which he writes from time to time.
The students laugh at him and make him tipsy; the street-boys pelt
him with ordure; the better cafés turn him from their doors. But
who knows? At least, this is how I see him:

MY BOOK

BEFORE I drink myself to death,
God, let me finish up my Book!
At night I fear, I fight for breath,
And wake up whiter than a spook;
And crawl off to a *bistro* near,
And drink until my brain is clear.

Rare Absinthe! Oh, it gives me strength
To write and write; and so I spend
Day after day, until at length
With joy and pain I'll write The End:
Then let this carcase rot; I give
The world my Book—my Book will live.

For every line is tense with truth,
There's hope and joy on every page;
A cheer, a clarion call to Youth,
A hymn, a comforter to Age:
All's there that I was meant to be,
My part divine, the God in me.

It's of my life the golden sum;
Ah! who that reads this Work of mine,
In stormy centuries to come,
Will dream I rooted with the swine?
Behold! I give mankind my best:
What does it matter, all the rest?

It's this that makes sublime my day;
It's this that makes me struggle on.
Oh, let them mock my mortal clay,
My spirit's deathless as the dawn;
Oh, let them shudder as they look . . .
I'll be immortal in my Book.

And so beside the sullen Seine
I fight with dogs for filthy food,
Yet know that from my sin and pain
Will soar serene a Something Good;
Exultantly from shame and wrong
A Right, a Glory, and a Song.

How charming it is, this Paris of the summer skies. Each morning I leap up with joy in my heart, all eager to begin the day of work. As I eat my breakfast and smoke my pipe, I ponder over my task. Then in the golden sunshine that floods my little attic, I pace up and down, absorbed and forgetful of the world. As I compose I speak the words aloud. There are difficulties to overcome; thoughts that will not fit their mould; rebellious rhymes. Ah! those moments of despair and defeat.

Then suddenly the mind grows lucid, imagination glows, the snarl unravels. In the end is always triumph and success. O, delectable *métier!* Who would not be a rhyme-smith in Paris, in Bohemia, in the heart of youth!

I have now finished my twentieth ballad. Five more and they will be done. In quiet corners of cafés, on benches of the Luxembourg, on the sunny Quays I read them over one by one. Here is my latest:

MY HOUR

Day after day behold me plying
My pen within an office drear;
The dullest dog, till homeward hying,
Then lo! I reign a king of cheer.

A throne have I of padded leather,
A little court of kiddies three,
A wife who smiles whate'er the weather,
A feast of muffins, jam and tea.

The table cleared, a romping battle,
A fairy tale, a "Children, bed,"
A kiss, a hug, a hush of prattle
(God save each little drowsy head!),
A cosy chat with wife a-sewing,
A silver lining clouds that lour,
Then she too goes, and with her going,
I come again into my Hour.

I poke the fire, I snugly settle,
My pipe I prime with proper care;
The water's purring in the kettle,
Rum, lemon, sugar, all are there.
And now the honest grog is steaming,
And now the trusty briar's aglow:
Alas! in smoking, drinking, dreaming,
How sadly swift the moments go!

Oh, golden hour! 'twixt love and duty,
All others I to others give;
But you are mine to yield to Beauty,
To glean Romance, to greatly live.

For in my easy-chair reclining . . .
I feel the sting of ocean spray;
And yonder wondrously are shining
The Magic Isles of Far Away.

Beyond the comber's crashing thunder
Strange beaches flash into my ken;
On jetties heaped head-high with plunder
I dance and dice with sailor-men.
Strange stars swarm down to burn above me
Strange shadows haunt, strange voices greet;
Strange women lure and laugh and love me,
And fling their bastards at my feet.

Oh, I would wish the wide world over,
In ports of passion and unrest,
To drink and drain, a tarry rover
With dragons tattooed on my chest,
With haunted eyes that hold red glories
Of foaming seas and crashing shores,
With lips that tell the strangest stories
Of sunken ships and gold moidores;

Till sick of storm and strife and slaughter,
Some ghostly night when hides the moon,
I slip into the milk-warm water,
And softly swim the stale lagoon.
Then through some jungle python-haunted,
Or plumed morass, or woodland wild,

I win my way with heart undaunted,
And all the wonder of a child.

The pathless plains shall swoon around me,
The forests frown, the floods appal;
The mountains tiptoe to confound me,
The rivers roar to speed my fall.
Wild dooms shall daunt, and dawns be gory,
And Death shall sit beside my knee;
Till after terror, torment, glory,
I win again the sea, the sea. . . .

Oh, anguish sweet! Oh, triumph splendid!
Oh, dreams adieu! my pipe is dead.
My glass is dry, my Hour is ended,
It's time indeed I stole to bed.
How peacefully the house is sleeping!
Ah! why should I strange fortunes plan!
To guard the dear ones in my keeping—
That's task enough for any man.

So though dim seas I'll ne'er go spoiling;
The red Tortugas never roam;
Please God! I'll keep the pot a-boiling,
And make at least a happy home.
My children's path shall gleam with roses,
Their grace abound, their joy increase.
And so my Hour divinely closes
With tender thoughts of praise and peace.

II

THE GARDEN OF THE LUXEMBOURG,
Late July, 1914.

When on some scintillating summer morning I leap lightly up to
the seclusion of my garret, I often think of those lines: "In the brave
days when I was twenty-one."

True, I have no loving, kind Lisette to pin her petticoat across
the pane, yet do I live in hope. Am I not in Bohemia the Magical,
Bohemia of Murger, of de Musset, of Verlaine? Shades of Mimi
Pinson, of Trilby, of all that immortal line of laughterful grisettes,
do not tell me that the days of love and fun are forever at an end!

Yes, youth is golden, but what of age? Shall it too not testify
to the rhapsody of existence? Let the years between be those of
struggle, of sufferance—of disillusion if you will; but let youth and
age affirm the ecstasy of being. Let us look forward all to a serene
sunset, and in the still skies "a late lark singing."

This thought comes to me as, sitting on a bench near the band-
stand, I see an old savant who talks to all the children. His clean-
shaven face is alive with kindliness; under his tall silk hat his white
hair falls to his shoulders. He wears a long black cape over a black
frock-coat, very neat linen, and a flowing tie of black silk. I call him
"Silvester Bonnard." As I look at him I truly think the best of life
are the years between sixty and seventy.

A SONG OF SIXTY-FIVE

BRAVE Thackeray has trolled of days when he was twenty-one,
And bounded up five flights of stairs, a gallant garreteer;
And yet again in mellow vein when youth was gaily run,
Has dipped his nose in Gascon wine, and told of Forty Year.

But if I worthy were to sing a richer, rarer time,
I'd tune my pipes before the fire and merrily I'd strive
To praise that age when prose again has given way to rhyme,
The Indian Summer days of life when I'll be Sixty-five.

For then my work will all be done, my voyaging be past,
And I'll have earned the right to rest where folding hills are
    green;
So in some glassy anchorage I'll make my cable fast,—
Oh, let the seas show all their teeth, I'll sit and smile serene.
The storm may bellow round the roof, I'll bide beside the fire,
And many a scene of sail and trail within the flame I'll see;
For I'll have worn away the spur of passion and desire . . .
Oh, yes, when I am Sixty-five, what peace will come to me.

I'll take my breakfast in my bed, I'll rise at half-past ten,
When all the world is nicely groomed, and full of golden song;
I'll smoke a bit and joke a bit, and read the news, and then
I'll potter round my peach-trees till I hear the luncheon gong.
And after that I think I'll doze an hour, well, maybe two,
And then I'll show some kindred soul how well my roses thrive;
I'll do the things I never yet have found the time to do. . . .
Oh, won't I be the busy man when I am Sixty-five!

I'll revel in my library; I'll read De Morgan's books;
I'll grow so garrulous I fear you'll write me down a bore;
I'll watch the ways of ants and bees in quiet sunny nooks,
I'll understand Creation as I never did before.

When gossips round the tea-cups talk I'll listen to it all;
On smiling days some kindly friend will take me for a drive;
I'll own a shaggy collie dog that dashes to my call:
I'll celebrate my second youth when I am Sixty-five.

Ah, though I've twenty years to go, I see myself quite plain,
A wrinkling, twinkling, rosy-cheeked, benevolent old chap;
I think I'll wear a tartan shawl and lean upon a cane;
I hope that I'll have silver hair beneath a velvet cap.
I see my little grandchildren a-romping round my knee;
So gay the scene, I almost wish 'twould hasten to arrive.
Let others sing of Youth and Spring, still will it seem to me
The golden time's the olden time, some time round Sixty-five.

From old men to children is but a step, and there too, in the shadow of the Fontaine de Medicis, I spend much of my time watching the little ones. Childhood, so innocent, so helpless, so trusting, is somehow pathetic to me.

There was one jolly little chap who used to play with a large white Teddy Bear. He was always with his mother, a sweet-faced woman, who followed his every movement with delight. I used to watch them both, and often spoke a few words.

Then one day I missed them, and it struck me I had not seen them for a week, even a month, maybe. After that I looked for them a time or two and soon forgot.

Then this morning I saw the mother in the rue D'Assas. She was alone and in deep black. I wanted to ask after the boy, but there was a look in her face that stopped me.

I do not think she will ever enter the garden of the Luxembourg again.

TEDDY BEAR

O Teddy Bear! with your head awry
And your comical twisted smile,
You rub your eyes—do you wonder why
You've slept such a long, long while?
As you lay so still in the cupboard dim,
And you heard on the roof the rain,
Were you thinking . . . what has become of *him?*
And when will he play again?

Did you sometimes long for a chubby hand,
And a voice so sweetly shrill?
O Teddy Bear! don't you understand
Why the house is awf'ly still?
You sit with your muzzle propped on your paws,
And your whimsical face askew.
Don't wait, don't wait for your friend . . . because
He's sleeping and sleeping too.

Aye, sleeping long. . . . You remember how
He stabbed our hearts with his cries?
And oh, the dew of pain on his brow,
And the deeps of pain in his eyes!
And, Teddy Bear! you remember, too,
As he sighed and sank to his rest,
How all of a sudden he smiled to you,
And he clutched you close to his breast.

I'll put you away, little Teddy Bear,
In the cupboard far from my sight;
Maybe he'll come and he'll kiss you there,
A wee white ghost in the night.
But me, I'll live with my love and pain
A weariful lifetime through;
And my Hope: will I see him again, again?
Ah, God! If I only knew!

After old men and children I am greatly interested in dogs. I will go out of my way to caress one who shows any desire to be friendly. There is a very filthy fellow who collects cigarette stubs on the Boul' Mich', and who is always followed by a starved yellow cur. The other day I came across them in a little side street. The man was stretched on the pavement brutishly drunk and dead to the world. The dog, lying by his side, seemed to look at me with sad, imploring eyes. Though all the world despise that man, I thought, this poor brute loves him and will be faithful unto death.

From this incident I wrote the verses that follow:

THE OUTLAW

A WILD and woeful race he ran
Of lust and sin by land and sea;
Until, abhorred of God and man,
They swung him from the gallows-tree.
And then he climbed the Starry Stair,
And dumb and naked and alone,
With head unbowed and brazen glare,
He stood before the Judgment Throne.

The Keeper of the Records spoke:
"This man, O Lord, has mocked Thy Name.
The weak have wept beneath his yoke,
The strong have fled before his flame.
The blood of babes is on his sword;
His life is evil to the brim:
Look down, decree his doom, O Lord!
Lo! there is none will speak for him."

The golden trumpets blew a blast
That echoed in the crypts of Hell,
For there was Judgment to be passed,
And lips were hushed and silence fell.
The man was mute; he made no stir
Erect before the Judgment Seat . . .
When all at once a mongrel cur
Crept out and cowered and licked his feet.

It licked his feet with whining cry.
Come Heav'n, come Hell, what did it care?
It leapt, it tried to catch his eye;
Its master, yea, its God was there.
Then, as a thrill of wonder sped
Through throngs of shining seraphim,
The Judge of All looked down and said:
"Lo! here is ONE who pleads for him.

"And who shall love of these the least,
And who by word or look or deed
Shall pity show to bird or beast,
By Me shall have a friend in need.
Aye, though his sin be black as night,
And though he stand mid men alone,
He shall be softened in My sight,
And find a pleader by My Throne.

"So let this man to glory win;
From life to life salvation glean;
By pain and sacrifice and sin,
Until he stand before Me—*clean*.
For he who loves the least of these
(And here I say and here repeat)
Shall win himself an angel's pleas
For Mercy at My Judgment Seat."

I take my exercise in the form of walking. It keeps me fit and leaves me free to think. In this way I have come to know Paris like my pocket. I have explored its large and little streets, its stateliness and its slums.

But most of all I love the Quays, between the leafage and the sunlit Seine. Like shuttles the little steamers dart up and down, weaving the water into patterns of foam. Cigar-shaped barges stream under the lacework of the many bridges and make me think of tranquil days and willow-fringed horizons.

But what I love most is the stealing in of night, when the sky takes on that strange, elusive purple; when eyes turn to the evening star and marvel at its brightness; when the Eiffel Tower becomes a strange, shadowy stairway yearning in impotent effort to the careless moon.

Here is my latest ballad, short if not very sweet:

THE WALKERS

(He speaks.)

WALKING, walking, oh, the joy of walking!
Swinging down the tawny lanes with head held high;
Striding up the green hills, through the heather stalking,
Swishing through the woodlands where the brown leaves lie;
Marvelling at all things—windmills gaily turning,
Apples for the cider-press, ruby-hued and gold;
Tails of rabbits twinkling, scarlet berries burning,
Wedge of geese high-flying in the sky's clear cold,
Lights in little windows, field and furrow darkling;
Home again returning, hungry as a hawk;
Whistling up the garden, ruddy-cheeked and sparkling,
Oh, but I am happy as I walk, walk, walk!

(She speaks.)

Walking, walking, oh, the curse of walking!
Slouching round the grim square, shuffling up the street,
Slinking down the by-way, all my graces hawking,
Offering my body to each man I meet.
Peering in the gin-shop where the lads are drinking,
Trying to look gay-like, crazy with the blues;

Halting in a doorway, shuddering and shrinking
(Oh, my draggled feather and my thin, wet shoes).
Here's a drunken drover: "Hullo, there, old dearie!"
No, he only curses, can't be got to talk. . . .
On and on till daylight, famished, wet and weary,
God in Heaven help me as I walk, walk, walk!

<h1 style="text-align:center">III</h1>

THE CAFE DE LA SOURCE,
Late in July, 1914.

The other evening MacBean was in a pessimistic mood.

"Why do you write?" he asked me gloomily.

"Obviously," I said, "to avoid starving. To produce something that will buy me food, shelter, raiment."

"If you were a millionaire, would you still write?"

"Yes," I said, after a moment's thought. "You get an idea. It haunts you. It seems to clamour for expression. It begins to obsess you. At last in desperation you embody it in a poem, an essay, a story. There! it is disposed of. You are at rest. It troubles you no more. Yes; if I were a millionaire I should write, if it were only to escape from my ideas."

"You have given two reasons why men write," said MacBean: "for gain, for self-expression. Then, again, some men write to amuse themselves, some because they conceive they have a mission in the world, some because they have real genius and are conscious they can enrich the literature of all time. I must say I don't know of any belonging to the latter class. We are living in an age of mediocrity. There is no writer of to-day who will be read twenty years after he is dead. That's a truth that must come home to the best of them."

"I guess they're not losing much sleep over it," I said.

"Take novelists," continued MacBean. "The line of first-class novelists ended with Dickens and Thackeray. Then followed some of the second class, Stevenson, Meredith, Hardy. And to-day we have three novelists of the third class, good, capable craftsmen. We can trust ourselves comfortably in their hands. We read and enjoy them, but do you think our children will?"

"Yours won't, anyway," I said.

"Don't be so sure. I may surprise you yet. I may get married and turn *bourgeois*."

The best thing that could happen to MacBean would be that. It might change his point of view. He is so painfully discouraging. I have never mentioned my ballads to him. He would be sure to throw cold water on them. And as it draws near to its end the thought of my book grows more and more dear to me. How I will get it published I know not; but I will. Then even if it doesn't sell, even if nobody reads it, I will be content. Out of this brief, perishable Me I will have made something concrete, something that will preserve my thought within its dusty covers long after I am dead and dust.

Here is one of my latest:

POOR PETER

Blind Peter Piper used to play
All up and down the city;
I'd often meet him on my way,
And throw a coin for pity.
But all amid his sparkling tones
His ear was quick as any
To catch upon the cobble-stones
The jingle of my penny.

And as upon a day that shone
He piped a merry measure:
"How well you play!" I chanced to say;
Poor Peter glowed with pleasure.
You'd think the words of praise I spoke
Were all the pay he needed;
The artist in the player woke,
The penny lay unheeded.

Now Winter's here; the wind is shrill,
His coat is thin and tattered;
Yet hark! he's playing trill on trill
As if his music mattered.
And somehow though the city looks
Soaked through and through with shadows,
He makes you think of singing brooks
And larks and sunny meadows.

Poor chap! he often starves, they say.
Well, well, I can believe it;
For when you chuck a coin his way
He'll let some street-boy thieve it.
I fear he freezes in the night;
My praise I've long repented,
Yet look! his face is all alight. . . .
Blind Peter seems contented.

A day later.

On the terrace of the Closerie de Lilas I came on Saxon Dane. He
was smoking his big briar and drinking a huge glass of brown beer.

The trees gave a pleasant shade, and he had thrown his sombrero on a chair. I noted how his high brow was bronzed by the sun and there were golden lights in his broad beard. There was something massive and imposing in the man as he sat there in brooding thought.

MacBean, he told me, was sick and unable to leave his room. Rheumatism. So I bought a cooked chicken and a bottle of Barsac, and mounting to the apartment of the invalid, I made him eat and drink. MacBean was very despondent, but cheered up greatly.

I think he rather dreads the future. He cannot save money, and all he makes he spends. He has always been a rover, often tried to settle down, but could not. Now I think he wishes for security. I fear, however, it is too late.

THE WISTFUL ONE

I SOUGHT the trails of South and North,
I wandered East and West;
But pride and passion drove me forth
And would not let me rest.

And still I seek, as still I roam,
A snug roof overhead;
Four walls, my own; a quiet home. . . .
"You'll have it—*when you're dead.*"

MacBean is one of Bohemia's victims. It is a country of the young. The old have no place in it. He will gradually lose his grip, go down and down. I am sorry. He is my nearest approach to a friend. I do not make them easily. I have deep reserves. I like solitude. I am never so surrounded by boon companions as when I am all alone.

But though I am a solitary, I realize the beauty of friendship, and on looking through my note-book I find the following:

IF YOU HAD A FRIEND

If you had a friend strong, simple, true,
Who knew your faults and who understood;
Who believed in the very best of you,
And who cared for you as a father would:
Who would stick by you to the very end,
Who would smile however the world might frown:
I'm sure you would try to please your friend,
You never would think to throw him down.

And supposing your friend was high and great,
And he lived in a palace rich and tall,
And sat like a King in shining state,
And his praise was loud on the lips of all;
Well then, when he turned to you alone,
And he singled you out from all the crowd,
And he called you up to his golden throne,
Oh, wouldn't you just be jolly proud?

If you had a friend like this, I say,
So sweet and tender, so strong and true,
You'd try to please him in every way,
You'd live at your bravest—now; wouldn't you?

His worth would shine in the words you penned;
You'd shout his praises . . . yet now it's odd!
You tell me you haven't got such a friend;
You haven't? I wonder . . . *What of God?*

To how few is granted the privilege of doing the work which lies closest to the heart, the work for which one is best fitted.

The happy man is he who knows his limitations, yet bows to no false gods.

MacBean is not happy. He is overridden by his appetites, and to satisfy them he writes stuff that in his heart he despises.

Saxon Dane is not happy. His dream exceeds his grasp. His twisted, tortured phrases mock the vague grandiosity of his visions.

I am happy. My talent is proportioned to my ambition. The things I like to write are the things I like to read. I prefer the lesser poets to the greater, the cackle of the barnyard fowl to the scream of the eagle. I lack the divinity of discontent.

True Contentment comes from within. It dominates circumstances. It is resignation wedded to philosophy, a Christian quality seldom attained except by the old.

There is such a one I sometimes see being wheeled about in the Luxembourg. His face is beautiful in its thankfulness.

THE CONTENTED MAN

"How good God is to me," he said;
"For have I not a mansion tall,
With trees and lawns of velvet tread,
And happy helpers at my call?

With beauty is my life abrim,
With tranquil hours and dreams apart;
You wonder that I yield to Him
That best of prayers, a grateful heart?"

"How good God is to me," he said;
"For look! though gone is all my wealth,
How sweet it is to earn one's bread
With brawny arms and brimming health.
Oh, now I know the joy of strife!
To sleep so sound, to wake so fit.
Ah yes, how glorious is life!
I thank Him for each day of it."

"How good God is to me," he said;
"Though health and wealth are gone, it's true;
Things might be worse, I might be dead,
And here I'm living, laughing too.
Serene beneath the evening sky
I wait, and every man's my friend;
God's most contented man am I . . .
He keeps me smiling to the End."

To-day the basin of the Luxembourg is bright with little boats.
Hundreds of happy children romp around it. Little ones everywhere;
yet there is no other city with so many childless homes.

THE SPIRIT OF THE UNBORN BABE

The Spirit of the Unborn Babe peered through the window-
    pane,
Peered through the window-pane that glowed like beacon in
    the night;
For, oh, the sky was desolate and wild with wind and rain;
And how the little room was crammed with cosiness and light!
Except the flirting of the fire there was no sound at all;
The Woman sat beside the hearth, her knitting on her knee;
The shadow of her husband's head was dancing on the wall;
She looked with staring eyes at it, she looked yet did not see.
She only saw a childish face that topped the table rim,
A little wistful ghost that smiled and vanished quick away;
And then because her tender eyes were flooding to the brim,
She lowered her head. . . . "Don't sorrow, dear," she heard him
    softly say;
"It's over now. We'll try to be as happy as before
(Ah! they who little children have, grant hostages to pain).
We gave Life chance to wound us once, but never, never
    more. . . ."
The Spirit of the Unborn Babe fled through the night again.

The Spirit of the Unborn Babe went wildered in the dark;
Like termagants the winds tore down and whirled it with the
    snow.
And then amid the writhing storm it saw a tiny spark,
A window broad, a spacious room all goldenly aglow,

A woman slim and Paris-gowned and exquisitely fair,
Who smiled with rapture as she watched her jewels catch the
    blaze;
A man in faultless evening dress, young, handsome, debonnaire,
Who smoked his cigarette and looked with frank admiring
    gaze.
"Oh, we are happy, sweet," said he; "youth, health, and wealth
    are ours.
What if a thousand toil and sweat that we may live at ease!
What if the hands are worn and torn that strew our path with
    flowers!
Ah, well! we did not make the world: let us not think of these.
Let's seek the beauty-spots of earth, Dear Heart, just you and I;
Let other women bring forth life with sorrow and with pain,
Above our door we'll hang the sign: *"No children need
    apply. . . ."*
The Spirit of the Unborn Babe sped through the night again.

The Spirit of the Unborn Babe went whirling on and on;
It soared above a city vast, it swept down to a slum;
It saw within a grimy house a light that dimly shone;
It peered in through a window-pane, and lo! a voice said:
    "Come!"
And so a little girl was born amid the dirt and din,
And lived in spite of everything, for life is ordered so;
A child whose eyes first opened wide to swinishness and sin,
A child whose love and innocence met only curse and blow.

And so in due and proper course she took the path of shame,
And gladly died in hospital, quite old at twenty years;
And when God comes to weigh it all, ah! whose shall be the
    blame
For all her maimed and poisoned life, her torture and her tears?
For oh, it is not what we do, but what we have not done!
And on that day of reckoning, when all is plain and clear,
What if we stand before the Throne, blood-guilty every
    one? . . .
Maybe the blackest sins of all are Selfishness and Fear.

IV

THE CAFE DE LA PAIX,
August 1, 1914.

Paris and I are out of tune. As I sit at this famous corner the faint
breeze is stale and weary; stale and weary, too, the faces that swirl
around me; while overhead the electric sign of Somebody's Chocolate
appears and vanishes with irritating insistency. The very trees seem
artificial, gleaming under the arc-lights with a raw viridity that rasps
my nerves.

"Poor little trees," I mutter, "growing in all this grime and glare,
your only dryads the loitering ladies with the complexions of such
brilliant certainty, your only Pipes of Pan orchestral echoes from the
clamorous cafés: Exiles of the forest! what know you of full-bosomed
winds, of red-embered sunsets, of the gentle admonition of spring rain!
Life, that would fain be a melody, seems here almost a malady. I
crave for the balm of Nature, the anodyne of solitude, the breath of
Mother Earth. Tell me, O wistful trees, what shall I do?"

Then that stale and weary wind rustles the leaves of the nearest sycamore, and I am sure it whispers: "Brittany."

So to-morrow I am off, off to the Land of Little Fields.

FINISTÈRE

HURRAH! I'm off to Finistère, to Finistère, to Finistère;
My satchel's swinging on my back, my staff is in my hand;
I've twenty *louis* in my purse, I know the sun and sea are there,
And so I'm starting out to-day to tramp the golden land.
I'll go alone and glorying, with on my lips a song of joy;
I'll leave behind the city with its canker and its care;
I'll swing along so sturdily—oh, won't I be the happy boy!
A-singing on the rocky roads, the roads of Finistère.

Oh, have you been to Finistère, and do you know a whin-grey
    town
That echoes to the clatter of a thousand wooden shoes?
And have you seen the fisher-girls go galivantin' up and down,
And watched the tawny boats go out, and heard the roaring
    crews?
Oh, would you sit with pipe and bowl, and dream upon some
    sunny quay,
Or would you walk the windy heath and drink the caller air;
Oh, would you seek a cradled cove and tussle with the topaz
    sea!—
Pack up your kit to-morrow, lad, and haste to Finistère.

Oh, I will go to Finistère, there's nothing that can hold me
back.

I'll laugh with Yves and Léon, and I'll chaff with Rose and
Jeanne;

I'll seek the little, quaint *buvette* that's kept by Mother
Merdrinac,

Who wears a cap of many frills, and swears just like a man.

I'll yarn with hearty, hairy chaps who dance and leap and crack
their heels;

Who swallow cupfuls of cognac and never turn a hair;

I'll watch the nut-brown boats come in with mullet, plaice
and conger eels,

The jewelled harvest of the sea they reap in Finistère.

Yes, I'll come back from Finistère with memories of shining
days,

Of scaly nets and salty men in overalls of brown;

Of ancient women knitting as they watch the tethered cattle
graze

By little nestling beaches where the gorse goes blazing down;

Of headlands silvering the sea, of Calvarys against the sky,

Of scorn of angry sunsets, and of Carnac grim and bare;

Oh, won't I have the leaping veins, and tawny cheek and sparkling eye,

When I come back to Montparnasse and dream of Finistère.

Two days later.

Behold me with staff and scrip, footing it merrily in the Land of
Pardons. I have no goal. When I am weary I stop at some *auberge;*

when I am rested I go on again. Neither do I put any constraint on my spirit. No subduing of the mind to the task of the moment. I dream to heart's content.

My dreams stretch into the future. I see myself a singer of simple songs, a laureate of the under-dogs. I will write books, a score of them. I will voyage far and wide. I will . . .

But there! Dreams are dangerous. They waste the time one should spend on making them come true. Yet when we do make them come true, we find the vision sweeter than the reality. How much of our happiness do we owe to dreams? I have in mind one old chap who used to herd the sheep on my uncle's farm.

OLD DAVID SMAIL

HE dreamed away his hours in school;
He sat with such an absent air,
The master reckoned him a fool,
And gave him up in dull despair.

When other lads were making hay
You'd find him loafing by the stream.
He'd take a book and slip away,
And just pretend to fish . . .and dream.

His brothers passed him in the race;
They climbed the hill and clutched the prize.
He did not seem to heed, his face
Was tranquil as the evening skies.

He lived apart, he spoke with few;
Abstractedly through life he went;
Oh, what he dreamed of no one knew,
And yet he seemed to be content.

I see him now, so old and grey,
His eyes with inward vision dim;
And though he faltered on the way,
Somehow I almost envied him.

At last beside his bed I stood:
"And is Life done so soon?" he sighed;
"It's been so rich, so full, so good,
I've loved it all . . ."—and so he died.

Another day.

Framed in hedgerows of emerald, the wheat glows with a caloric
fervour, as if gorged with summer heat. In the vivid green of pastures
old women are herding cows. Calm and patient are their faces as with
gentle industry they bend over their knitting. One feels that they are
necessary to the landscape.

To gaze at me the field-workers suspend the magnificent lethargy of
their labours. The men with the reaping-hooks improve the occasion
by another pull at the cider bottle under the stook; the women raise
apathetic brown faces from the sheaf they are tying; everyone is a study
in deliberation, though the crop is russet ripe and crying to be cut.

Then on I go again amid high banks overgrown with fern and honeysuckle. Sometimes I come on an old mill that seems to have been
constructed by Constable, so charmingly does Nature imitate Art. By
the deserted house, half drowned in greenery, the velvety wheel, dipping

in the crystal water, seems to protest against this prolongation of its toil.

Then again I come on its brother, the Mill of the Wind, whirling its arms so cheerily, as it turns its great white stones for its master, the floury miller by the door.

These things delight me. I am in a land where Time has lagged, where simple people timorously hug the Past. How far away now seems the welter and swelter of the city, the hectic sophistication of the streets. The sense of wonder is strong in me again, the joy of looking at familiar things as if one were seeing them for the first time.

THE WONDERER

I wish that I could understand
The moving marvel of my Hand;
I watch my fingers turn and twist,
The supple bending of my wrist,
The dainty touch of finger-tip,
The steel intensity of grip;
A tool of exquisite design,
With pride I think: "It's mine! It's mine!"

Then there's the wonder of my Eyes,
Where hills and houses, seas and skies,
In waves of light converge and pass,
And print themselves as on a glass.
Line, form and colour live in me;
I am the Beauty that I see;
Ah! I could write a book of size
About the wonder of my Eyes.

What of the wonder of my Heart,
That plays so faithfully its part?
I hear it running sound and sweet;
It does not seem to miss a beat;
Between the cradle and the grave
It never falters, stanch and brave.
Alas! I wish I had the art
To tell the wonder of my Heart.

Then oh! but how can I explain
The wondrous wonder of my Brain?
That marvellous machine that brings
All consciousness of wonderings;
That lets me from myself leap out
And watch my body walk about;
It's hopeless—all my words are vain
To tell the wonder of my Brain.

But do not think, O patient friend,
Who read these stanzas to the end,
That I myself would glorify. . . .
You're just as wonderful as I,
And all Creation in our view
Is quite as marvellous as you.
Come, let us on the sea-shore stand
And wonder at a grain of sand;
And then into the meadow pass
And marvel at a blade of grass;

Or cast our vision high and far
And thrill with wonder at a star;
A host of stars—night's holy tent
Huge-glittering with wonderment.

If wonder is in great and small,
Then what of Him Who made it all?
In eyes and brain and heart and limb
Let's see the wondrous work of Him.
In house and hill and sward and sea,
In bird and beast and flower and tree,
In everything from sun to sod,
The wonder and the awe of God.

August 9, 1914.

For some time the way has been growing wilder. Thick-set hedges
have yielded to dykes of stone, and there is every sign that I am ap-
proaching the rugged region of the coast. At each point of vantage I
can see a Cross, often a relic of the early Christians, stumpy and
corroded. Then I come on a slab of grey stone upstanding about
fifteen feet. Like a sentinel on that solitary plain it overwhelms me
with a sense of mystery.

But as I go on through this desolate land these stones become more
and more familiar. Like soldiers they stand in rank, extending over
the moor. The sky is cowled with cloud, save where a sullen sunset
shoots blood-red rays across the plain. Bathed in that sinister light
stands my army of stone, and a wind swooping down seems to wail
amid its ranks. As in a glass darkly I can see the skin-clad men, the
women with the tangled hair, the beast-like feast, the cowering terror
of the night. Then the sunset is cut off suddenly, and a clammy mist

shrouds that silent army. So it is almost with a shudder I take my last look at the Stones of Carnac.

But now my pilgrimage is drawing to an end. A painter friend who lives by the sea has asked me to stay with him awhile. Well, I have walked a hundred miles, singing on the way. I have dreamed and dawdled, planned, exulted. I have drunk buckets of cider, and eaten many an omelette that seemed like a golden glorification of its egg. It has all been very sweet, but it will also be sweet to loaf awhile.

OH, IT IS GOOD

Oh, it is good to drink and sup,
And then beside the kindly fire
To smoke and heap the faggots up,
And rest and dream to heart's desire.

Oh, it is good to ride and run,
To roam the greenwood wild and free;
To hunt, to idle in the sun,
To leap into the laughing sea.

Oh, it is good with hand and brain
To gladly till the chosen soil,
And after honest sweat and strain
To see the harvest of one's toil.

Oh, it is good afar to roam,
And seek adventure in strange lands;
Yet oh, so good the coming home,
The velvet love of little hands.

So much is good. . . . We thank Thee, God,
For all the tokens Thou hast given,
That here on earth our feet have trod
Thy little shining trails of Heaven.

V

August 10, 1914.

I am living in a little house so near the sea that at high tide I can
see on my bedroom wall the reflected ripple of the water. At night I
waken to the melodious welter of waves; or maybe there is a great stillness, and then I know that the sand and sea-grass are lying naked to the
moon. But soon the tide returns, and once more I hear the roistering
of the waves.

Calvert, my friend, is a lover as well as a painter of nature. He
rises with the dawn to see the morning mist kindle to coral and the sun's
edge clear the hill-crest. As he munches his coarse bread and sips his
white wine, what dreams are his beneath the magic changes of the sky!
He will paint the same scene under a dozen conditions of light. He
has looked so long for Beauty that he has come to see it everywhere.

I love this friendly home of his. A peace steals over my spirit, and
I feel as if I could stay here always. Some day I hope that I, too, may
have such a one, and that I may write like this:

I HAVE SOME FRIENDS

I HAVE some friends, some worthy friends,
And worthy friends are rare:
These carpet slippers on my feet,
That padded leather chair;
This old and shabby dressing-gown,
So well the worse of wear.

I have some friends, some honest friends,
And honest friends are few;
My pipe of briar, my open fire,
A book that's not too new;
My bed so warm that nights of storm
I love to listen to.

I have some friends, some good, good friends,
Who faithful are to me:
My wrestling partner when I rise,
The big and burly sea;
My little boat that's riding there
So saucy and so free.

I have some friends, some golden friends,
Whose worth will not decline:
A tawny Irish terrier, a purple shading pine,
A little red-roofed cottage that
So proudly I call mine.

All other friends may come and go,
All other friendships fail;
But these, the friends I've worked to win,
Oh, they will never stale;
And comfort me till Time shall write
The finish to my tale.

Calvert tries to paint more than the thing he sees; he tries to paint
behind it, to express its spirit. He believes that Beauty is God made

v*

manifest, and that when we discover Him in Nature we discover Him in ourselves.

But Calvert did not always see thus. At one time he was a Pagan, content to paint the outward aspect of things. It was after his little child died he gained in vision. Maybe the thought that the dead are lost to us was too unbearable. He had to believe in a coming together again.

THE QUEST

I sought Him on the purple seas,
I sought Him on the peaks aflame;
Amid the gloom of giant trees
And canyons lone I called His Name;
The wasted ways of earth I trod:
In vain! In vain! I found not God.

I sought Him in the hives of men,
The cities grand, the hamlets grey,
The temples old beyond my ken,
The tabernacles of to-day;
All life that is, from cloud to clod,
I sought. . . . Alas! I found not God.

Then after roamings far and wide,
In streets and seas and deserts wild,
I came to stand at last beside
The death-bed of my little child.
Lo! as I bent beneath the rod
I raised my eyes . . . and there was God.

A golden mile of sand swings hammock-like between two tusks of rock. The sea is sleeping sapphire that wakes to cream and crash upon the beach. There is a majesty in the detachment of its lazy waves, and it is good in the night to hear its friendly roar. Good, too, to leap forth with the first sunshine and fall into its arms, to let it pummel the body to living ecstasy and send one to breakfast glad-eyed and glowing.

Behind the house the greensward slopes to a wheat-field that is like a wall of gold. Here I lie and laze away the time, or dip into a favourite book, Stevenson's *Letters* or Belloc's *Path to Rome*. Bees drone in the wild thyme; a cuckoo keeps calling, a lark spills jewelled melody. Then there is a seeming silence, but it is the silence of a deeper sound.

After all, Silence is only man's confession of his deafness. Like Death, like Eternity, it is a word that means nothing. So lying there I hear the breathing of the trees, the crepitation of the growing grass, the seething of the sap and the movements of innumerable insects. Strange how I think with distaste of the spurious glitter of Paris, of my garret, even of my poor little book.

I watch the wife of my friend gathering poppies in the wheat. There is a sadness in her face, for it is only a year ago they lost their little one. Often I see her steal away to the village graveyard, sitting silent for long and long.

THE COMFORTER

As I sat by my baby's bed
That's open to the sky,
There fluttered round and round my head
A radiant butterfly.

And as I wept—of hearts that ache
The saddest in the land—
It left a lily for my sake,
And lighted on my hand.

I watched it, oh, so quietly,
And though it rose and flew,
As if it fain would comfort me
It came and came anew.

Now, where my darling lies at rest,
I do not dare to sigh,
For look! there gleams upon my breast
A snow-white butterfly.

My friends will have other children, and if some day they should read this piece of verse, perhaps they will think of the city lad who used to sit under the old fig-tree in the garden and watch the lizards sun themselves on the time-worn wall.

THE OTHER ONE

"GATHER around me, children dear;
The wind is high and the night is cold;
Closer, little ones, snuggle near;
Let's seek a story of ages old;
A magic tale of a bygone day,
Of lovely ladies and dragons dread;
Come, for you're all so tired of play,
We'll read till it's time to go to bed."

So they all are glad, and they nestle in,
And squat on the rough old nursery rug,
And they nudge and hush as I begin,
And the fire leaps up and all's so snug;

And there I sit in the big arm-chair,
And how they are eager and sweet and wise,
And they cup their chins in their hands and stare
At the heart of the flame with thoughtful eyes.

And then, as I read by the ruddy glow
And the little ones sit entranced and still . . .
He's drawing near, ah! I know, I know
He's listening too, as he always will.
He's there—he's standing beside my knee;
I see him so well, my wee, wee son. . . .
Oh, children dear, don't look at me—
I'm reading now for—the Other One.

For the firelight glints in his golden hair,
And his wondering eyes are fixed on my face,
And he rests on the arm of my easy-chair,
And the book's a blur and I lose my place:
And I touch my lips to his shining head,
And my voice breaks down and—the story's done. . . .
Oh, children, kiss me and go to bed:
Leave me to think of the Other One.

Of the One who will never grow up at all,
Who will always be just a child at play,
Tender and trusting and sweet and small,
Who will never leave me and go away;
Who will never hurt me and give me pain;
Who will comfort me when I'm all alone;

A heart of love that's without a stain,
Always and always my own, my own.

Yet a thought shines out from the dark of pain,
And it gives me hope to be reconciled:
That each of us must be born again,
And live and die as a little child;
So that with souls all shining white,
White as snow and without one sin,
We may come to the Gates of Eternal Light,
Where only children may enter in.

So, gentle mothers, don't ever grieve
Because you have lost, but kiss the rod;
From the depths of your woe be glad, believe
You've given an angel unto God.
Rejoice! You've a child whose youth endures,
Who comes to you when the day is done,
Wistful for love, oh, yours, just yours,
Dearest of all, the Other One.

CATASTROPHE

BRITTANY,
August First, 1914.

And now I fear I must write in another strain. Up to this time
I have been too happy. I have existed in a magic Bohemia, largely of
my own making. Hope, faith, enthusiasm have been mine. Each
day has had its struggle, its failure, its triumph. However, that is all

ended. During the past week we have lived breathlessly. For in spite of the exultant sunshine our spirits have been under a cloud, a deepening shadow of horror and calamity. . . . WAR.

Even as I write, in our little village steeple the bells are ringing madly, and in every little village steeple all over the land. As he listens, the harvester checks his scythe on the swing; the clerk throws down his pen; the shopkeeper puts up his shutters. Only in the cafés there is a clamour of voices and a drowning of care.

For here every man must fight, every home give tribute. There is no question, no appeal. By heredity and discipline all minds are shaped to this great hour. So to-morrow each man will seek his barracks and become a soldier as completely as if he had never been anything else. With the same docility as he dons his baggy red trousers will he let some muddle-headed General hurl him to destruction for some dubious gain. To-day a father, a home-maker; to-morrow fodder for cannon. So they all go without hesitation, without bitterness; and the great military machine that knows not humanity swings them to their fate. I marvel at the sense of duty, the resignation, the sacrifice. It is magnificent, it is FRANCE.

And the Women. Those who wait and weep. Ah! to-day I have not seen one who did not weep. Yes, one. She was very old, and she stood by her garden gate with her hand on the uplifted latch. As I passed she looked at me with eyes that did not see. She had no doubt sons and grandsons who must fight, and she had good reason, perhaps, to remember the war of *soixante-dix*. When I passed an hour later she was still there, her hand on the uplifted latch.

August 30th.

The men have gone. Only remain greybeards, women and children. Calvert and I have been helping our neighbours to get in the harvest. No doubt we aid; but there with the old men and children a sense of uneasiness and even shame comes over me. I would like to return to Paris, but the railway is mobilized. Each day I grow more discontented. Up there in the red North great things are doing and I am out of it. I am thoroughly unhappy.

Then Calvert comes to me with a plan. He has a Ford car. We will all three go to Paris. He intends to offer himself and his car to the Red Cross. His wife will nurse. So we are very happy at the solution, and to-morrow we are off.

PARIS.

Back again. Closed shutters, deserted streets. How glum everything is! Those who are not mobilized seem uncertain how to turn. Everyone buys the papers and reads grimly of disaster. No news is bad news.

I go to my garret as to a beloved friend. Everything is just as I left it, so that it seems I have never been away. I sigh with relief and joy. I will take up my work again. Serene above the storm I will watch and wait. Although I have been brought up in England I am American born. My country is not concerned.

So, going to the Dôme Café, I seek some of my comrades. Strange! They have gone.´ MacBean, I am told, is in Scotland. By dyeing his hair and lying about his age he has managed to enlist in the Seaforth Highlanders. Saxon Dane too. He has joined the Foreign Legion, and even now may be fighting.

Well, let them go. I will keep out of the mess. But why did they go? I wish I knew. War is murder. Criminal folly. Against Humanity. Imperialism is at the root of it. We are fools and dupes. Yes, I will think and write of other things. . . .

MacBean has enlisted.

I hate violence. I would not willingly cause pain to anything breathing. I would rather be killed than kill. I will stand above the Battle and watch it from afar.

Dane is in the Foreign Legion.

How disturbing it all is! One cannot settle down to anything. Every day I meet men who tell the most wonderful stories in the most casual way. I envy them. I too want to have experiences, to live where life's beat is most intense. But that's a poor reason for going to war.

And yet, though I shrink from the idea of fighting, I might in some way help those who are. MacBean and Dane, for example. Sitting lonely in the Dôme, I seem to see their ghosts in the corner. MacBean listening with his keen, sarcastic smile, Saxon Dane banging his great hairy fist on the table till the glasses jump. Where are they now? Living a life that I will never know. When they come back, if they ever do, shall I not feel shamed in their presence? Oh, this filthy war! Things were going on so beautifully. We were all so happy, so full of ambition, of hope; laughing and talking over pipe and bowl, and in our garrets seeking to realize our dreams. Ah, these days will never come again!

Then, as I sit there, Calvert seeks me out. He has joined an ambulance corps that is going to the Front. Will I come in?

"Yes," I say; "I'll do anything."

So it is all settled. To-morrow I give up my freedom.

PART FOUR

WINTER

I

The Somme Front,
January, 1915.

THERE is an avenue of noble beeches leading to the Chateau, and in the shadow of each glimmers the pale oblong of an ambulance. We have to keep them thus concealed, for only yesterday morning a Taube flew over. The beggars are rather partial to Red Cross cars. One of our chaps, taking in a load of wounded, was chased and pelted the other day.

The Chateau seems all spires and towers, the glorified dream of a Parisian pastrycook. On its terrace figures in khaki are lounging. They are the volunteers, the owner-drivers of the Corps, many of them men of wealth and title. Curious to see one who owns all the coal in two counties proudly signing for his *sou* a day; or another, who lives in a Fifth Avenue palace, contentedly sleeping on the straw-strewn floor of a hovel.

Here is a rhyme I have made of such a one:

PRISCILLA

JERRY MACMULLEN the millionaire,
Driving a red-meat bus out there—
How did he win his *Croix de Guerre*?
Bless you, that's all old stuff:
Beast of a night on the Verdun road,
Jerry stuck with a woful load,
Stalled in the mud where the red lights glowed,
Prospect devilish tough.

"Little Priscilla" he called his car,
Best of our battered bunch by far,
Branded with many a bullet scar,
Yet running so sweet and true.
Jerry he loved her, knew her tricks;
Swore: "She's the beat of the best big six,
And if ever I get in a deuce of a fix
Priscilla will pull me through."

"Looks pretty rotten right now," says he:
"Hanged if the devil himself could see.
Priscilla, it's up to you and me
To show 'em what we can do."
Seemed that Priscilla just took the word;
Up with a leap like a horse that's spurred,
On with the joy of a homing bird,
Swift as the wind she flew.

Shell-holes shoot at them out of the night;
A lurch to the left, a wrench to the right,
Hands grim-gripping and teeth clenched tight,
Eyes that glare through the dark.
"Priscilla, you're doing me proud this day;
Hospital's only a league away,
And, honey, I'm longing to hit the hay,
So hurry, old girl. . . . But hark!"

Howl of a shell, harsh, sudden, dread;
Another . . . another . . . "Strike me dead

If the Huns ain't strafing the road ahead
So the convoy can't get through!
A barrage of shrap, and us alone;
Four rush-cases—you hear 'em moan?
Fierce old messes of blood and bone . . .
Priscilla, what shall we do?"

Again it seems that Priscilla hears.
With a rush and a roar her way she clears,
Straight at the hell of flame she steers,
Full at its heart of wrath.
Fury of death and dust and din!
Havoc and horror! She's in, she's in;
She's almost over, she'll win, she'll win!
Woof! Crump! right in the path.

Little Priscilla skids and stops,
Jerry MacMullen sways and flops;
Bang in his map the crash he cops;
Shriek from the car: "Mon Dieu!"
One of the *blessés* hears him say,
Just at the moment he faints away:
"Reckon this isn't my lucky day,
Priscilla, it's up to you."

Sergeant raps on the doctor's door;
"Car in the court with *couchés* four;
Driver dead on the dashboard floor;
Strange how the bunch got here."

"No," says the Doc, "this chap's alive;
But tell me, how could a man contrive
With both arms broken, a car to drive?
Thunder of God! it's queer."

Same little *blessé* makes a speil;
Says he: "When I saw our driver reel,
A Strange Shape leapt to the driving wheel
And sped us safe through the night."
But Jerry, he says in his drawling tone:
"Rats! Why, Priscilla came in on her own.
Bless her, she did it alone, alone. . . ."
Hanged if I know who's right.

As I am sitting down to my midday meal an orderly gives me a
telegram:

Hill 71. Two couchés. Send car at once.

The uplifted country-side is a checker-board of green and grey, and,
except where groves of trees rise like islands, cultivated to the last
acre. But as we near the firing-line all efforts to till the land cease,
and the ungathered beets of last year have grown to seed. Amid rank
unkempt fields I run over a road that is pitted with obus-holes; I pass
a line of guns painted like snakes, and drawn by horses dyed khaki-
colour; then soldiers coming from the trenches, mud-caked and ineffably
weary; then a race over a bit of road that is exposed; then, buried in
the hill-side, the dressing station.

The two wounded are put into my car. From hip to heel one is
swathed in bandages; the other has a great white turban on his head,
with a red patch on it that spreads and spreads. They stare dully, but

make no sound. As I crank the car there is a shrill screaming noise.
. . . About thirty yards away I hear an explosion like a mine-blast,
followed by a sudden belch of coal-black smoke. I stare at it in a
dazed way. Then the doctor says: "Don't trouble to analyse your sen-
sations. Better get off. You're only drawing their fire."

Here is one of my experiences:

A CASUALTY

That boy I took in the car last night,
With the body that awfully sagged away,
And the lips blood-crisped, and the eyes flame-bright,
And the poor hands folded and cold as clay—
Oh, I've thought and I've thought of him all the day.

For the weary old doctor says to me:
"He'll only last for an hour or so.
Both of his legs below the knee
Blown off by a bomb. . . . So, lad, go slow,
And please remember, he doesn't know."

So I tried to drive with never a jar;
And there was I cursing the road like mad,
When I hears a ghost of a voice from the car:
"Tell me, old chap, have I 'copped it' bad?"
So I answers "No," and he says, "I'm glad."

"Glad," says he, "for at twenty-two
Life's so splendid, I hate to go.

There's so much good that a chap might do,
And I've fought from the start and I've suffered so.
'Twould be hard to get knocked out now, you know."

"Forget it," says I; then I drove awhile,
And I passed him a cheery word or two;
But he didn't answer for many a mile,
So just as the hospital hove in view,
Says I: "Is there nothing that I can do?"

Then he opens his eyes and he smiles at me;
And he takes my hand in his trembling hold:
"Thank you—you're far too kind," says he:
"I'm awfully comfy—stay . . . let's see:
I fancy my blanket's come unrolled—
My *feet*, please wrap 'em—they're cold . . . they're cold."

There is a city that glitters on the plain. Afar off we can see its tall cathedral spire, and there we often take our wounded from the little village hospitals to the rail-head. Tragic little buildings, these emergency hospitals—town-halls, churches, schools; their cots are never empty, their surgeons never still.

So every day we get our list of cases and off we go, a long line of cars swishing through the mud. Then one by one we branch off to our village hospital, puzzling out the road on our maps. Arrived there, we load up quickly.

The wounded make no moan. They lie, limp, heavily bandaged, with bare legs and arms protruding from their blankets. They do not know where they are going; they do not care. Like live stock, they are labelled and numbered. An orderly brings along their battle-scarred equipment, throwing open their rifles to see that no charge remains. Sometimes they shake our hands and thank us for the drive.

In the streets of the city I see French soldiers wearing the *fourragère*. It is a cord of green, yellow or red, and corresponds to the *Croix de Guerre*, the *Médaille militaire* and the Legion of Honour. The red is the highest of all, and has been granted only to one or two regiments. This incident was told to me by a man who saw it:

THE BLOOD-RED *FOURRAGERE*

WHAT was the blackest sight to me
Of all that campaign?
A naked woman tied to a tree
With jagged holes where her breasts should be,
Rotting there in the rain.

On we pressed to the battle fray,
Dogged and dour and spent.
Sudden I heard my Captain say:
"*Voilà!* Kultur has passed this way,
And left us a monument."

So I looked and I saw our Colonel there,
And his grand head, snowed with the years,
Unto the beat of the rain was bare;
And, oh, there was grief in his frozen stare,
And his cheeks were stung with tears!

Then at last he turned from the woful tree,
And his face like stone was set;
"Go, march the Regiment past," said he,
"That every father and son may see,
And none may ever forget."

Oh, the crimson strands of her hair downpoured
Over her breasts of woe;
And our grim old Colonel leaned on his sword,
And the men filed past with their rifles lowered,
Solemn and sad and slow.

But I'll never forget till the day I die,
As I stood in the driving rain,
And the jaded columns of men slouched by,
How amazement leapt into every eye,
Then fury and grief and pain.

And some would like madmen stand aghast,
With their hands upclenched to the sky;
And some would cross themselves as they passed,
And some would curse in a scalding blast,
And some like children cry.

Yea, some would be sobbing, and some would pray,
And some hurl hateful names;
But the best had never a word to say;
They turned their twitching faces away,
And their eyes were like hot flames.

They passed; then down on his bended knee
The Colonel dropped to the Dead:
"Poor martyred daughter of France!" said he,
"O dearly, dearly avenged you'll be
Or ever a day be sped!"

Now they hold that we are the best of the best,
And each of our men may wear,
Like a gash of crimson across his chest,
As one fierce-proved in the battle-test,
The blood-red *Fourragère*.

For each as he leaps to the top can see,
Like an etching of blood on his brain,
A wife or a mother lashed to a tree,
With two black holes where her breasts should be,
Left to rot in the rain.

So we fight like fiends, and of us they say
That we neither yield nor spare.
Oh, we have the bitterest debt to pay. . . .
Have we paid it?—Look—how we wear to-day
Like a trophy, gallant and proud and gay,
Our blood-red *Fourragère*.

It is often weary waiting at the little *poste de secours*. Some of us play solitaire, some read a "sixpenny," some doze or try to talk in bad French to the *poilus*. Around us is discomfort, dirt and drama.

For my part, I pass the time only too quickly, trying to put into
verse the incidents and ideas that come my way. In this way I hope
to collect quite a lot of stuff which may some day see itself in print.

Here is one of my efforts:

JIM

NEVER knew Jim, did you? Our boy Jim?
Bless you, there was the likely lad;
Supple and straight and long of limb,
Clean as a whistle, and just as glad.
Always laughing, wasn't he, dad?
Joy, pure joy to the heart of him,
And, oh, but the soothering ways he had,
                      Jim, our Jim!

But I see him best as a tiny tot,
A bonny babe, though it's me that speaks;
Laughing there in his little cot,
With his sunny hair and his apple cheeks.
And my! but the blue, blue eyes he'd got,
And just where his wee mouth dimpled dim
Such a fairy mark like a beauty spot—
                      That was Jim.

Oh, the war, the war! How my eyes were wet!
But he says: "Don't be sorrowing, mother dear;
You never knew me to fail you yet,
And I'll be back in a year, a year."

'Twas at Mons he fell, in the first attack;
For so they said, and their eyes were dim;
But I laughed in their faces: "He'll come back,
                              Will my Jim."

Now, we'd been wedded for twenty year,
And Jim was the only one we'd had;
So when I whispered in father's ear,
He wouldn't believe me—would you, dad?
There! I must hurry . . . hear him cry?
My new little baby. . . . See! that's him.
What are we going to call him? Why,
                              Jim, just Jim.

Jim! For look at him laughing there
In the same old way in his tiny cot,
With his rosy cheeks and his sunny hair,
And look, just look . . . his beauty spot
In the selfsame place. . . . Oh, I can't explain
And of course you think it's a mother's whim,
But I know, I know it's my boy again,
                              Same wee Jim.

Just come back as he said he would;
Come with his love and his heart of glee.
Oh, I cried and I cried, but the Lord was good;
From the shadow of Death he set Jim free.
So I'll have him all over again, you see.

Can you wonder my mother-heart's a-brim?
Oh, how happy we're going to be!

                              Aren't we, Jim?

                    II

In Picardy,
January, 1915.

The road lies amid a malevolent heath. It seems to lead us right into the clutch of the enemy; for the star-shells, that at first were bursting overhead, gradually encircle us. The fields are strangely sinister; the splintered trees are like giant tooth picks. There is a lisping and a twanging overhead.

As we wait at the door of the dugout that serves as a first-aid dressing station, I gaze up into that mysterious dark, so alive with musical vibrations. Then a small shadow detaches itself from the greater shadow, and a grey-bearded sentry says to me: "You'd better come in out of the bullets."

So I keep under cover, and presently they bring my load. Two men drip with sweat as they carry their comrade. I can see that they all three belong to the Foreign Legion. I think for a moment of Saxon Dane. How strange if some day I should carry him! Half fearfully I look at my passenger, but he is a black man. Such things only happen in fiction.

This is what I have written of the finest troops in the Army of France:

KELLY OF THE LEGION

Now Kelly was no fighter;
He loved his pipe and glass;
An easygoing blighter,
Who lived in Montparnasse.

But 'mid the tavern tattle
He heard some guinney say:
"When France goes forth to battle,
The Legion leads the way.

> *"The scourings of creation,*
> *Of every sin and station,*
> *The men who've known damnation,*
> *Are picked to lead the way."*

Well, Kelly joined the Legion;
They marched him day and night;
They rushed him to the region
Where largest loomed the fight.
"Behold your mighty mission,
Your destiny," said they;
"By glorious tradition
The Legion leads the way.

> *"With tattered banners flying*
> *With trail of dead and dying,*
> *On! On! All hell defying,*
> *The Legion sweeps the way."*

With grim, hard-bitten faces,
With jests of savage mirth,
They swept into their places,
The men of iron worth;

Their blooded steel was flashing;
They swung to face the fray;
Then rushing, roaring, crashing,
The Legion cleared the way.

The trail they blazed was gory;
Few lived to tell the story;
Through death they plunged to glory;
But, oh, they cleared the way!

Now Kelly lay a-dying,
And dimly saw advance,
With split new banner flying,
The *fantassins* of France.
Then up amid the *mêlée*
He rose from where he lay;
"Come on, me boys," says Kelly,
"The Layjun lades the way!"

Aye, while they faltered, doubting
(Such flames of doom were spouting),
He caught them, thrilled them, shouting:
"The Layjun lades the way!"

They saw him slip and stumble,
Then stagger on once more;
They marked him trip and tumble,
A mass of grime and gore;

They watched him blindly crawling
Amid hell's own affray,
And calling, calling, calling:
"The Layjun lades the way!"

> *And even while they wondered,*
> *The battle-wrack was sundered;*
> *To Victory they thundered,*
> *But . . . Kelly led the way.*

Still Kelly kept agoing;
Berserker-like he ran;
His eyes with fury glowing,
A lion of a man;
His rifle madly swinging,
His soul athirst to slay,
His slogan ringing, ringing,
"The Layjun lades the way!"

> *Till in a pit death-baited,*
> *Where Huns with Maxims waited,*
> *He plunged . . . and there, blood-sated,*
> *To death he stabbed his way.*

Now Kelly was a fellow
Who simply loathed a fight:
He loved a tavern mellow,
Grog hot and pipe alight;

I'm sure the Show appalled him,
And yet without dismay,
When Death and Duty called him,
He up and led the way.

> So in Valhalla drinking
> (If heroes meek and shrinking
> Are suffered there), I'm thinking
> 'Tis Kelly leads the way.

We have just had one of our men killed, a young sculptor of immense promise.

When one thinks of all the fine work he might have accomplished, it seems a shame. But, after all, to-morrow it may be the turn of any of us. If it should be mine, my chief regret will be for work undone. Ah! I often dream of how I will go back to the Quarter and take up the old life again. How sweet it will all seem. But first I must earn the right. And if ever I do go back, how I will find Bohemia changed! Missing how many a face!

It was in thinking of our lost comrade I wrote the following:

THE THREE TOMMIES

THAT Barret, the painter of pictures, what feeling for colour he
    had!
And Fanning, the maker of music, such melodies mirthful
    and mad!

And Harley, the writer of stories, so whimsical, tender and glad!
To hark to their talk in the trenches, high heart unfolding to heart,
Of the day when the war would be over, and each would be true to his part,
Upbuilding a Palace of Beauty to the wonder and glory of Art . . .

Yon's Barret, the painter of pictures, yon carcass that rots on the wire;
His hand with its sensitive cunning is crisped to a cinder with fire;
His eyes with their magical vision are bubbles of glutinous mire.

Poor Fanning! He sought to discover the symphonic note of a shell;
There are bits of him broken and bloody, to show you the place where it fell;
I've reason to fear on his exquisite ear the rats have been banqueting well.

And speaking of Harley, the writer, I fancy I looked on him last,
Sprawling and staring and writhing in the roar of the battle blast;
Then a mad gun-team crashed over, and scattered his brains as it passed.

Oh, Harley and Fanning and Barret, they were bloody good
    mates o' mine;
Their bodies are empty bottles; Death has guzzled the wine;
What's left of them's filth and corruption. . . . Where is the
    Fire Divine?

I'll tell you. . . . At night in the trenches, as I watch and I
    do my part,
Three radiant spirits I'm seeing, high heart revealing to heart,
And they're building a peerless palace to the splendour and
    triumph of Art.

Yet, alas! for the fame of Barret, the glory he might have
    trailed!
And alas! for the name of Fanning, a star that beaconed and
    paled,
Poor Harley, obscure and forgotten. . . . Well, who shall say
    that they failed!

No, each did a Something Grander than ever he dreamed to do;
And as for the work unfinished, all will be paid their due;
The broken ends will be fitted, the balance struck will be true.

So painters, and players, and penmen, I tell you: Do as you
    please;
Let your fame outleap on the trumpets, you'll never rise up
    to these—
To three grim and gory Tommies, down, down on your bended
    knees.

Daventry, the sculptor, is buried in a little graveyard near one of our posts. Just now our section of the line is quiet, so I often go and sit there. Stretching myself on a flat stone, I dream for hours.

Silence and solitude! How good the peace of it all seems! Around me the grasses weave a pattern, and half hide the hundreds of little wooden crosses. Here is one with a single name:

AUBREY.

Who was Aubrey I wonder? Then another:

To Our Beloved Comrade.

Then one which has attached to it, in the cheapest of little frames, the crude water-colour daub of a child, three purple flowers standing in a yellow vase. Below it, painfully printed, I read:

To My Darling Papa—Thy Little Odette.

And beyond the crosses many fresh graves have been dug. With hungry open mouths they wait. Even now I can hear the guns that are going to feed them. Soon there will be more crosses, and more and more. Then they will cease, and wives and mothers will come here to weep.

Ah! Peace so precious must be bought with blood and tears. Let us honour and bless the men who pay, and envy them the manner of their dying; for not all the jewelled orders on the breasts of the living can vie in glory with the little wooden cross the humblest of these has won. . . .

THE TWA JOCKS

SAYS Bauldy MacGreegor frae Gleska tae Hecky MacCrimmon
    frae Skye:
"That's whit I hate maist aboot fetchin'—it make ye sae deevilish
    dry;

Noo jist hae a keek at yon ferm-hoose them Gairmans are
    poundin' sae fine,
Weel, think o' it, doon in the dunnie there's bottles and bottles
    o' wine.
A' hell's fairly belchin' oot yonner, but oh, lad, I'm ettlin'
    tae try. . . ."
"If it's poose she'll be with ye whateffer," says Hecky MacCrim-
mon frae Skye.

Says Bauldy MacGreegor frae Gleska: "Whit price fur a funeral
    wreath?
We're dodgin' a' kinds o' destruction, an' jist by the skin o' oor
    teeth.
Here, spread yersel oot on yer belly, and slither along in the
    glaur;
Confoond ye, ye big Hielan' deevil! Ye don't realize there's
    a war.
Ye think that ye're back in Dunvegan, and herdin, the wee
    bits o' kye."
"She'll neffer trink wine in Dunfegan," says Hecky MacCrim-
mon frae Skye.

Says Bauldy MacGreegor frae Gleska: "Thank goodness! the
    ferm-hoose at last;
There's no muckle left but the celler, an' even that's vanishin'
    fast.
Look oot, there's the corpse o' a wumman, sair mangelt and
    deid by her lane.

Quick! Strike a match. . . . Whit did I tell ye! A hale
    bonny box o' shampane;
Jist knock the heid aff o' a bottle. . . . Haud on, mon, I'm
    hearing a cry. . . ."
*"She'll think it's a wean that wass greetin'," says Hecky Mac-
Crimmon frae Skye.*

Says Bauldy MacGreegor frae Gleska: "Ma conscience! I'm
    hanged but yer richt.
It's yin o' thae waifs of the war-field, a' sobbin' and shakin'
    wi fricht.
Wheesht noo, dear, we're no gaun tae hurt ye. We're takin'
    ye hame, my wee doo!
We've got tae get back wi' her, Hecky. Whit mercy we
    didna get fou!
We'll no touch a drap o' that likker—that's hard, man, ye canna
    deny. . . ."
*"It's the last thing she'll think o' denyin'," says Hecky Mac-
Crimmon frae Skye.*

Says Bauldy MacGreegor frae Gleska: "If I should get struck
    frae the rear,
Ye'll tak' and ye'll shield the wee lassie, and rin for the lines
    like a deer.
God! Wis that the breenge o' a bullet? I'm thinkin' it's
    cracket ma spine.
I'm doon on ma knees in the glabber; I'm fearin', auld man,
    I've got mine.

Here, quick! Pit yer erms roon the lassie. Noo, rin, lad!
    good luck and good-bye. . . .
"Hoots, mon! it's ye baith she'll be takin'," says Hecky Mac-
    Crimmon frae Skye.

Says Corporal Muckle frae Rannoch: "Is that no' a picture
    tae frame?
Twa sair woundit Jocks wi' a lassie jist like ma wee Jeannie
    at hame.
We're prood o' ye baith, ma brave heroes. We'll gie ye a
    medal, I think."
Says Bauldy MacGreegor frae Gleska: "I'd raither ye gied me
    a drink.
I'll no speak for Private MacCrimmon, but oh, mon, I'm
    perishin' dry. . . ."
"She'll wush that Loch Lefen wass whuskey," says Hecky
    MacCrimmon frae Skye.

III

NEAR ALBERT,
February, 1915.

    Over the spine of the ridge a horned moon of reddish hue peers
through the splintered, hag-like trees. Where the trenches are, rockets
are rising, green and red. I hear the coughing of the maxims, the
peevish nagging of the rifles, the boom of a "heavy" and the hollow
sound of its exploding shell.

Running the car into the shadow of a ruined house, I try to sleep. But a battery starts to blaze away close by, and the flame lights up my shelter. Near me some soldiers are in deep slumber; one stirs in his sleep as a big rat runs over him, and I know by experience that when one is sleeping a rat feels as heavy as a sheep.

But how *can* one possibly sleep? Out there in the dark there is the wild tattoo of a thousand rifles; and hark! that dull roar is the explosion of a mine. There! the purring of the rapid firers. Desperate things are doing. There will be lots of work for me before this night is over. What a cursed place!

As I cannot sleep, I think of a story I heard to-day. It is of a Canadian Colonel, and in my mind I shape it like this:

HIS BOYS

"I'm going, Billy, old fellow. Hist, lad! Don't make any noise.
There's Boches to beat all creation, the pitch of a bomb away.
I've fixed the note to your collar, you've got to get back to my Boys,
You've got to get back to warn 'em before it's the break of day."

The order came to go forward to a trench-line traced on the map;
I knew the brass-hats had blundered, I knew and I told 'em so;
I knew if I did as they ordered I would tumble into a trap,
And I tried to explain, but the answer came like a pistol: "Go."

Then I thought of the Boys I commanded—I always called
    them "my Boys"—
The men of my own recruiting, the lads of my countryside;
Tested in many a battle, I knew their sorrows and joys,
And I loved them all like a father, with more than a father's
    pride.

To march my Boys to a shambles as soon as the dawn of day;
To see them helplessly slaughtered, if all that I guessed was
    true;
My Boys that trusted me blindly, I thought and I tried to pray,
And then I arose and I muttered: "It's either them or it's you."

I rose and I donned my rain-coat; I buckled my helmet tight.
I remember you watched me, Billy, as I took my cane in
    my hand;
I vaulted over the sandbags into the pitchy night,
Into the pitted valley that served us as No Man's Land.

I strode out over the hollow of hate and havoc and death,
From the heights the guns were angry, with a vengeful snarling
    of steel;
And once in a moment of stillness I heard hard panting breath,
And I turned . . . it was you, old rascal, following hard on
    my heel.

I fancy I cursed you, Billy; but not so much as I ought!
And so we went forward together, till we came to the valley rim,

And then a star-shell sputtered . . . it was even worse than
    I thought,
For the trench they told me to move in was packed with
    Boche to the brim.

They saw me too, and they got me; they peppered me till
    I fell;
And there I scribbled my message with my life-blood ebbing
    away;
"Now, Billy, you fat old duffer, you've got to get back
    like hell;
And get them to cancel that order before it's the dawn of day.

"Billy, old boy, I love you, I kiss your shiny black nose;
Now, home there. . . . Hurry, you devil, or I'll cut you to
    ribands. . . . See . . ."
Poor brute! he's off! and I'm dying. . . . I go as a soldier goes.
I'm happy. My Boys, God bless 'em! . . . It had to be them
    or me.

Ah! I never was intended for a job like this. I realize it more
and more every day, but I will stick it out till I break down. To be
nervous, over-imaginative, terribly sensitive to suffering, is a poor
equipment for the man who starts out to drive wounded on the
battlefield. I am haunted by the thought that my car may break
down when I have a load of wounded. Once indeed it did, and a
man died while I waited for help. Now I never look at what is
given me. It might unnerve me.

I have been at it for over six months without a rest. When an attack has been going on I have worked day and night, until as I drove I wanted to fall asleep at the wheel.

The winter has been trying; there is rain one day, frost the next. Mud up to the axles. One sleeps in lousy barns or dripping dugouts. Cold, hunger, dirt, I know them all singly and together. My only consolation is that the war must soon be over, and that I will have helped. When I have time and am not too tired, I comfort myself with scribbling.

THE BOOBY-TRAP

I'm crawlin' out in the mangolds to bury wot's left o' Joe—
Joe, my pal, and a good un (God! 'ow it rains and rains).
I'm sick o' seein' him lyin' like a 'eap o' offal, and so
I'm crawlin' out in the beet-field to bury 'is last remains.

'E might 'a bin makin' munitions—'e 'adn't no need to go;
An' I tells 'im strite, but 'e arnsers, "'Tain't no use chewin'
    the fat;
I've got to be doin' me dooty wiv the rest o' the boys" . . .
    an' so
Yon's 'im, yon blob on the beet-field wot I'm tryin' so 'ard
    to git at.

There was five of us lads from the brickyard; 'Enry was
    gassed at Bapome,
Sydney was drowned in a crater, 'Erbert was 'alved by a shell;
Joe was the pick o' the posy, might 'a bin sifely at 'ome,
Only son of 'is mother, 'er a widder as well.

z

She used to sell bobbins and buttons—'ad a plice near the
     Waterloo Road;
A little, old, bent-over lydy, wiv glasses an' silvery 'air;
Must tell 'er I planted 'im nicely, cheer 'er up like . . .
     (Well, I'm blowed,
That bullet near catched me a biffer)—I'll see the old gel if I'm
     spared.

She'll tike it to 'eart, pore ol' lydy, fer 'e was 'er 'ope and 'er
     joy;
'Is dad used to drink like a knot-'ole, she kept the 'ome goin',
     she did:
She pinched and she scriped fer 'is scoolin', 'e was sich a fine
     'andsome boy
·('Alf Flanders seems packed on me panties)—'e's 'andsome no
     longer, pore kid!

This bit o' a board that I'm packin' and draggin' around
     in the mire,
I was tickled to death when I found it. Says I, " 'Ere's a
     nice little glow."
I was chilled and wet through to the marrer, so I started to
     make me a fire;
And then I says: "No; 'ere, Goblimy, it'll do for a cross for Joe."

Well, 'ere 'e is. Gawd! 'Ow one chinges a-lyin' six weeks in
     the rain.

Joe, me old pal, 'ow I'm sorry; so 'elp me, I wish I could pray.

An' now I 'ad best get a-diggin' 'is grave (it seems more like a drain)—

And I 'opes that the Boches won't git me till I gits 'im safe planted away.

> (*As he touches the body there is a tremendous explosion. He falls back shattered.*)

A booby-trap! Ought to 'a known it! If that's not a bastardly trick!

Well, one thing, I won't be long goin'. Gawd! I'm a 'ell of a sight.

Wish I'd died fightin' and killin'; that's wot it is makes me sick. . . .

Ah, Joe! we'll be pushin' up dysies . . . together, old Chummie . . . good-night!

To-day I heard that MacBean had been killed in Belgium. I believe he turned out a wonderful soldier. Saxon Dane, too, has been missing for two months. We know what that means.

It is odd how one gets callous to death, a mediæval callousness. When we hear that the best of our friends have gone West, we have a moment of the keenest regret; but how soon again we find the heart to laugh! The saddest part of loss, I think, is that one so soon gets over it.

Is it that we fail to realize it all? Is it that it seems a strange and hideous dream, from which we will awake and rub our eyes?

Oh, how I feel bitter as the days go by! It is creeping more and more into my verse. Read this:

BONEHEAD BILL

I WONDER 'oo and wot 'e was,
That 'Un I got so slick.
I couldn't see 'is face because
The night was 'ideous thick.
I just made out among the black
A blinkin' wedge o' white;
Then *biff!* I guess I got 'im *crack*—
The man I killed last night.

I wonder if account o' me
Some wench will go unwed,
And 'eaps o' lives will never be,
Because 'e's stark and dead?
Or if 'is missis damns the war,
And by some candle light,
Tow-headed kids are prayin' for
The Fritz I copped last night.

I wonder, 'struth, I wonder why
I 'ad that 'orful dream?
I saw up in the giddy sky
The gates o' God agleam;
I saw the gates o' 'eaven shine
Wiv everlastin' light:
And then . . . I knew that I'd got mine,
As 'e got 'is last night.

702

Aye, bang beyond the broodin' mists
Where spawn the mother stars,
I 'ammered wiv me bloody fists
Upon them golden bars;
I 'ammered till a devil's doubt
Fair froze me wiv affright:
To fink wot God would say about
The bloke I corpsed last night.

I 'ushed; I wilted wiv despair,
When, like a rosy flame,
I sees a angel standin' there
'Oo calls me by me name.
'E 'ad such soft, such shiny eyes;
'E 'eld 'is 'and and smiled;
And through the gates o' Paradise
'E led me like a child.

'E led me by them golden palms
Wot 'ems that jewelled street;
And seraphs was a-singin' psalms,
You've no ideer 'ow sweet;
Wiv cheroobs crowdin' closer round
Than peas is in a pod,
'E led me to a shiny mound
Where beams the throne o' God.

And then I 'ears God's werry voice:
"Bill Fagan, 'ave no fear.
Stand up and glory and rejoice
For 'im 'oo led you 'ere."
And in a nip I seemed to see:
Aye, like a flash o' light,
My angel pal I knew to be
The chap I plugged last night.

Now, I don't claim to understand—
They calls me Bonehead Bill;
They shoves a rifle in me 'and,
And shows me 'ow to kill.
Me job's to risk me life and limb,
But . . . be it wrong or right,
This cross I'm makin', it's for 'im,
The cove I croaked last night.

IV

A LAPSE OF TIME AND A WORD OF EXPLANATION

THE AMERICAN HOSPITAL, NEUILLY,
January, 1919.

Four years have passed and it is winter again. Much has happened.
When I last wrote, on the Somme in 1915, I was sickening with
typhoid fever. All that spring I was in hospital.

Nevertheless, I was sufficiently recovered to take part in the Champagne battle in the Fall of that year, and to 'carry on" during the following winter. It was at Verdun I got my first wound.

In the spring of 1917 I again served with my Corps; but on the entry of the United States into the War I joined the army of my country. In the Argonne I had my left arm shot away.

As far as time and health permitted, I kept a record of these years, and also wrote much verse. All this, however, has disappeared under circumstances into which there is no need to enter here. The loss was a cruel one, almost more so than that of my arm; for I have neither the heart nor the power to rewrite this material.

And now, in default of something better, I have bundled together this manuscript, and have added to it a few more verses, written in hospitals. Let it represent me. If I can find a publisher for it, *tant mieux*. If not, I will print it at my own cost, and anyone who cares for a copy can write to me—

STEPHEN POORE,
12 *bis,* RUE DES PETITS MOINEAUX,
PARIS.

MICHAEL

"THERE'S something in your face, Michael, I've seen it all the day;
There's something quare that wasn't there when first ye wint away. . . ."

"It's just the Army life, mother, the drill, the left and right,
That puts the stiffinin' in yer spine and locks yer jaw up tight. . . ."

"There's something in your eyes, Michael, an' how they stare
　　and stare—
You're lookin' at me now, me boy, as if I wasn't there. . . ."

"It's just the things I've seen, mother, the sights that come
　　and come,
A bit o' broken, bloody pulp that used to be a chum. . . ."

"There's something on your heart, Michael, that makes ye
　　wake at night,
And often when I hear ye moan, I trimble in me fright. . . ."

"It's just a man I killed, mother, a mother's son like me;
It seems he's always hauntin' me, he'll never let me be. . . ."

"But maybe he was bad, Michael, maybe it was right
To kill the inimy you hate in fair and honest fight. . . ."

"I did not hate at all, mother; he never did me harm;
I think he was a lad like me, who worked upon a farm. . . ."

"And what's it all about, Michael; why did you have to go,
A quiet, peaceful lad like you, and we were happy so? . . ."

"It's thim that's up above, mother, it's thim that sits an' rules;
We've got to fight the wars they make, it's us as are the
　　fools. . . ."

"And what will be the end, Michael, and what's the use, I say,
Of fightin' if whoever wins it's us that's got to pay? . . ."

"Oh, it will be the end, mother, when lads like him and me,
That sweat to feed the ones above, decide that we'll be
     free. . . ."

"And when will that day come, Michael, and when will fightin'
     cease,
And simple folks may till their soil and live and love in
     peace? . . ."

"It's coming soon and soon, mother, it's nearer every day,
When only men who earn their wage will have a word to say;
When all who gain their honest bread in every land and soil
Will claim the Brotherhood of Man, the Comradeship of Toil;
When we, the Workers, all demand: 'What are WE fighting
     for?' . . .
Then, then we'll end that stupid crime, that devil's madness—
     War."

THE   WIFE

"TELL Annie I'll be home in time
To help her with her Christmas-tree."
That's what he wrote, and hark! the chime
Of Christmas bells, and where is he?
And how the house is dark and sad,
And Annie's sobbing on my knee!

The page beside the candle-flame
With cruel type was overfilled;
I read and read until a name
Leapt at me and my heart was stilled:
My eye crept up the column—up
Unto its hateful heading: *Killed*.

And there was Annie on the stair:
"And will he not be long?" she said.
Her eyes were bright and in her hair
She'd twined a bit of riband red;
And every step was daddy's sure,
Till tired out she went to bed.

And there alone I sat so still,
With staring eyes that did not see;
The room was desolate and chill,
And desolate the heart of me;
Outside I heard the news-boys shrill:
"Another Glorious Victory!"

A victory. . . .   Ah! what care I?
A thousand victories are vain.
Here in my ruined home I cry
From out my black despair and pain,
I'd rather, rather damned defeat,
And have my man with me again.

They talk to us of pride and power,
Of Empire vast beyond the sea;
As here beside my hearth I cower,
What mean such words as these to me?
Oh, will they lift the clouds that lour,
Or light my load in years to be?

What matters it to us poor folk?
Who win or lose, it's we who pay.
Oh, I would laugh beneath the yoke
If I had *him* at home to-day;
One's home before one's country comes:
Aye, so a million women say.

"Hush, Annie dear, don't sorrow so."
(How can I tell her?)   "See, we'll light
With tiny star of purest glow
Each little candle pink and white."
(They make mistakes.   I'll try to think
I did not read that name aright.)

Come, dearest one; come, let us pray
Beside our gleaming Christmas-tree;
Just fold your little hands and say
These words so softly after me:
"God pity mothers in distress,
And little children fatherless."

"God pity mothers in distress,
And little children fatherless."

          *   *   *   *   *

What's that?—a step upon the stair;
A shout!—the door thrown open wide!
My hero and my man is there,
And Annie's leaping by his side. . . .
The room reels round, I faint, I fall. . . .
"O God! Thy world is glorified."

VICTORY STUFF

WHAT d'ye think, lad; what d'ye think,
As the roaring crowds go by?
As the banners flare and the brasses blare
And the great guns rend the sky?
As the women laugh like they'd all gone mad,
And the champagne glasses clink:
Oh, you're grippin' me hand so tightly, lad,
I'm a-wonderin': what d'ye think?

D'ye think o' the boys we used to know,
And how they'd have topped the fun?
Tom and Charlie, and Jack and Joe—
Gone now, every one.

How they'd have cheered as the joy-bells chime,
And they grabbed each girl for a kiss!
And now—they're rottin' in Flanders slime,
And they gave their lives—for *this*.

Or else d'ye think of the many a time
We wished we too was dead,
Up to our knees in the freezin' grime,
With the fires of hell overhead.
When the youth and the strength of us sapped away,
And we cursed in our rage and pain—
And yet—we haven't a word to say. . . .
We're glad. We'd do it again.

I'm scared that they pity us. Come, old boy,
Let's leave them their flags and their fuss.
We'd surely be hatin' to spoil their joy
With the sight of such wrecks as us.
Let's slip away quietly, you and me,
And we'll talk of our chums out there:
You with your eyes that'll never see,
Me that's wheeled in a chair.

WAS IT YOU?

"HULLO, young Jones! with your tie so gay
And your pen behind your ear;
Will you mark my cheque in the usual way?
For I'm overdrawn, I fear."

Then you look at me in a manner bland,
As you turn your ledger's leaves,
And you hand it back with a soft white hand,
And the air of a man who grieves. . . .

"Was it you, young Jones, was it you I saw
(And I think I see you yet)
With a live bomb gripped in your grimy paw
And your face to the parapet?
With your lips asnarl and your eyes gone mad
With a fury that thrilled you through. . . .
Oh, I look at you now and I think, my lad,
Was it you, young Jones, was it you?

"Hullo, young Smith, with your well-fed look
And your coat of dapper fit,
Will you recommend me a decent book
With nothing of War in it?"
Then you smile as you polish a finger-nail,
And your eyes serenely roam,
And you suavely hand me a thrilling tale
By a man who stayed at home.

"Was it you, young Smith, was it you I saw
In the battle's storm and stench,
With a roar of rage and a wound red-raw
Leap into the reeking trench?

As you stood like a fiend on the firing-shelf
And you stabbed and hacked and slew. . . .
Oh, I look at you and I ask myself,
Was it you, young Smith, was it you?

"Hullo, old Brown, with your ruddy cheek
And your tummy's rounded swell,
Your garden's looking jolly *chic*
And your kiddies awf'ly well.
Then you beam at me in your cheery way
As you swing your water-can;
And you mop your brow and you blithely say:
'What about golf, old man?'

"*Was it you, old Brown, was it you I saw*
Like a bull-dog stick to your gun,
A cursing devil of fang and claw
When the rest were on the run?
Your eyes aflame with the battle-hate. . . .
As you sit in the family pew,
And I see you rising to pass the plate,
I ask: Old Brown, was it you?

"Was it me and you? Was it you and me?
(Is that grammar, or is it not?)
Who grovelled in filth and misery,
Who gloried and groused and fought?

Which is the wrong and which is the right?
Which is the false and the true?
The man of peace or the man of fight?
Which is the ME and the you?"

V

LES GRANDS MUTILES

I saw three wounded of the war:
And the first had lost his eyes;
And the second went on wheels and had
No legs below the thighs;
And the face of the third was featureless,
And his mouth ran cornerwise.

So I made a rhyme about each one,
And this is how my fancies run.

THE SIGHTLESS MAN

Out of the night a crash,
A roar, a rampart of light;
A flame that leaped like a lash,
Searing for ever my sight;
Out of the night a flash,
Then, oh, for ever the Night!

Here in the dark I sit,
I who so loved the sun;
Supple and strong and fit,
In the dark till my days be done;
Aye, that's the hell of it,
Stalwart and twenty-one.

Marie is stanch and true,
Willing to be my wife;
Swears she has eyes for two . . .
Aye, but it's long, is Life.
What is a lad to do
With his heart and his brain at strife?

There now, my pipe is out;
No one to give me a light;
I grope and I grope about. . . .
Well, it is nearly night;
Sleep may resolve my doubt,
Help me to reason right. . . .

(He sleeps and dreams.)

I heard them whispering there by the bed . . .
Oh, but the ears of the blind are quick!
Every treacherous word they said
Was a stab of pain and my heart turned sick.
Then lip met lip and they looked at me,
Sitting bent by the fallen fire,

And they laughed to think that I couldn't see;
But I felt the flame of their hot desire.
He's helping Marie to work the farm,
A dashing, upstanding chap, they say;
And look at me with my flabby arm,
And the fat of sloth, and my face of clay—
Look at me as I sit and sit,
By the side of a fire that's seldom lit,
Sagging and weary the livelong day,
When everyone else is out on the field,
Sowing the seed for a golden yield,
Or tossing around the new-mown hay. . . .

Oh, the shimmering wheat that frets the sky,
Gold of plenty and blue of hope,
I'm seeing it all with an inner eye
As out of the door I grope and grope.
And I hear my wife and her lover there,
Whispering, whispering, round the rick,
Mocking me and my sightless stare,
As I fumble and stumble everywhere,
Slapping and tapping with my stick;
Old and weary at thirty-one,
Heartsick, wishing it all was done.

Oh, I'll tap my way around to the byre,
And I'll hear the cows as they chew their hay;
There at least there is none to tire,
There at least I am not in the way.

And they'll look at me with their velvet eyes
And I'll stroke their flanks with my woman's hand,
And they'll answer to me with soft replies,
And somehow I fancy they'll understand.
And the horses too, they knew me well;
I'm sure that they pity my wretched lot,
And the big fat ram with the jingling bell . . .
Oh, the beasts are the only friends I've got.
And my old dog, too, he loves me more,
I think, than ever he did before.
Thank God for the beasts that are all so kind,
That know and pity the helpless blind!

Ha! they're coming, the loving pair.
My hand's a-shake as my pipe I fill.
What if I steal on them unaware
With a reaping-hook, to kill, to kill? . . .
I'll do it . . . they're there in the mow of hay,
I hear them saying: "He's out of the way!"
Hark! how they're kissing and whispering. . . .
Closer I creep . . . I crouch . . . I spring. . . .

(He wakes.)

Ugh! What a horrible dream I've had!
And it isn't real . . . I'm glad, I'm glad!
Marie is good and Marie is true . . .
But now I know what it's best to do.

I'll sell the farm and I'll seek my kind,
I'll live apart with my fellow-blind,
And we'll eat and drink, and we'll laugh and joke,
And we'll talk of our battles, and smoke and smoke;
And brushes of bristle we'll make for sale,
While one of us reads a book of Braille.
And there will be music and dancing too,
And we'll seek to fashion our life anew;
And we'll walk the highways hand in hand,
The Brotherhood of the Sightless Band;
Till the years at last shall bring respite
And our night is lost in the Greater Night.

THE LEGLESS MAN

(The Dark Side.)

*My mind goes back to Fumin Wood, and how we stuck
it out,*
*Eight days of hunger, thirst and cold, mowed down by steel
and flame;*
*Waist-deep in mud and mad with woe, with dead men all
about,*
We fought like fiends and waited for relief that never came.
Eight days and nights they rolled on us in battle-frenzied mass!
*"Debout les morts!" We hurled them back. By God! they
did not pass.*

They pinned two medals on my chest, a yellow and a brown,
And lovely ladies made me blush, such pretty words they said.
I felt a cheerful man, almost, until my eyes went down,
And there I saw the blankets—how they sagged upon my bed.
And then again I drank the cup of sorrow to the dregs:
Oh, they can keep their medals if they give me back my legs.

I think of how I used to run and leap and kick the ball
And ride and dance and climb the hills and frolic in the sea;
And all the thousand things that now I'll never do at all. . . .
Alas! there's nothing left in life, it often seems to me.
And as the nurses lift me up and strap me in my chair,
If they would chloroform me off, by God I wouldn't care.

Ah yes! we're "heroes all" to-day—they point to us with pride;
To-day their hearts go out to us, the tears are in their eyes!
But wait a bit; to-morrow they will blindly look aside;
They'll cease to talk of what they owe, the dues of sacrifice
(One hates to be reminded of an everlasting debt).
It's all in human nature. Ah! the world will soon forget.

My mind goes back to where I lay wound-rotted on the plain,
And ate the muddy mangold roots, and drank the drops of
      dew,
And dragged myself for miles and miles when every move
      was pain,
And over me the carrion-crows were retching as they flew.

Oh, ere I closed my eyes and stuck my rifle in the air
I wish that those who picked me up had passed and left me
*   there.*

(The Bright Side.)

Oh, one gets used to everything!
I hum a merry song,
And up the street and round the square
I wheel my chair along;
For look you, how my chest is sound
And how my arms are strong!

Oh, one gets used to anything!
It's awkward at the first,
And jolting o'er the cobbles gives
A man a grievous thirst;
But of all ills that one must bear
That's surely not the worst.

For there's the café open wide,
And there they set me up;
And there I smoke my *caporal*
Above my cider cup;
And play *manille* a while before
I hurry home to sup.

At home the wife is waiting me
With smiles and pigeon-pie;
And little Zi-Zi claps her hands
With laughter loud and high;
And if there's cause to growl, I fail
To see the reason why.

And all the evening by the lamp
I read some tale of crime,
Or play my old accordion
With Marie keeping time,
Until we hear the hour of ten
From out the steeple chime.

Then in the morning bright and soon,
No moment do I lose;
Within my little cobbler's shop
To gain the silver *sous*
(Good luck one has no need of legs
To make a pair of shoes).

And every Sunday—oh, it's then
I am the happy man;
They wheel me to the river-side,
And there with rod and can
I sit and fish and catch a dish
Of *goujons* for the pan.

Aye, one gets used to everything,
And doesn't seem to mind;
Maybe I'm happier than most
Of my two-legged kind;
For look you at the darkest cloud,
Lo! how it's silver lined.

THE FACELESS MAN

I'm dead.
Officially I'm dead. Their hope is past.
How long I stood as missing! Now, at last,
                              I'm dead.
Look in my face—no likeness can you see,
No tiny trace of him they knew as "me."
How terrible the change!
Even my eyes are strange.
So keyed are they to pain,
That if I chanced to meet
My mother in the street
She'd look at me in vain.

When she got home I think she'd say:
"I saw the saddest sight to-day—
A *poilu* with no face at all.
Far better in the fight to fall
Than go through life like that, I think.
Poor fellow! how he made me shrink.

No face. Just eyes that seemed to stare
At me with anguish and despair.
This ghastly war! I'm almost cheered
To think my son who disappeared,
My boy so handsome and so gay,
Might have come home like him to-day."

I'm dead. I think it's better to be dead
When little children look at you with dread;
And when you know your coming home again
Will only give the ones who love you pain.
Ah! who can help but shrink? One cannot blame.
They see the hideous husk, not, not the flame
Of sacrifice and love that burns within;
While souls of satyrs, raddled through with sin,
Have bodies fair and excellent to see.
Mon Dieu! how different we all would be
If this our flesh was ordained to express
Our spirit's beauty or its ugliness.

(Oh, you who look at me with fear to-day,
And shrink despite yourselves, and turn away—
It was for you I suffered woe accurst;
For you I braved red battle at its worst;
For you I fought and bled and maimed and slew;
                              For you, for you.
For you I faced hell-fury and despair;
The reeking horror of it all I knew:

I flung myself into the furnace there;
I faced the flame that scorched me with its glare;
I drank unto the dregs the devil's brew—
Look at me now—for *you* and *you* and *you*. . . .)

*   *   *   *   *   *

I'm thinking of the time we said good-bye:
We took our dinner in Duval's that night,
Just little Jacqueline, Lucette and I;
We tried our very utmost to be bright.
We laughed. And yet our eyes, they weren't gay.
I sought all kinds of cheering things to say.
"Don't grieve," I told them. "Soon the time will pass;
My next permission will come quickly round;
We'll all meet at the Gare du Montparnasse;
Three times I've come already, safe and sound."
(But oh, I thought, it's harder every time,
After a home that seems like Paradise,
To go back to the vermin and the slime,
The weariness, the want, the sacrifice.
"Pray God," I said, "the war may soon be done,
But no, oh never, never till we've won!")

Then to the station quietly we walked;
I had my rifle and my haversack,
My heavy boots, my blankets on my back;
And though it hurt us, cheerfully we talked.
We chatted bravely at the platform gate.

I watched the clock. My train must go at eight.
One minute to the hour . . . we kissed good-bye,
Then, oh, they both broke down, with piteous cry
I went. . . . Their way was barred; they could not pass.
I looked back as the train began to start;
Once more I ran with anguish at my heart
And through the bars I kissed my little lass. . . .

Three years have gone; they've waited day by day;
I never came. I did not even write.
For when I saw my face was such a sight
I thought that I had better . . . stay away.
And so I took the name of one who died,
A friendless friend who perished by my side.
In Prussian prison camps three years of hell,
I hugged my secret; oh, I kept it well!
And now I'm free, but none shall ever know;
They think I died out there . . . it's better so.

To-day I met my wife in widow's weeds.
I brushed her arm. She did not even look.
So white, so pinched her face, my heart still bleeds,
And at the touch of her, oh, how I shook!
And then last night I passed the window where
They sat together; I could see them clear,
The lamplight softly gleaming on their hair,
And all the room so full of cosy cheer.
My wife was sewing, while my daughter read;
I even saw my portrait on the wall.

I wanted to rush in, to tell them all;
And then I cursed myself: "You're dead, you're dead!"
God! how I watched them from the darkness there,
Clutching the dripping branches of a tree,
Peering as close as ever I might dare,
And sobbing, sobbing, oh, so bitterly!

But no, it's folly; and I mustn't stay,
To-morrow I am going far away.
I'll find a ship and sail before the mast;
In some wild land I'll bury all the past.
I'll live on lonely shores and there forget,
Or tell myself that there has never been
The gay and tender courage of Lucette,
The little loving arms of Jacqueline.

A lonely man upon a lonely isle,
Sometimes I'll look towards the North and smile
To think they're happy, and they both believe
I died for France, and that I lie at rest;
And for my glory's sake they've ceased to grieve,
And hold my memory sacred. Ah! that's best.
And in that thought I'll find my joy and peace
As there alone I wait the Last Release.

L'ENVOI

We've finished up the filthy war;
We've won what we were fighting for . . .
(Or have we?   I don't know).
But anyway I have my wish:
I'm back upon the old Boul' Mich',
And how my heart's aglow!
Though in my coat's an empty sleeve,
Ah! do not think I ever grieve
(The pension for it, I believe,
Will keep me on the go).

So I'll be free to write and write,
And give my soul to sheer delight,
Till joy is almost pain;
To stand aloof and watch the throng,
And worship youth and sing my song
Of faith and hope again;
To seek for beauty everywhere,
To make each day a living prayer
That life may not be vain.

727

To sing of things that comfort me,
The joy in mother-eyes, the glee
Of little ones at play;
The blessed gentleness of trees,
Of old men dreaming at their ease
Soft afternoons away;
Of violets and swallows' wings,
Of wondrous, ordinary things
In words of every day.

To rhyme of rich and rainy nights,
When like a legion leap the lights
And take the town with gold;
Of taverns quaint where poets dream,
Of cafés gaudily agleam,
And vice that's overbold;
Of crystal shimmer, silver sheen,
Of soft and soothing nicotine,
Of wine that's rich and old.

Of gutters, chimney-tops and stars,
Of apple-carts and motor-cars,
The sordid and sublime;
Of wealth and misery that meet
In every great and little street,
Of glory and of grime;
Of all the living tide that flows—
From princes down to puppet shows—
I'll make my humble rhyme.

So if you like the sort of thing
Of which I also like to sing,
Just give my stuff a look;
And if you don't, no harm is done—
In writing it I've had my fun;
Good luck to you and everyone—
And so . . .

HERE ENDS MY BOOK

Printed in Great Britain by
Lowe & Brydone (Printers) Limited